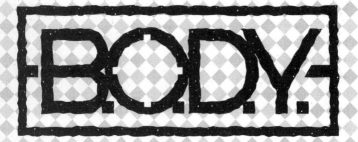

Vol. 7

Story & Art by
Ao Mimori

Contents

The Story Thus Far...

Ryoko falls hard for Ryunosuke, the quiet, bespectacled cutie who sits next to her in class. Then she learns that he moonlights as a host—a guy who dates women for money! Soft-spoken bookworm by day, aggressive ladies' man by night, Ryu may be more than the inexperienced Ryoko can handle. But she can't seem to get him out of her head...or her heart...

Ryoko finds out why Ryunosuke lives alone: his dad is a globe-trotting photographer, and his mom moved to the U.S. to work as a medical researcher. What's more, his parents are divorced, and they don't get along... especially where Ryunosuke is concerned. When Ryoko makes a bad first impression, Ryu's no-nonsense mom lays down the law: her son is forbidden to date Ryoko!

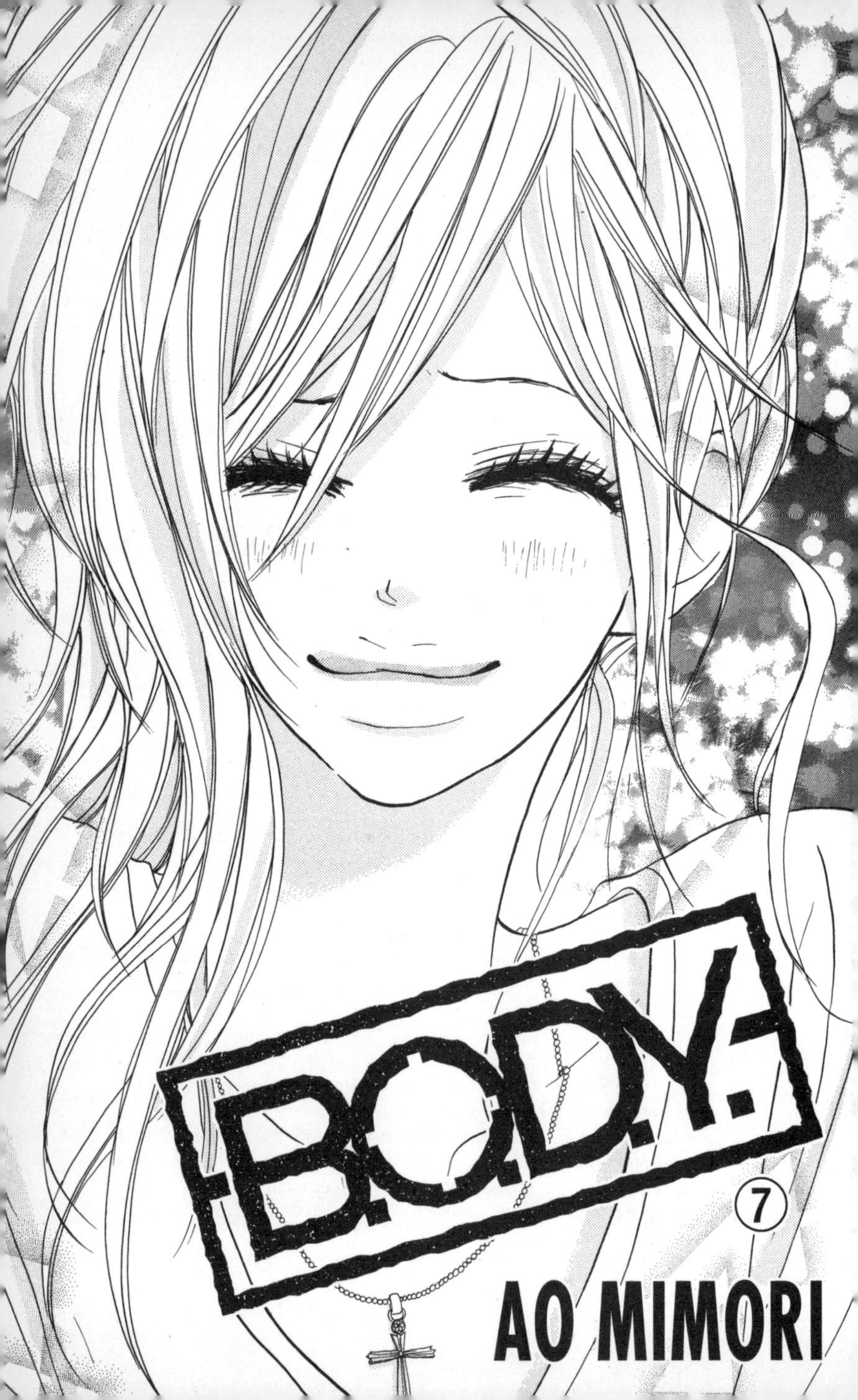
B.O.D.Y.
7
AO MIMORI

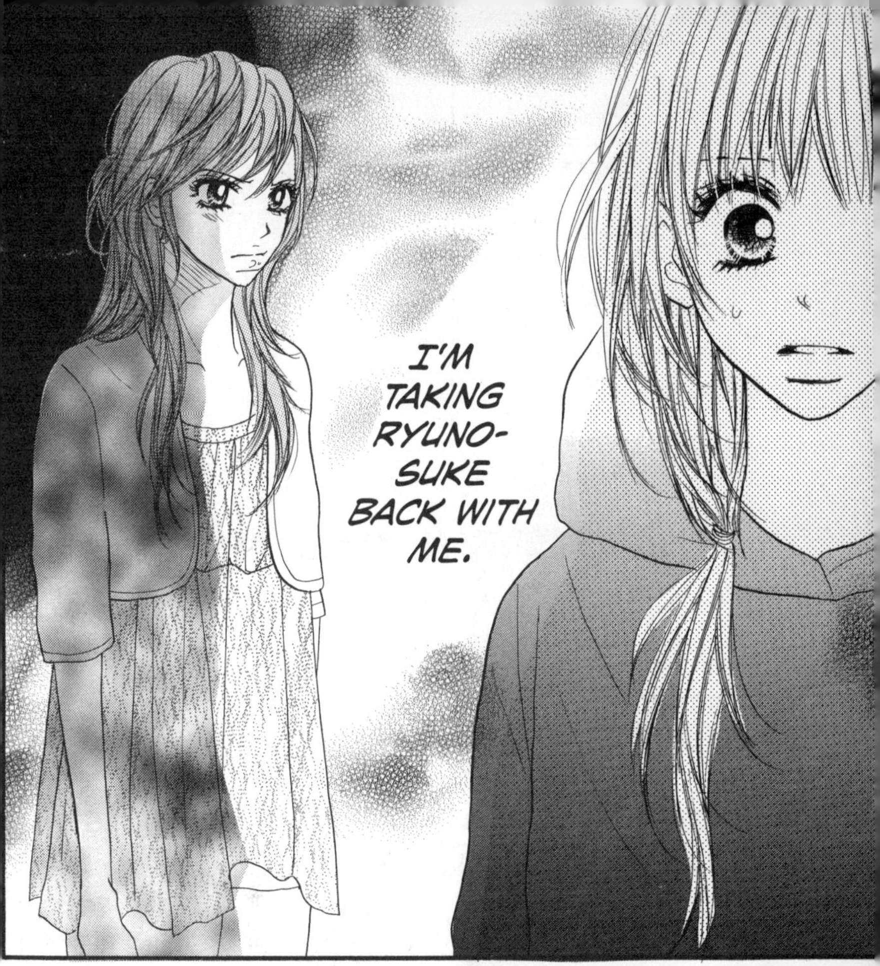
I'M TAKING RYUNO-SUKE BACK WITH ME.

FAN MAIL CORNER

I WANNA INCLUDE AS MUCH AS I CAN, SO LET'S GO!

☆

A boy asked me out, but I told him, "I have Ryunosuke. Actually you're not as cute as Ryunosuke," and rejected him. He was speechless.
M.E., Chiba

WHOA... EVEN HER FRIEND SAID, "YEAH! RYUNOSUKE'S WAY BETTER!" TO THE GUY WHO ASKED HER OUT, I'M SO SORRY!

☆

I have a crush on K. in the class next to mine. He looks like Ryunosuke!! I can't choose between the two!! Or should I give up on both and go for you, Ms. Mimori?
K.I., Hiroshima

UM... THIS LETTER IS WRONG IN SO MANY WAYS... BUT WHAT THE HECK! PICK ME!

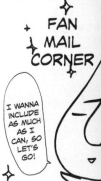

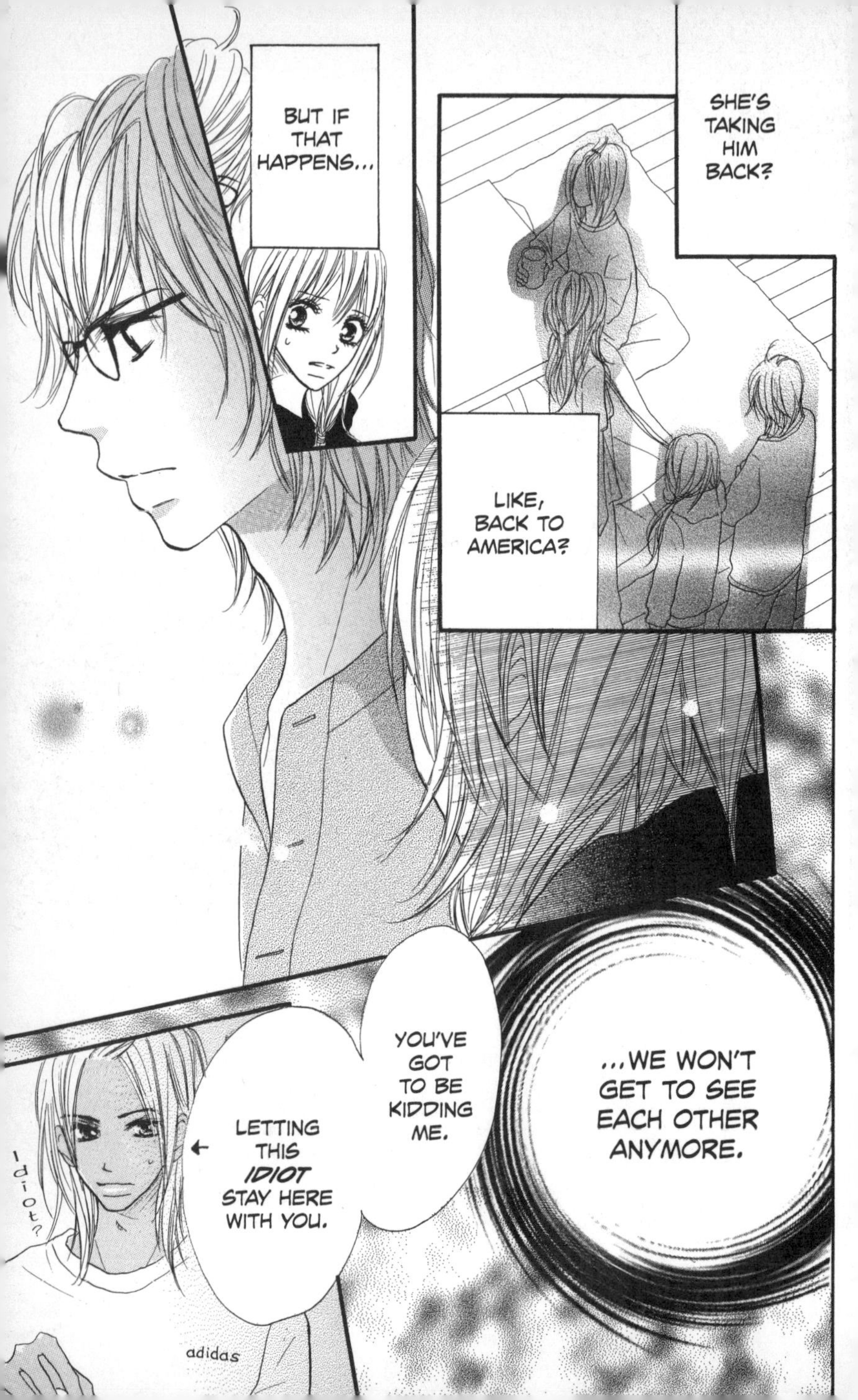

SHE'S TAKING HIM BACK?
LIKE, BACK TO AMERICA?
BUT IF THAT HAPPENS...
...WE WON'T GET TO SEE EACH OTHER ANYMORE.
YOU'VE GOT TO BE KIDDING ME.
LETTING THIS IDIOT STAY HERE WITH YOU.
Idiot?
adidas

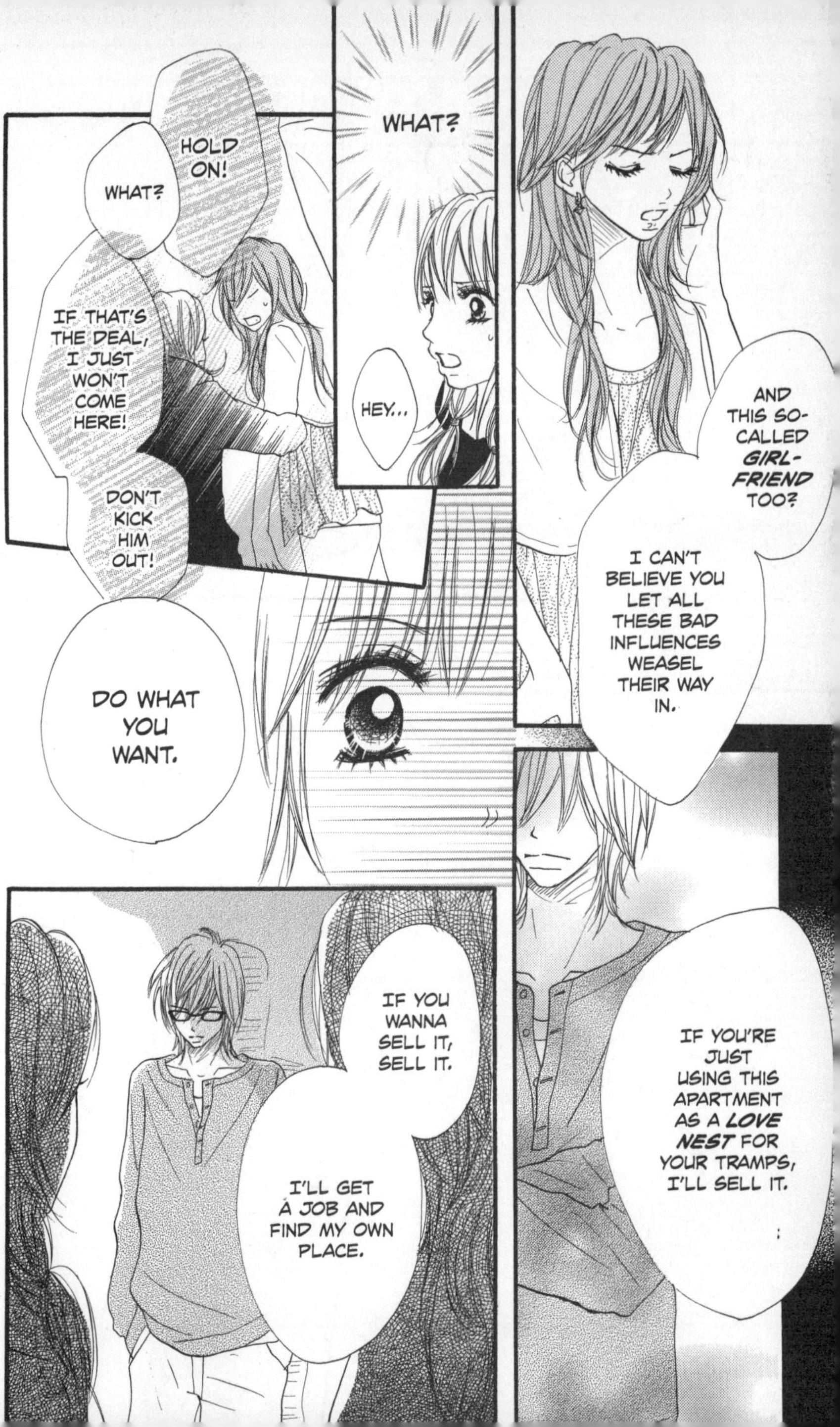
AND THIS SO-CALLED GIRL-FRIEND TOO?
I CAN'T BELIEVE YOU LET ALL THESE BAD INFLUENCES WEASEL THEIR WAY IN.
IF YOU'RE JUST USING THIS APARTMENT AS A LOVE NEST FOR YOUR TRAMPS, I'LL SELL IT.
WHAT?
HEY...
HOLD ON!
WHAT?
IF THAT'S THE DEAL, I JUST WON'T COME HERE!
DON'T KICK HIM OUT!
DO WHAT YOU WANT.
IF YOU WANNA SELL IT, SELL IT.
I'LL GET A JOB AND FIND MY OWN PLACE.

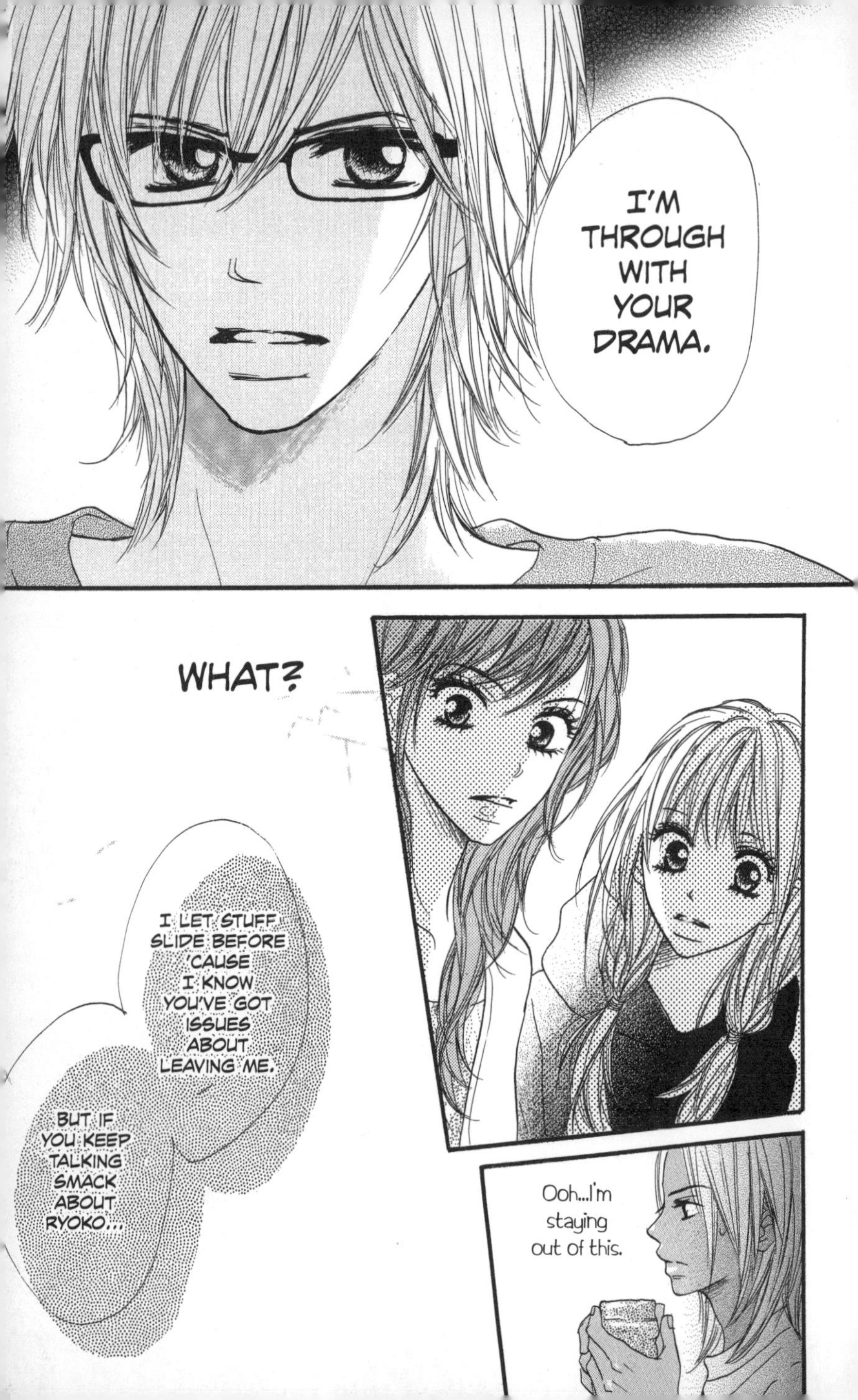
I'M THROUGH WITH YOUR DRAMA.
WHAT?
I LET STUFF SLIDE BEFORE 'CAUSE I KNOW YOU'VE GOT ISSUES ABOUT LEAVING ME.
BUT IF YOU KEEP TALKING SMACK ABOUT RYOKO...
Ooh...I'm staying out of this.

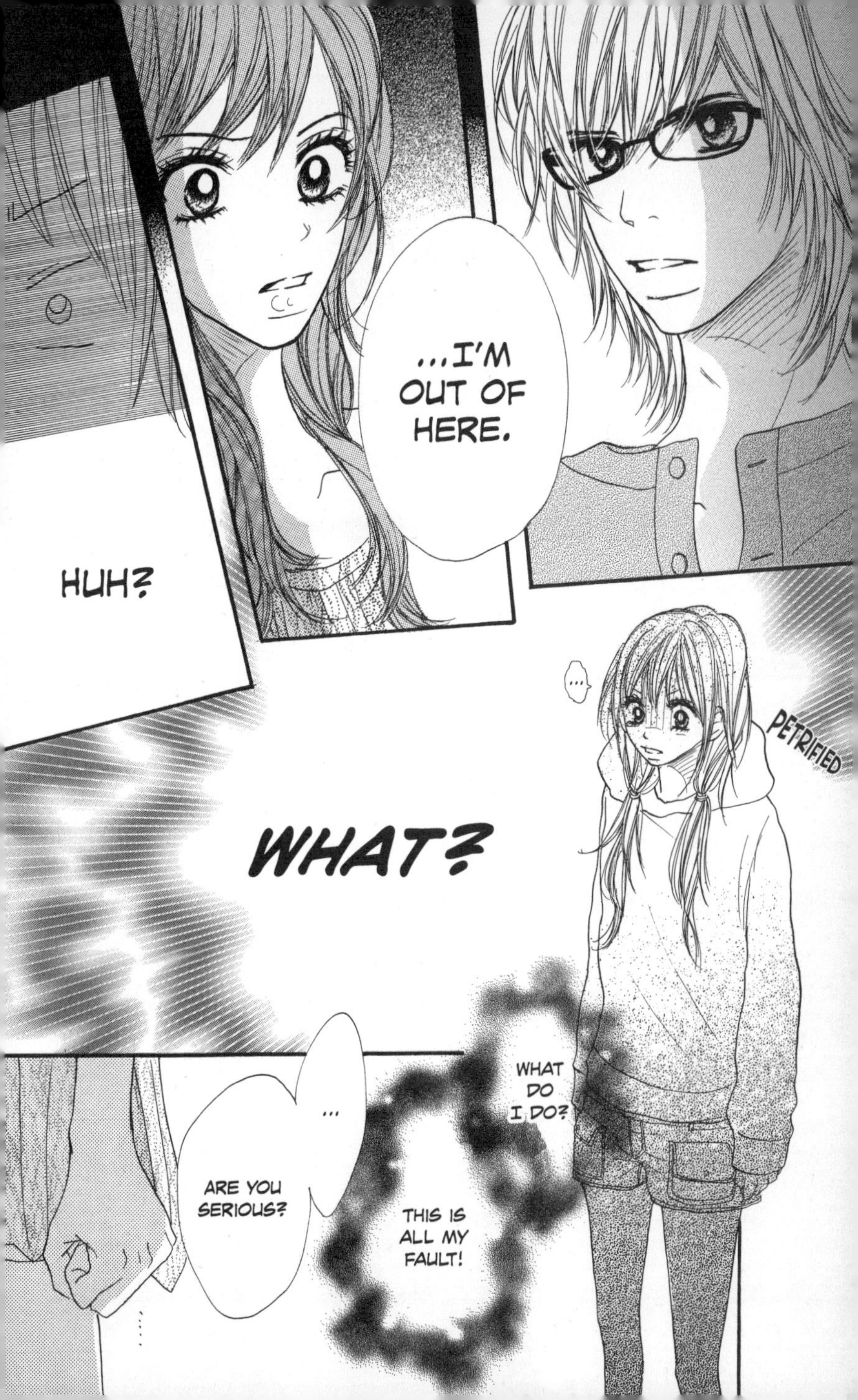
...I'M OUT OF HERE.
HUH?
...
PETRIFIED
WHAT?
WHAT DO I DO?
THIS IS ALL MY FAULT!
...
ARE YOU SERIOUS?
...

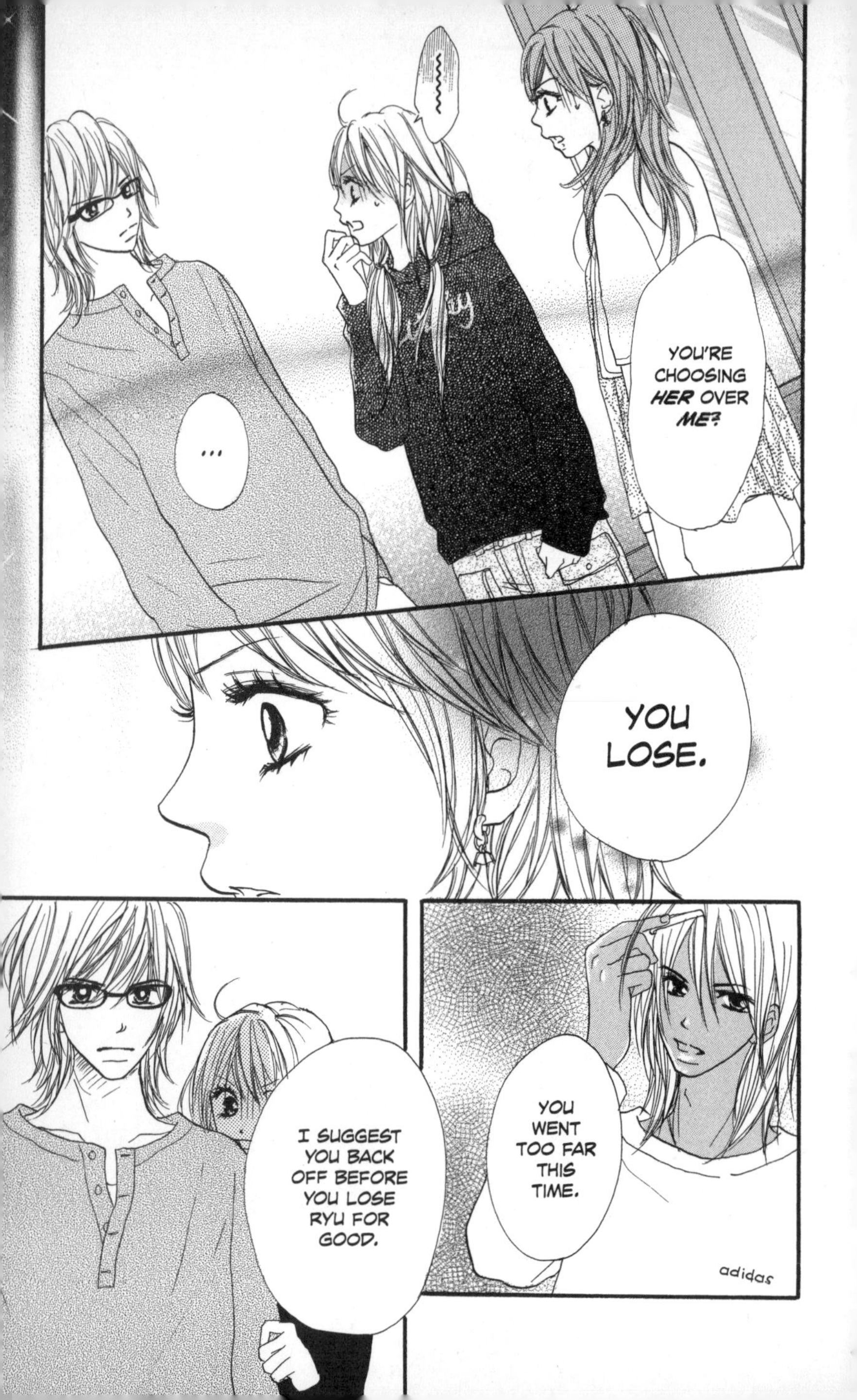
YOU'RE CHOOSING *HER* OVER *ME*?
...
YOU LOSE.
YOU WENT TOO FAR THIS TIME.
adidas
I SUGGEST YOU BACK OFF BEFORE YOU LOSE RYU FOR GOOD.

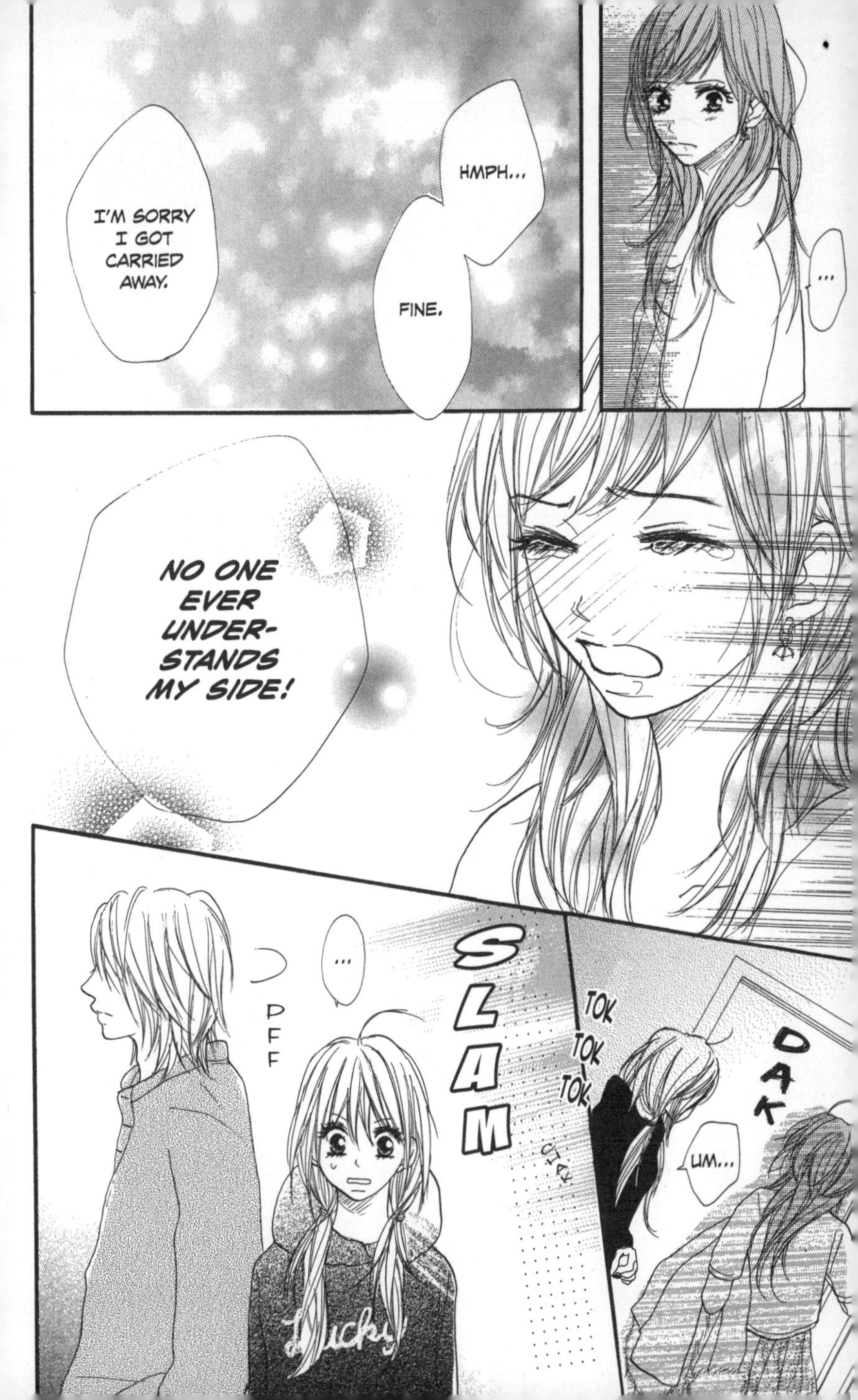
...
HMPH...
FINE.
I'M SORRY I GOT CARRIED AWAY.
NO ONE EVER UNDER-STANDS MY SIDE!
DAK
TOK TOK TOK
UM...
SLAM
...
PFF

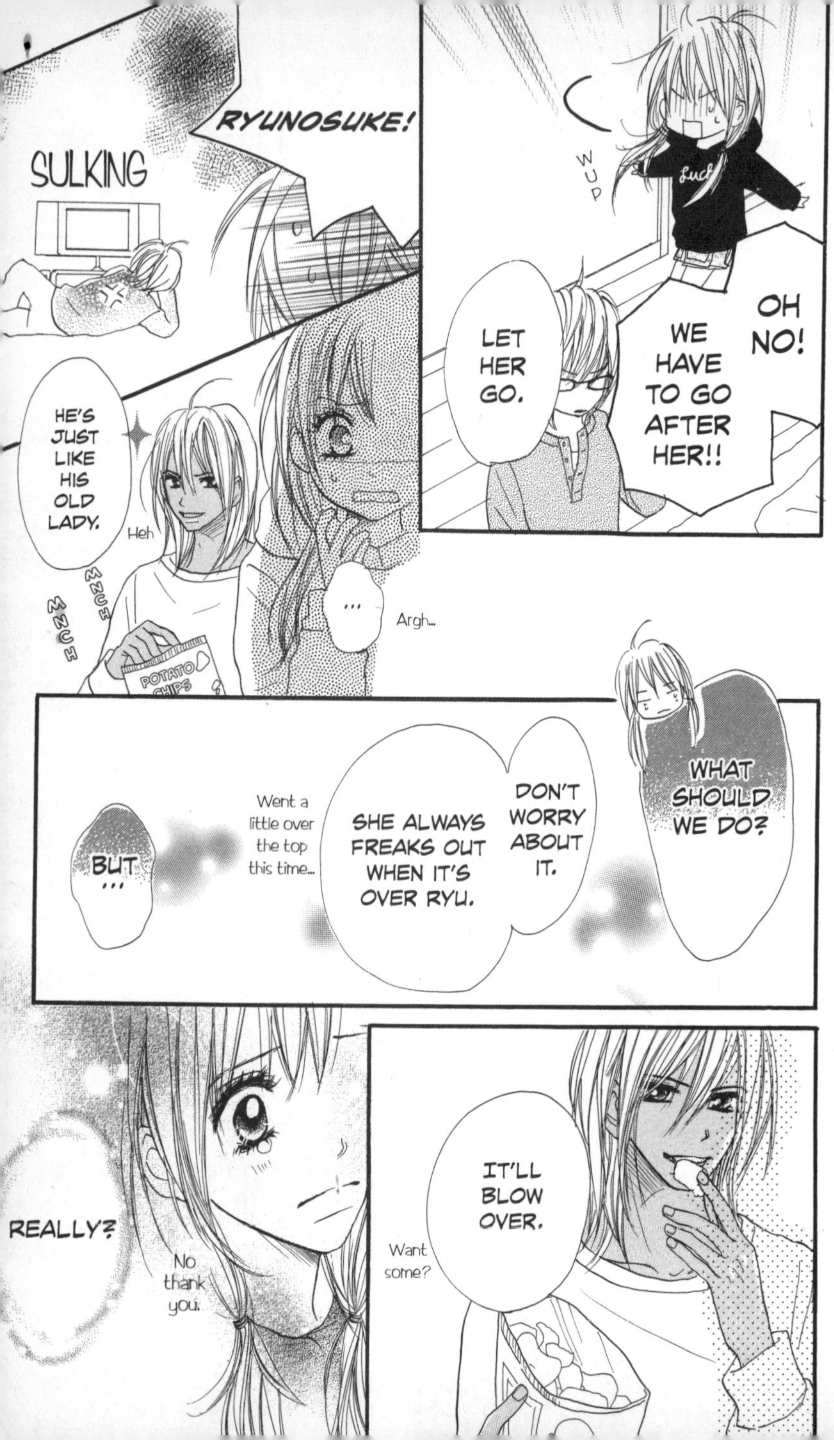
WUP
OH NO!
WE HAVE TO GO AFTER HER!!
LET HER GO.
RYUNOSUKE!
SULKING
Argh...
...
HE'S JUST LIKE HIS OLD LADY.
Heh
MNCH MNCH
POTATO CHIPS
WHAT SHOULD WE DO?
DON'T WORRY ABOUT IT.
SHE ALWAYS FREAKS OUT WHEN IT'S OVER RYU.
Went a little over the top this time...
BUT...
IT'LL BLOW OVER.
Want some?
REALLY?
No thank you.

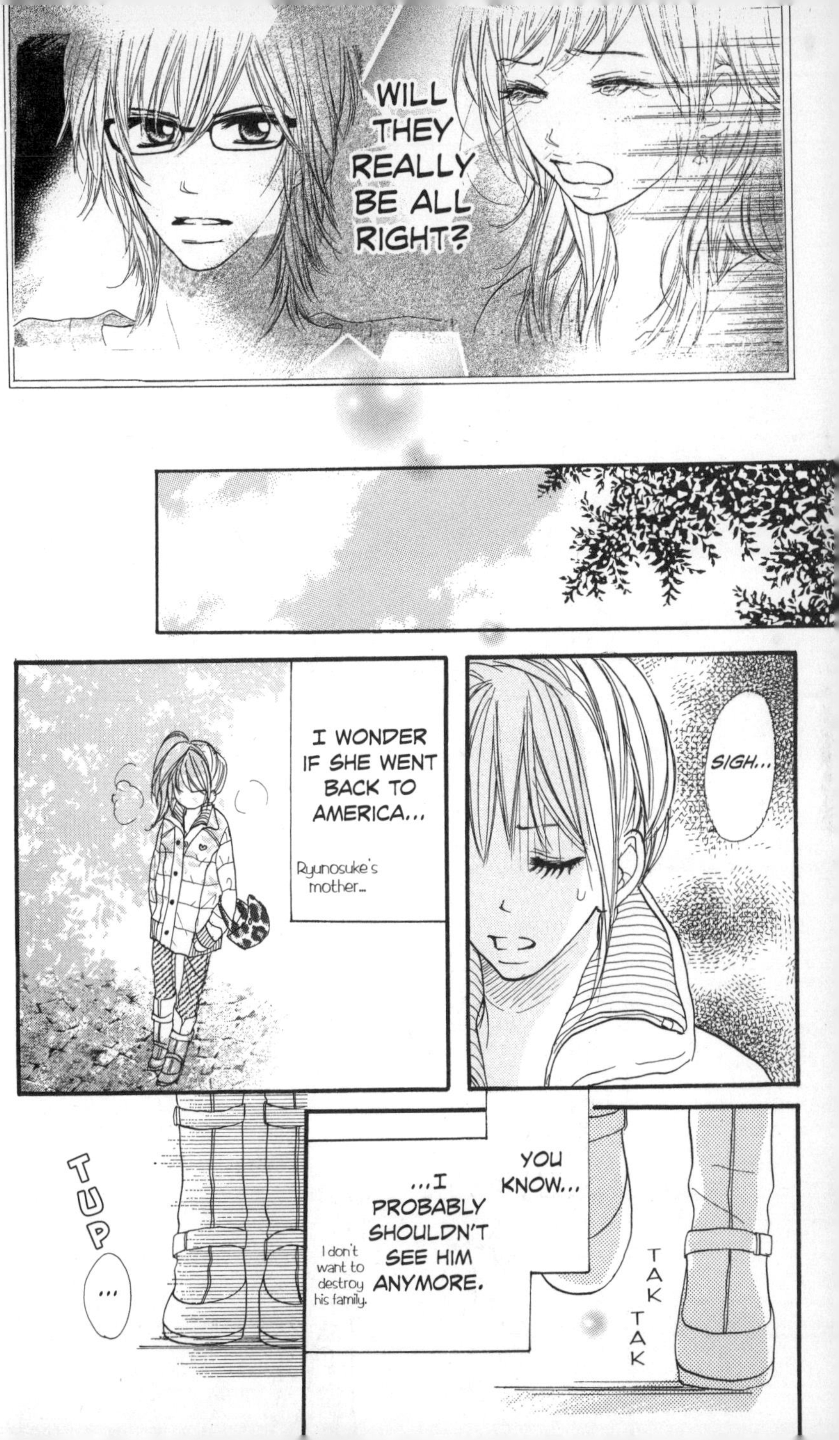
WILL THEY REALLY BE ALL RIGHT?
SIGH...
I WONDER IF SHE WENT BACK TO AMERICA...
Ryunosuke's mother...
TAK TAK
YOU KNOW...
...I PROBABLY SHOULDN'T SEE HIM ANYMORE.
I don't want to destroy his family.
TUP
...

HEH

① How are you all doing? Ao Mimori here. To those of you who started with volume 7 and those who have been reading all along, thank you!!
I'm grateful to everyone who picks up a copy!! TUP

Thanks to all of you, there will soon be a...

✧B.O.D.Y.✧
✧DRAMA CD!!✧

Yay Yay WUP WUP WUP WUP

Okay...A drama CD is like an anime without the pictures. Voice actors play the characters and there are sound effects... sorry for the terrible explanation.

Mm...

Please check it out if you can spare the cash!! It costs a bit more than the manga so don't go overboard.
But I know you'll like it!

More details to follow...

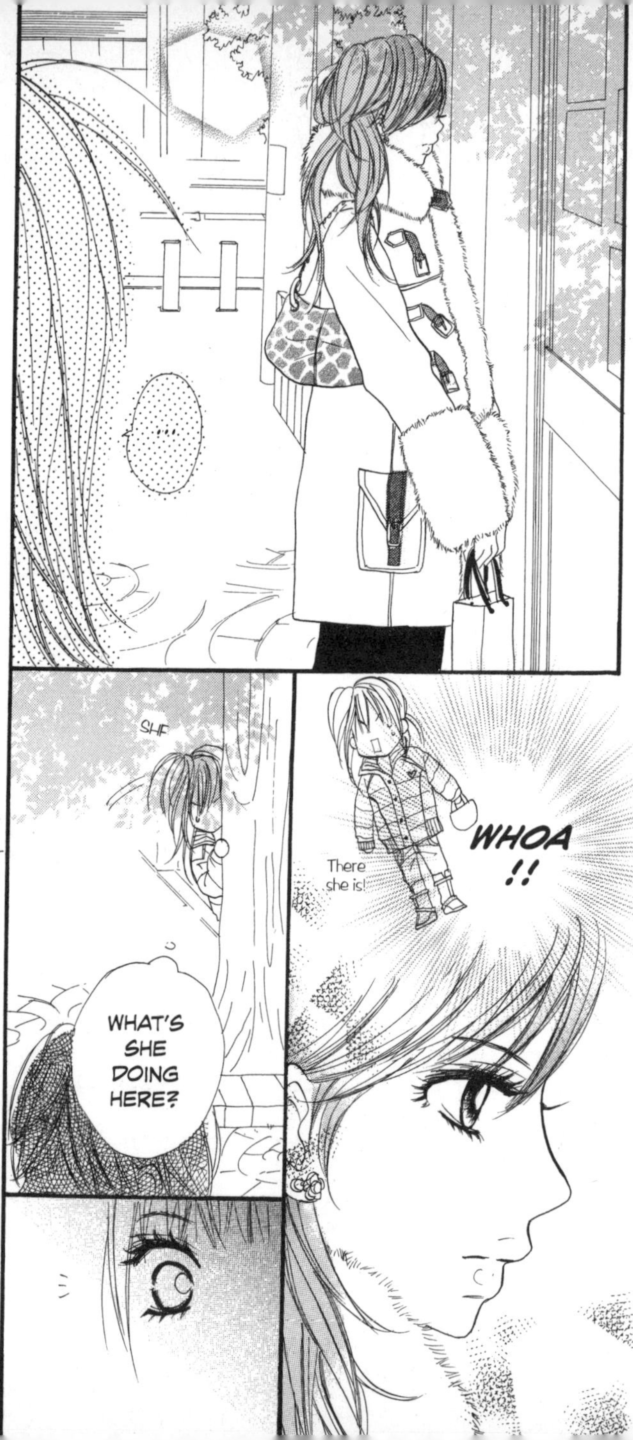
...
WHOA!!
There she is!
SHF
WHAT'S SHE DOING HERE?

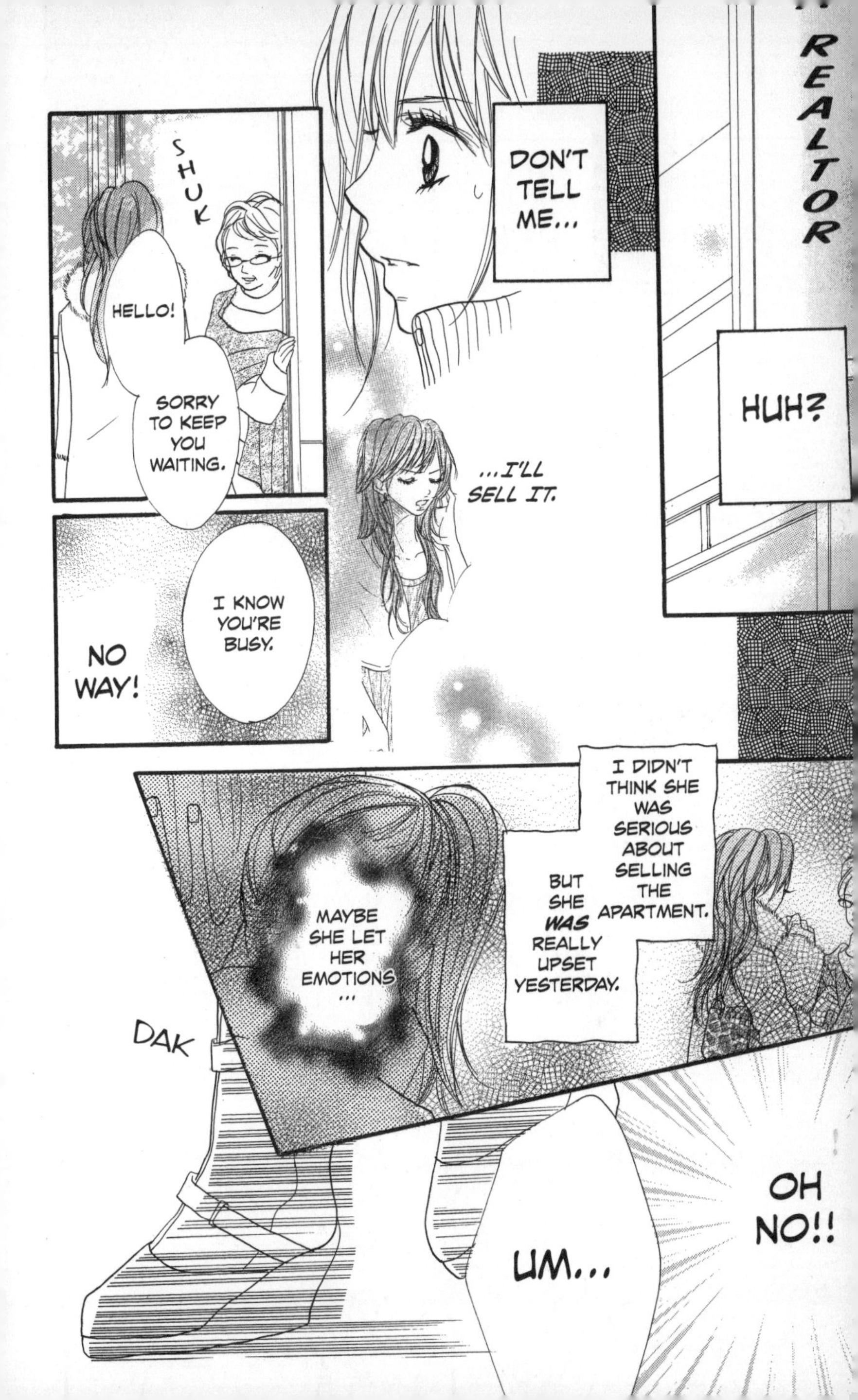
REALTOR
HUH?
DON'T TELL ME...
...I'LL SELL IT.
SHUK
HELLO!
SORRY TO KEEP YOU WAITING.
I KNOW YOU'RE BUSY.
NO WAY!
I DIDN'T THINK SHE WAS SERIOUS ABOUT SELLING THE APARTMENT.
BUT SHE WAS REALLY UPSET YESTERDAY.
MAYBE SHE LET HER EMOTIONS ...
DAK
OH NO!!
UM...

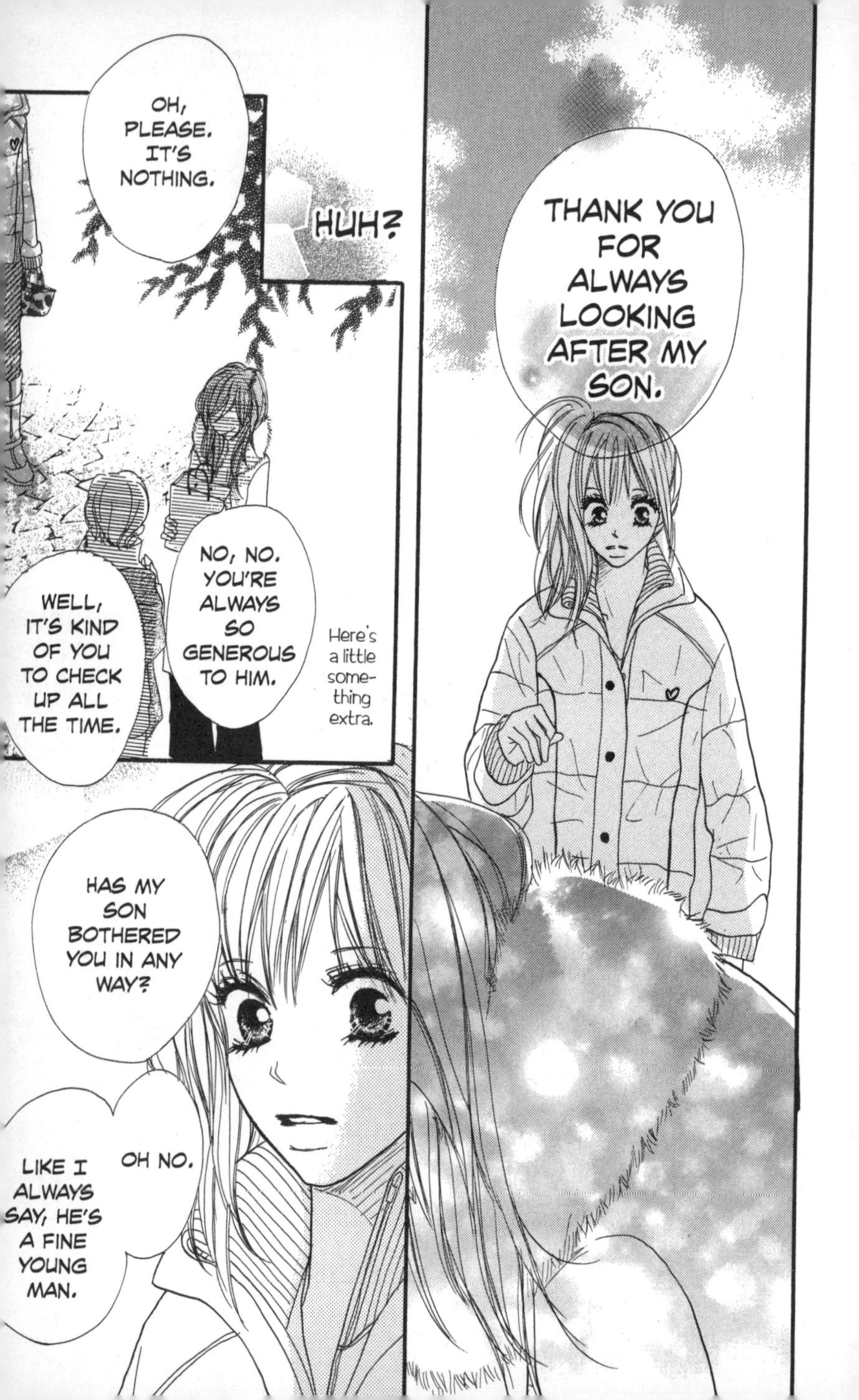
THANK YOU FOR ALWAYS LOOKING AFTER MY SON.
OH, PLEASE. IT'S NOTHING.
HUH?
Here's a little something extra.
NO, NO. YOU'RE ALWAYS SO GENEROUS TO HIM.
WELL, IT'S KIND OF YOU TO CHECK UP ALL THE TIME.
HAS MY SON BOTHERED YOU IN ANY WAY?
OH NO.
LIKE I ALWAYS SAY, HE'S A FINE YOUNG MAN.

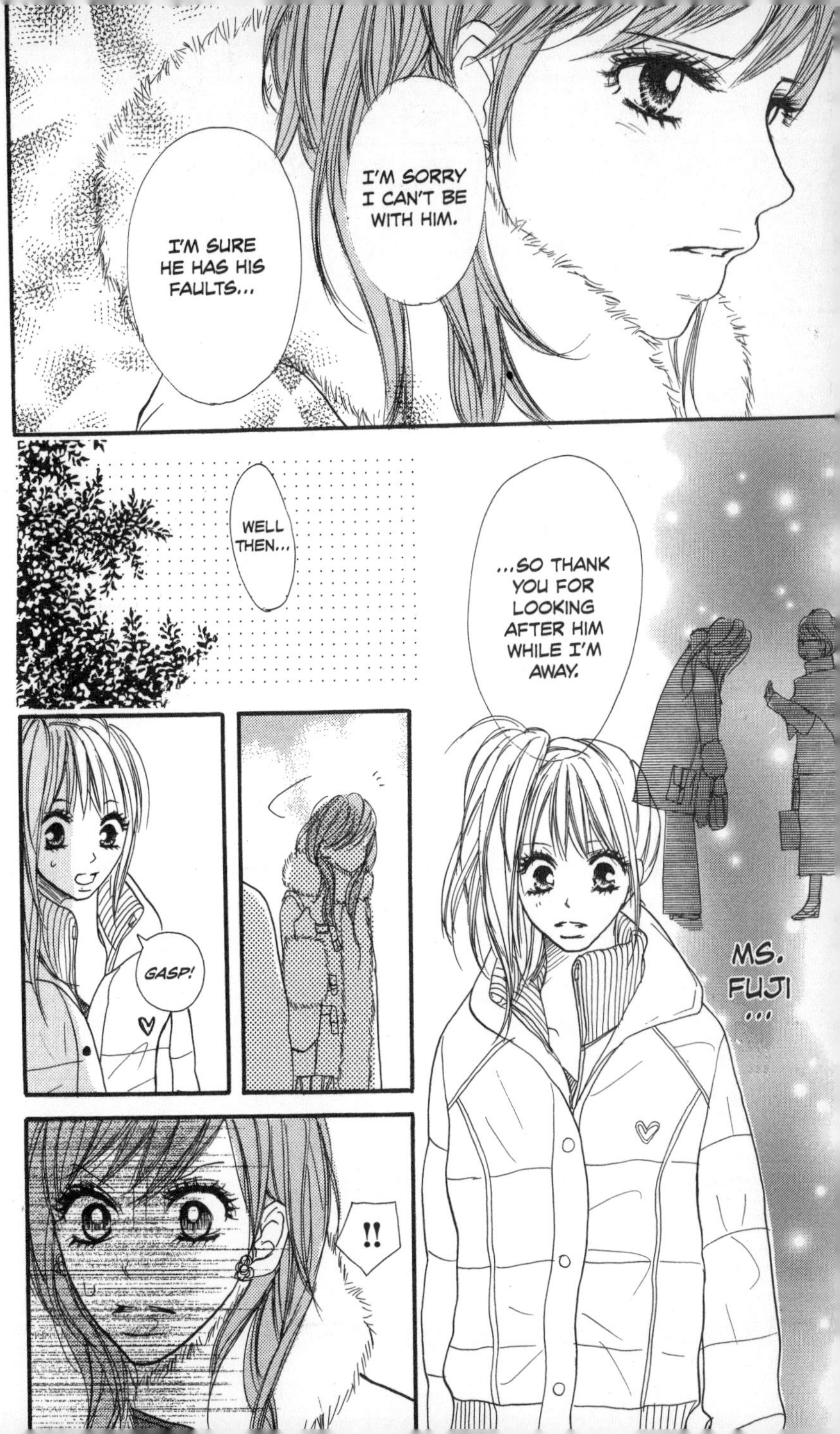
I'M SORRY I CAN'T BE WITH HIM.
I'M SURE HE HAS HIS FAULTS...
...SO THANK YOU FOR LOOKING AFTER HIM WHILE I'M AWAY.
MS. FUJI ...
WELL THEN...
GASP!
!!

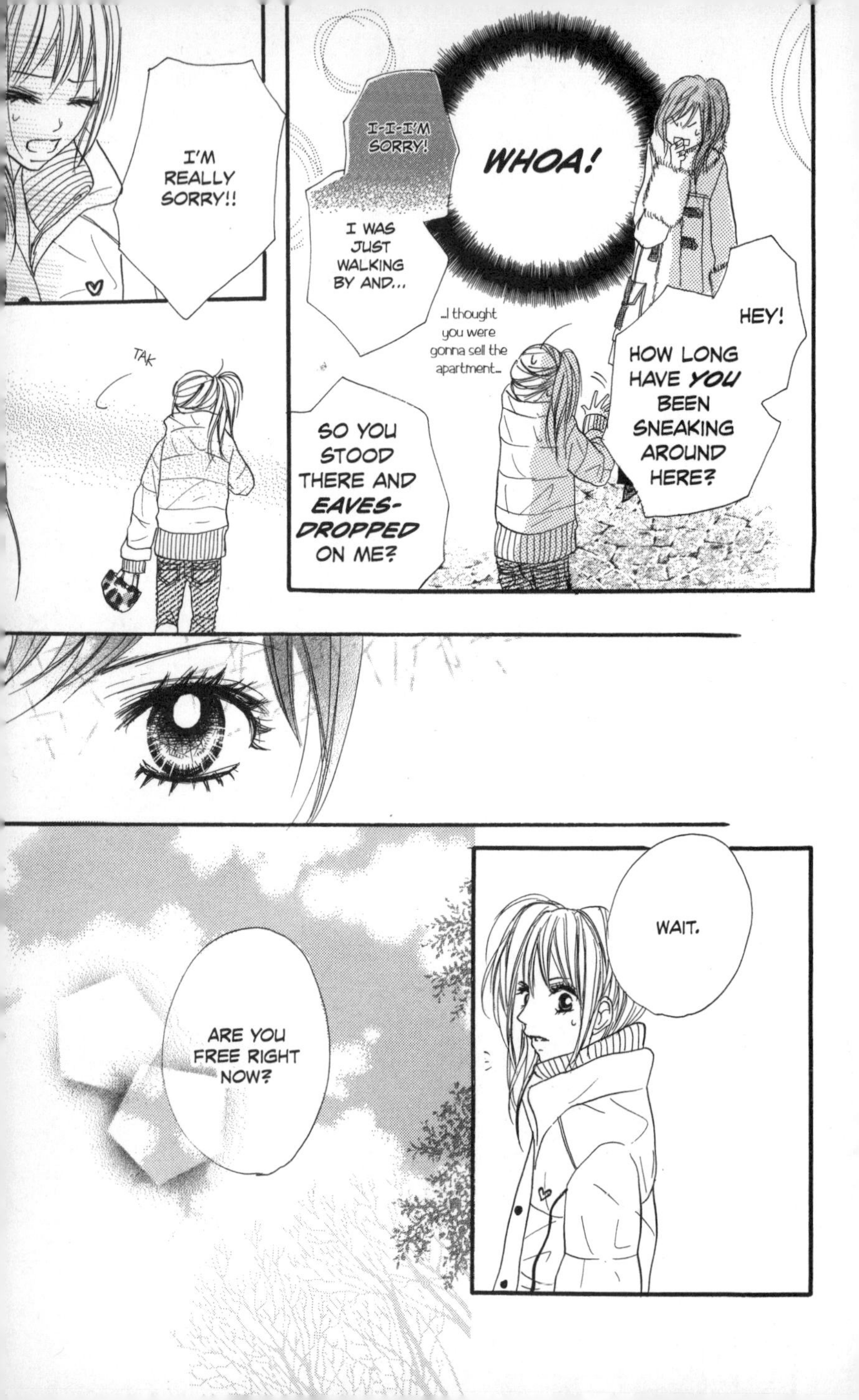
WHOA!
I-I-I'M SORRY!
I WAS JUST WALKING BY AND...
HEY! HOW LONG HAVE YOU BEEN SNEAKING AROUND HERE?
...I thought you were gonna sell the apartment...
SO YOU STOOD THERE AND EAVES-DROPPED ON ME?
I'M REALLY SORRY!!
TAK
WAIT.
ARE YOU FREE RIGHT NOW?

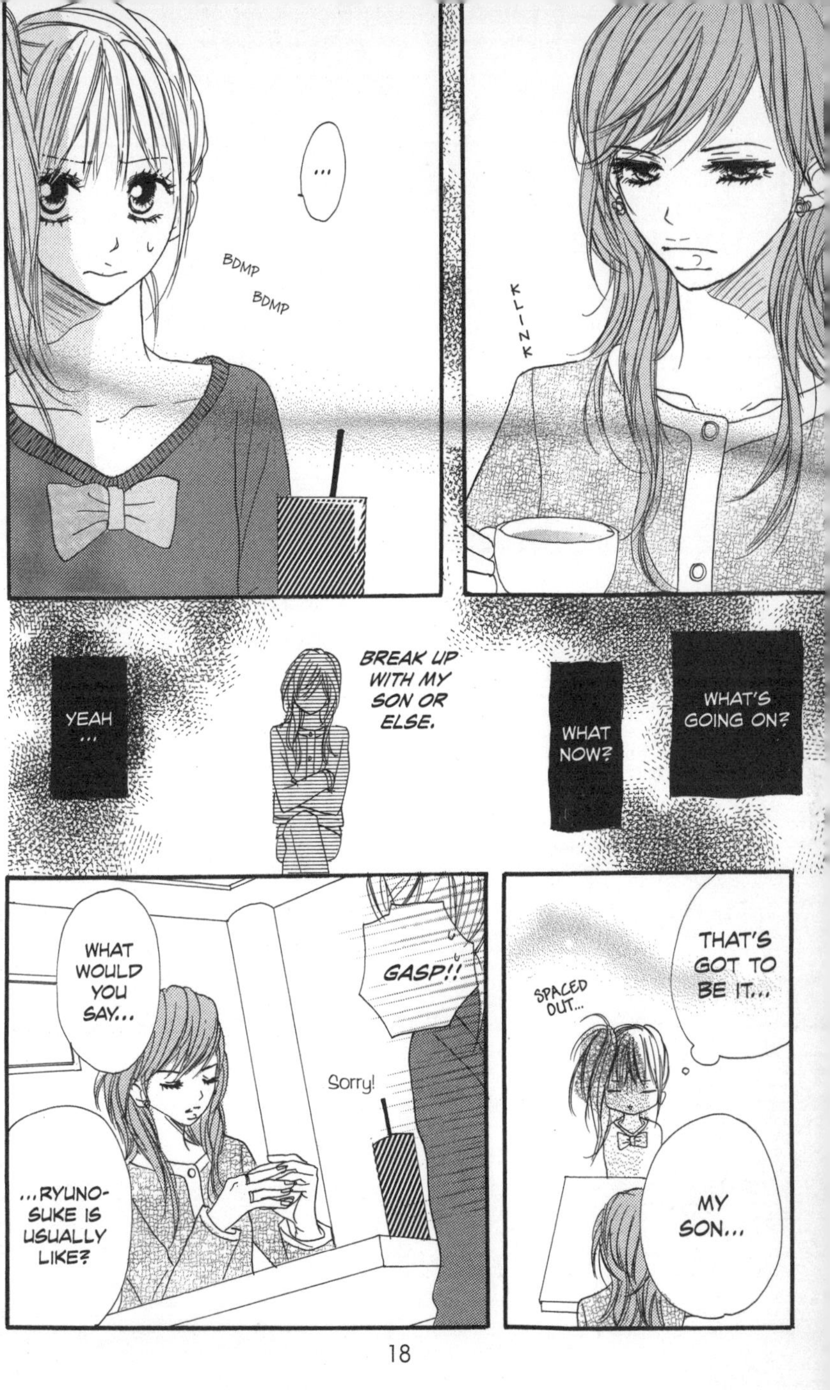
K-L-I-N-K
...
BDMP
BDMP
WHAT'S GOING ON?
WHAT NOW?
BREAK UP WITH MY SON OR ELSE.
YEAH...
THAT'S GOT TO BE IT...
SPACED OUT...
MY SON...
GASP!!
WHAT WOULD YOU SAY...
Sorry!
...RYUNO-SUKE IS USUALLY LIKE?

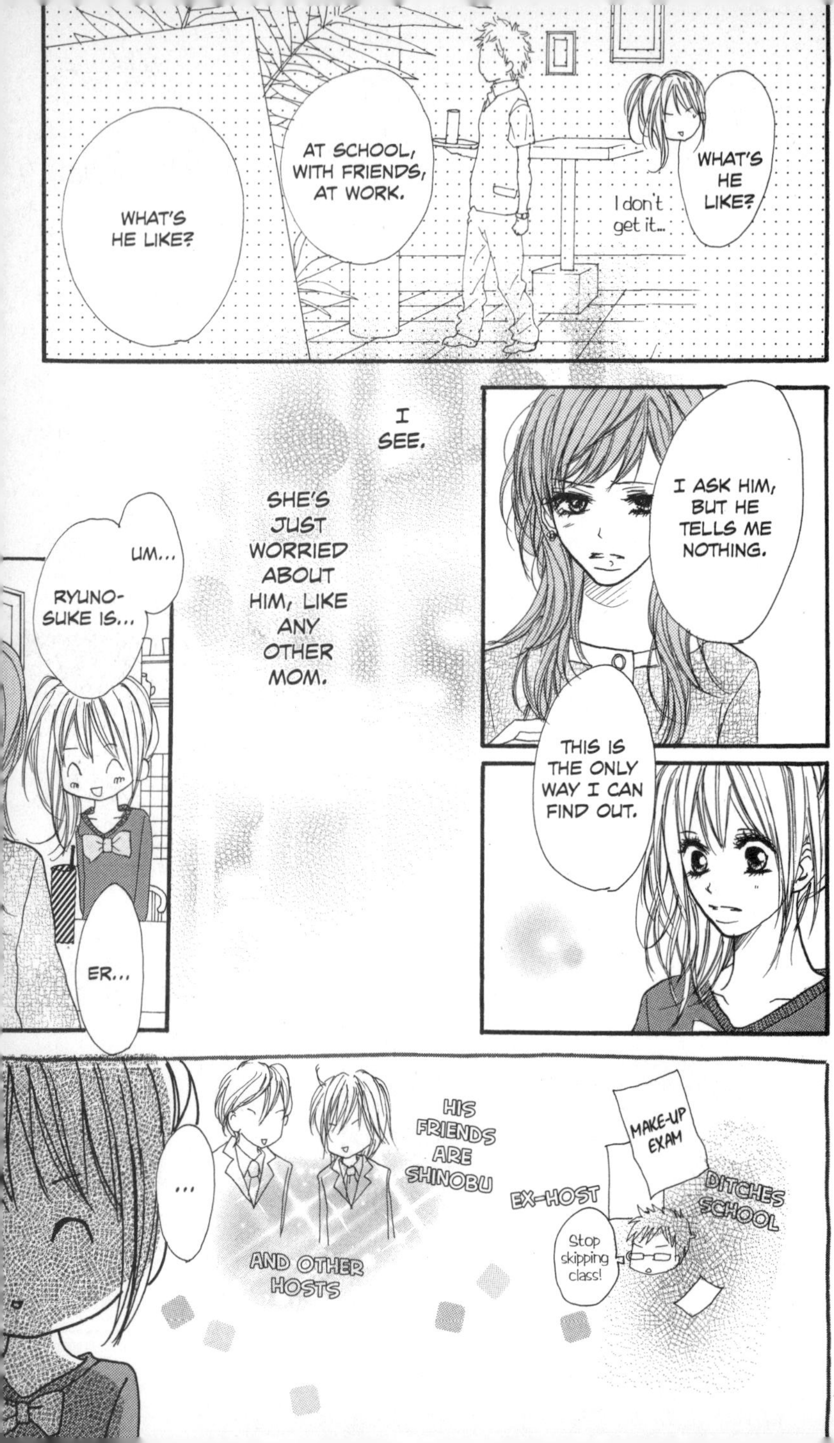
WHAT'S HE LIKE?
I don't get it...
AT SCHOOL, WITH FRIENDS, AT WORK.
WHAT'S HE LIKE?
I ASK HIM, BUT HE TELLS ME NOTHING.
THIS IS THE ONLY WAY I CAN FIND OUT.
I SEE.
SHE'S JUST WORRIED ABOUT HIM, LIKE ANY OTHER MOM.
UM...
RYUNO-SUKE IS...
ER...
DITCHES SCHOOL
MAKE-UP EXAM
Stop skipping class!
EX-HOST
HIS FRIENDS ARE SHINOBU
AND OTHER HOSTS
...

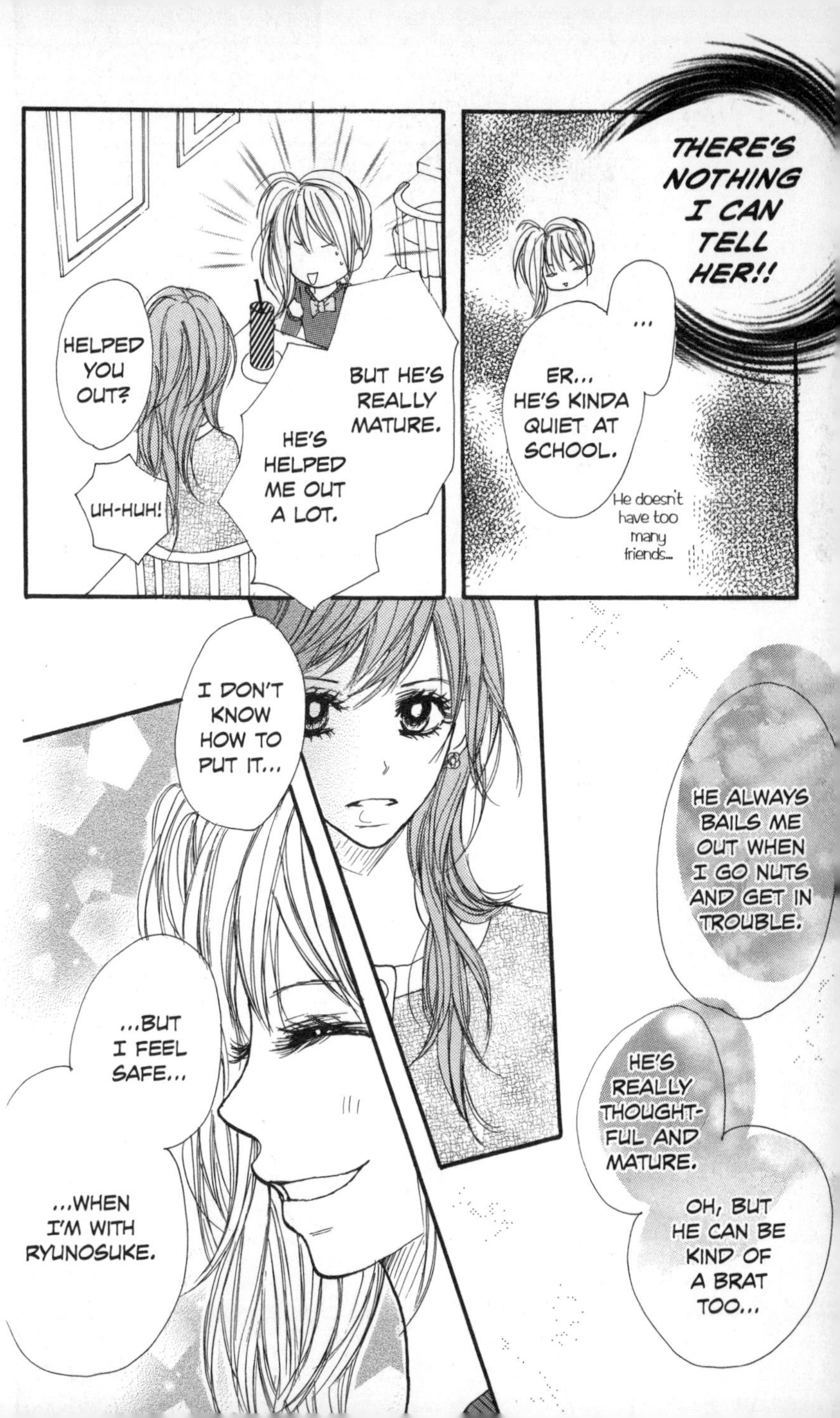
THERE'S NOTHING I CAN TELL HER!!
...
ER... HE'S KINDA QUIET AT SCHOOL.
He doesn't have too many friends...
BUT HE'S REALLY MATURE.
HE'S HELPED ME OUT A LOT.
HELPED YOU OUT?
UH-HUH!
I DON'T KNOW HOW TO PUT IT...
HE ALWAYS BAILS ME OUT WHEN I GO NUTS AND GET IN TROUBLE.
HE'S REALLY THOUGHT-FUL AND MATURE.
OH, BUT HE CAN BE KIND OF A BRAT TOO...
...BUT I FEEL SAFE...
...WHEN I'M WITH RYUNOSUKE.

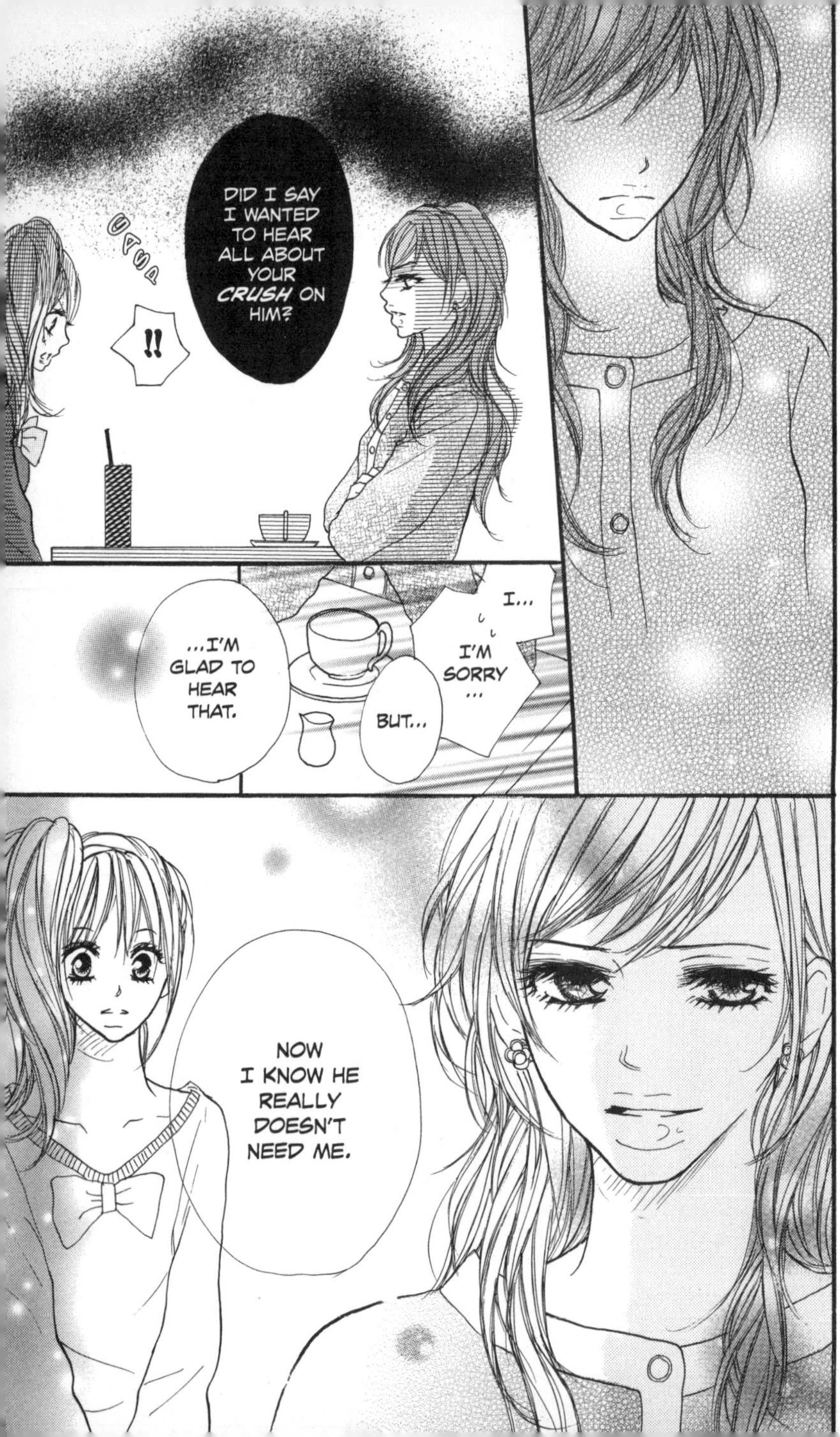
DID I SAY I WANTED TO HEAR ALL ABOUT YOUR *CRUSH* ON HIM?
!!
I...
I'M SORRY...
BUT...
...I'M GLAD TO HEAR THAT.
NOW I KNOW HE REALLY DOESN'T NEED ME.

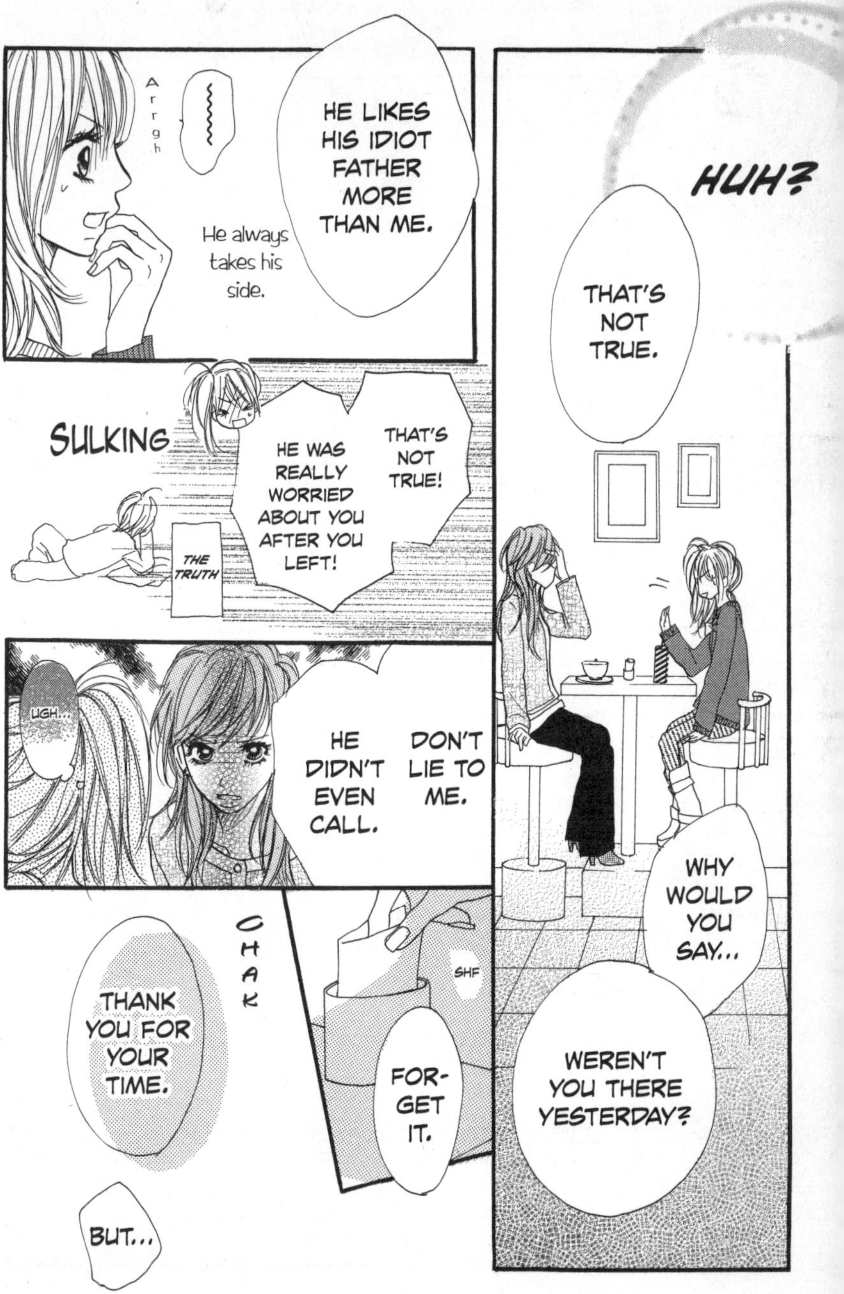
HUH?
THAT'S NOT TRUE.
WHY WOULD YOU SAY...
WEREN'T YOU THERE YESTERDAY?
HE LIKES HIS IDIOT FATHER MORE THAN ME.
Arrgh
He always takes his side.
THAT'S NOT TRUE!
HE WAS REALLY WORRIED ABOUT YOU AFTER YOU LEFT!
SULKING
THE TRUTH
DON'T LIE TO ME.
HE DIDN'T EVEN CALL.
UGH...
SHF
CHAK
FOR-GET IT.
THANK YOU FOR YOUR TIME.
BUT...

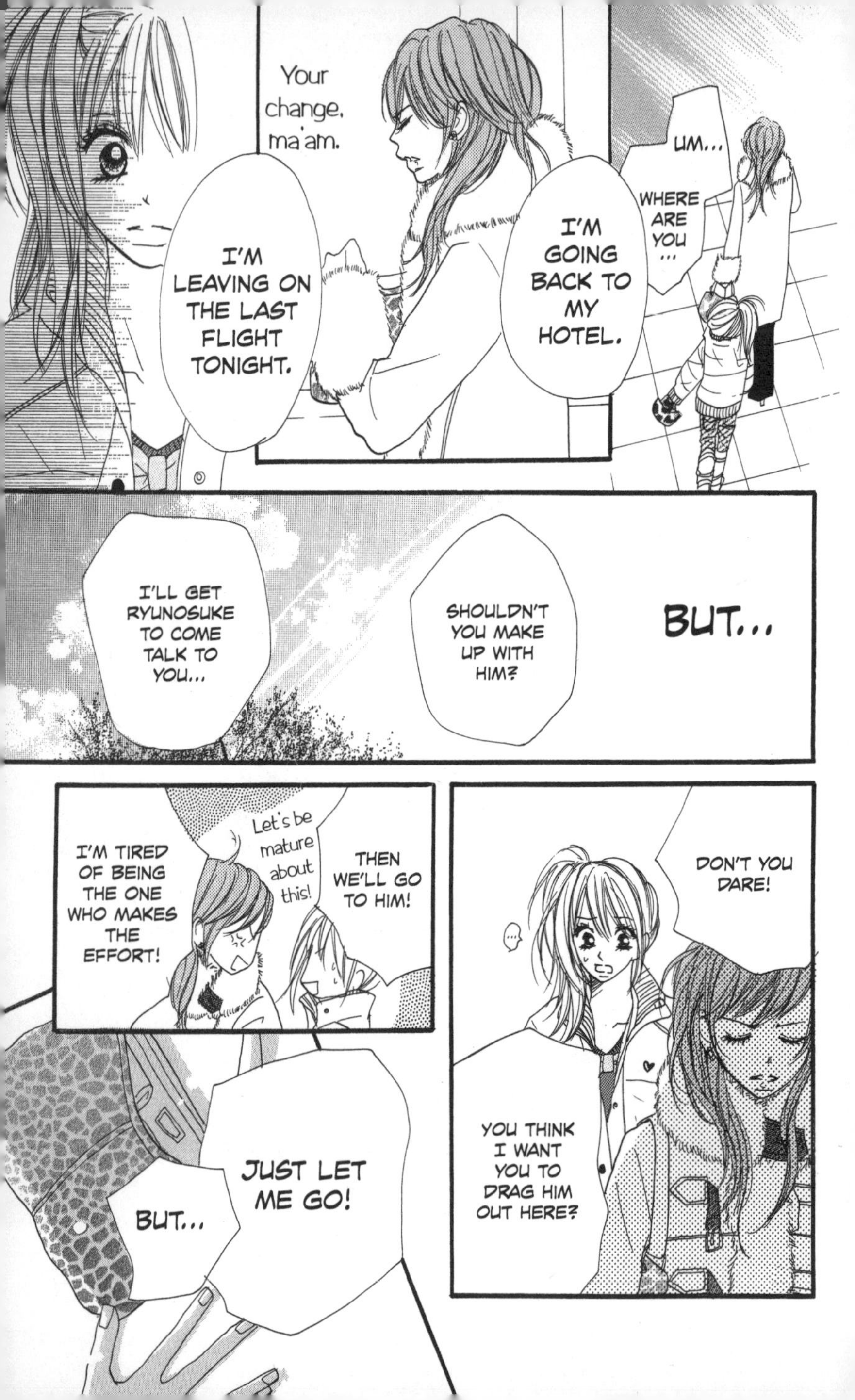
UM...
WHERE ARE YOU ...
Your change, ma'am.
I'M GOING BACK TO MY HOTEL.
I'M LEAVING ON THE LAST FLIGHT TONIGHT.
BUT...
SHOULDN'T YOU MAKE UP WITH HIM?
I'LL GET RYUNOSUKE TO COME TALK TO YOU...
DON'T YOU DARE!
...
YOU THINK I WANT YOU TO DRAG HIM OUT HERE?
THEN WE'LL GO TO HIM!
Let's be mature about this!
I'M TIRED OF BEING THE ONE WHO MAKES THE EFFORT!
JUST LET ME GO!
BUT...

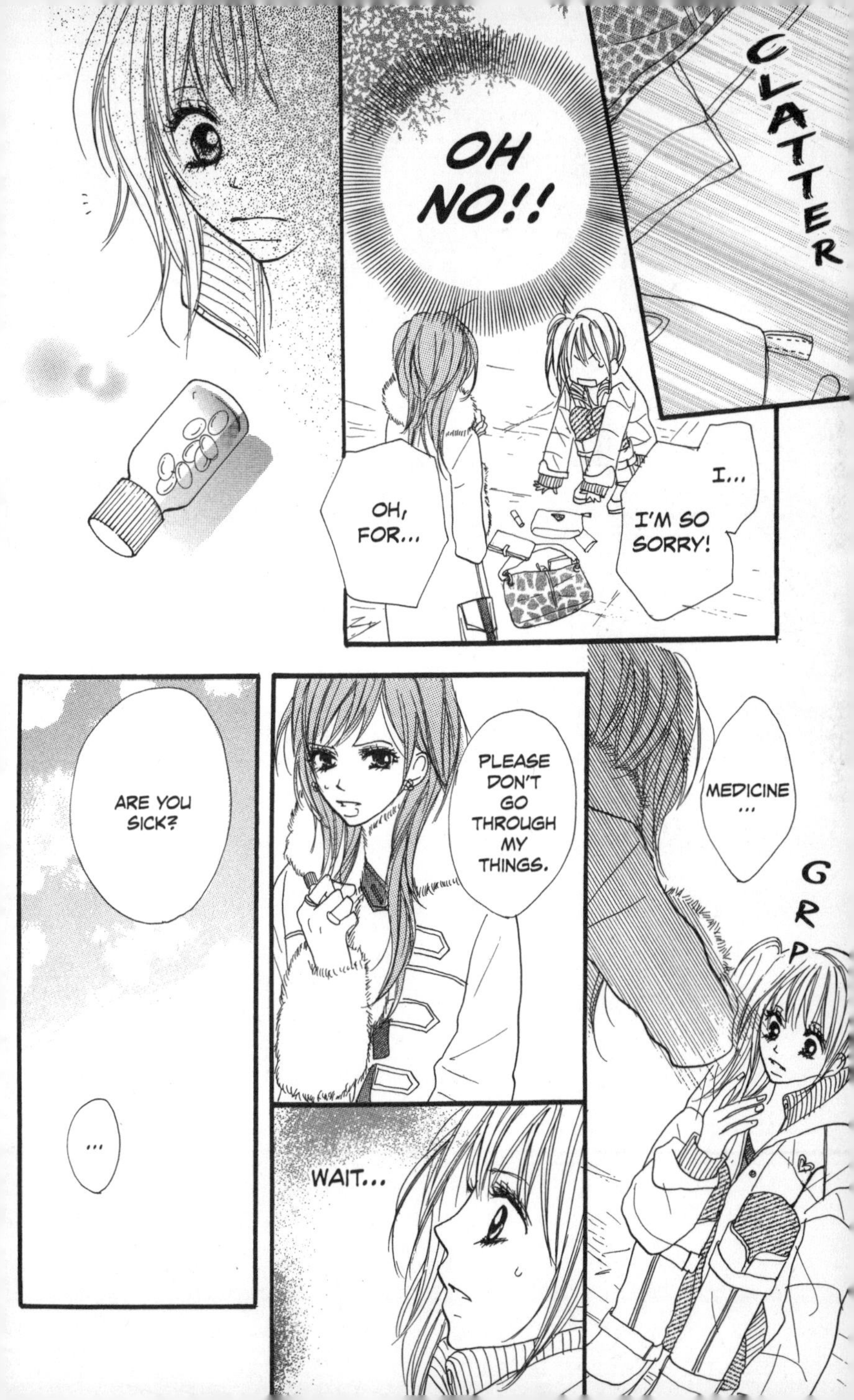
CLATTER
OH NO!!
I... I'M SO SORRY!
OH, FOR...
MEDICINE ...
GRP
PLEASE DON'T GO THROUGH MY THINGS.
WAIT...
ARE YOU SICK?
...

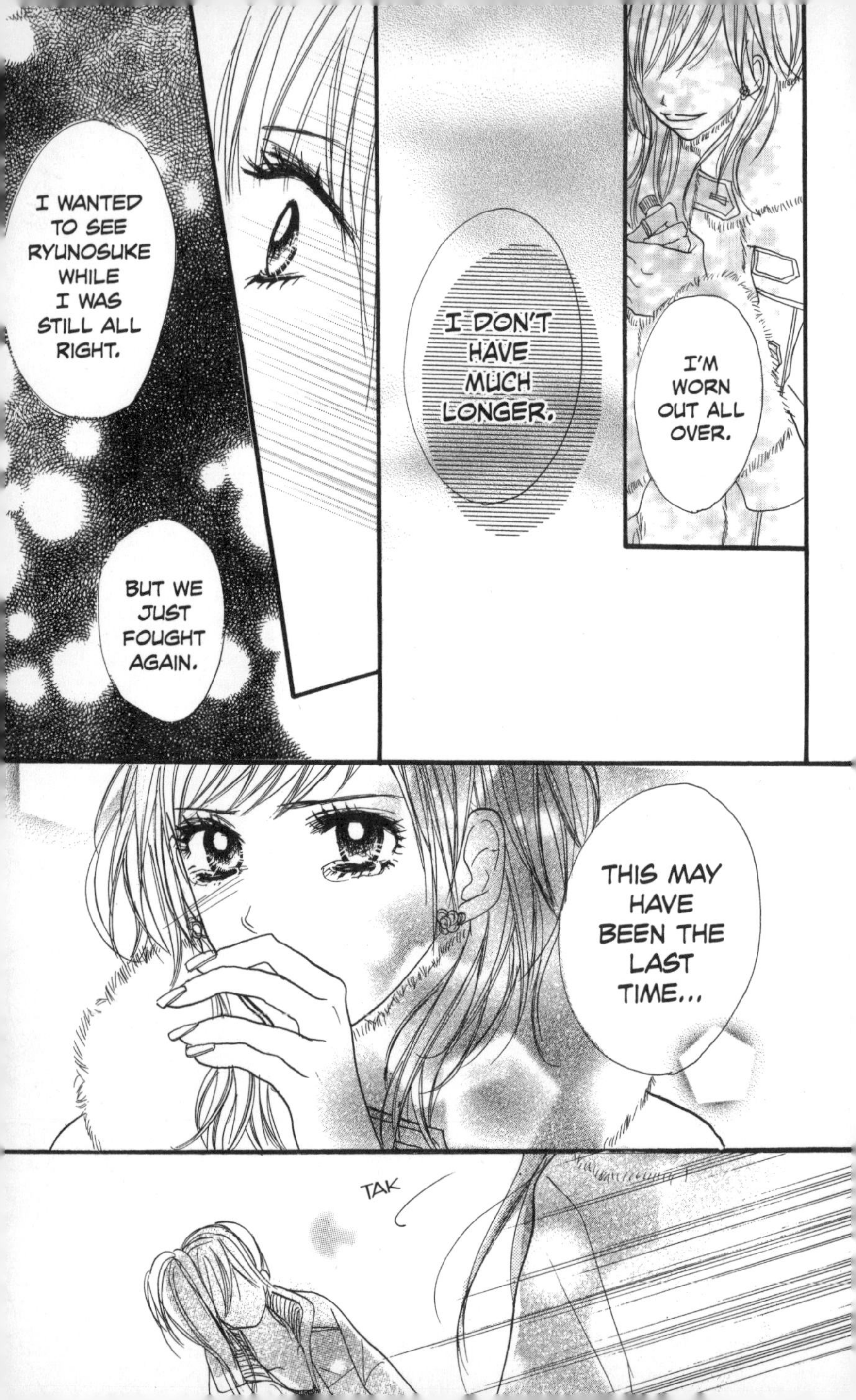
I'M WORN OUT ALL OVER.
I DON'T HAVE MUCH LONGER.
I WANTED TO SEE RYUNOSUKE WHILE I WAS STILL ALL RIGHT.
BUT WE JUST FOUGHT AGAIN.
THIS MAY HAVE BEEN THE LAST TIME...
TAK

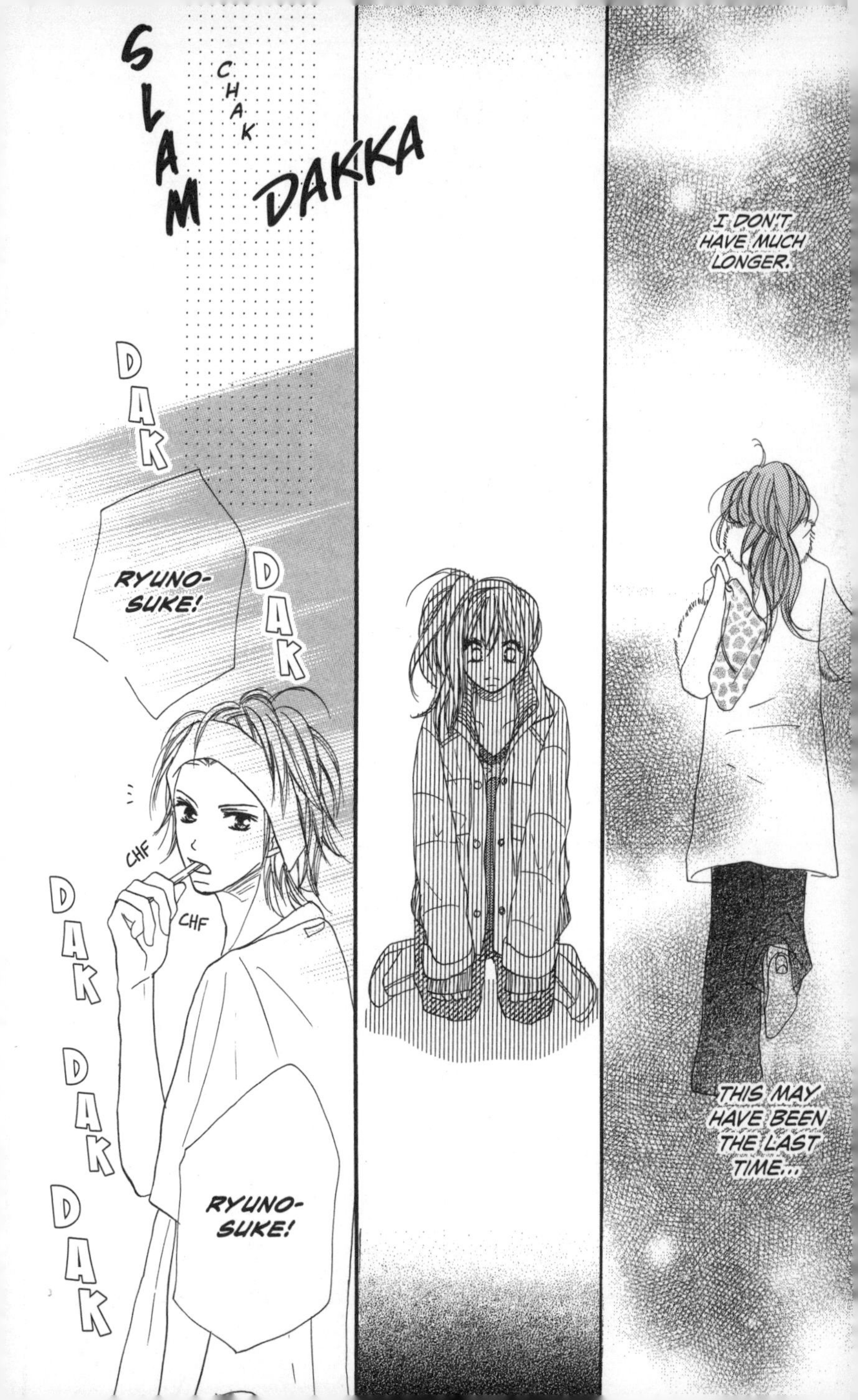
I DON'T HAVE MUCH LONGER.
THIS MAY HAVE BEEN THE LAST TIME...
SLAM
CHAK
DAKKA
DAK
RYUNO-SUKE!
DAK
CHF
CHF
DAK
DAK
DAK
RYUNO-SUKE!

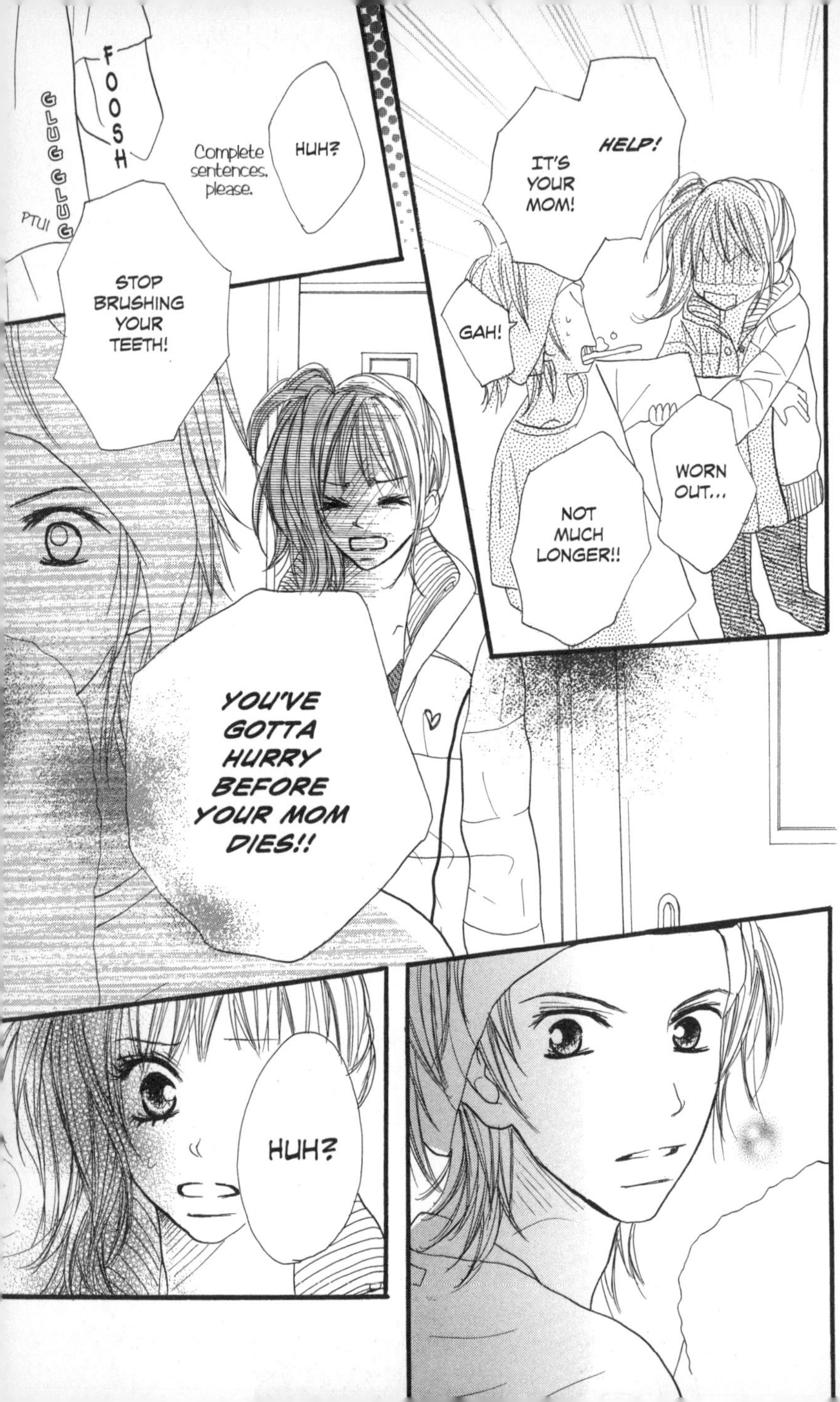
HELP!
IT'S YOUR MOM!
GAH!
WORN OUT...
NOT MUCH LONGER!!
HUH?
Complete sentences, please.
FOOSH
GLUGGLUGG
PTUI
STOP BRUSHING YOUR TEETH!
YOU'VE GOTTA HURRY BEFORE YOUR MOM DIES!!
HUH?

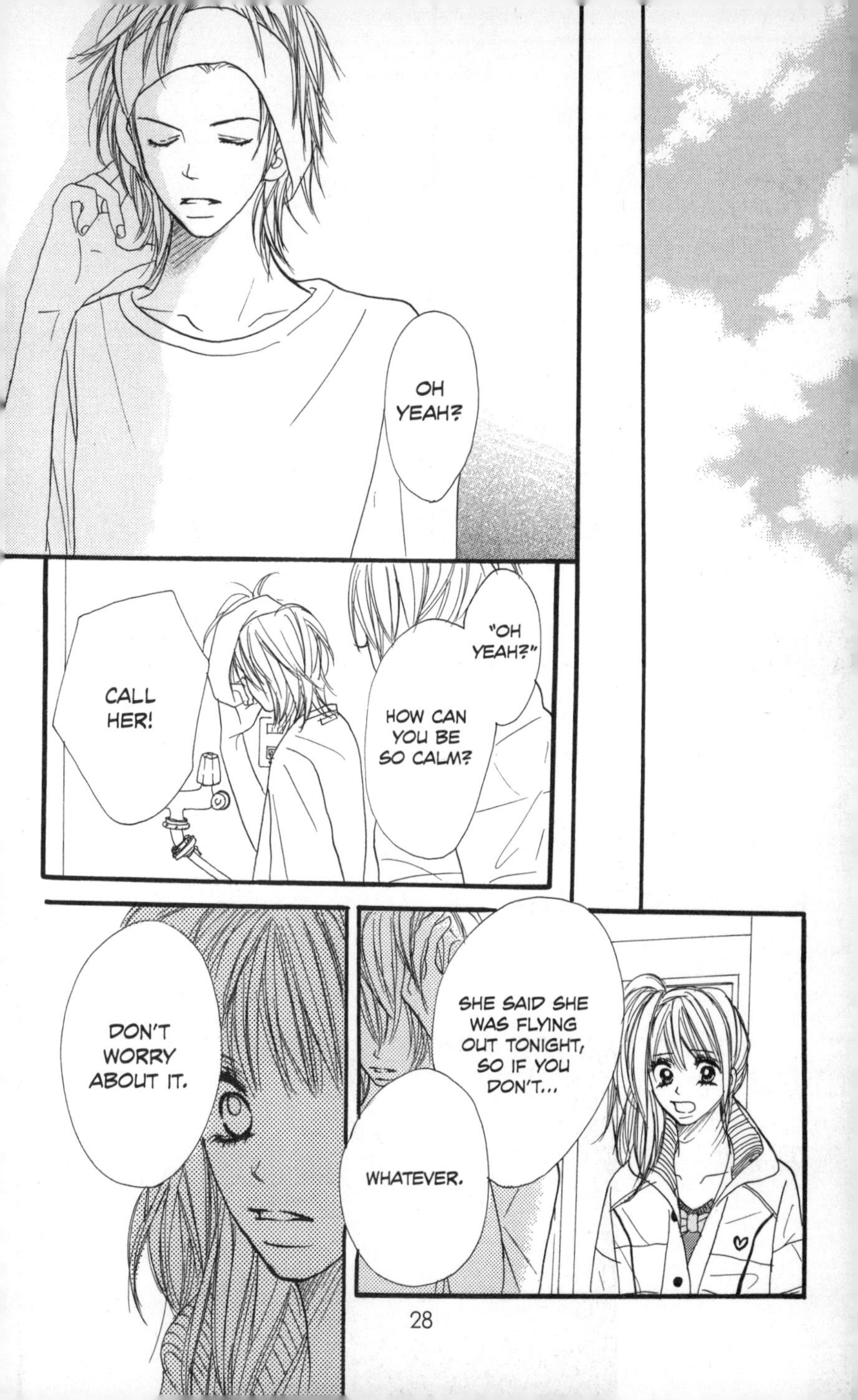
OH YEAH?
"OH YEAH?"
HOW CAN YOU BE SO CALM?
CALL HER!
SHE SAID SHE WAS FLYING OUT TONIGHT, SO IF YOU DON'T...
WHATEVER.
DON'T WORRY ABOUT IT.

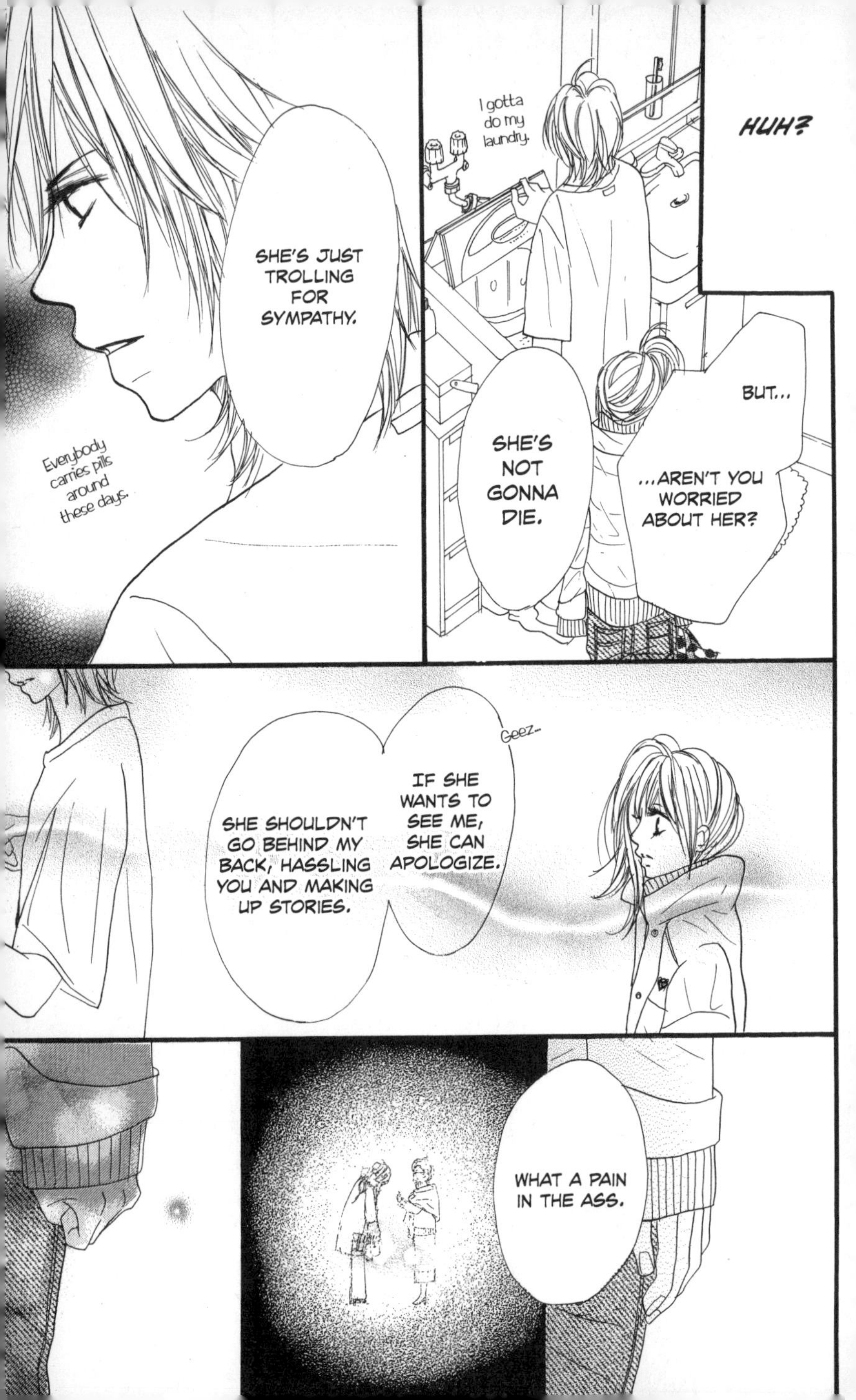
HUH?
I gotta do my laundry.
BUT... ...AREN'T YOU WORRIED ABOUT HER?
SHE'S NOT GONNA DIE.
SHE'S JUST TROLLING FOR SYMPATHY.
Everybody carries pills around these days.
Geez...
IF SHE WANTS TO SEE ME, SHE CAN APOLOGIZE.
SHE SHOULDN'T GO BEHIND MY BACK, HASSLING YOU AND MAKING UP STORIES.
WHAT A PAIN IN THE ASS.

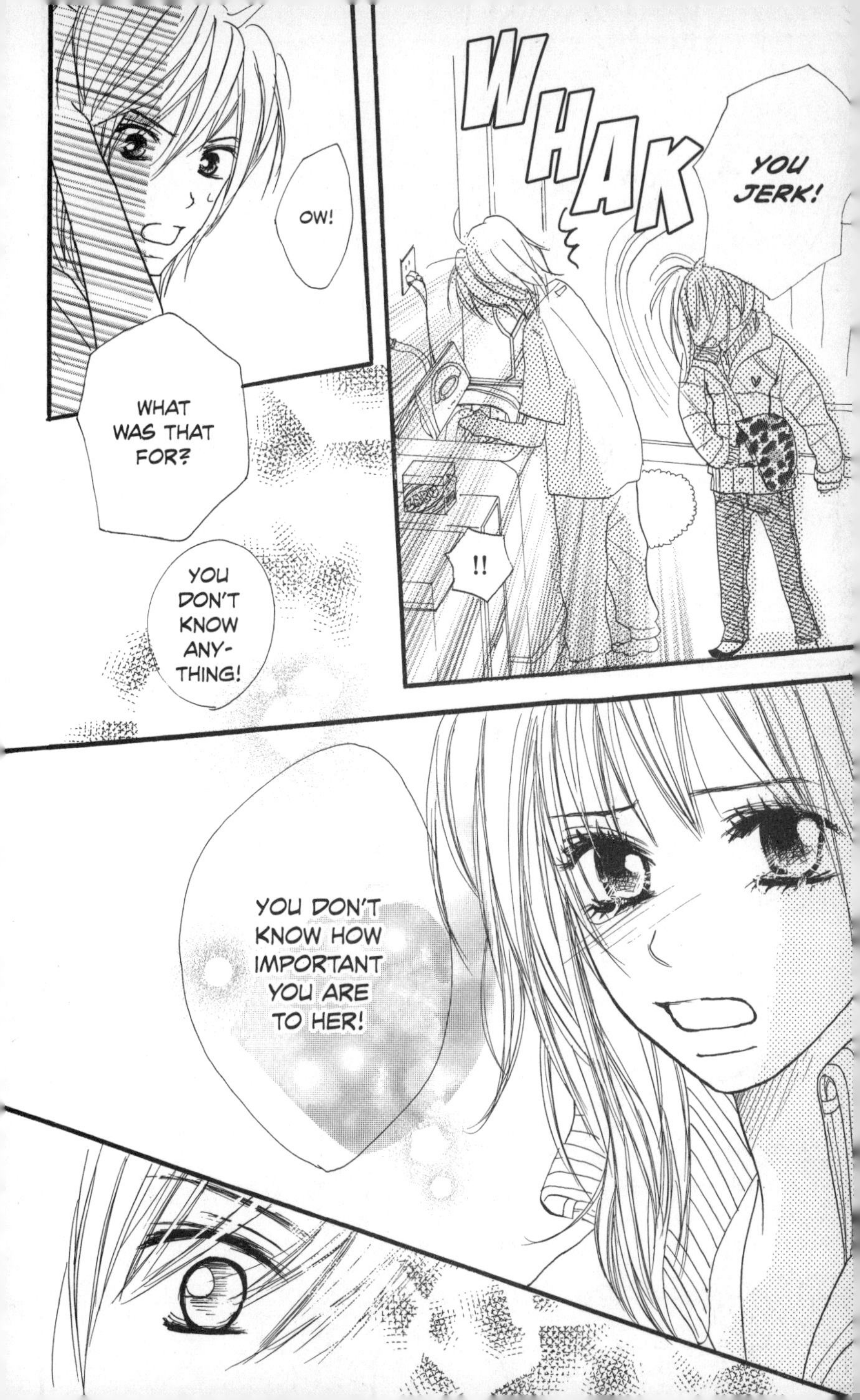
YOU JERK!
WHAK
!!
OW!
WHAT WAS THAT FOR?
YOU DON'T KNOW ANYTHING!
YOU DON'T KNOW HOW IMPORTANT YOU ARE TO HER!

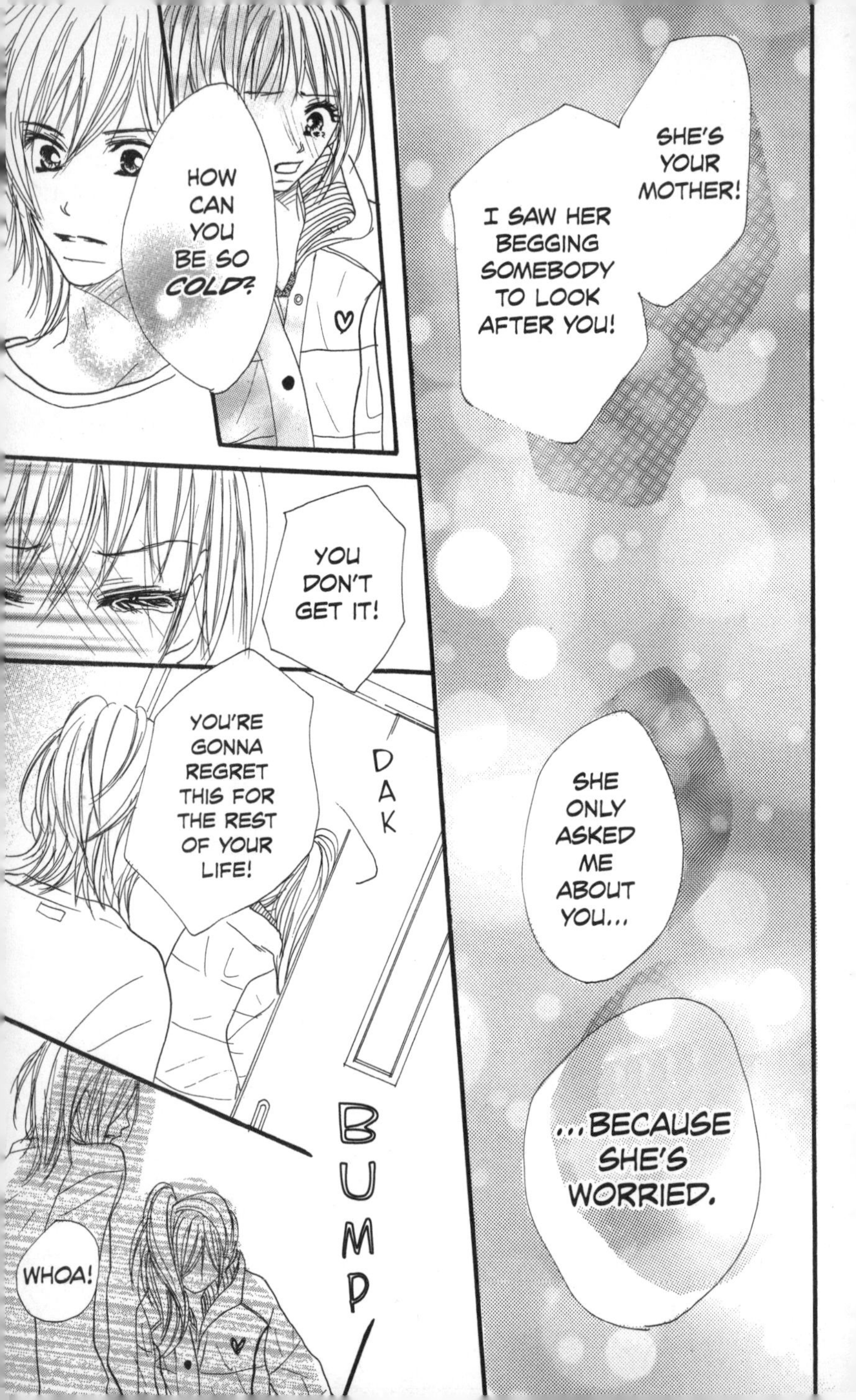
SHE'S YOUR MOTHER!
I SAW HER BEGGING SOMEBODY TO LOOK AFTER YOU!
SHE ONLY ASKED ME ABOUT YOU...
...BECAUSE SHE'S WORRIED.
HOW CAN YOU BE SO COLD?
YOU DON'T GET IT!
YOU'RE GONNA REGRET THIS FOR THE REST OF YOUR LIFE!
DAK
BUMP
WHOA!

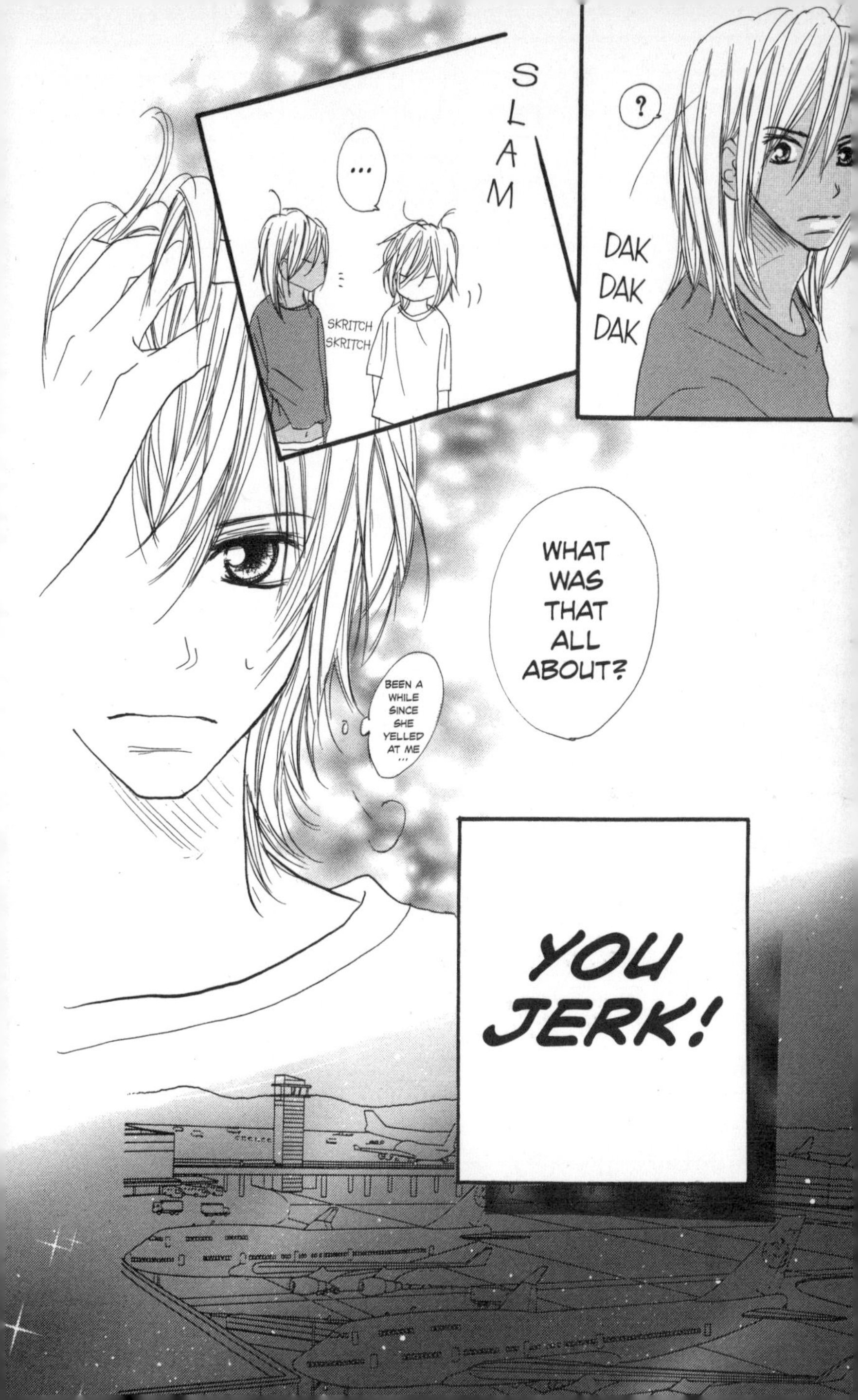
?
DAK DAK DAK
SLAM
...
SKRITCH SKRITCH
WHAT WAS THAT ALL ABOUT?
BEEN A WHILE SINCE SHE YELLED AT ME...
YOU JERK!

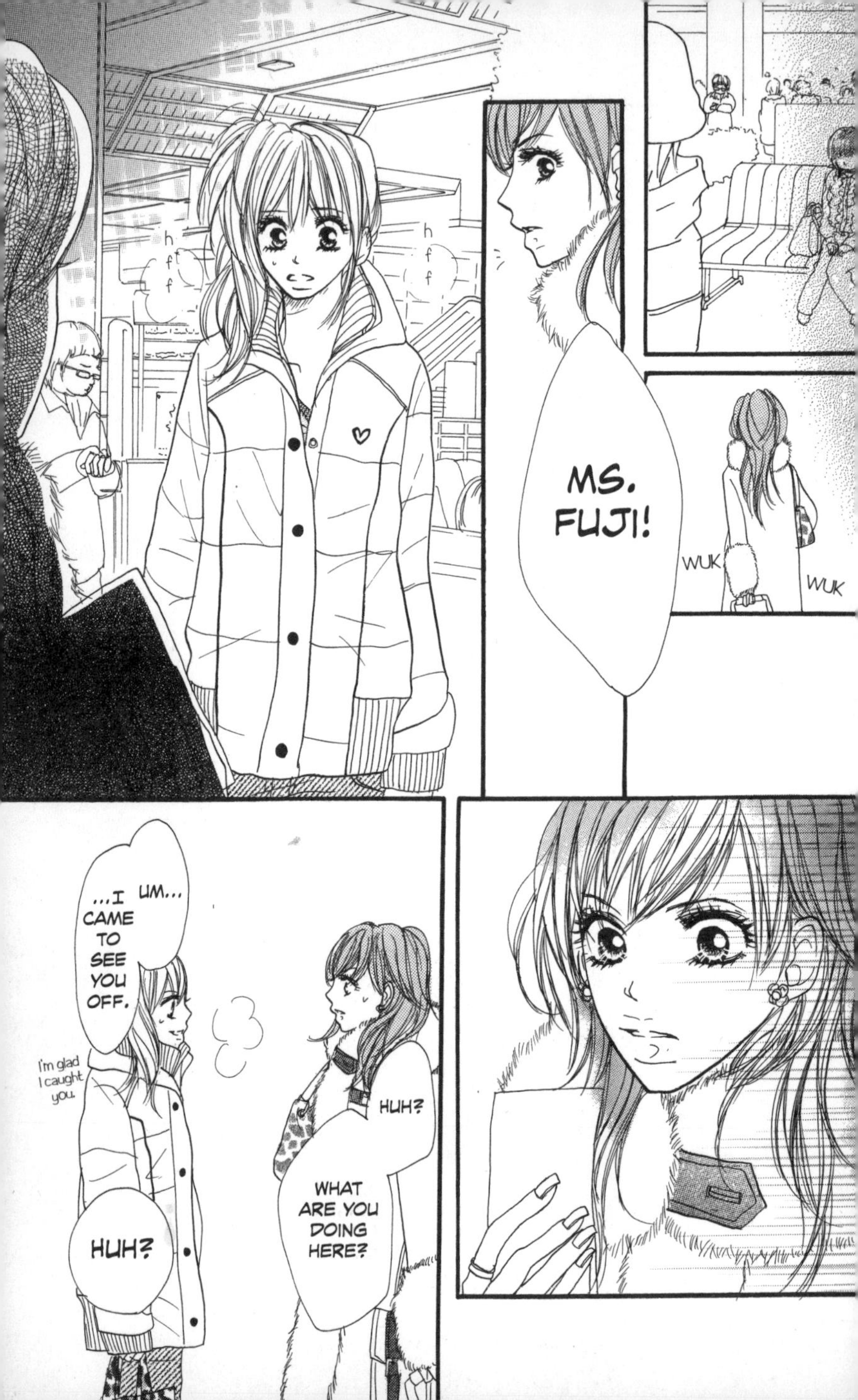
WUK
WUK
MS. FUJI!
h f f
h f f
HUH?
WHAT ARE YOU DOING HERE?
HUH?
UM... ...I CAME TO SEE YOU OFF.
I'm glad I caught you.

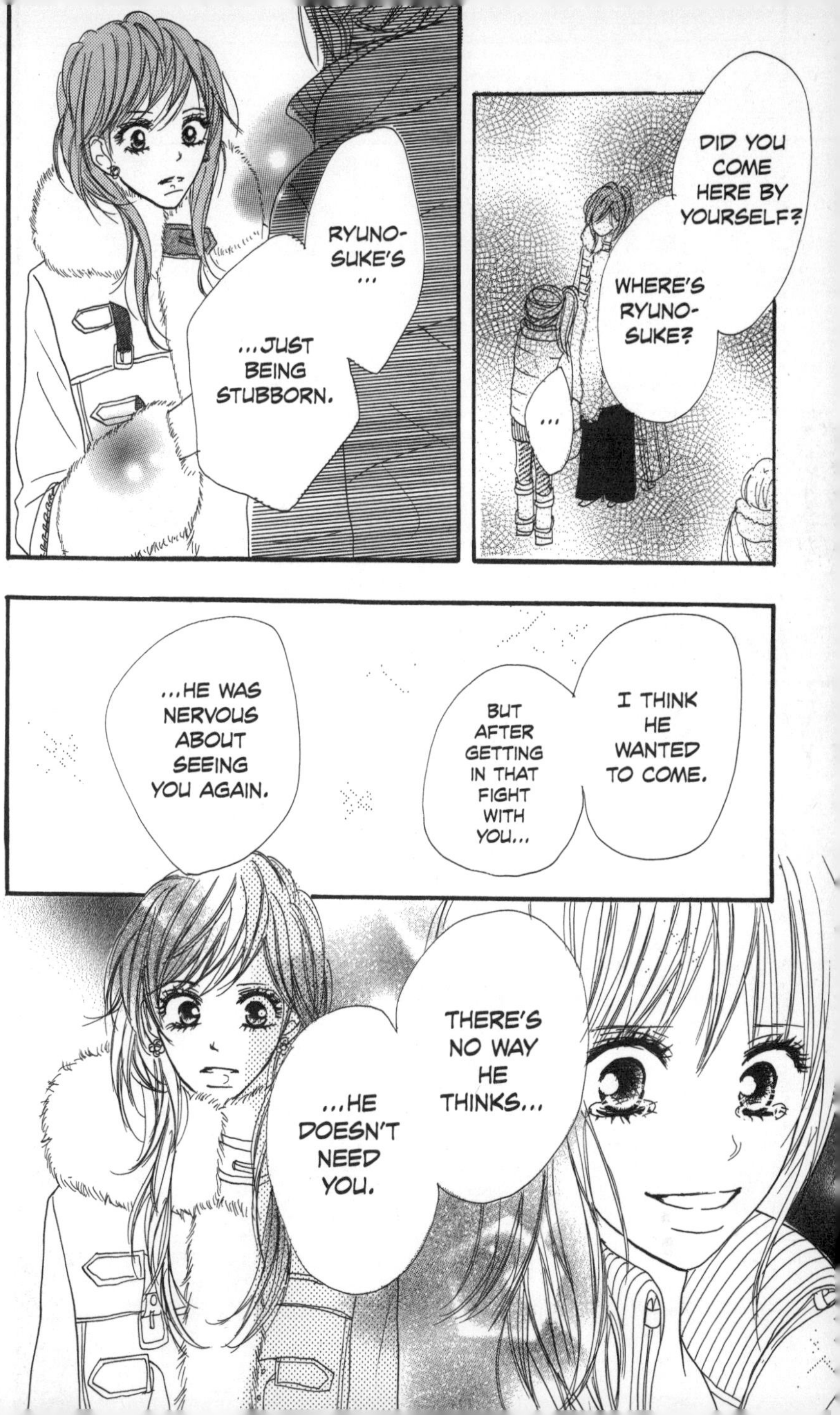
DID YOU COME HERE BY YOURSELF?
WHERE'S RYUNOSUKE?
...
RYUNOSUKE'S...
...JUST BEING STUBBORN.
I THINK HE WANTED TO COME.
BUT AFTER GETTING IN THAT FIGHT WITH YOU...
...HE WAS NERVOUS ABOUT SEEING YOU AGAIN.
THERE'S NO WAY HE THINKS...
...HE DOESN'T NEED YOU.

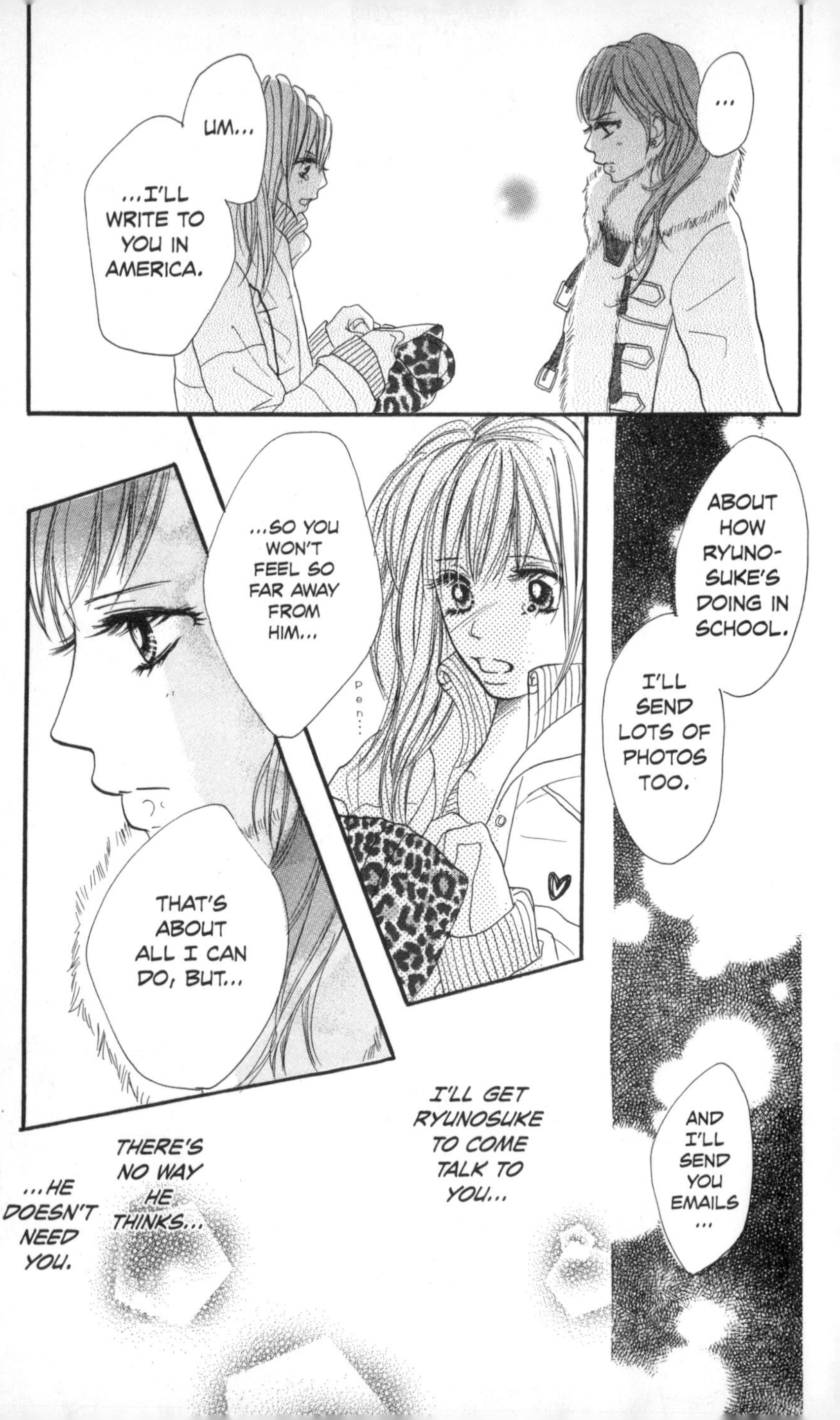
...
UM...
...I'LL WRITE TO YOU IN AMERICA.
ABOUT HOW RYUNO-SUKE'S DOING IN SCHOOL.
I'LL SEND LOTS OF PHOTOS TOO.
AND I'LL SEND YOU EMAILS...
...SO YOU WON'T FEEL SO FAR AWAY FROM HIM...
Pen...
THAT'S ABOUT ALL I CAN DO, BUT...
I'LL GET RYUNOSUKE TO COME TALK TO YOU...
THERE'S NO WAY HE THINKS...
...HE DOESN'T NEED YOU.

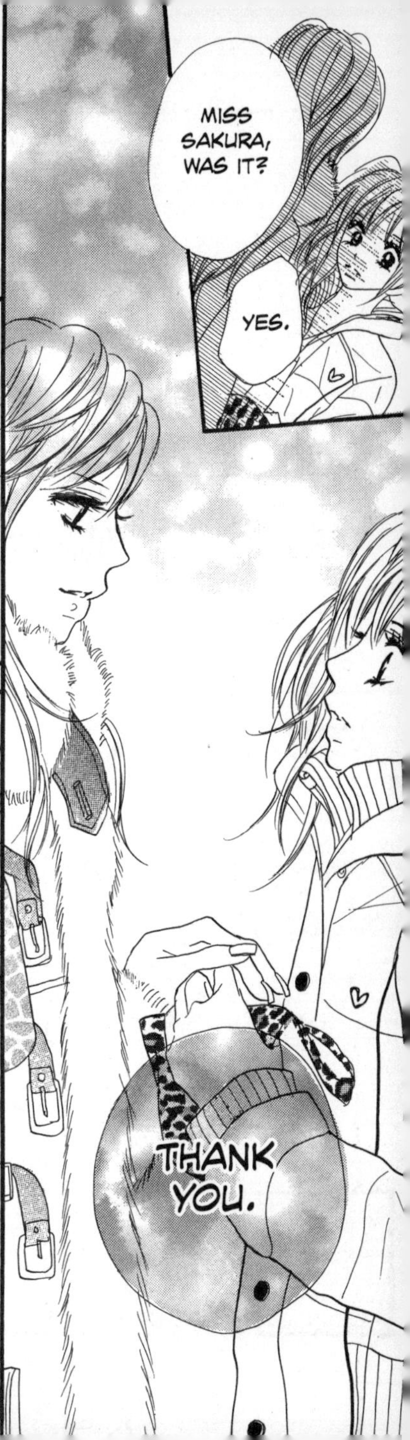
MISS SAKURA, WAS IT?
YES.
THANK YOU.
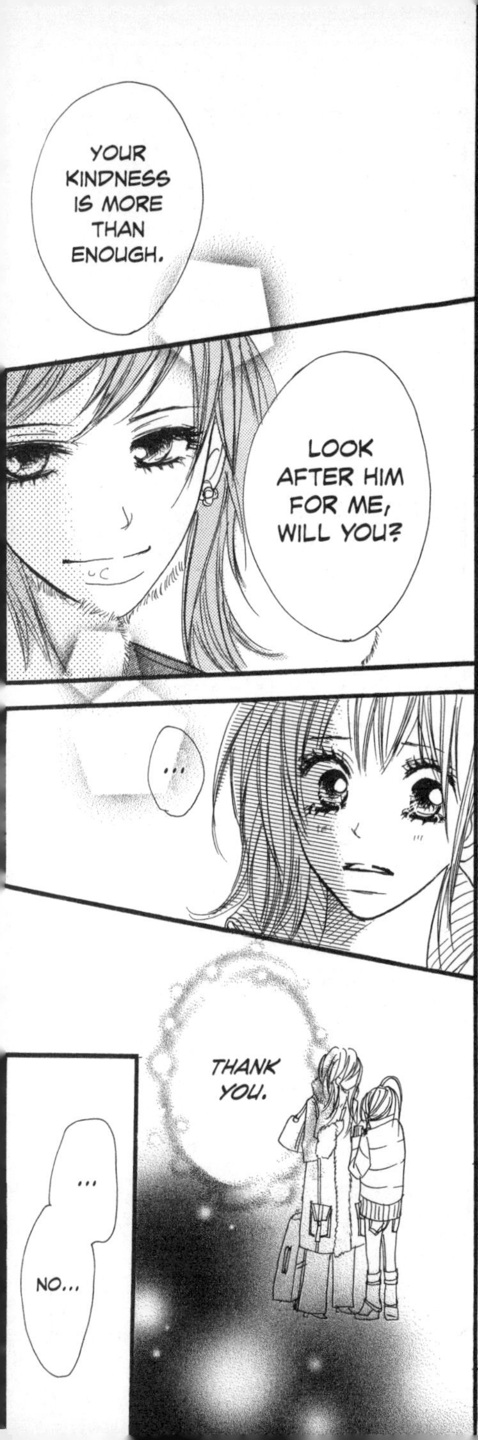
YOUR KINDNESS IS MORE THAN ENOUGH.
LOOK AFTER HIM FOR ME, WILL YOU?
...
THANK YOU.
... NO...

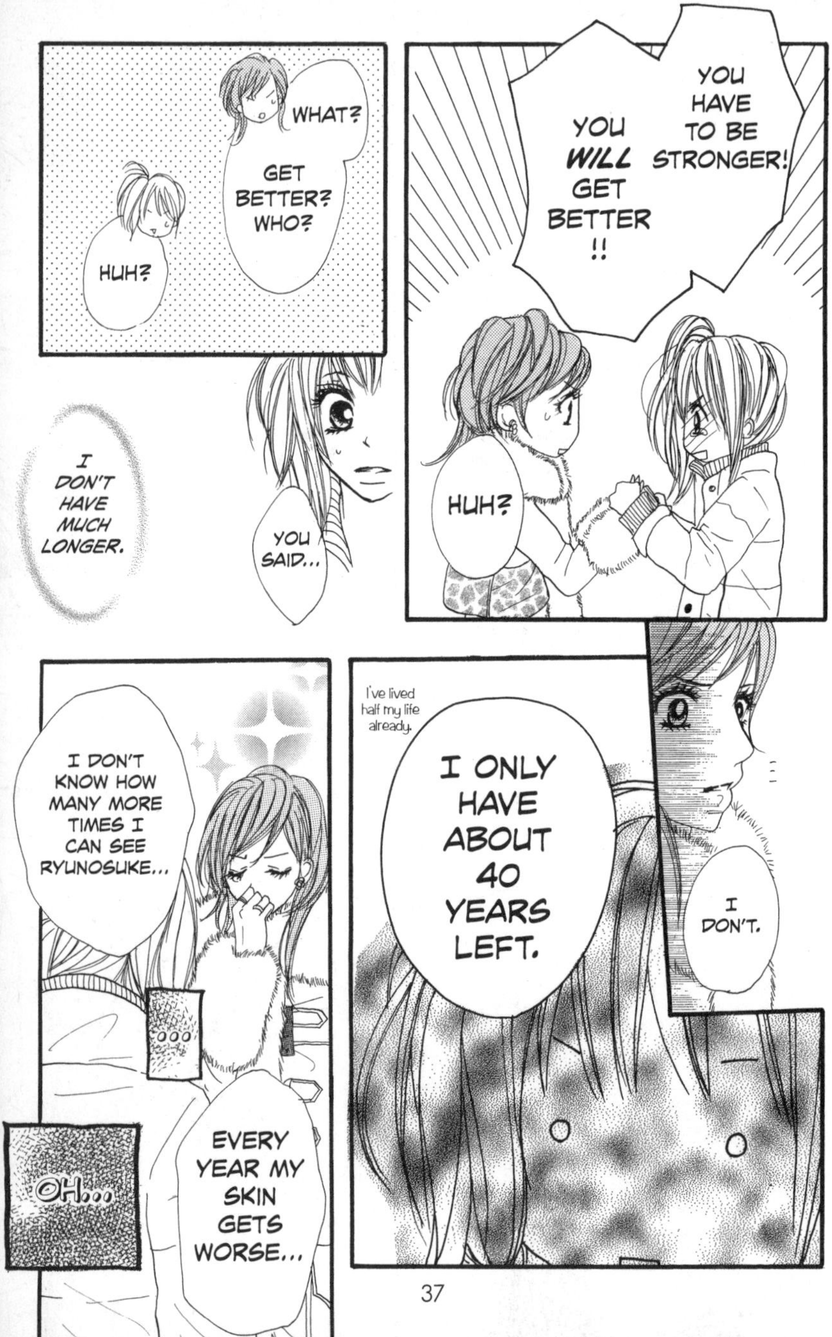
YOU HAVE TO BE STRONGER!
YOU ***WILL*** GET BETTER!!
HUH?
WHAT?
GET BETTER? WHO?
HUH?
YOU SAID...
I DON'T HAVE MUCH LONGER.
I DON'T.
I've lived half my life already.
I ONLY HAVE ABOUT 40 YEARS LEFT.
I DON'T KNOW HOW MANY MORE TIMES I CAN SEE RYUNOSUKE...
...
EVERY YEAR MY SKIN GETS WORSE...
OH...

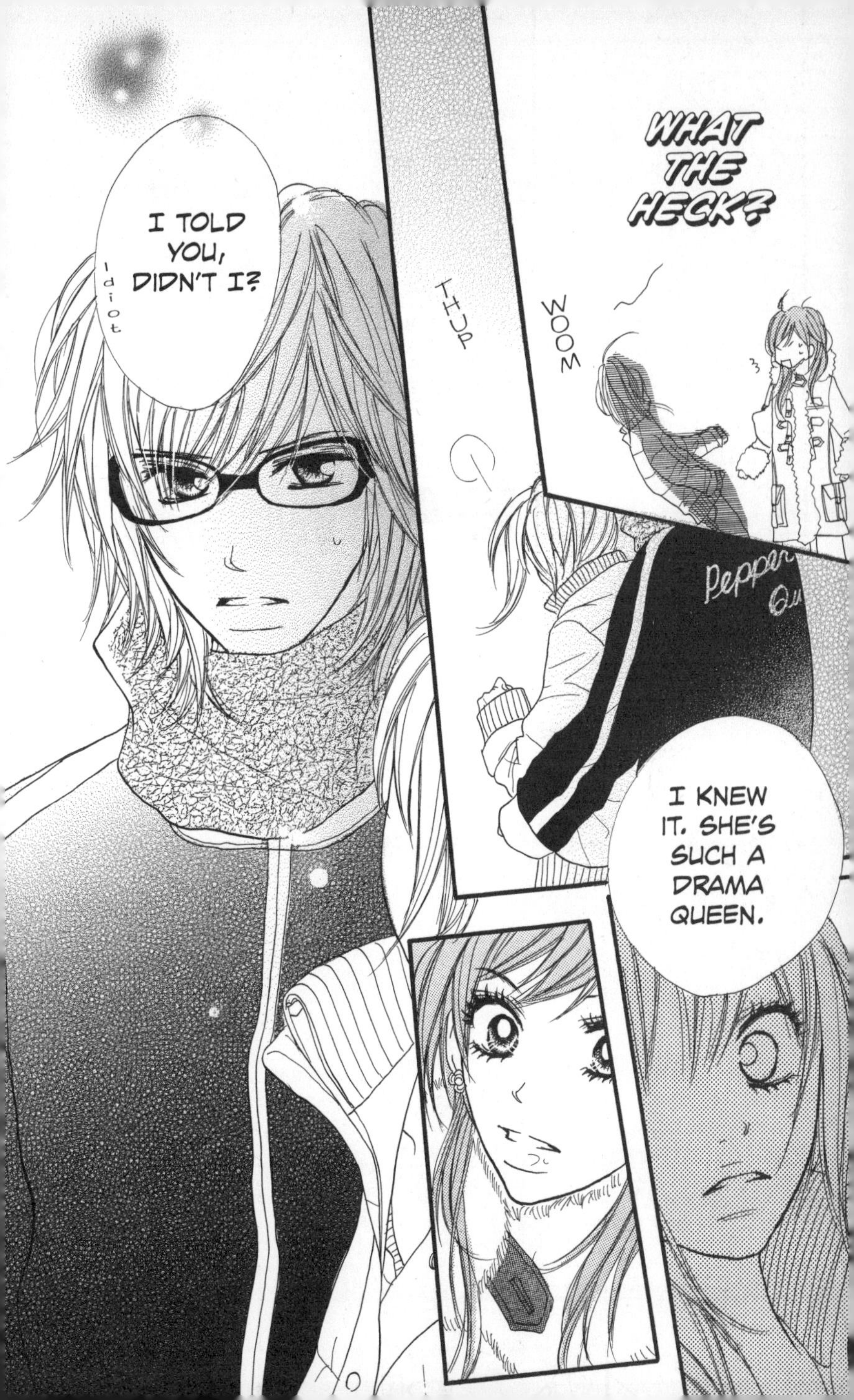
WHAT THE HECK?
WOOM
THUP
Pepper
I TOLD YOU, DIDN'T I?
idiot
I KNEW IT. SHE'S SUCH A DRAMA QUEEN.

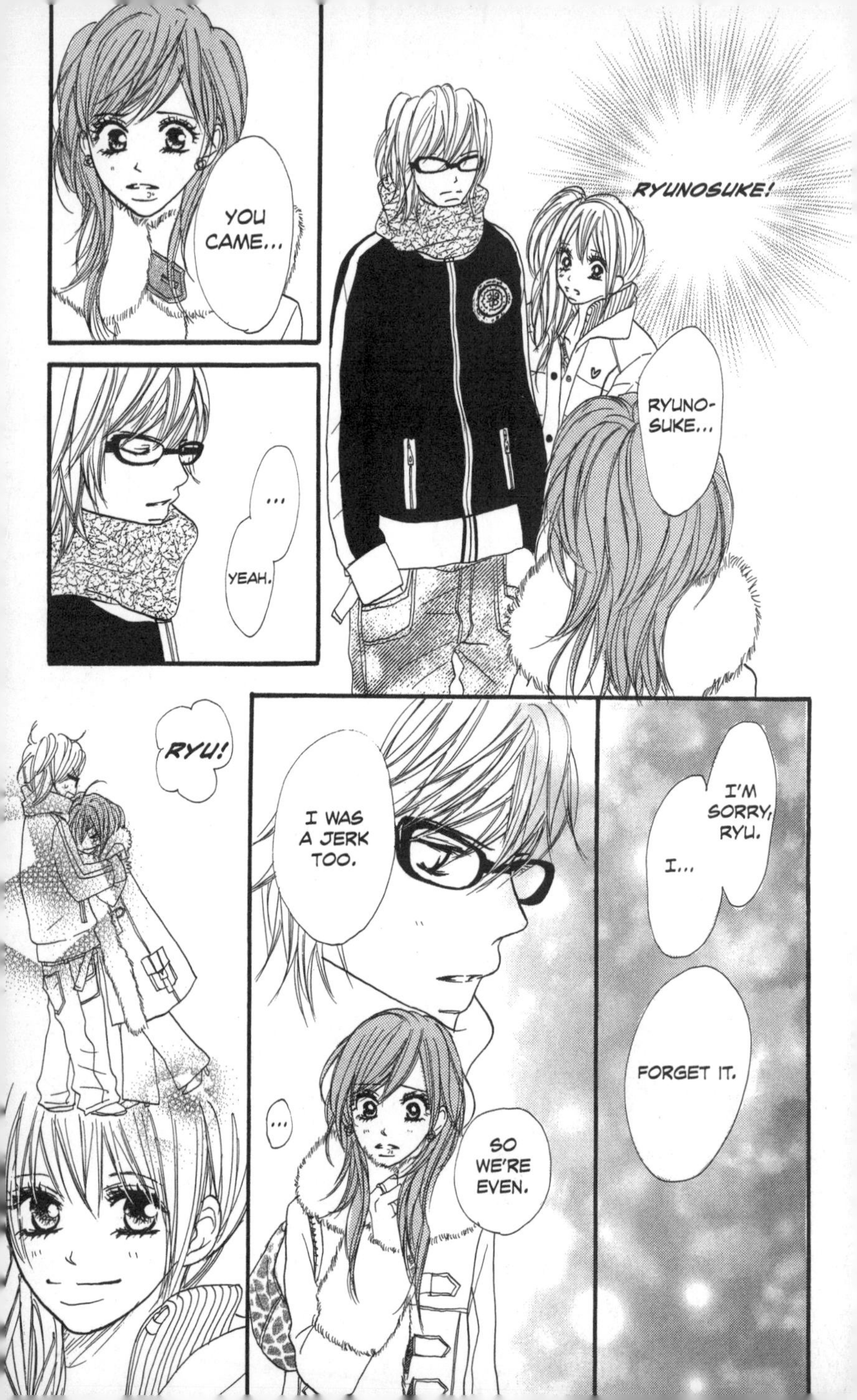
RYUNOSUKE!
RYUNO-SUKE...
YOU CAME...
...
YEAH.
I'M SORRY, RYU.
I...
FORGET IT.
I WAS A JERK TOO.
SO WE'RE EVEN.
...
RYU!

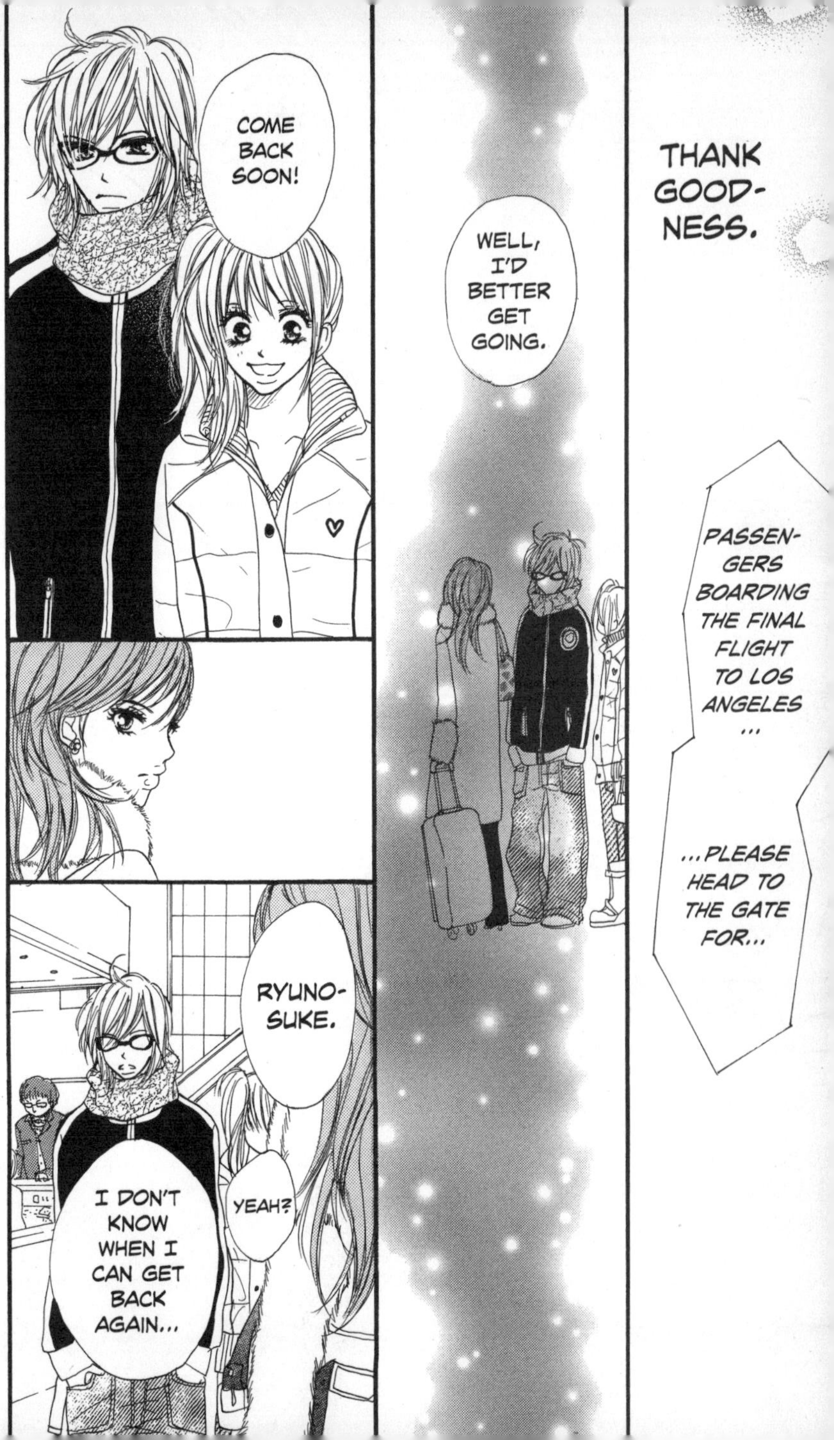
THANK GOOD-NESS.
PASSEN-GERS BOARDING THE FINAL FLIGHT TO LOS ANGELES ...
...PLEASE HEAD TO THE GATE FOR...
WELL, I'D BETTER GET GOING.
COME BACK SOON!
RYUNO-SUKE.
YEAH?
I DON'T KNOW WHEN I CAN GET BACK AGAIN...

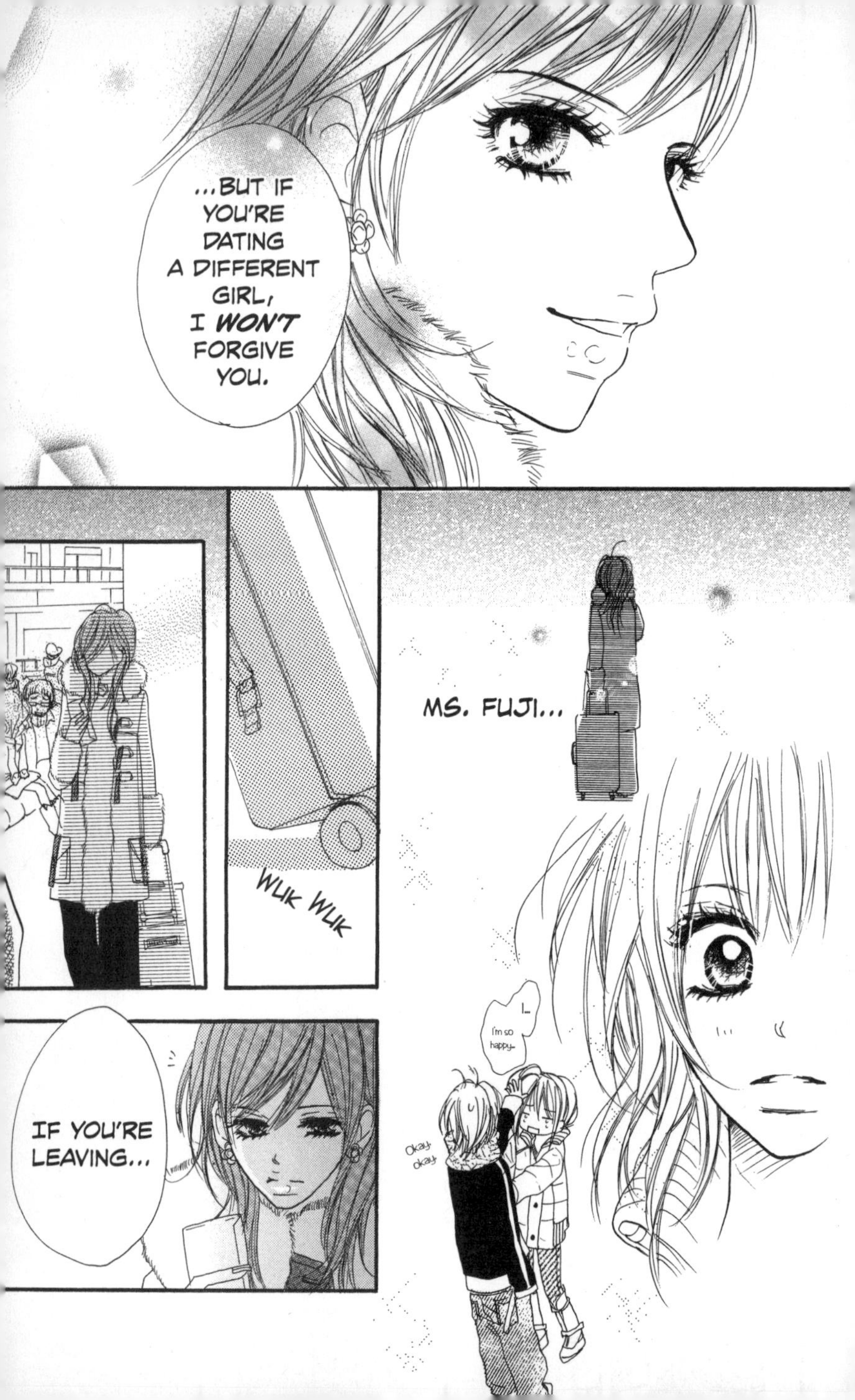
...BUT IF YOU'RE DATING A DIFFERENT GIRL, I WON'T FORGIVE YOU.
MS. FUJI...
I...
I'm so happy...
Okay, okay.
WUK WUK
IF YOU'RE LEAVING...

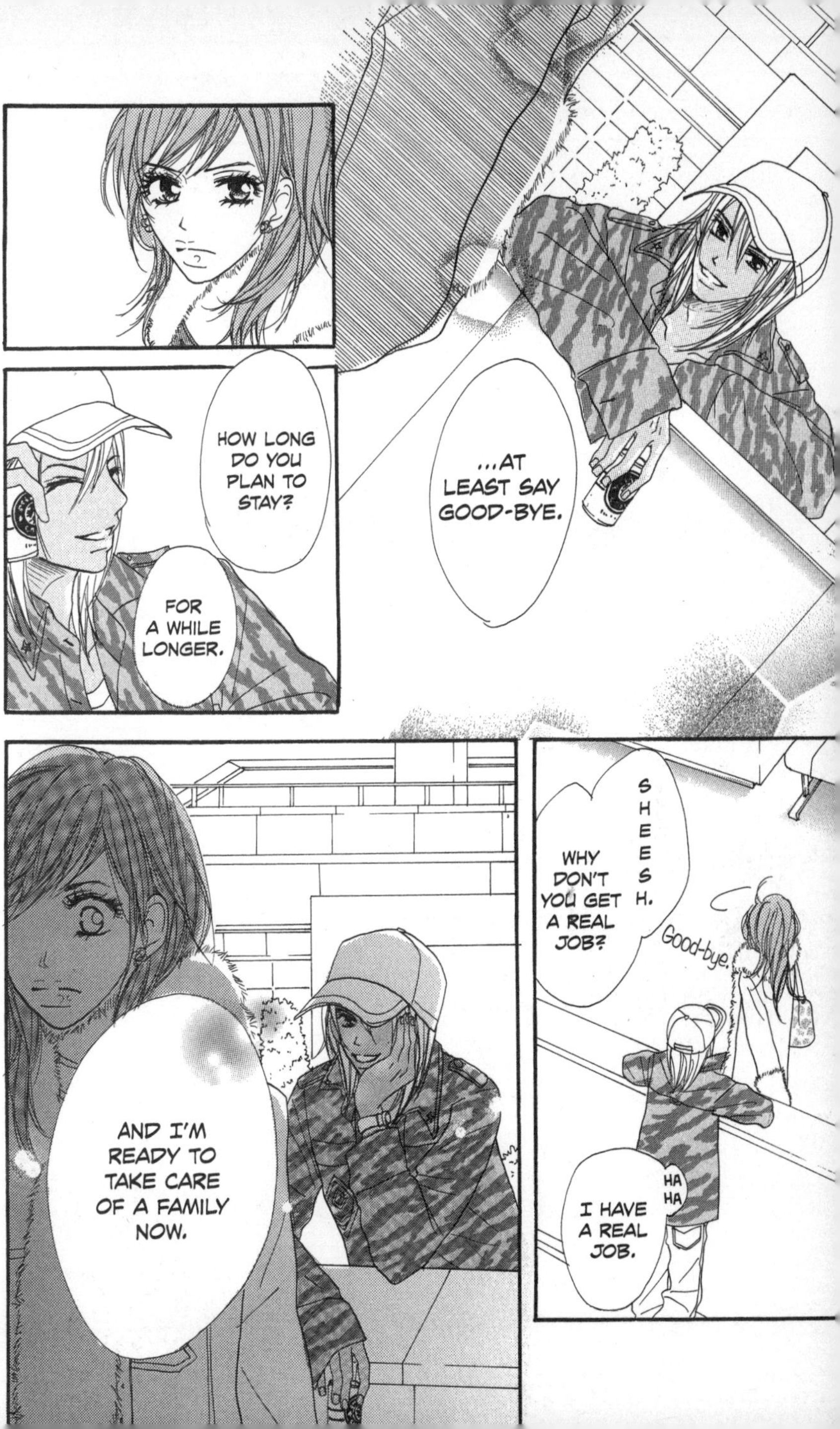
...AT LEAST SAY GOOD-BYE.
HOW LONG DO YOU PLAN TO STAY?
FOR A WHILE LONGER.
SHEESH.
WHY DON'T YOU GET A REAL JOB?
Good-bye.
HA HA
I HAVE A REAL JOB.
AND I'M READY TO TAKE CARE OF A FAMILY NOW.

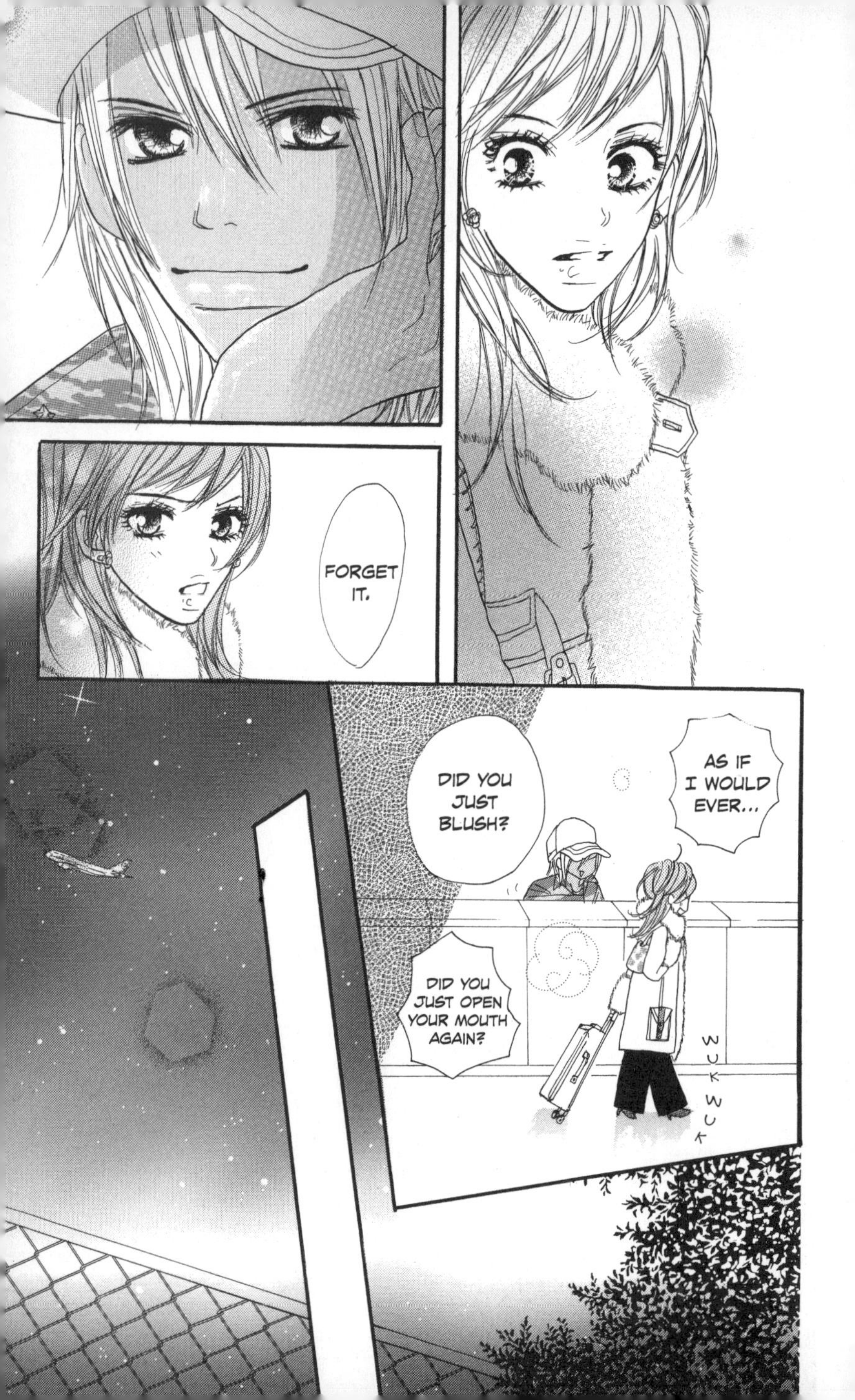
FORGET IT.
AS IF I WOULD EVER...
DID YOU JUST BLUSH?
DID YOU JUST OPEN YOUR MOUTH AGAIN?
WUK WUK

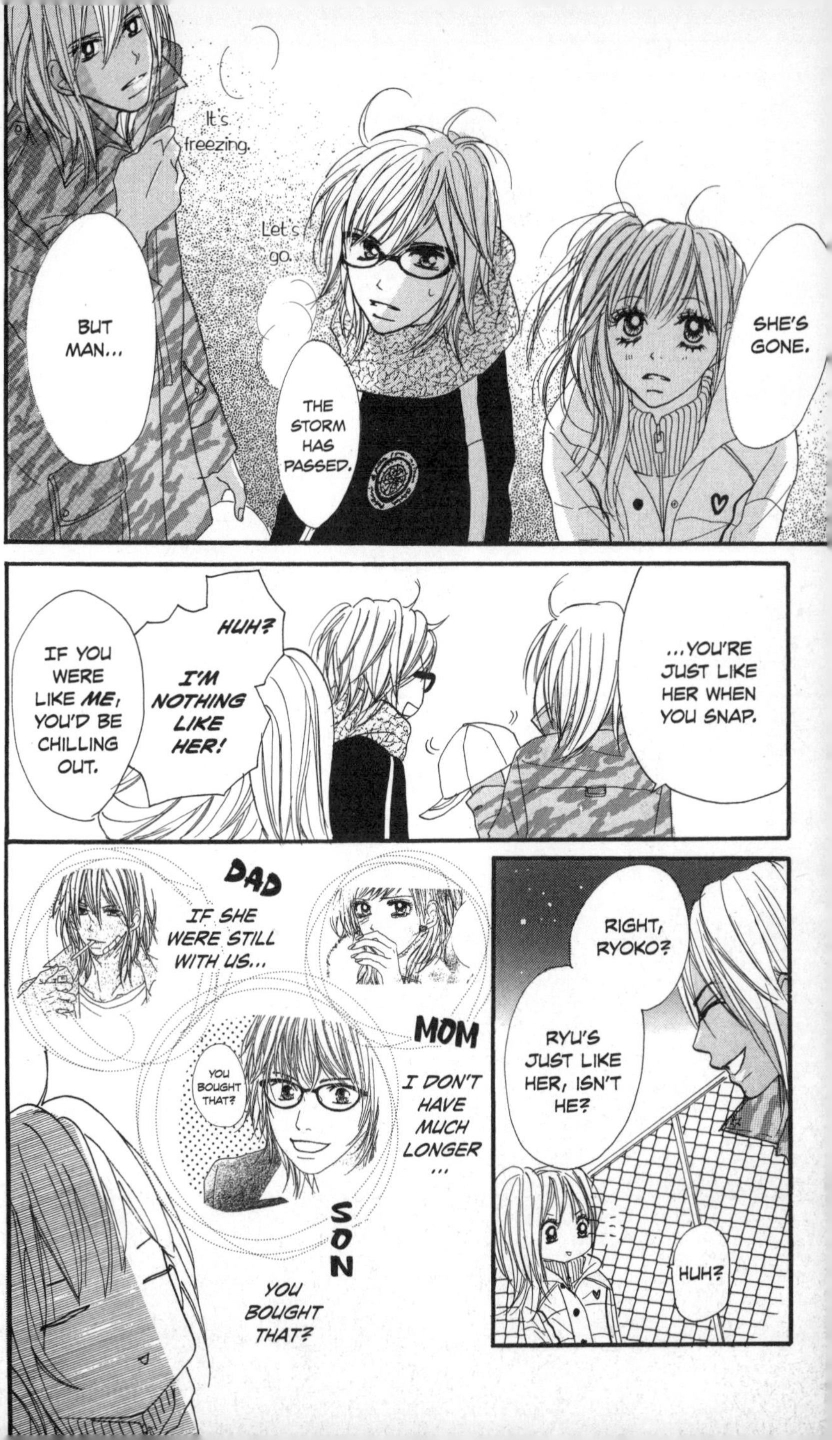
SHE'S GONE.
Let's go.
THE STORM HAS PASSED.
It's freezing.
BUT MAN...
...YOU'RE JUST LIKE HER WHEN YOU SNAP.
HUH?
I'M NOTHING LIKE HER!
IF YOU WERE LIKE ME, YOU'D BE CHILLING OUT.
RIGHT, RYOKO?
RYU'S JUST LIKE HER, ISN'T HE?
HUH?
DAD
IF SHE WERE STILL WITH US...
MOM
I DON'T HAVE MUCH LONGER...
YOU BOUGHT THAT?
SON
YOU BOUGHT THAT?

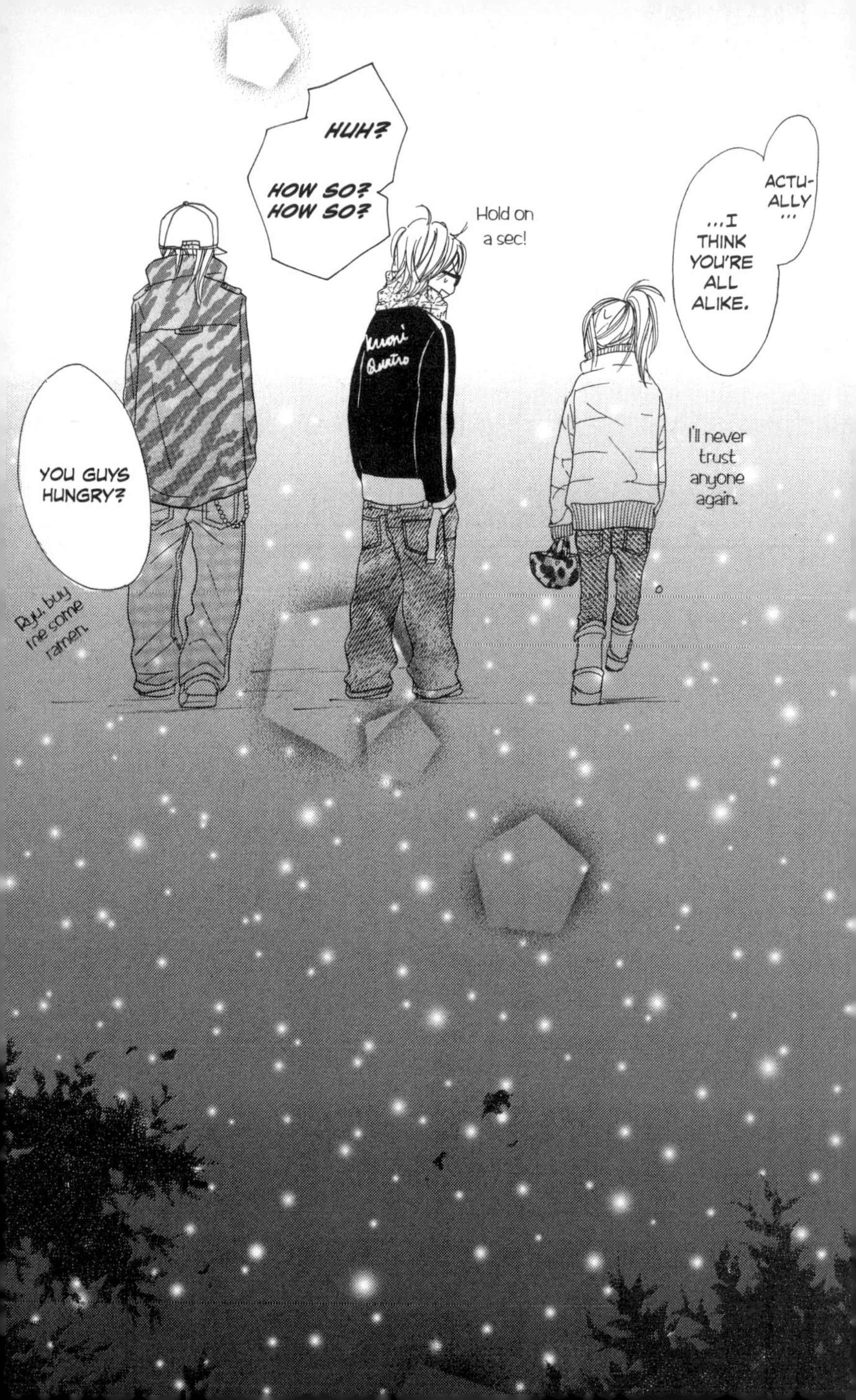
ACTU-ALLY...
...I THINK YOU'RE ALL ALIKE.
I'll never trust anyone again.
Hold on a sec!
HUH?
HOW SO? HOW SO?
YOU GUYS HUNGRY?
Ryu, buy me some ramen.

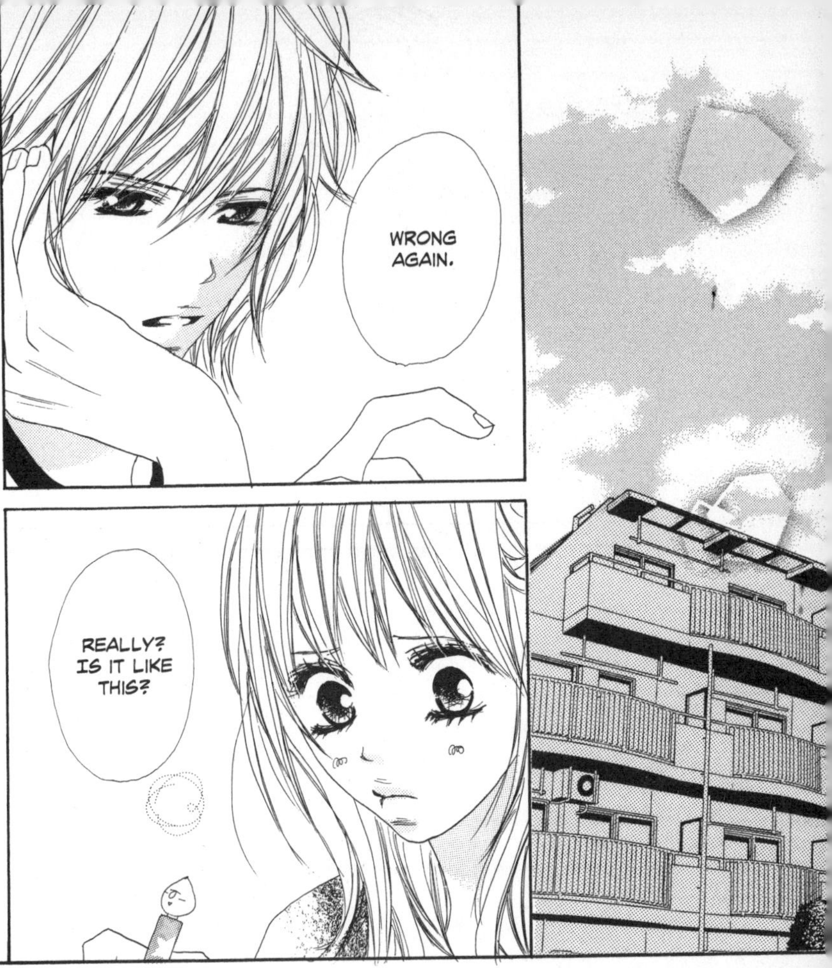
WRONG AGAIN.
REALLY? IS IT LIKE THIS?

I hope you stay kind of a secret. I don't want you to get really famous and be known by everybody... (cry) Sorry for feeling this way. (cry)

K.K., Gifu

AWW... I WANNA GIVE YOU A BIG HUG!! IF I WAS A GUY AND MY GIRLFRIEND SAID THAT TO ME I'D PROPOSE TO HER IN TWO SECONDS. DON'T WORRY, I WON'T BE GOING ANYWHERE! ♡

I uber-love *B.O.D.Y.*!! I especially love the storyline in Volumes 4 and 5 where Ryunosuke risks his life for Ryoko!! Whenever I recommend it to a friend I always tell them, "It's uber-good so just read it!!"

M.N., Hokkaido

YOU'RE UBER-CUTE. ♡ MY HEART TWINGES WHEN I READ LETTERS WRITTEN IN LOCAL DIALECTS LIKE KANSAI ♡ AND KYUSHU. I HAVE A BORING TOKYO ACCENT, SO I GET JEALOUS.

I'VE ALSO BEEN GETTING LETTERS FROM GIRLS TELLING ME THEIR BROTHERS AND BOYFRIENDS ARE READING *B.O.D.Y.* ♡ I WELCOME MALE READERS! OF COURSE GIRLS ARE WELCOME TOO. ♡

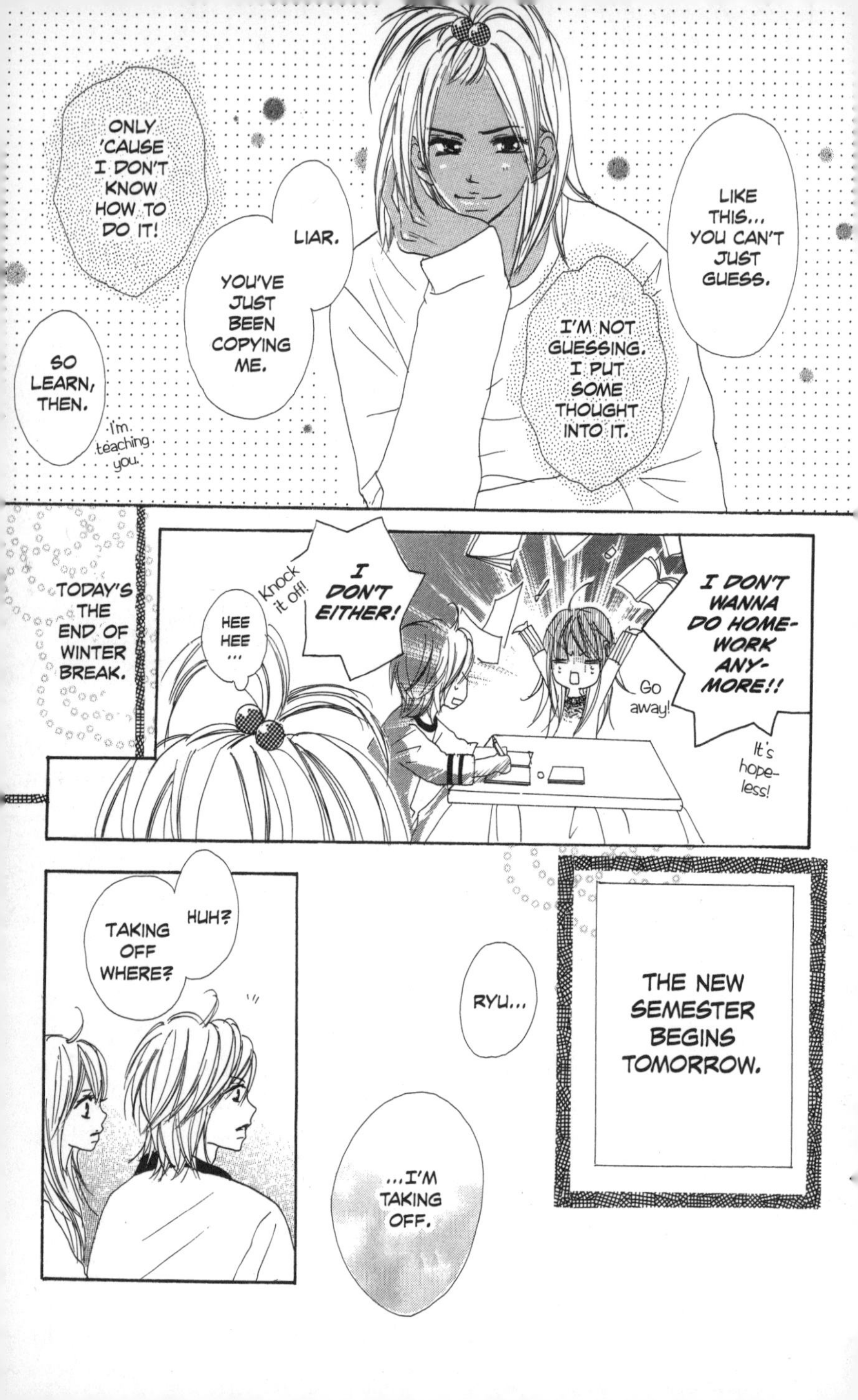
LIKE THIS... YOU CAN'T JUST GUESS.
I'M NOT GUESSING. I PUT SOME THOUGHT INTO IT.
LIAR.
YOU'VE JUST BEEN COPYING ME.
ONLY 'CAUSE I DON'T KNOW HOW TO DO IT!
SO LEARN, THEN.
I'm teaching you.
I DON'T WANNA DO HOME-WORK ANY-MORE!!
Go away!
It's hope-less!
I DON'T EITHER!
Knock it off!
HEE HEE...
TODAY'S THE END OF WINTER BREAK.
THE NEW SEMESTER BEGINS TOMORROW.
RYU...
...I'M TAKING OFF.
HUH?
TAKING OFF WHERE?

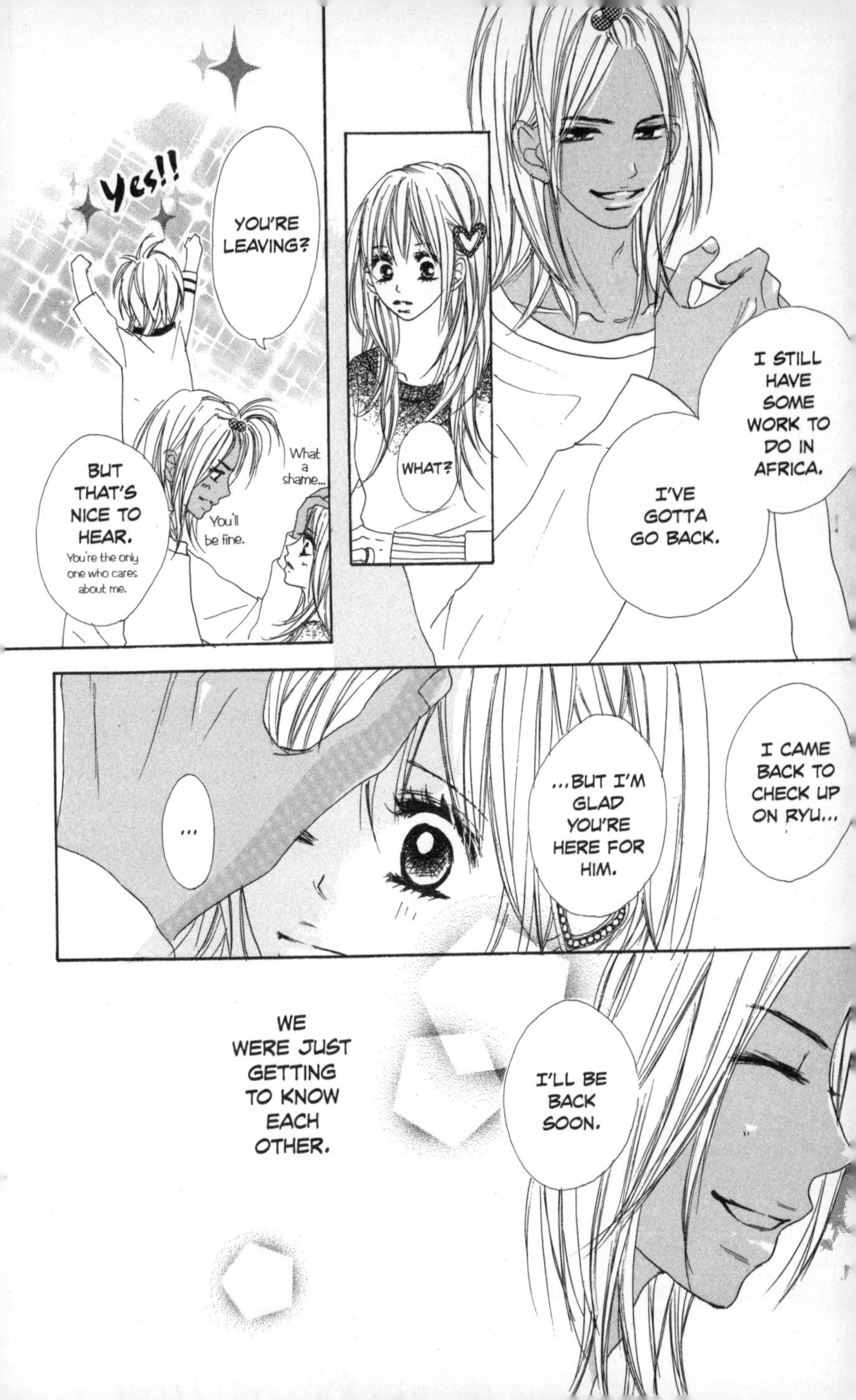
I STILL HAVE SOME WORK TO DO IN AFRICA.
I'VE GOTTA GO BACK.
WHAT?
YOU'RE LEAVING?
Yes!!
What a shame...
You'll be fine.
BUT THAT'S NICE TO HEAR.
You're the only one who cares about me.
I CAME BACK TO CHECK UP ON RYU...
...BUT I'M GLAD YOU'RE HERE FOR HIM.
...
I'LL BE BACK SOON.
WE WERE JUST GETTING TO KNOW EACH OTHER.

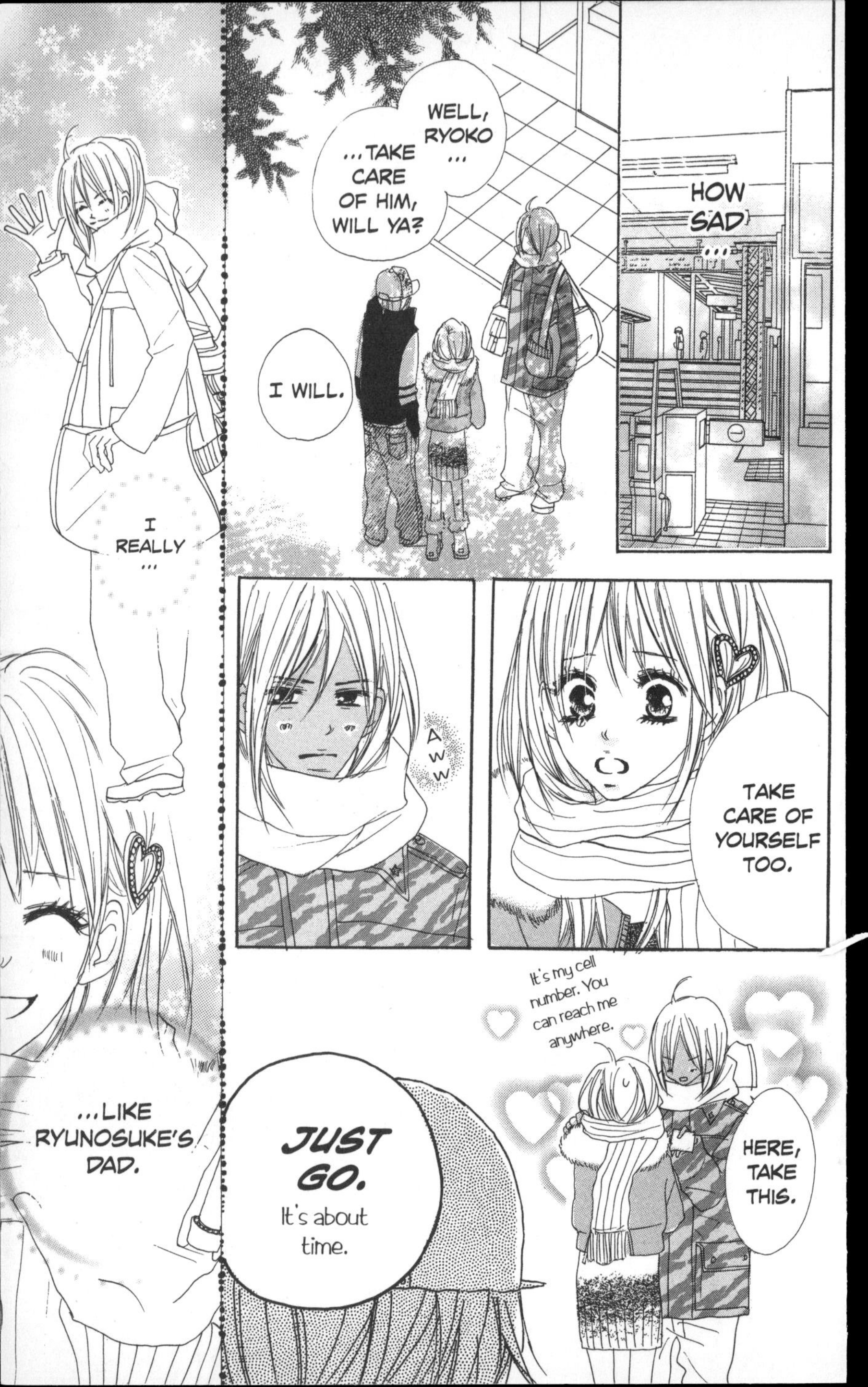
HOW SAD...
WELL, RYOKO...
...TAKE CARE OF HIM, WILL YA?
I WILL.
TAKE CARE OF YOURSELF TOO.
AWW
HERE, TAKE THIS.
It's my cell number. You can reach me anywhere.
JUST GO.
It's about time.
I REALLY...
...LIKE RYUNOSUKE'S DAD.

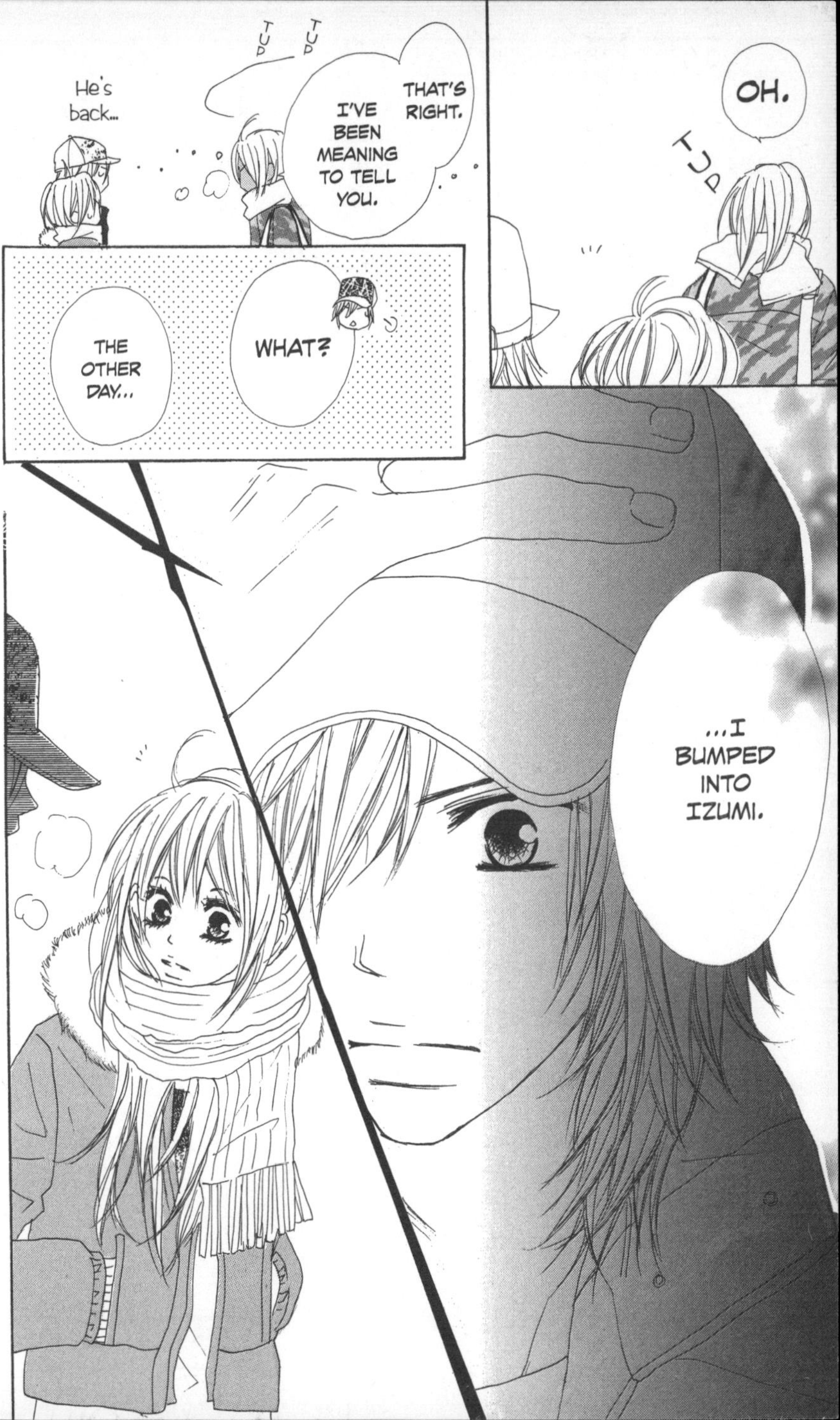
OH.
TUP
TUP
TUP
THAT'S RIGHT.
I'VE BEEN MEANING TO TELL YOU.
He's back...
WHAT?
THE OTHER DAY...
...I BUMPED INTO IZUMI.

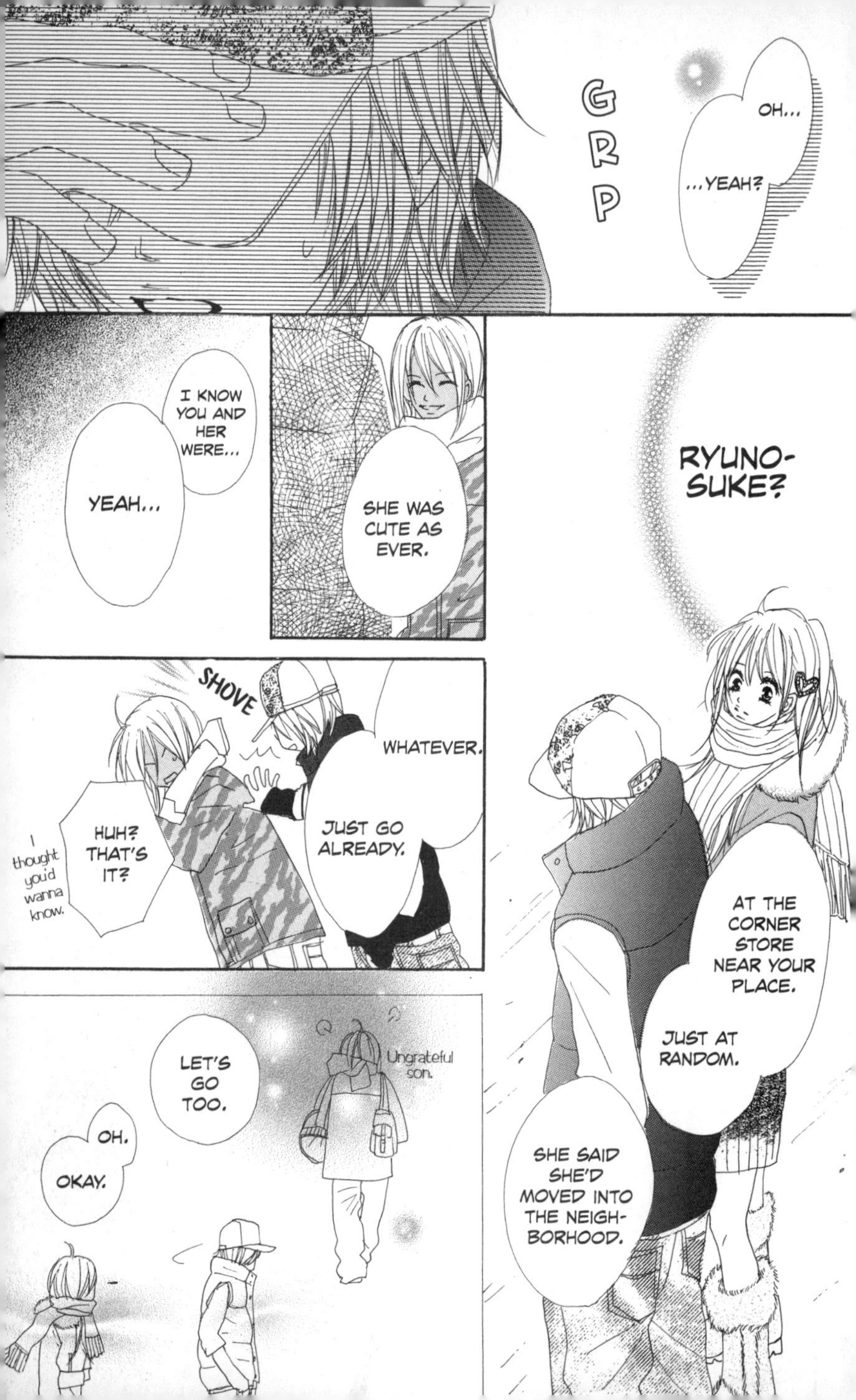
OH...
...YEAH?
GRP
RYUNO-SUKE?
AT THE CORNER STORE NEAR YOUR PLACE.
JUST AT RANDOM.
SHE SAID SHE'D MOVED INTO THE NEIGH-BORHOOD.
SHE WAS CUTE AS EVER.
I KNOW YOU AND HER WERE...
YEAH...
SHOVE
WHATEVER.
JUST GO ALREADY.
HUH? THAT'S IT?
I thought you'd wanna know.
LET'S GO TOO.
Ungrateful son.
OH.
OKAY.

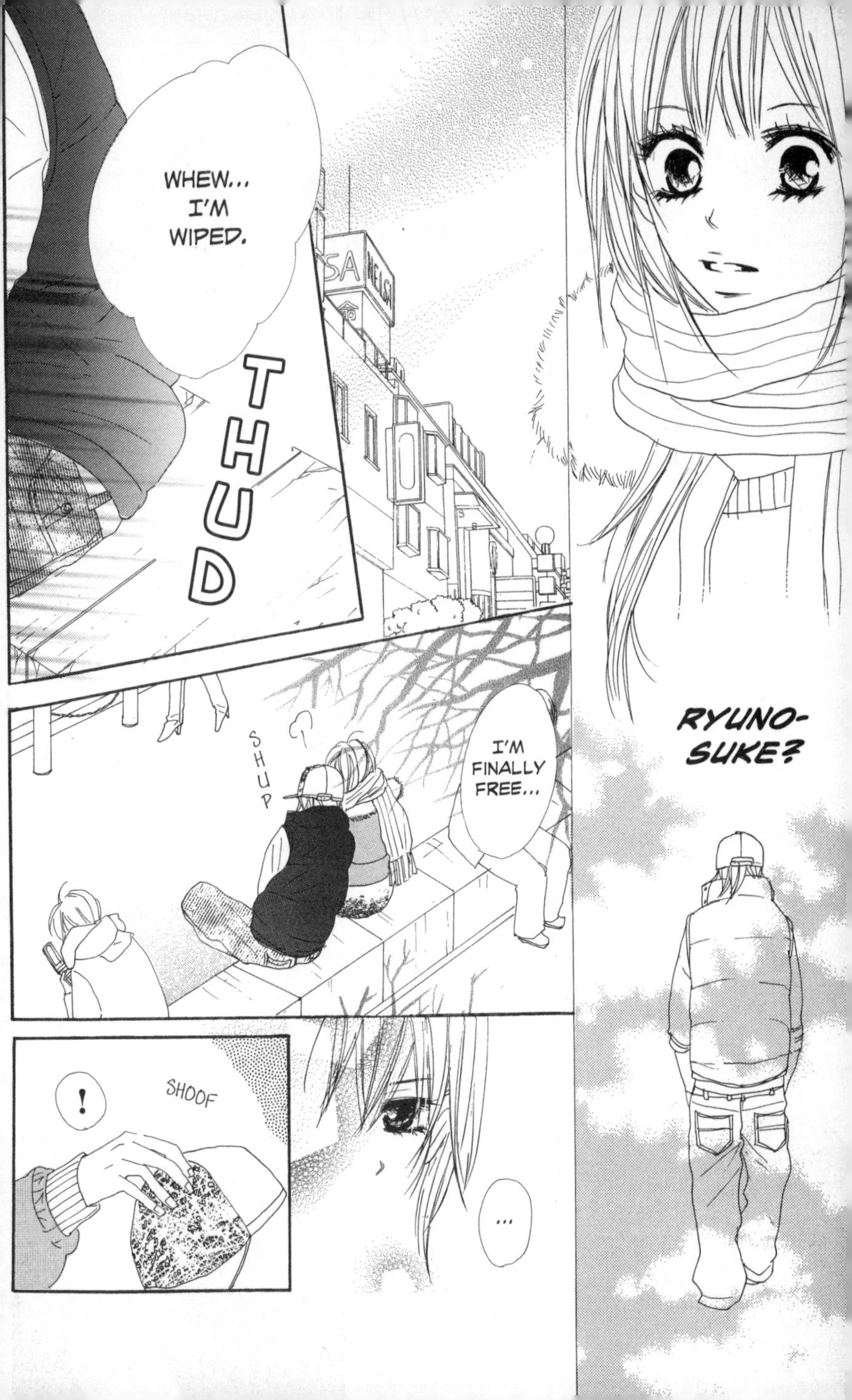
RYUNO-
SUKE?
WHEW... I'M WIPED.
THUD
SHUP
I'M FINALLY FREE...
...
!
SHOOF

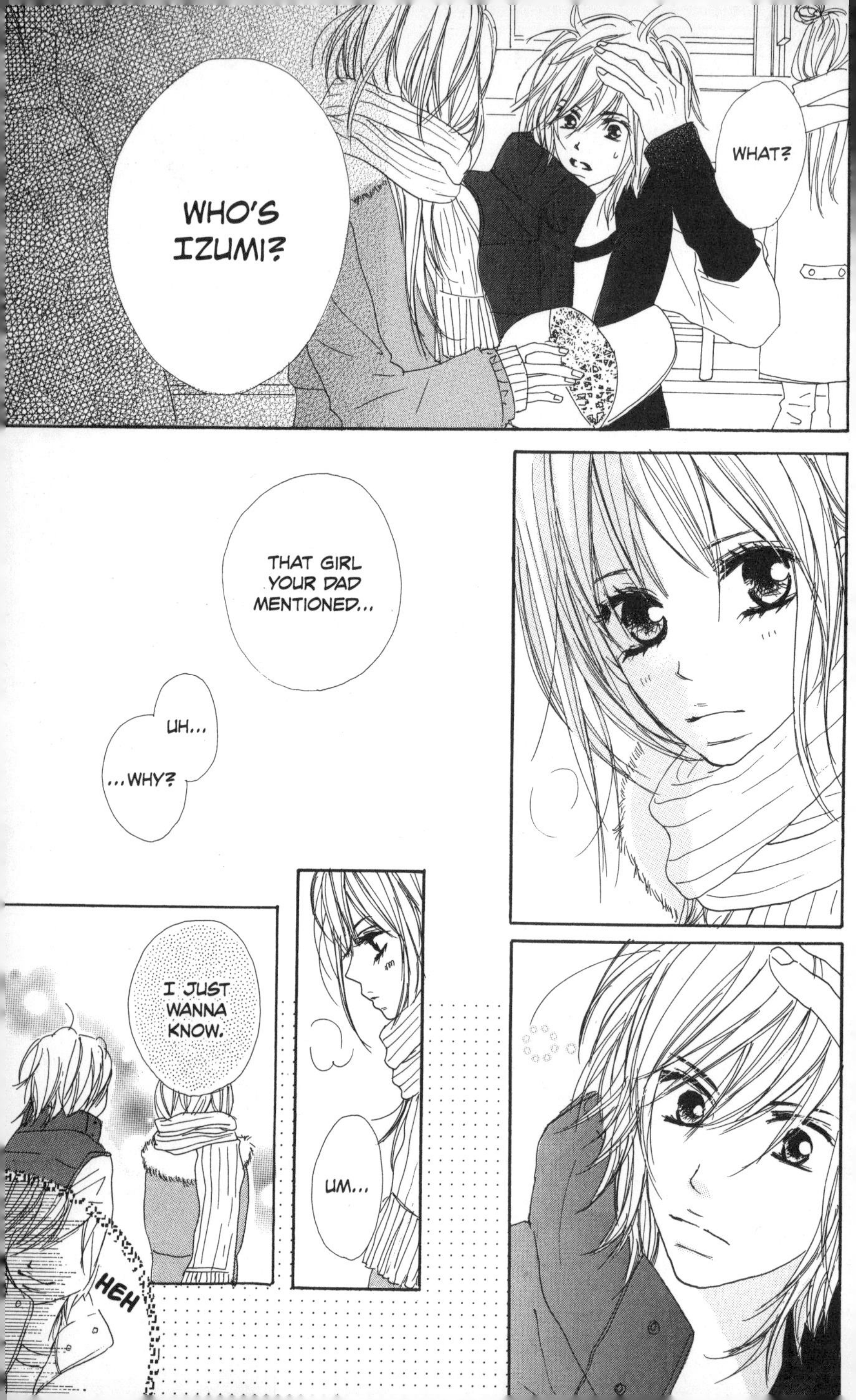
WHAT?
WHO'S IZUMI?
THAT GIRL YOUR DAD MENTIONED...
UH...
...WHY?
UM...
I JUST WANNA KNOW.
HEH

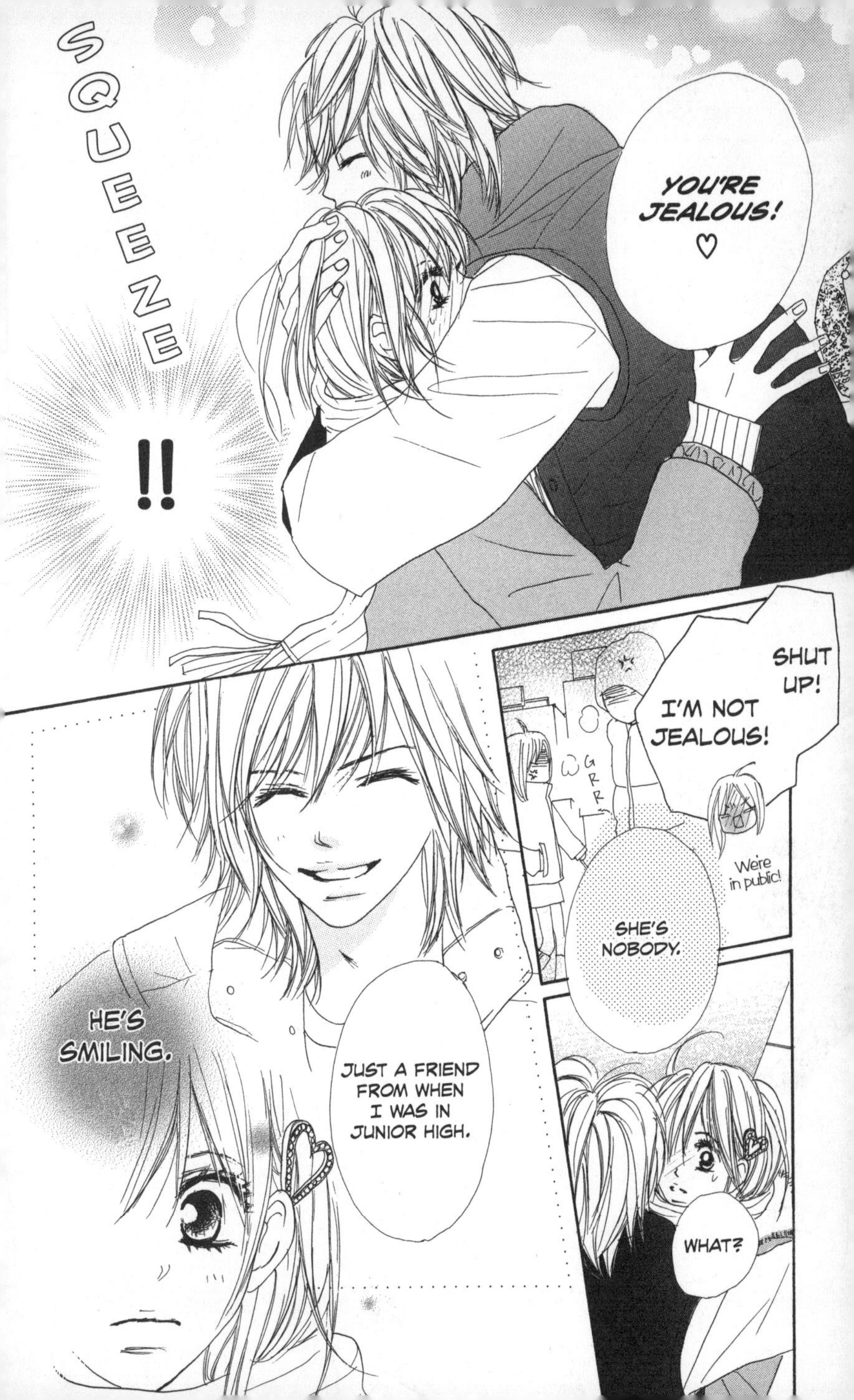
YOU'RE JEALOUS! ♡
SQUEEZE
!!
SHUT UP!
I'M NOT JEALOUS!
GRR
We're in public!
WHAT?
SHE'S NOBODY.
JUST A FRIEND FROM WHEN I WAS IN JUNIOR HIGH.
HE'S SMILING.

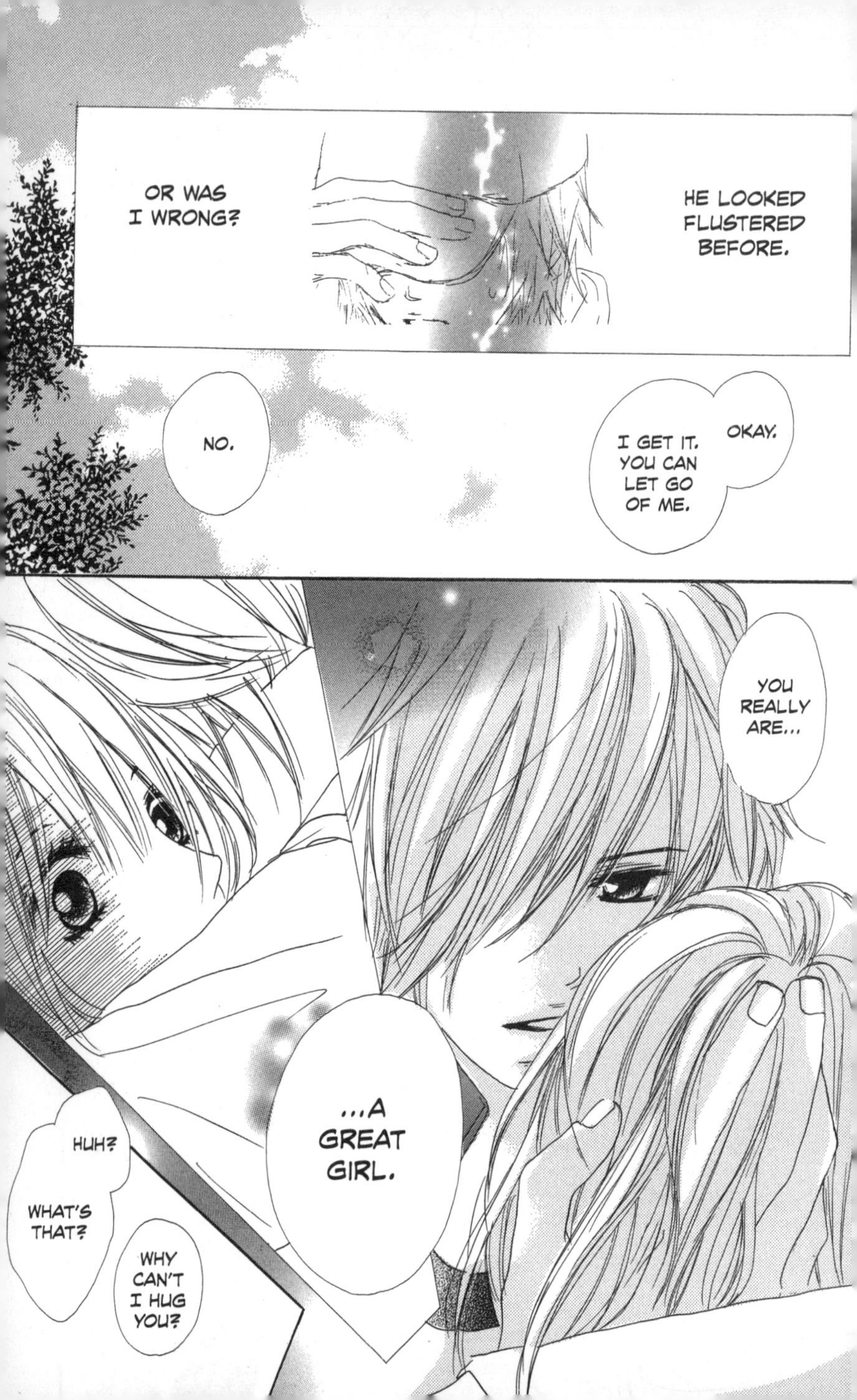
HE LOOKED FLUSTERED BEFORE.
OR WAS I WRONG?
OKAY.
I GET IT. YOU CAN LET GO OF ME.
NO.
YOU REALLY ARE...
...A GREAT GIRL.
HUH?
WHAT'S THAT?
WHY CAN'T I HUG YOU?

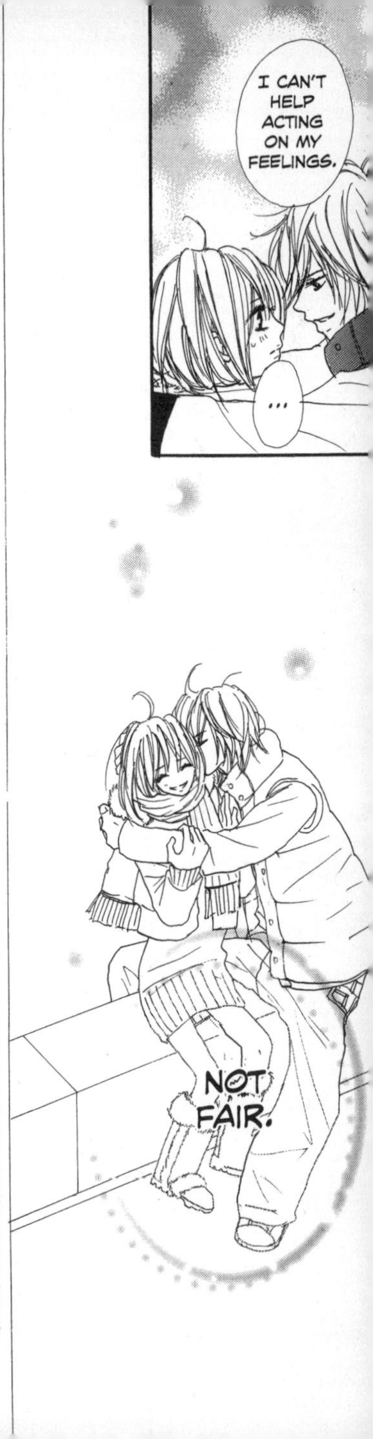
I CAN'T HELP ACTING ON MY FEELINGS.
...
NOT FAIR.

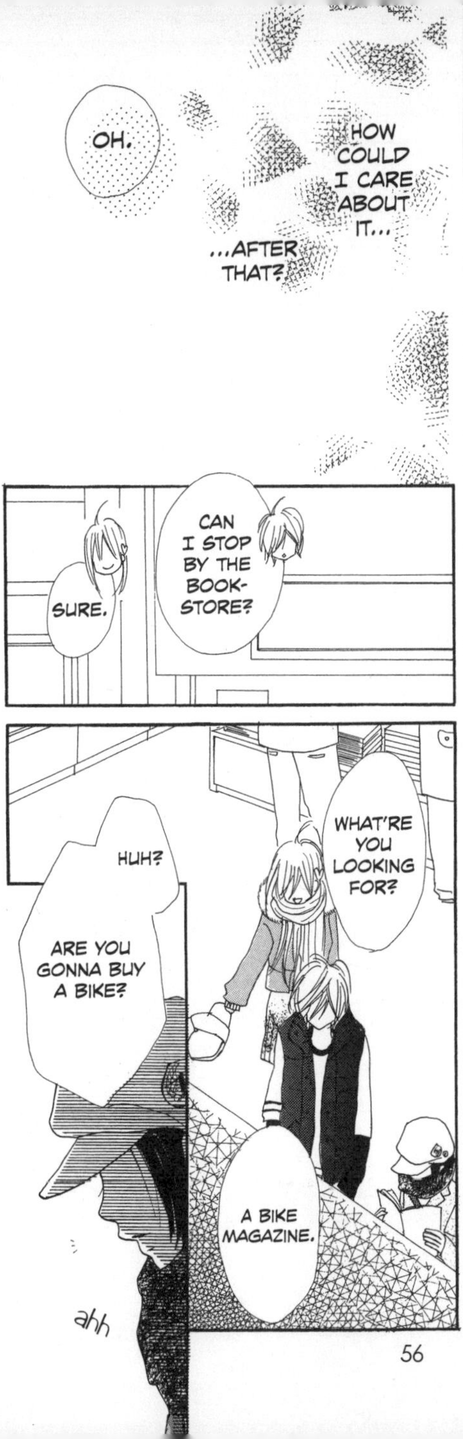
OH.
HOW COULD I CARE ABOUT IT...
...AFTER THAT?
CAN I STOP BY THE BOOK-STORE?
SURE.
WHAT'RE YOU LOOKING FOR?
A BIKE MAGAZINE.
HUH?
ARE YOU GONNA BUY A BIKE?
ahh

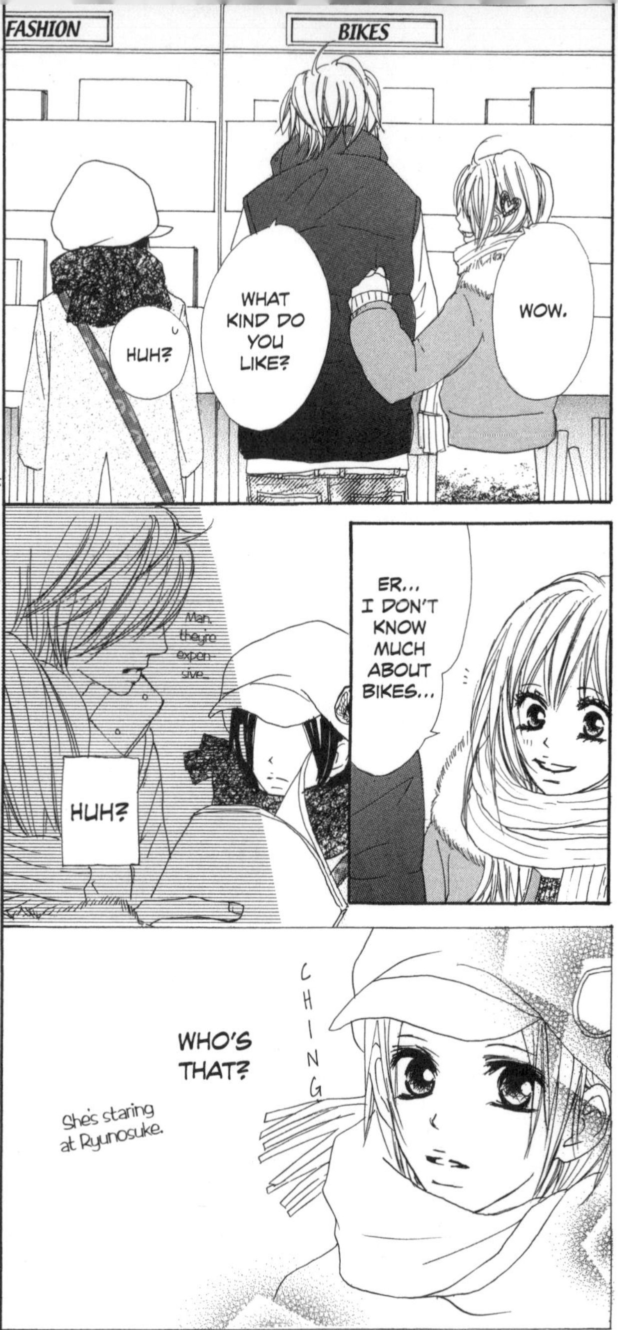
FASHION
BIKES
WOW.
WHAT KIND DO YOU LIKE?
HUH?
ER... I DON'T KNOW MUCH ABOUT BIKES...
Man, they're expen-sive...
HUH?
WHO'S THAT?
CHING
She's staring at Ryunosuke.

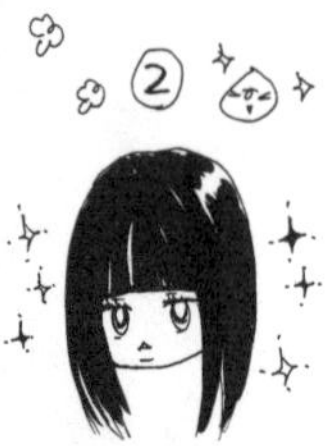
2

The drawing above is Sadako from Karuho Shiina's *Kimi ni Todoke*. She's really cute... especially when Karuho draws her like this. It's so funny. I'm always laughing my butt off every month...I love her. But when I tried to draw her, this is what I ended up with!! To Karuho and all you Karuho fans, I'm sorry!

Also, as I was drawing this, I got a text from Karuho!! I just sent a photo of the drawing to her. I wonder if she'll get mad...

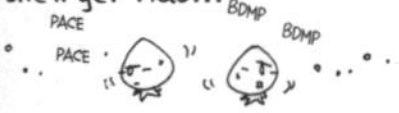
PACE
PACE
BDMP
BDMP

Wow! That's so cute! Thank you! It makes me really happy!

That's what she said! She's so, so nice!!!!

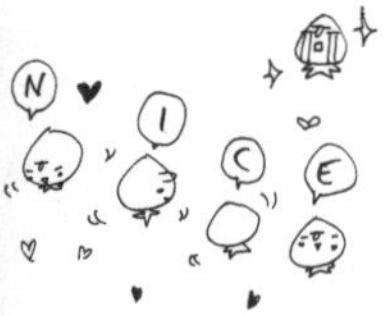
N
I
C
E

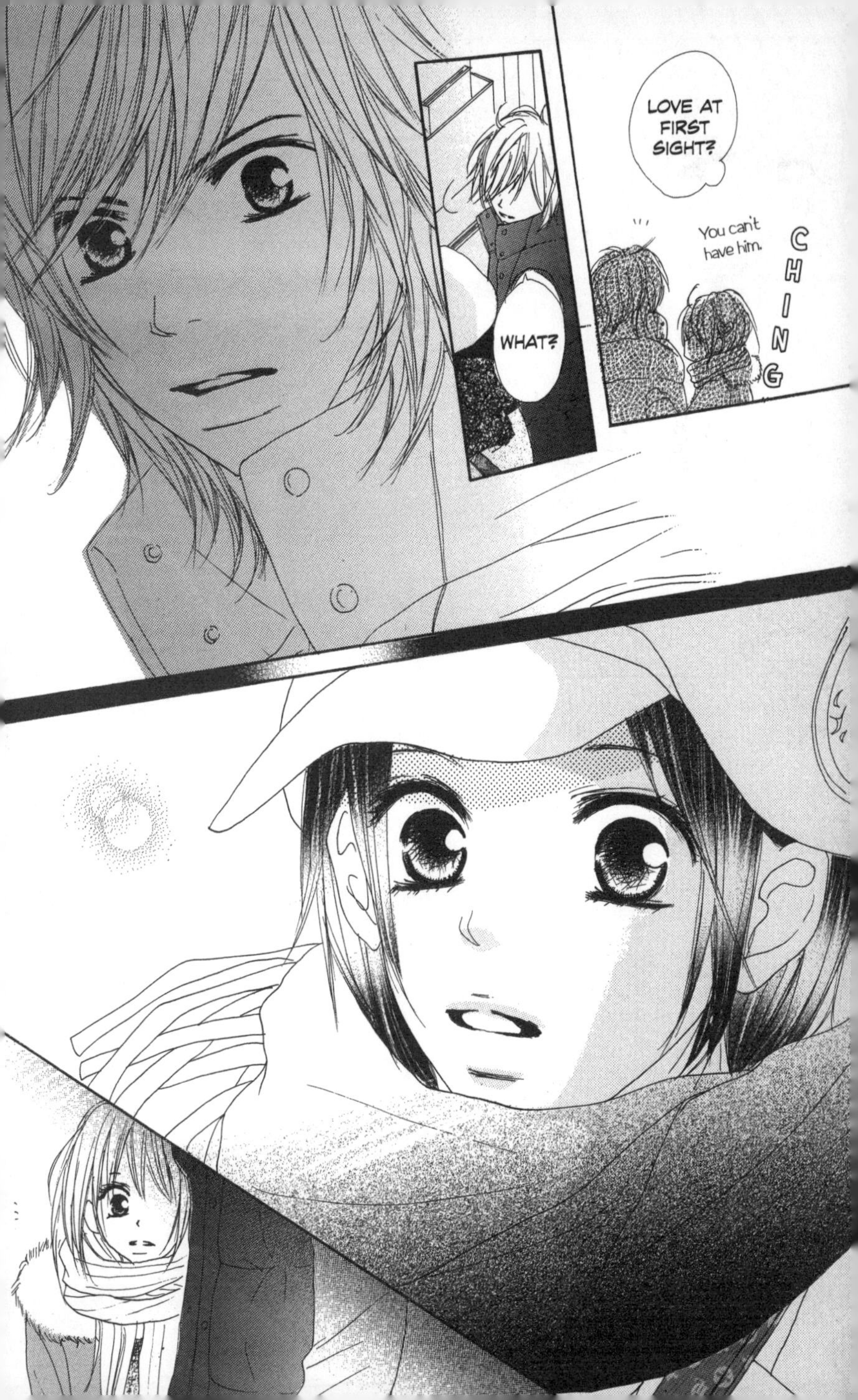
LOVE AT FIRST SIGHT?
You can't have him.
CHING
WHAT?

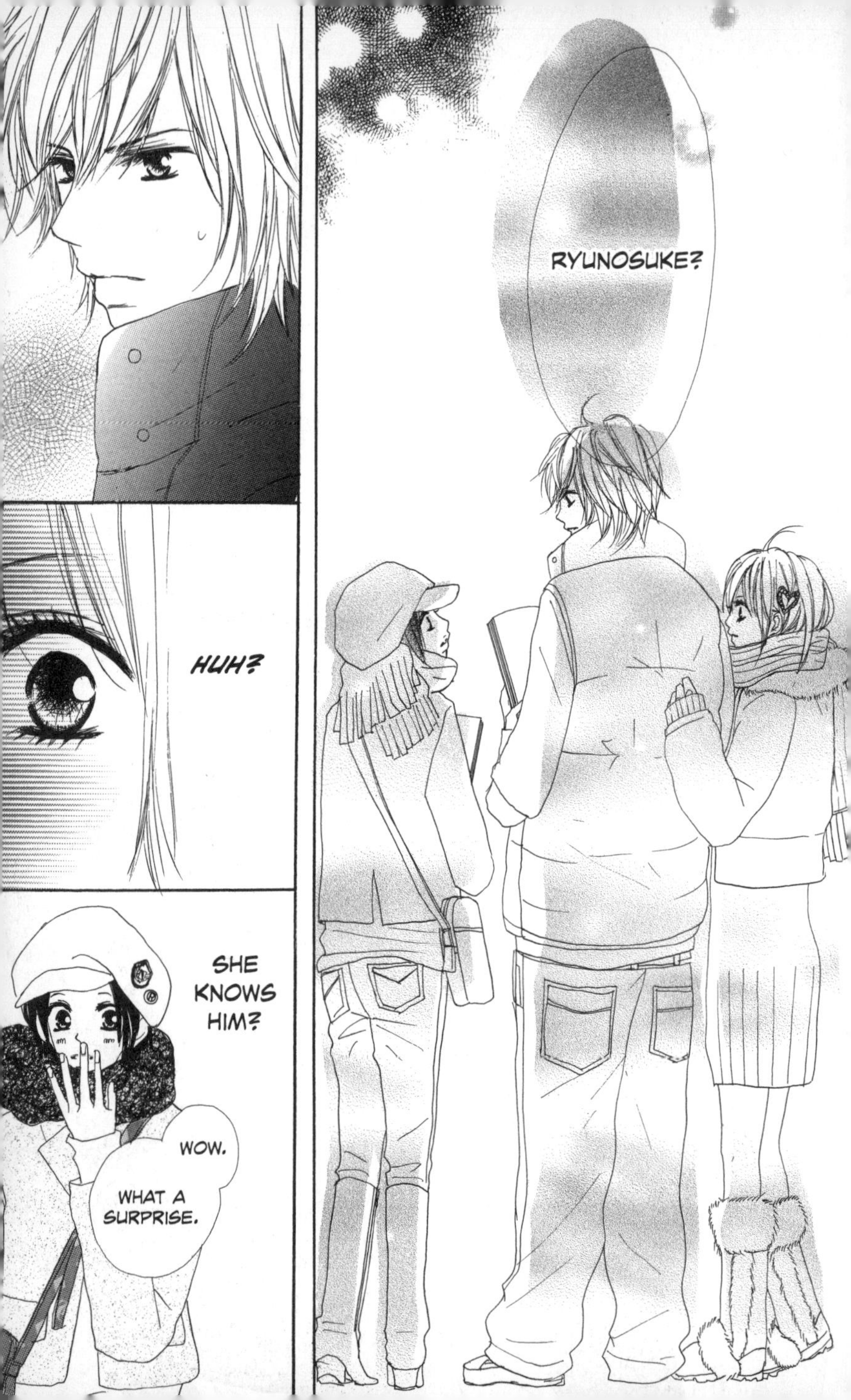
RYUNOSUKE?
HUH?
SHE KNOWS HIM?
WOW.
WHAT A SURPRISE.

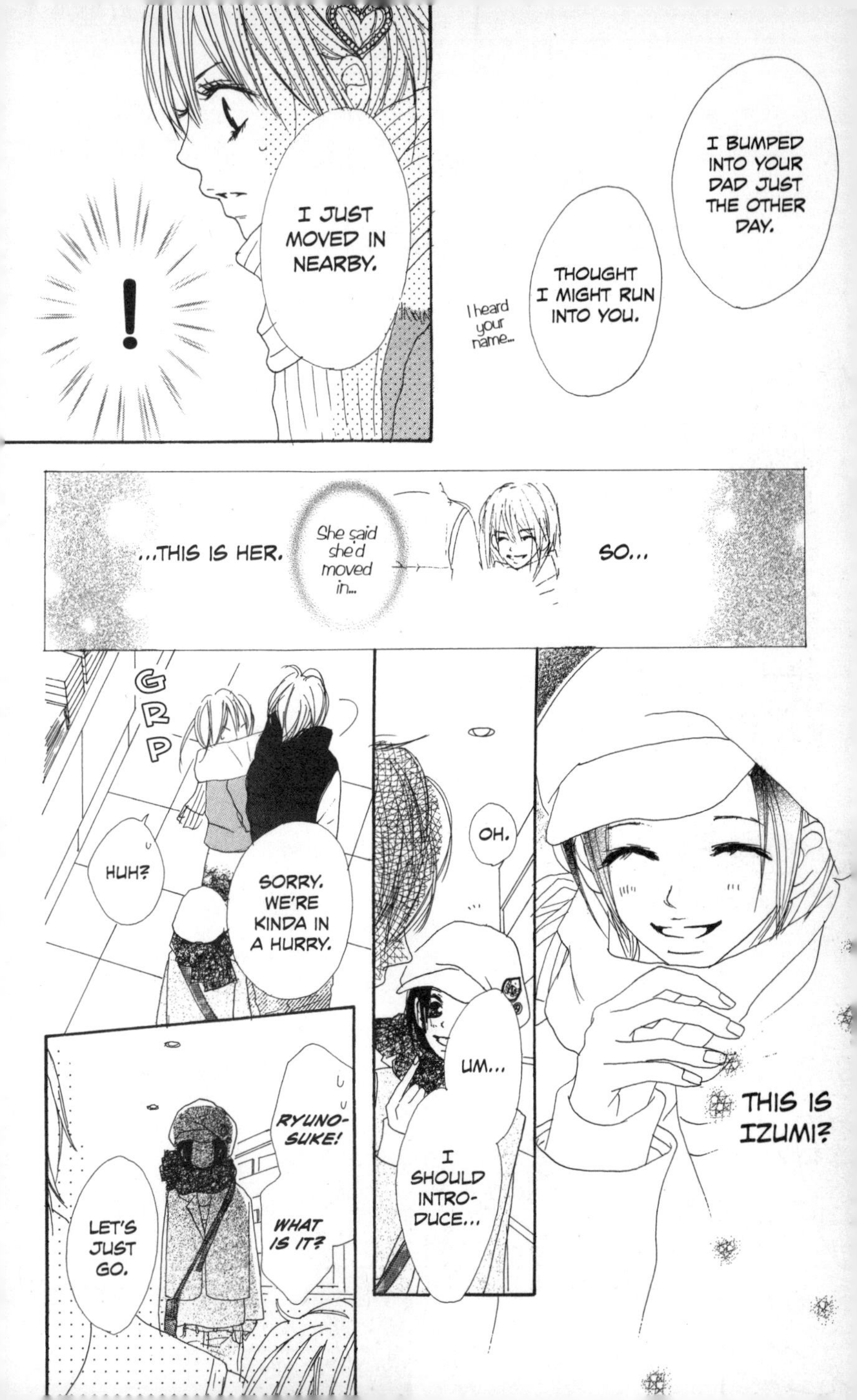
I BUMPED INTO YOUR DAD JUST THE OTHER DAY.
THOUGHT I MIGHT RUN INTO YOU.
I heard your name...
I JUST MOVED IN NEARBY.
!
SO...
She said she'd moved in...
...THIS IS HER.
THIS IS IZUMI?
OH.
UM...
I SHOULD INTRO-DUCE...
GRP
SORRY. WE'RE KINDA IN A HURRY.
HUH?
RYUNO-SUKE!
WHAT IS IT?
LET'S JUST GO.

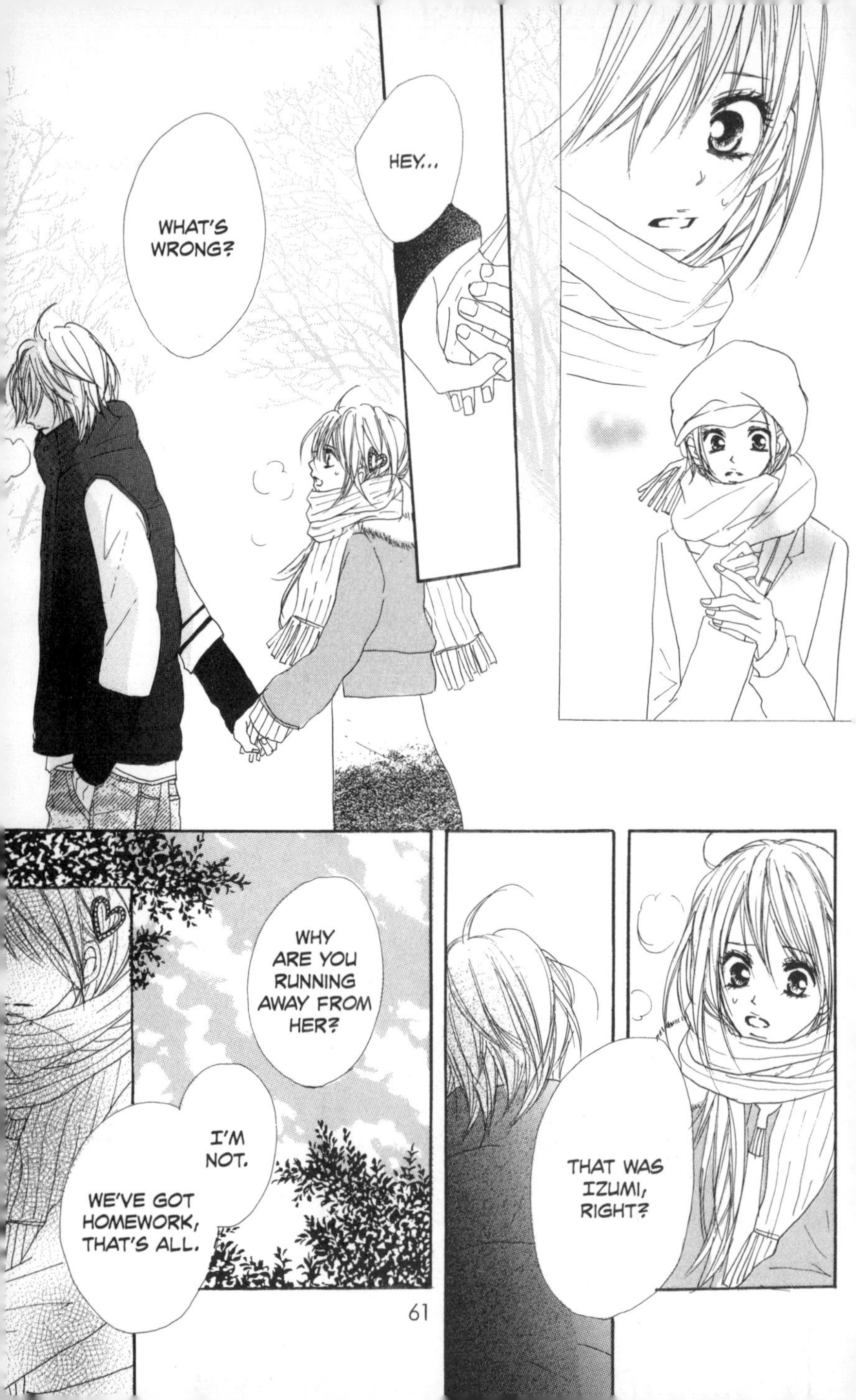
HEY...
WHAT'S WRONG?
THAT WAS IZUMI, RIGHT?
WHY ARE YOU RUNNING AWAY FROM HER?
I'M NOT.
WE'VE GOT HOMEWORK, THAT'S ALL.

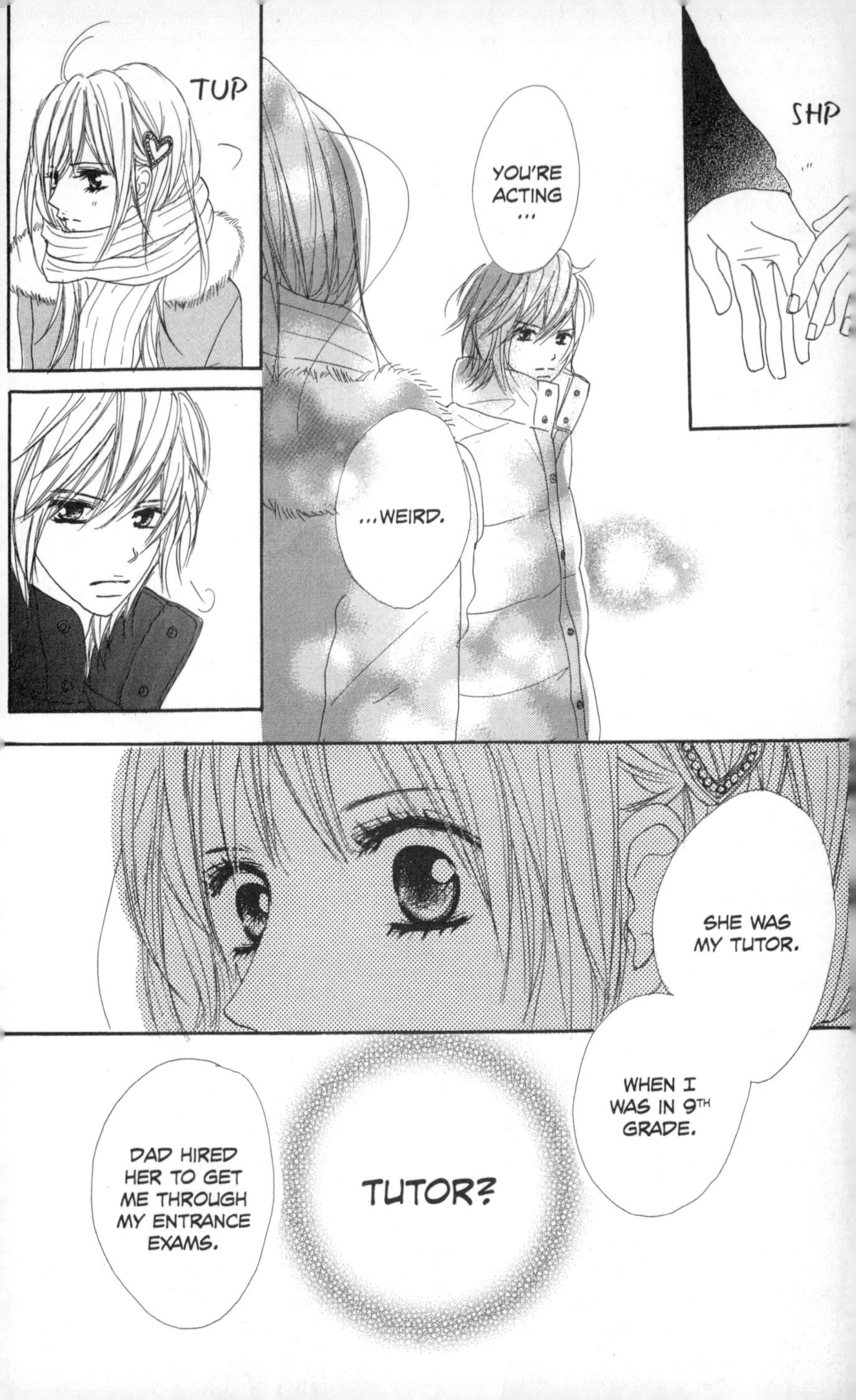
SHP
YOU'RE ACTING ...
...WEIRD.
TUP
SHE WAS MY TUTOR.
WHEN I WAS IN 9TH GRADE.
TUTOR?
DAD HIRED HER TO GET ME THROUGH MY ENTRANCE EXAMS.

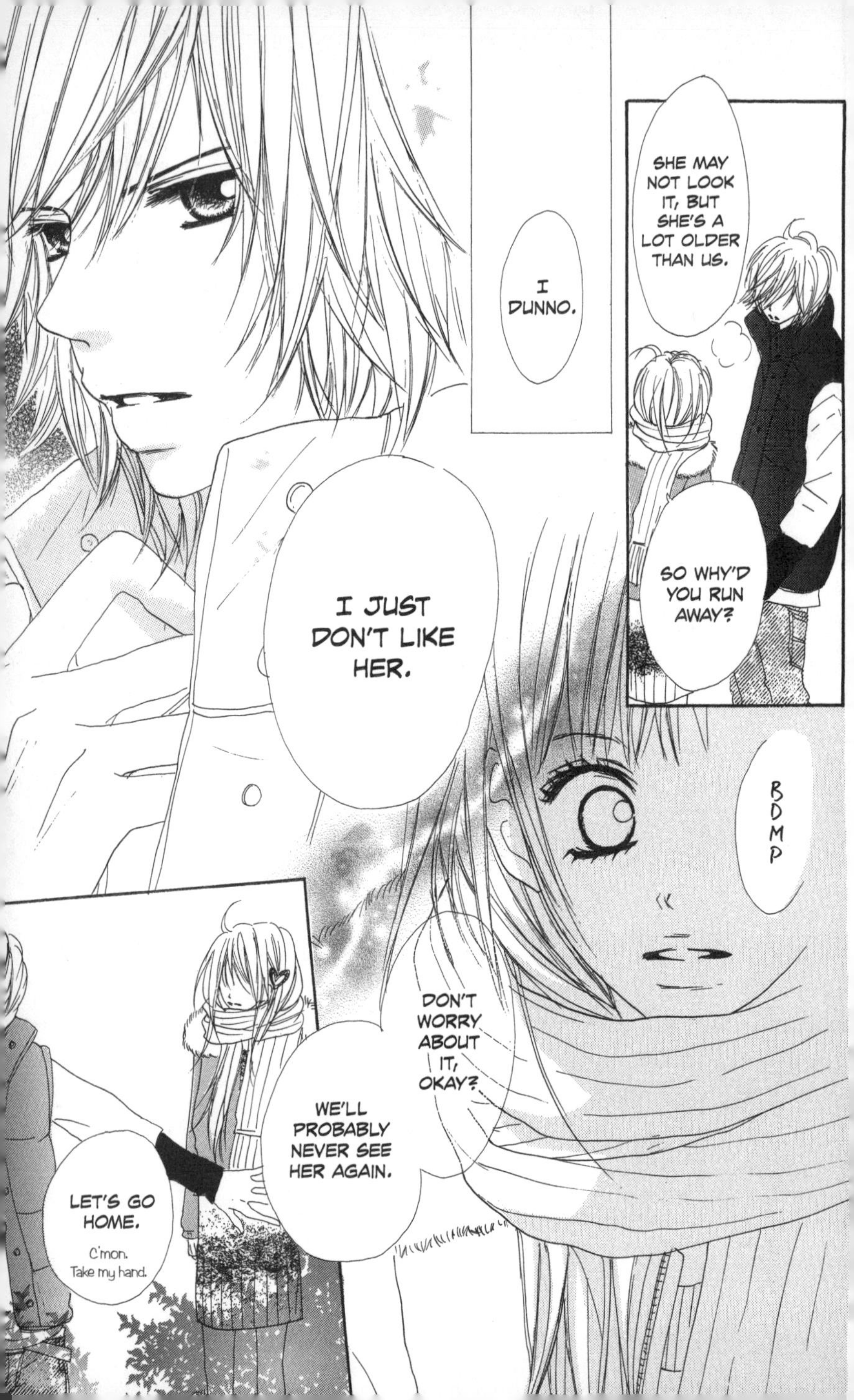
SHE MAY NOT LOOK IT, BUT SHE'S A LOT OLDER THAN US.
I DUNNO.
SO WHY'D YOU RUN AWAY?
I JUST DON'T LIKE HER.
BDMP
DON'T WORRY ABOUT IT, OKAY?
WE'LL PROBABLY NEVER SEE HER AGAIN.
LET'S GO HOME.
C'mon. Take my hand.

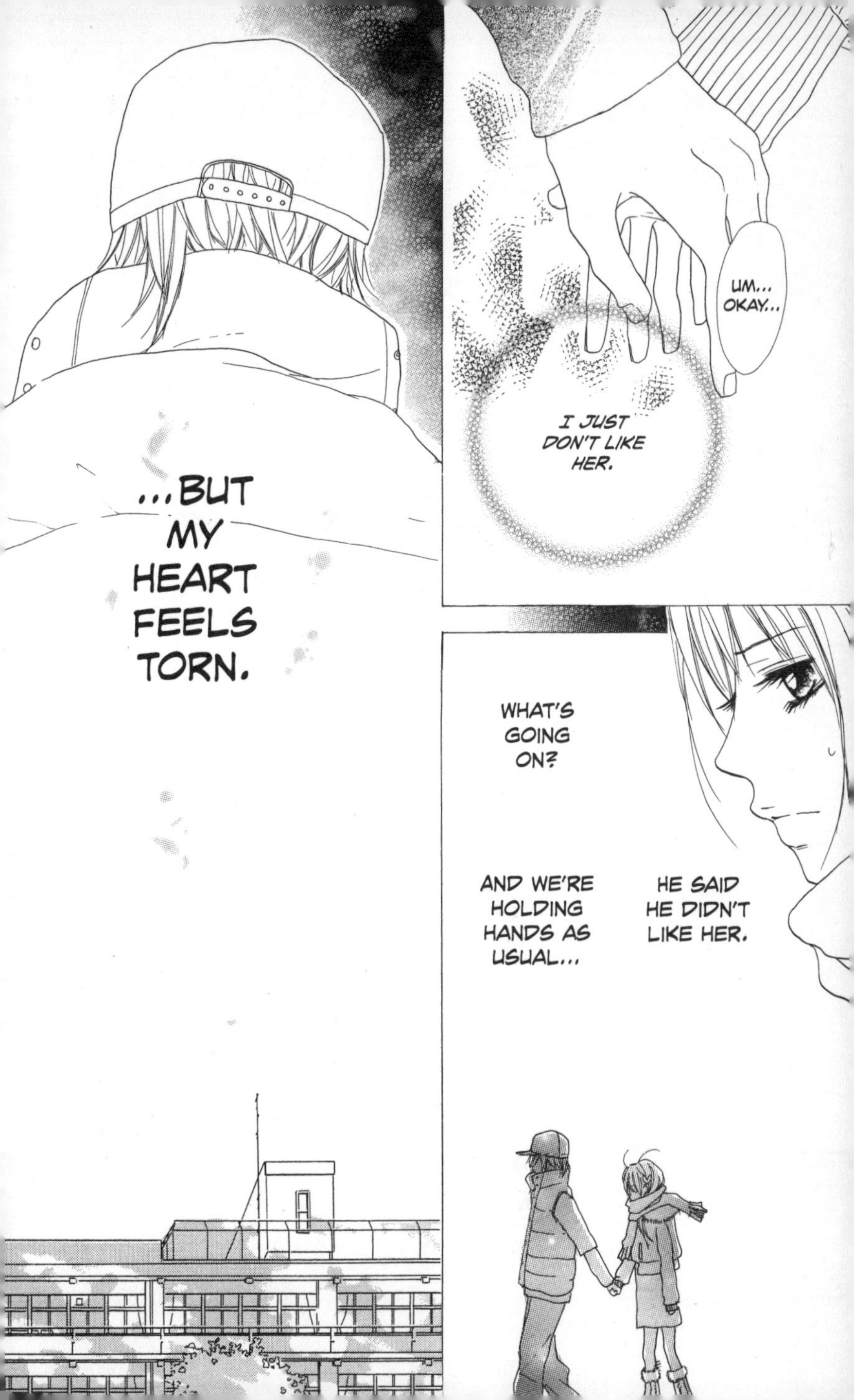
UM... OKAY...
I JUST DON'T LIKE HER.
WHAT'S GOING ON?
HE SAID HE DIDN'T LIKE HER.
AND WE'RE HOLDING HANDS AS USUAL...
...BUT MY HEART FEELS TORN.

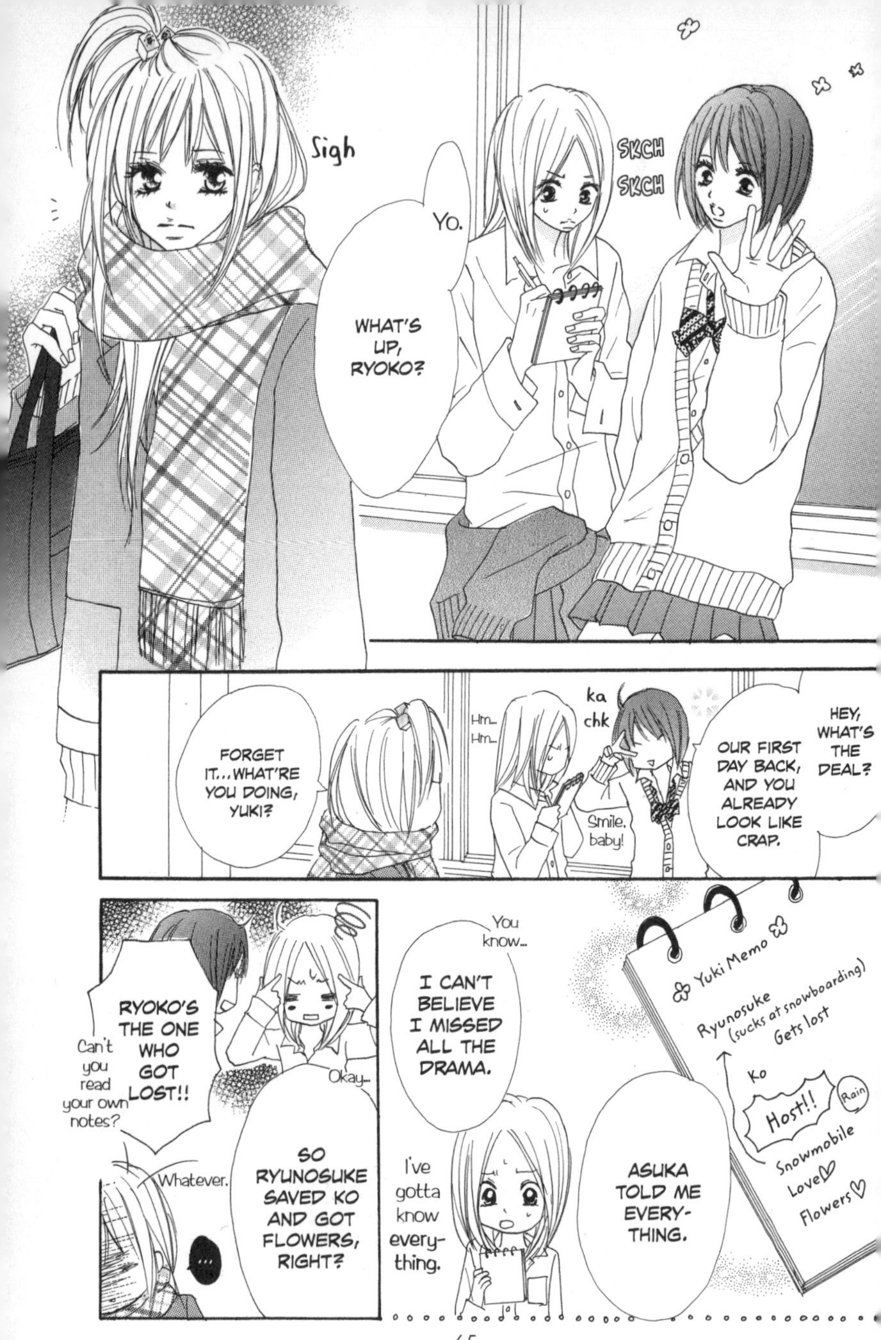
SKCH
SKCH
Yo.
WHAT'S UP, RYOKO?
Sigh
HEY, WHAT'S THE DEAL?
OUR FIRST DAY BACK, AND YOU ALREADY LOOK LIKE CRAP.
ka chk
Smile, baby!
Hm... Hm...
FORGET IT... WHAT'RE YOU DOING, YUKI?
Yuki Memo
Ryunosuke (sucks at snowboarding) Gets lost
Ko
Host!!
Rain
Snowmobile
Love♡
Flowers♡
ASUKA TOLD ME EVERY-THING.
You know...
I CAN'T BELIEVE I MISSED ALL THE DRAMA.
I've gotta know every-thing.
SO RYUNOSUKE SAVED KO AND GOT FLOWERS, RIGHT?
Okay...
RYOKO'S THE ONE WHO GOT LOST!!
Can't you read your own notes?
Whatever.
...

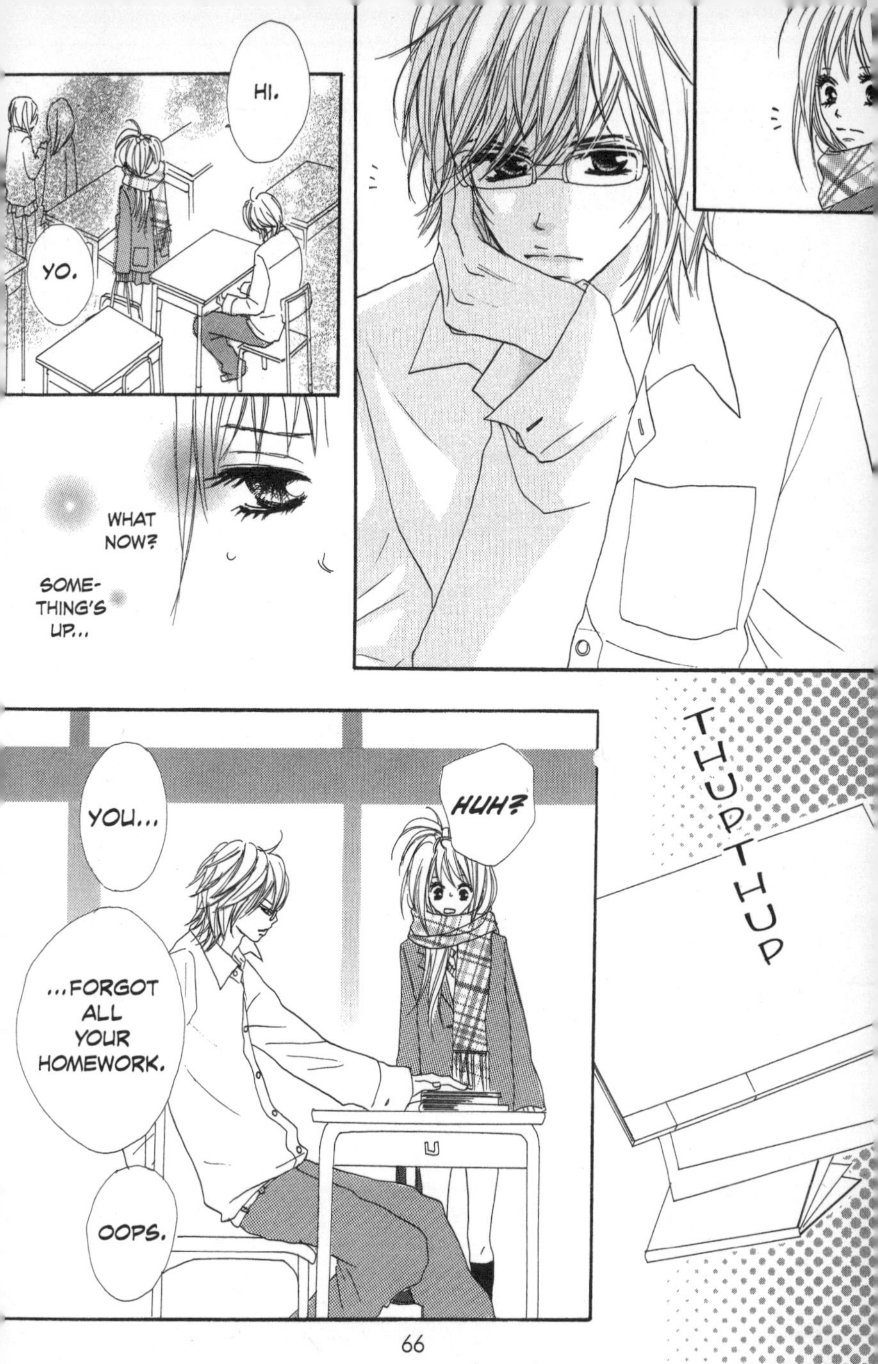
HI.
YO.
WHAT NOW?
SOME-THING'S UP...
THUP THUP
HUH?
YOU...
...FORGOT ALL YOUR HOMEWORK.
OOPS.

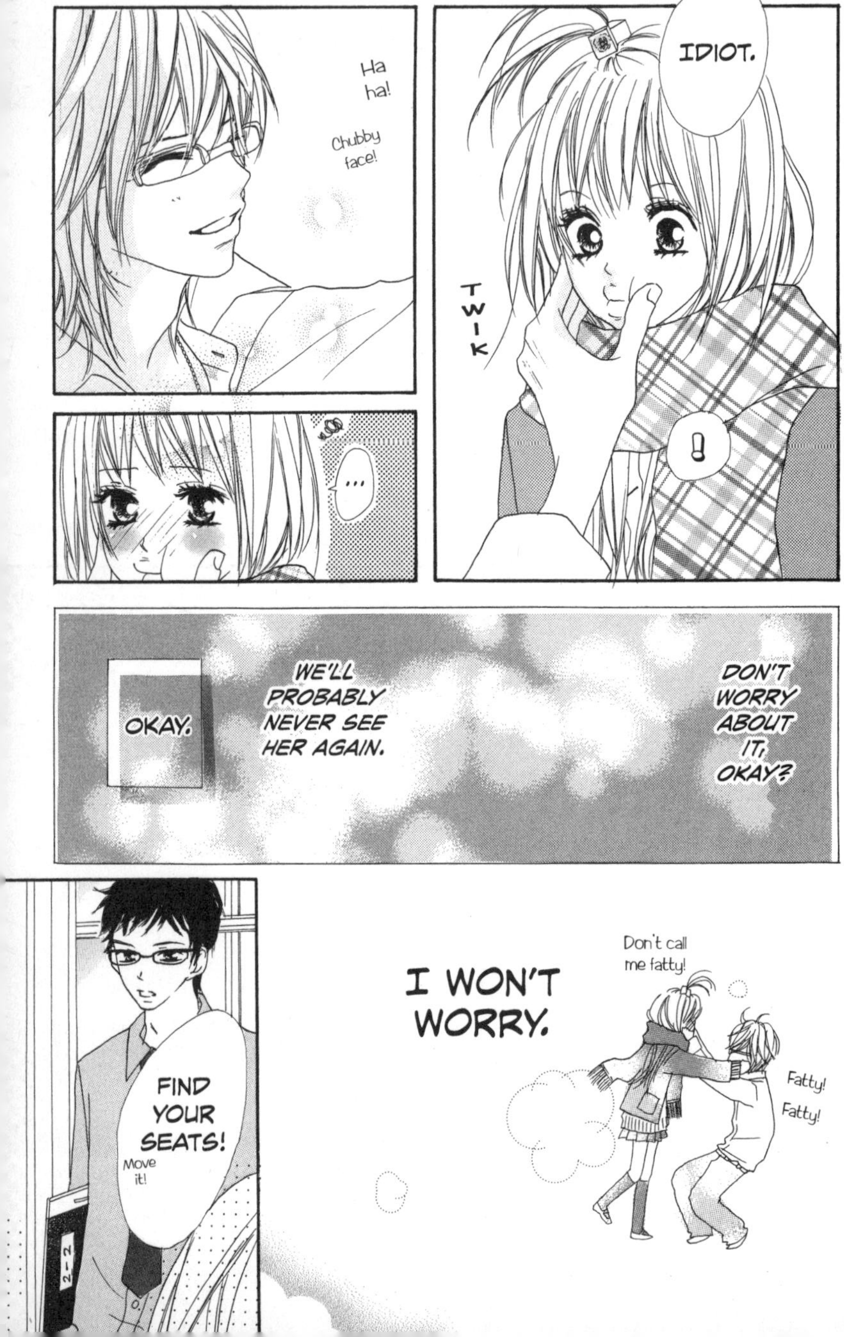
IDIOT.
TWIK
!
Ha ha!
Chubby face!
...
DON'T WORRY ABOUT IT, OKAY?
WE'LL PROBABLY NEVER SEE HER AGAIN.
OKAY.
Fatty! Fatty!
Don't call me fatty!
I WON'T WORRY.
FIND YOUR SEATS!
Move it!
2-2

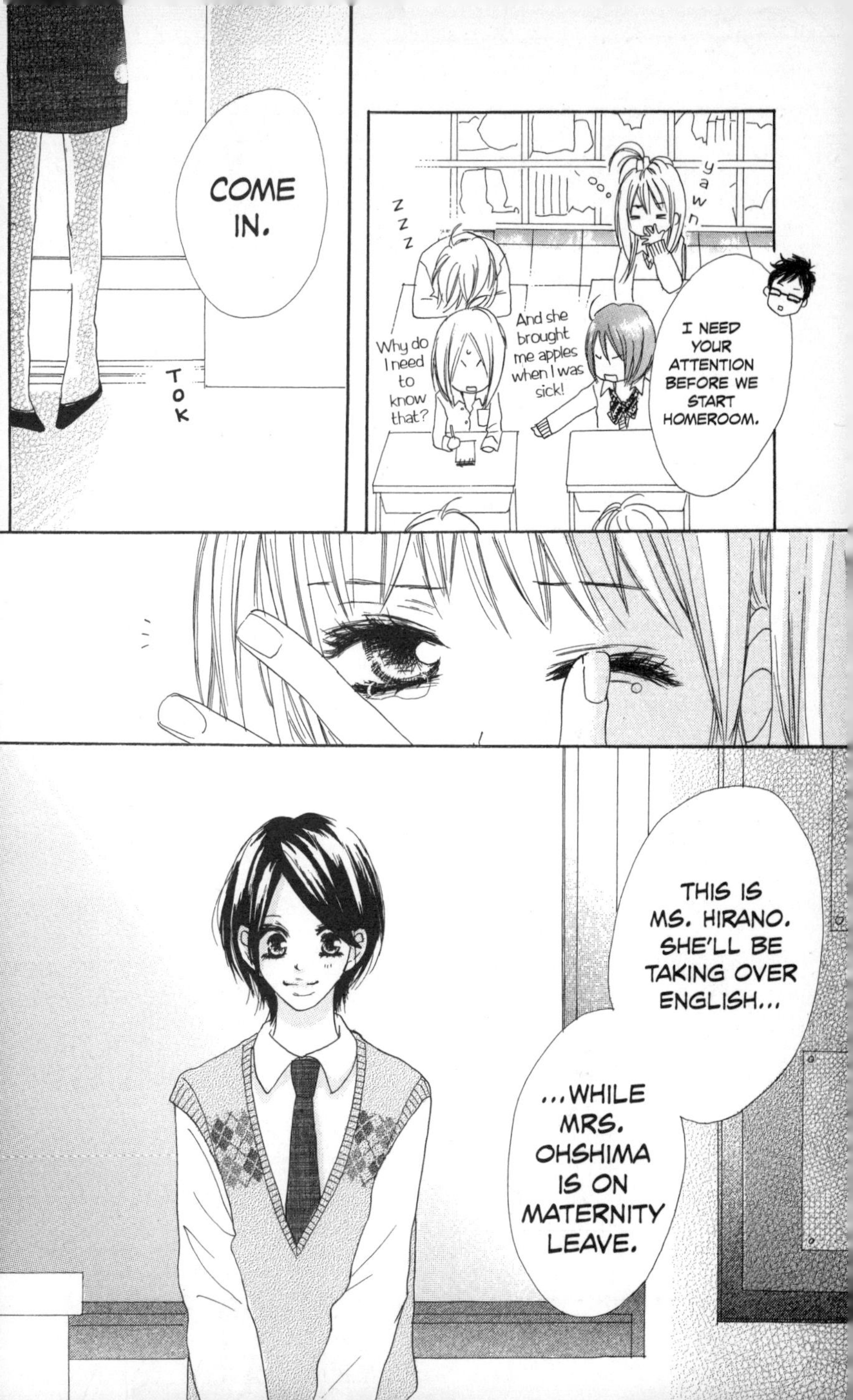
yawn
I NEED YOUR ATTENTION BEFORE WE START HOMEROOM.
And she brought me apples when I was sick!
Why do I need to know that?
ZZZ
COME IN.
TOK
THIS IS MS. HIRANO. SHE'LL BE TAKING OVER ENGLISH...
...WHILE MRS. OHSHIMA IS ON MATERNITY LEAVE.

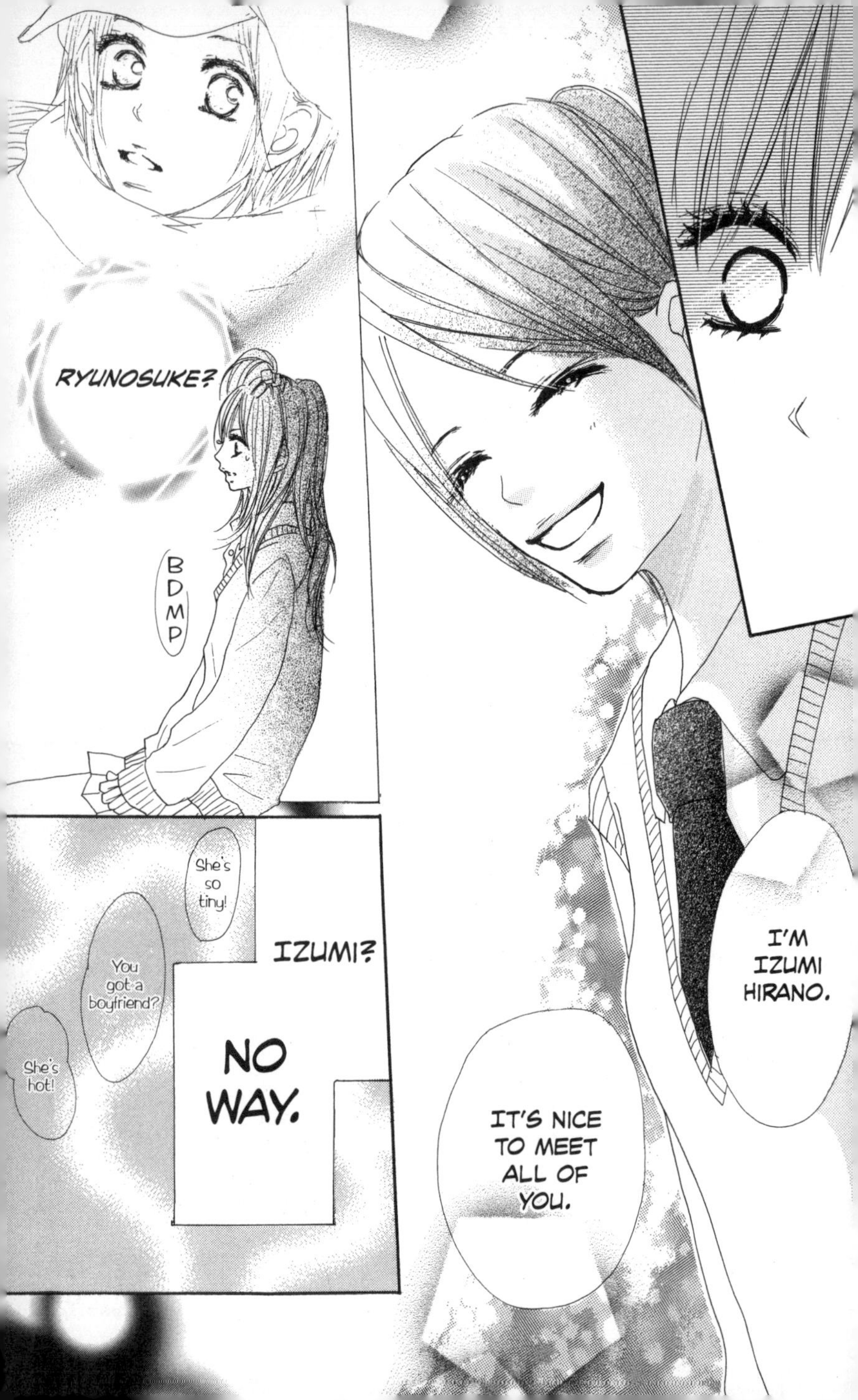
I'M IZUMI HIRANO.
IT'S NICE TO MEET ALL OF YOU.
RYUNOSUKE?
BDMP
IZUMI?
NO WAY.
She's so tiny!
You got a boyfriend?
She's hot!

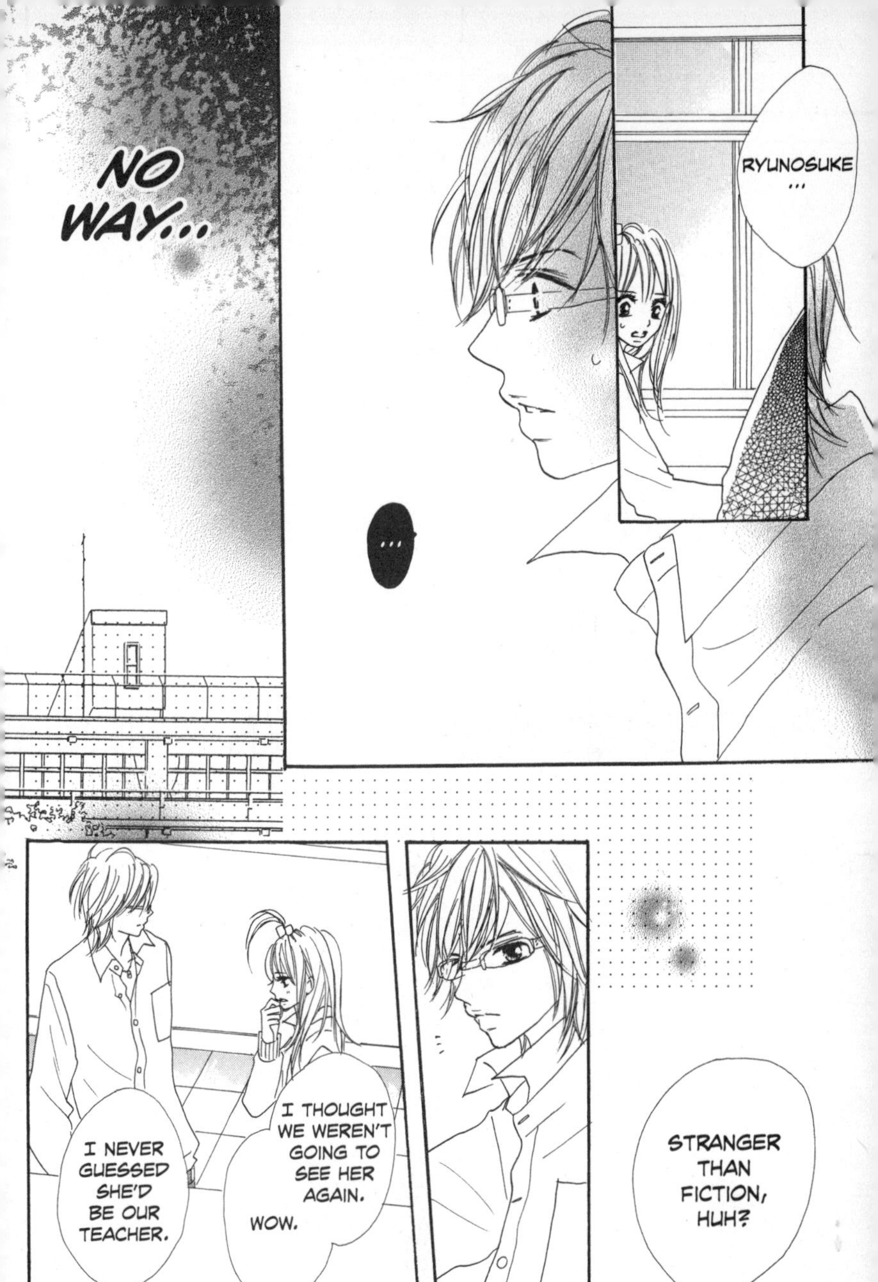
RYUNOSUKE ...
...
NO WAY...
STRANGER THAN FICTION, HUH?
I THOUGHT WE WEREN'T GOING TO SEE HER AGAIN.
WOW.
I NEVER GUESSED SHE'D BE OUR TEACHER.

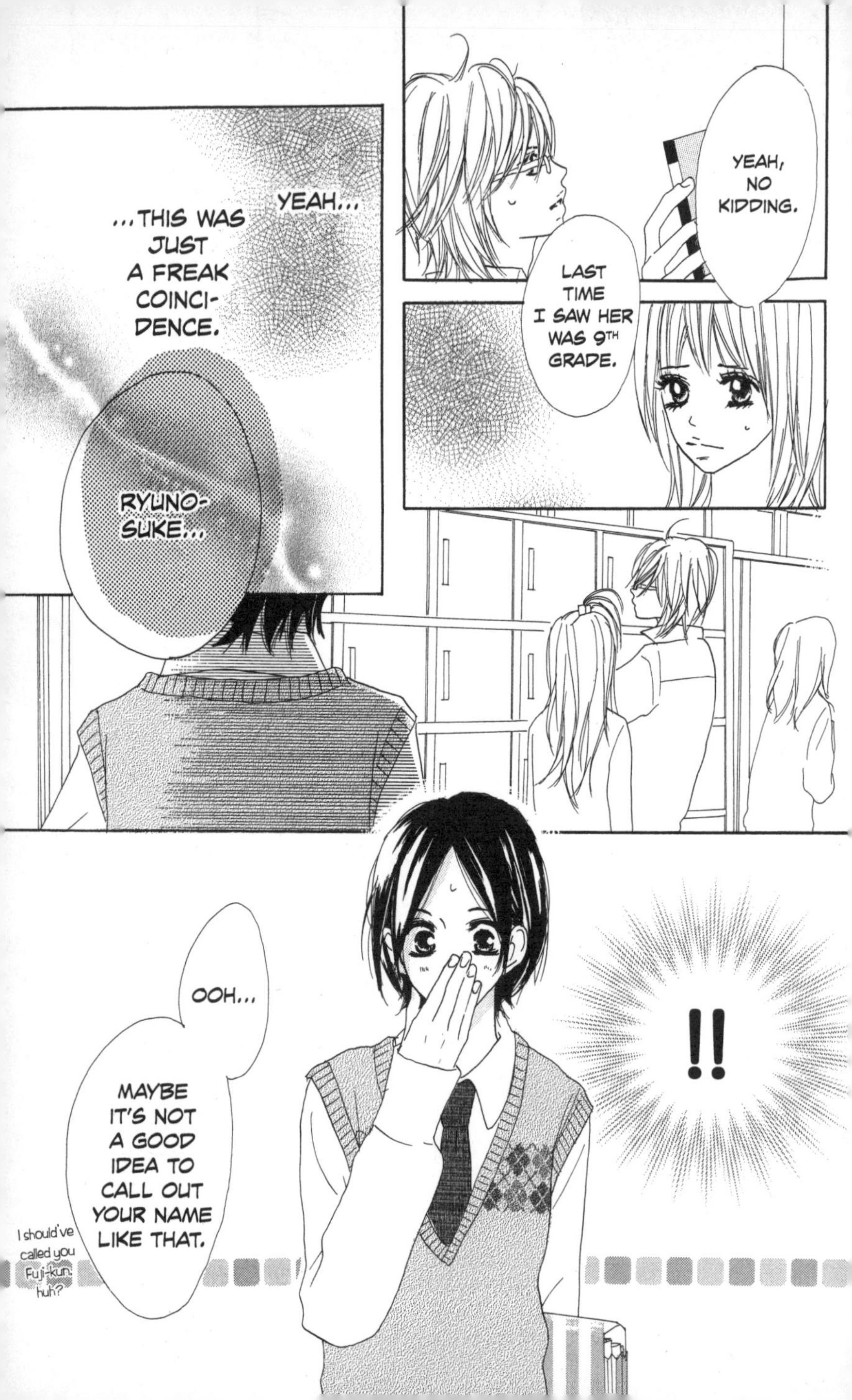

YEAH, NO KIDDING.
LAST TIME I SAW HER WAS 9TH GRADE.
YEAH...
...THIS WAS JUST A FREAK COINCIDENCE.
RYUNOSUKE...
!!
OOH...
MAYBE IT'S NOT A GOOD IDEA TO CALL OUT YOUR NAME LIKE THAT.
I should've called you Fuji-kun, huh?

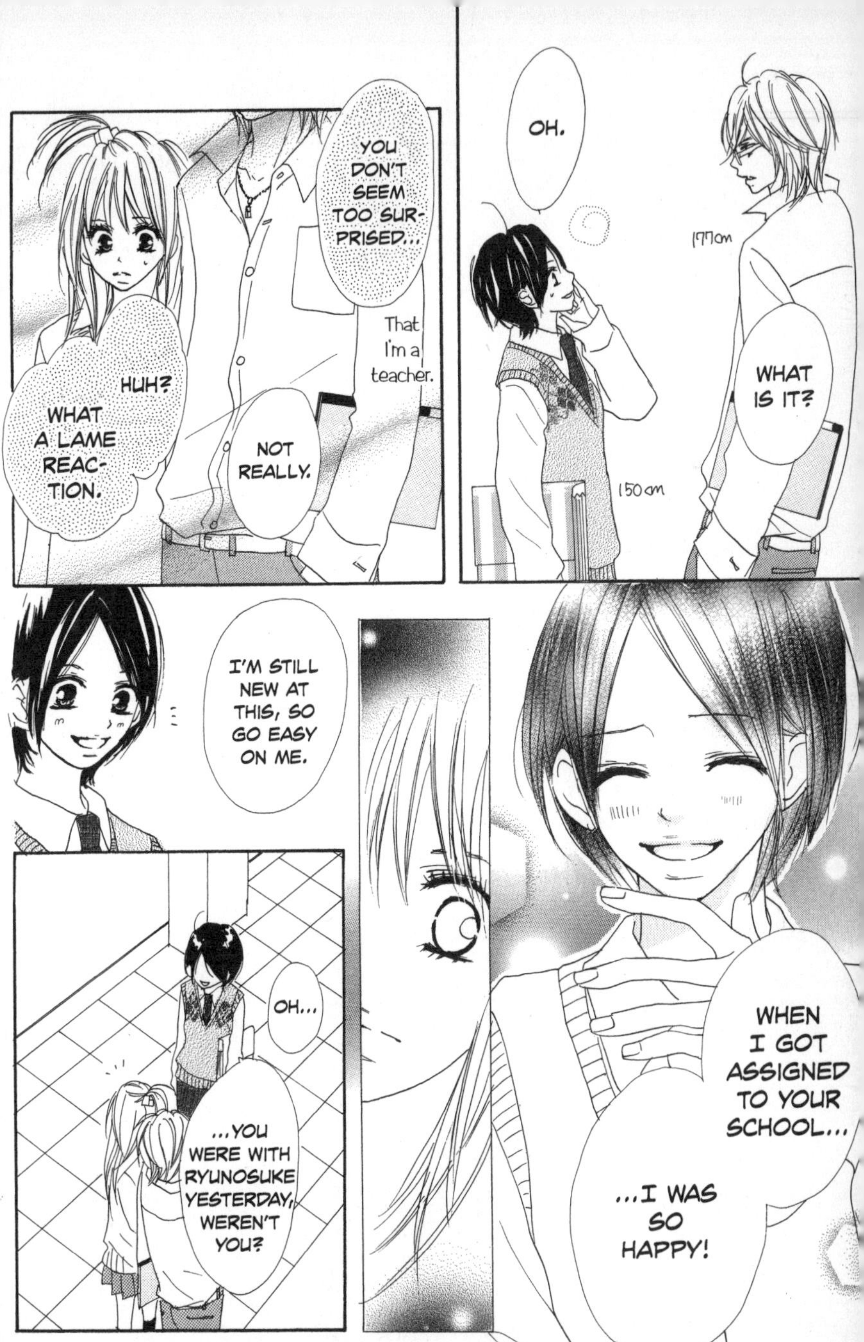
OH.
WHAT IS IT?
177cm
150cm
YOU DON'T SEEM TOO SURPRISED...
That I'm a teacher.
NOT REALLY.
HUH? WHAT A LAME REACTION.
WHEN I GOT ASSIGNED TO YOUR SCHOOL...
...I WAS SO HAPPY!
I'M STILL NEW AT THIS, SO GO EASY ON ME.
OH...
...YOU WERE WITH RYUNOSUKE YESTERDAY, WEREN'T YOU?

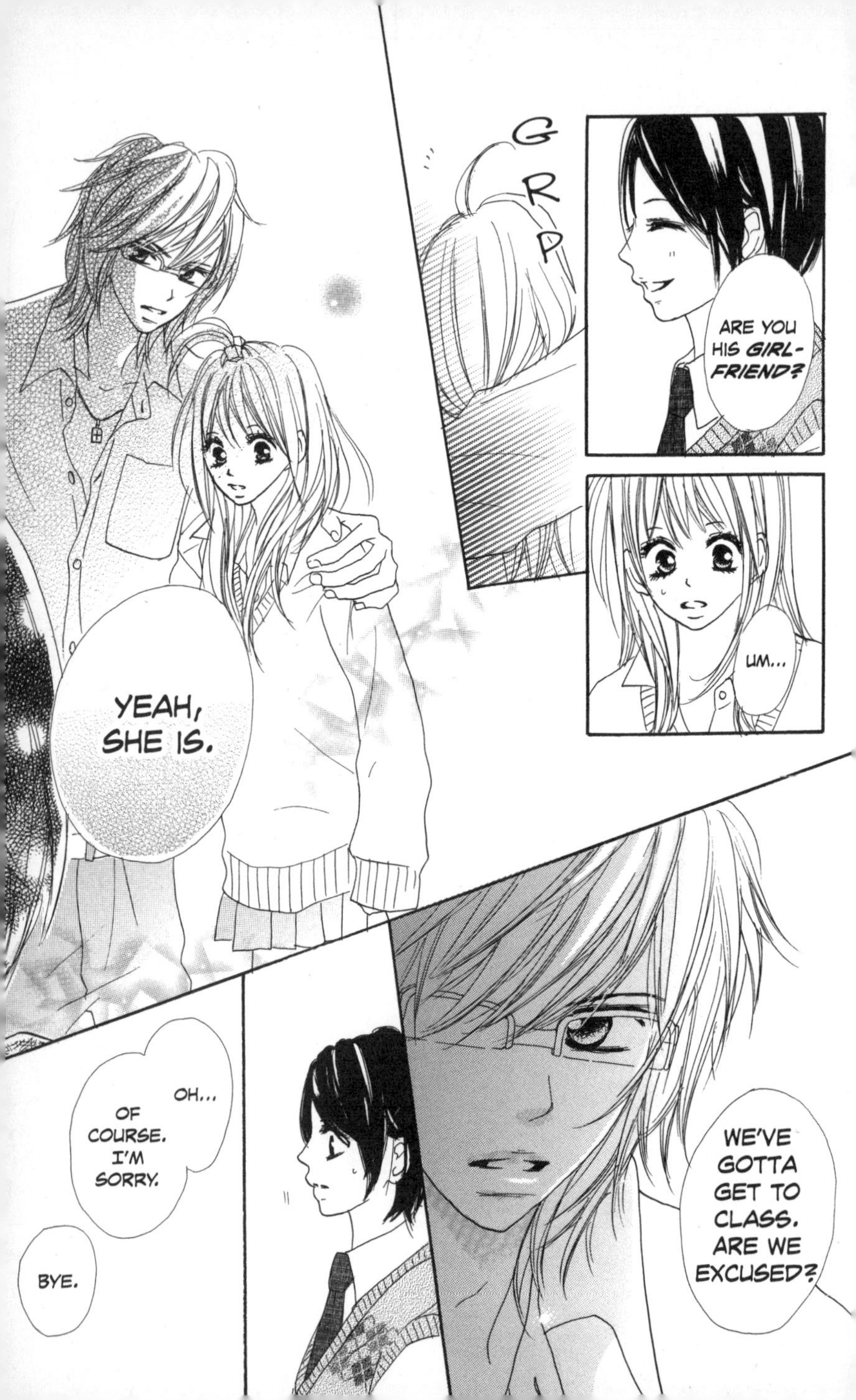
ARE YOU HIS *GIRL-FRIEND?*
UM...
G R P
YEAH, SHE IS.
WE'VE GOTTA GET TO CLASS. ARE WE EXCUSED?
OH... OF COURSE. I'M SORRY.
BYE.

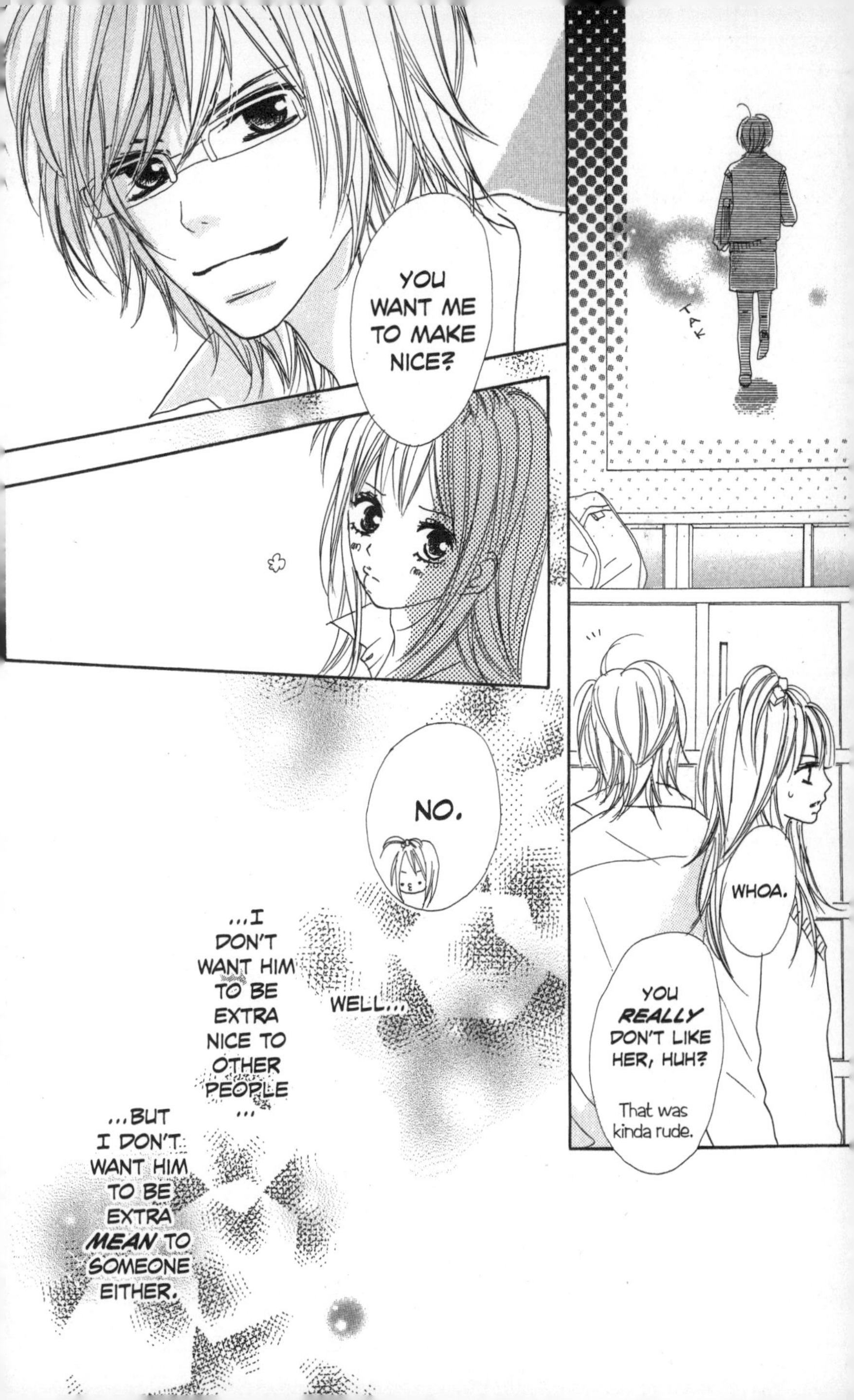
TAK
WHOA.
YOU *REALLY* DON'T LIKE HER, HUH?
That was kinda rude.
YOU WANT ME TO MAKE NICE?
NO.
WELL...
...I DON'T WANT HIM TO BE EXTRA NICE TO OTHER PEOPLE...
...BUT I DON'T WANT HIM TO BE EXTRA *MEAN* TO SOMEONE EITHER.

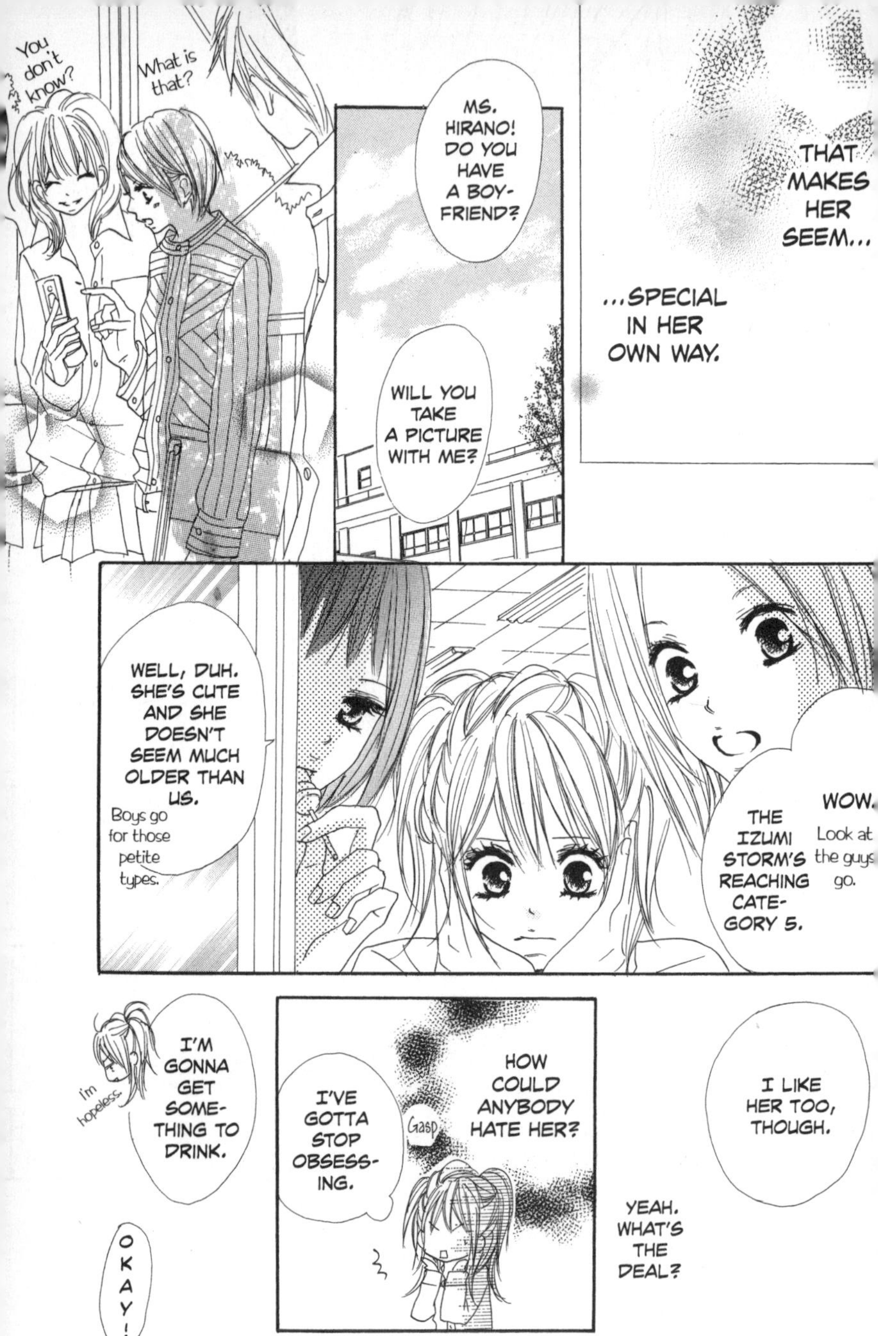
THAT MAKES HER SEEM...
...SPECIAL IN HER OWN WAY.
MS. HIRANO! DO YOU HAVE A BOY-FRIEND?
WILL YOU TAKE A PICTURE WITH ME?
What is that?
You don't know?
WOW.
Look at the guys go.
THE IZUMI STORM'S REACHING CATE-GORY 5.
WELL, DUH. SHE'S CUTE AND SHE DOESN'T SEEM MUCH OLDER THAN US.
Boys go for those petite types.
I LIKE HER TOO, THOUGH.
YEAH. WHAT'S THE DEAL?
HOW COULD ANYBODY HATE HER?
Gasp
I'VE GOTTA STOP OBSESS-ING.
I'M GONNA GET SOME-THING TO DRINK.
I'm hopeless.
OKAY!

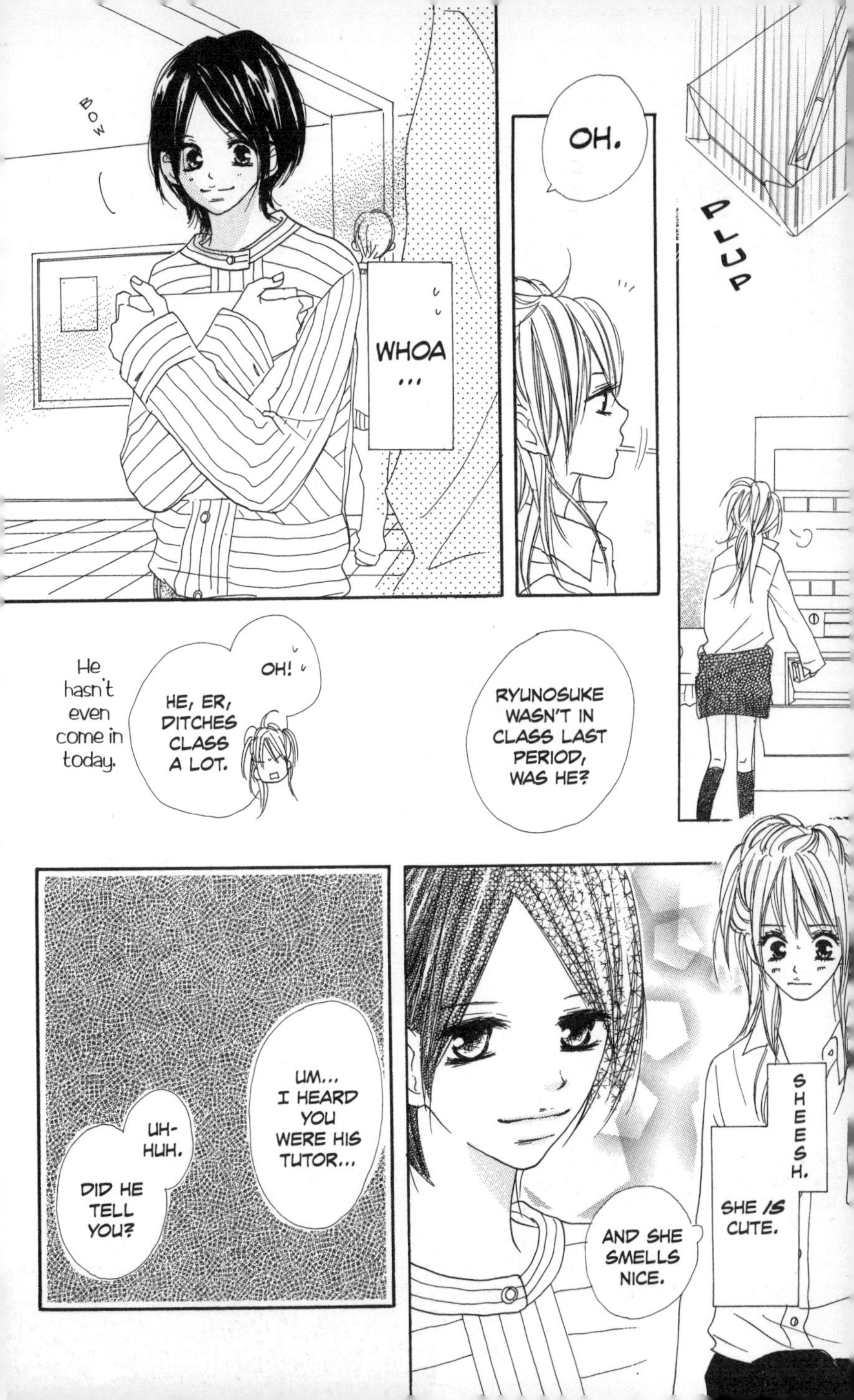
PLUP
OH.
WHOA...
BOW
RYUNOSUKE WASN'T IN CLASS LAST PERIOD, WAS HE?
OH!
HE, ER, DITCHES CLASS A LOT.
He hasn't even come in today.
SHEESH.
SHE *IS* CUTE.
AND SHE SMELLS NICE.
UM... I HEARD YOU WERE HIS TUTOR...
UH-HUH.
DID HE TELL YOU?

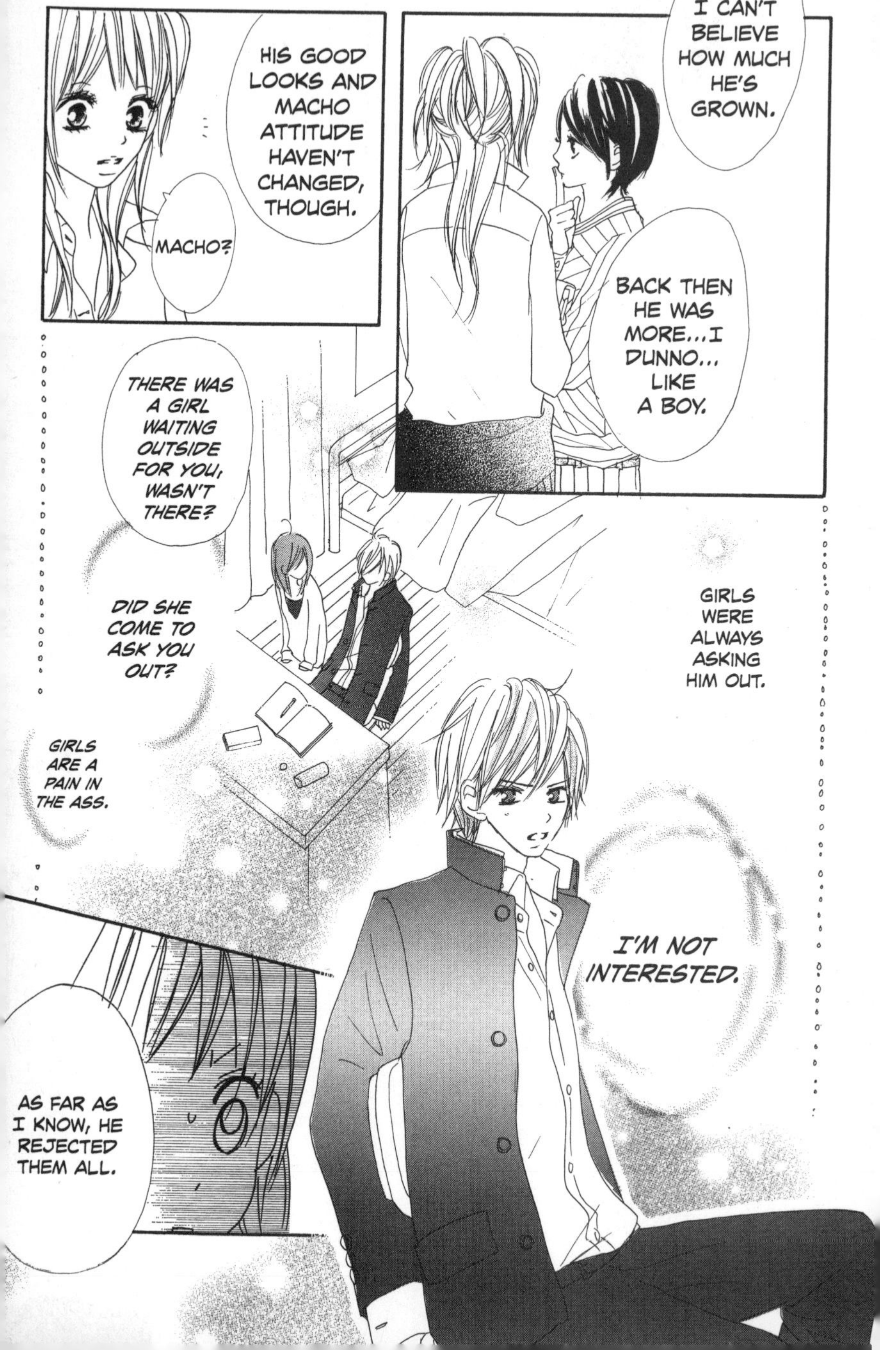
I CAN'T BELIEVE HOW MUCH HE'S GROWN.
BACK THEN HE WAS MORE...I DUNNO... LIKE A BOY.
HIS GOOD LOOKS AND MACHO ATTITUDE HAVEN'T CHANGED, THOUGH.
MACHO?
GIRLS WERE ALWAYS ASKING HIM OUT.
THERE WAS A GIRL WAITING OUTSIDE FOR YOU, WASN'T THERE?
DID SHE COME TO ASK YOU OUT?
I'M NOT INTERESTED.
GIRLS ARE A PAIN IN THE ASS.
AS FAR AS I KNOW, HE REJECTED THEM ALL.

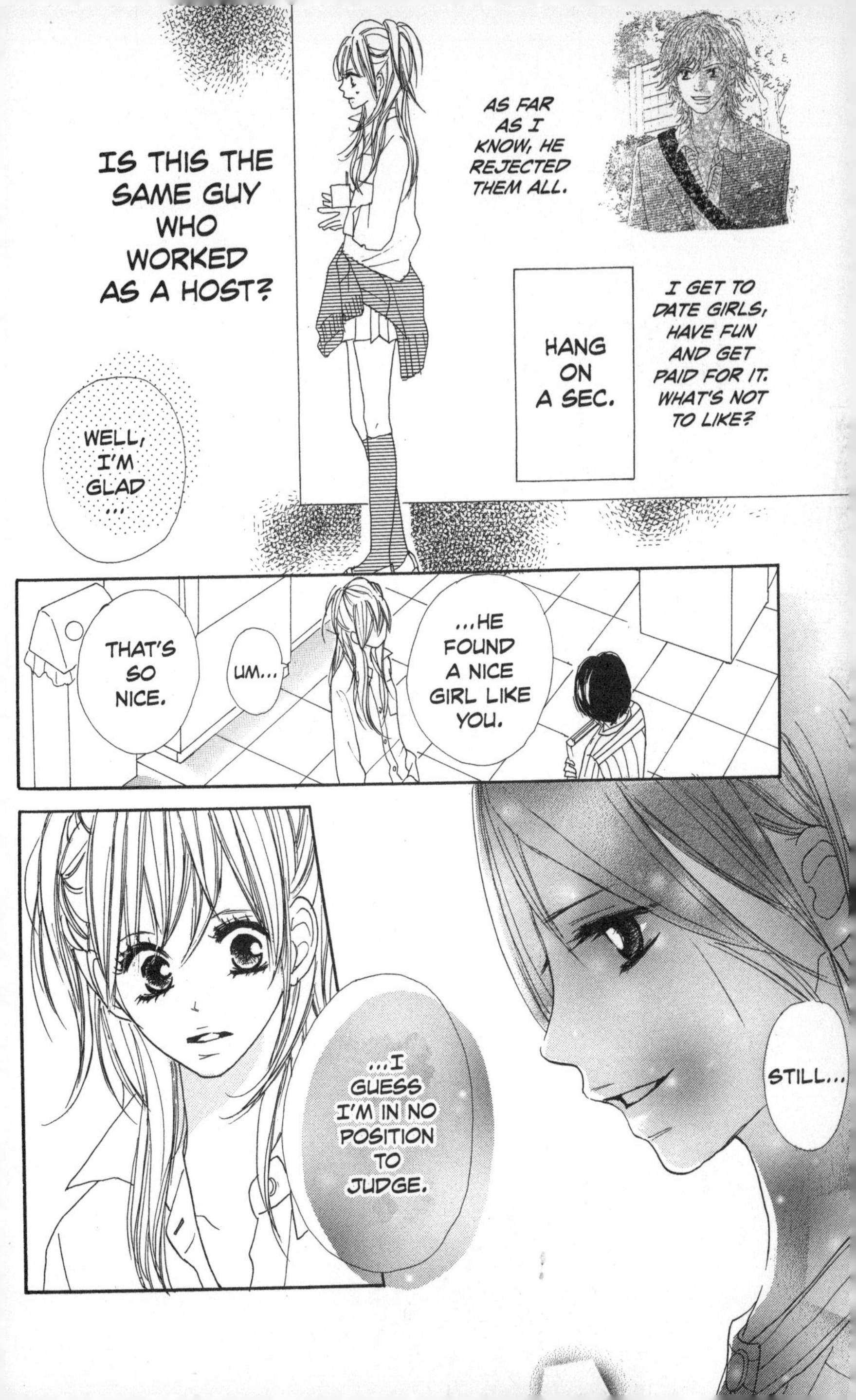
AS FAR AS I KNOW, HE REJECTED THEM ALL.
I GET TO DATE GIRLS, HAVE FUN AND GET PAID FOR IT. WHAT'S NOT TO LIKE?
HANG ON A SEC.
IS THIS THE SAME GUY WHO WORKED AS A HOST?
WELL, I'M GLAD...
...HE FOUND A NICE GIRL LIKE YOU.
UM...
THAT'S SO NICE.
STILL...
...I GUESS I'M IN NO POSITION TO JUDGE.

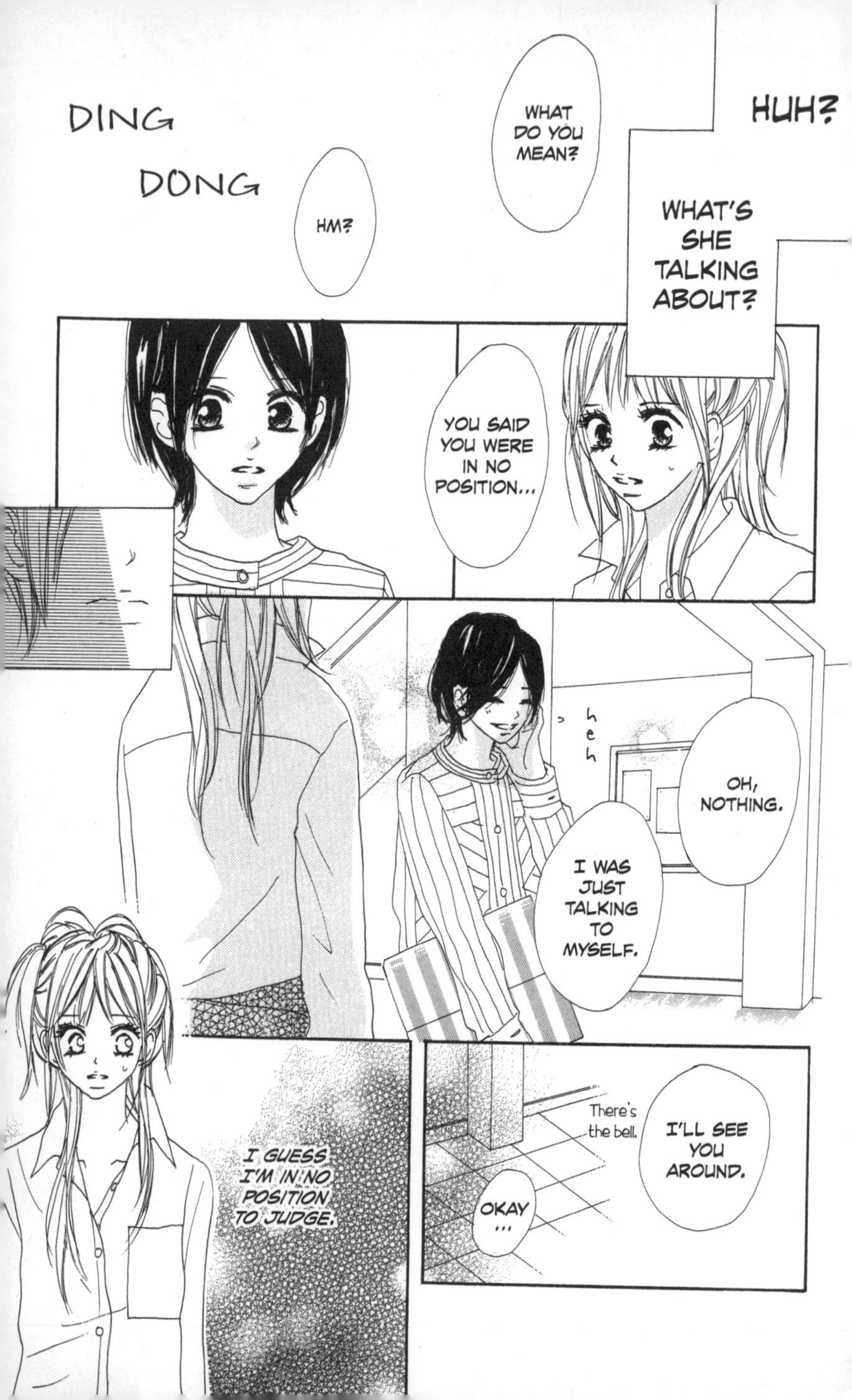
HUH?
WHAT'S SHE TALKING ABOUT?
WHAT DO YOU MEAN?
HM?
DING DONG
YOU SAID YOU WERE IN NO POSITION...
heh
OH, NOTHING.
I WAS JUST TALKING TO MYSELF.
I'LL SEE YOU AROUND.
There's the bell.
OKAY...
I GUESS I'M IN NO POSITION TO JUDGE.

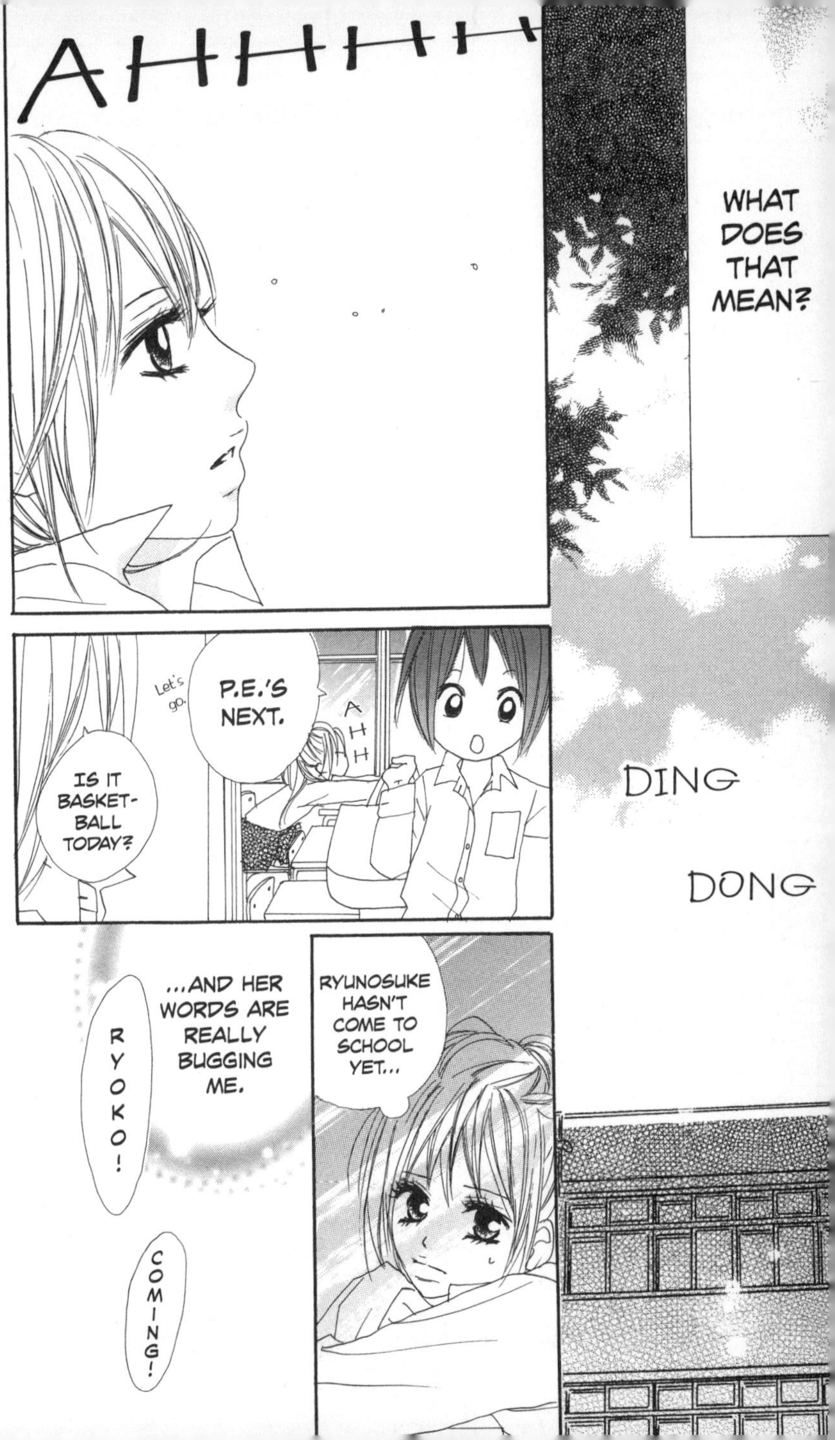

WHAT DOES THAT MEAN?
DING
DONG
AHHHHHH
P.E.'S NEXT.
Let's go.
AHH
IS IT BASKET-BALL TODAY?
RYUNOSUKE HASN'T COME TO SCHOOL YET...
...AND HER WORDS ARE REALLY BUGGING ME.
RYOKO!
COMING!

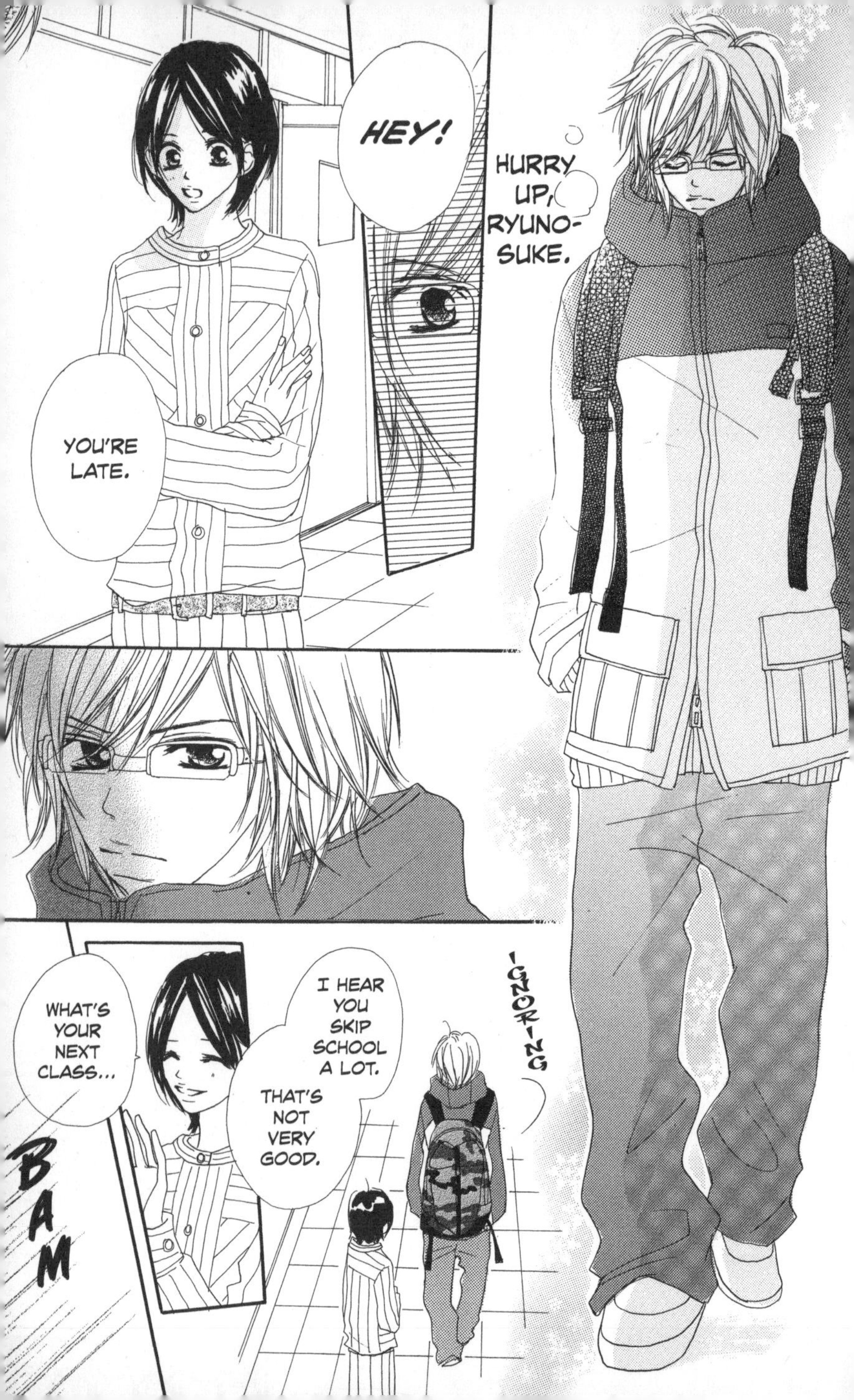
HURRY UP, RYUNOSUKE.
HEY!
YOU'RE LATE.
IGNORING
I HEAR YOU SKIP SCHOOL A LOT.
THAT'S NOT VERY GOOD.
WHAT'S YOUR NEXT CLASS...
BAM

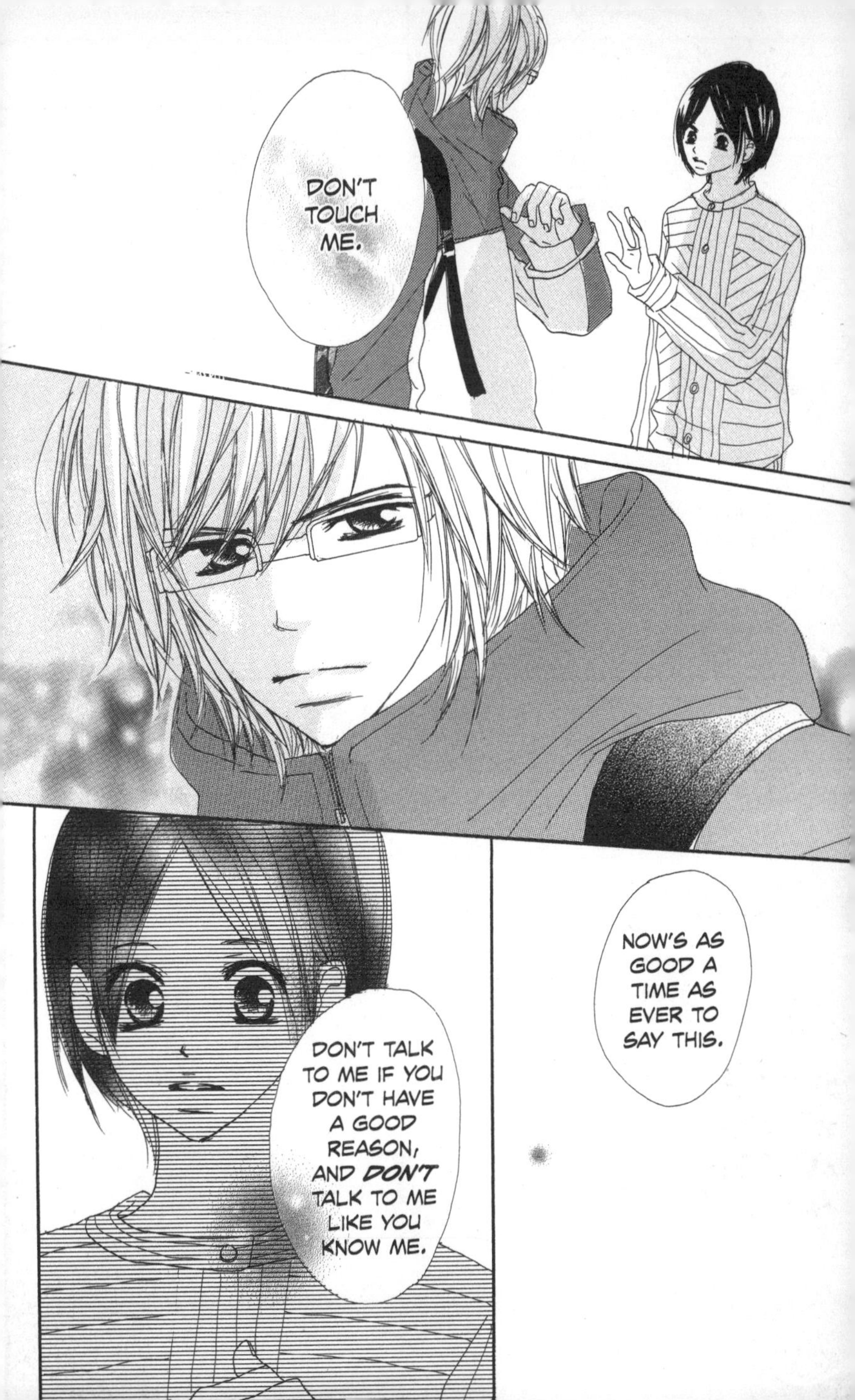
DON'T TOUCH ME.
NOW'S AS GOOD A TIME AS EVER TO SAY THIS.
DON'T TALK TO ME IF YOU DON'T HAVE A GOOD REASON, AND *DON'T* TALK TO ME LIKE YOU KNOW ME.

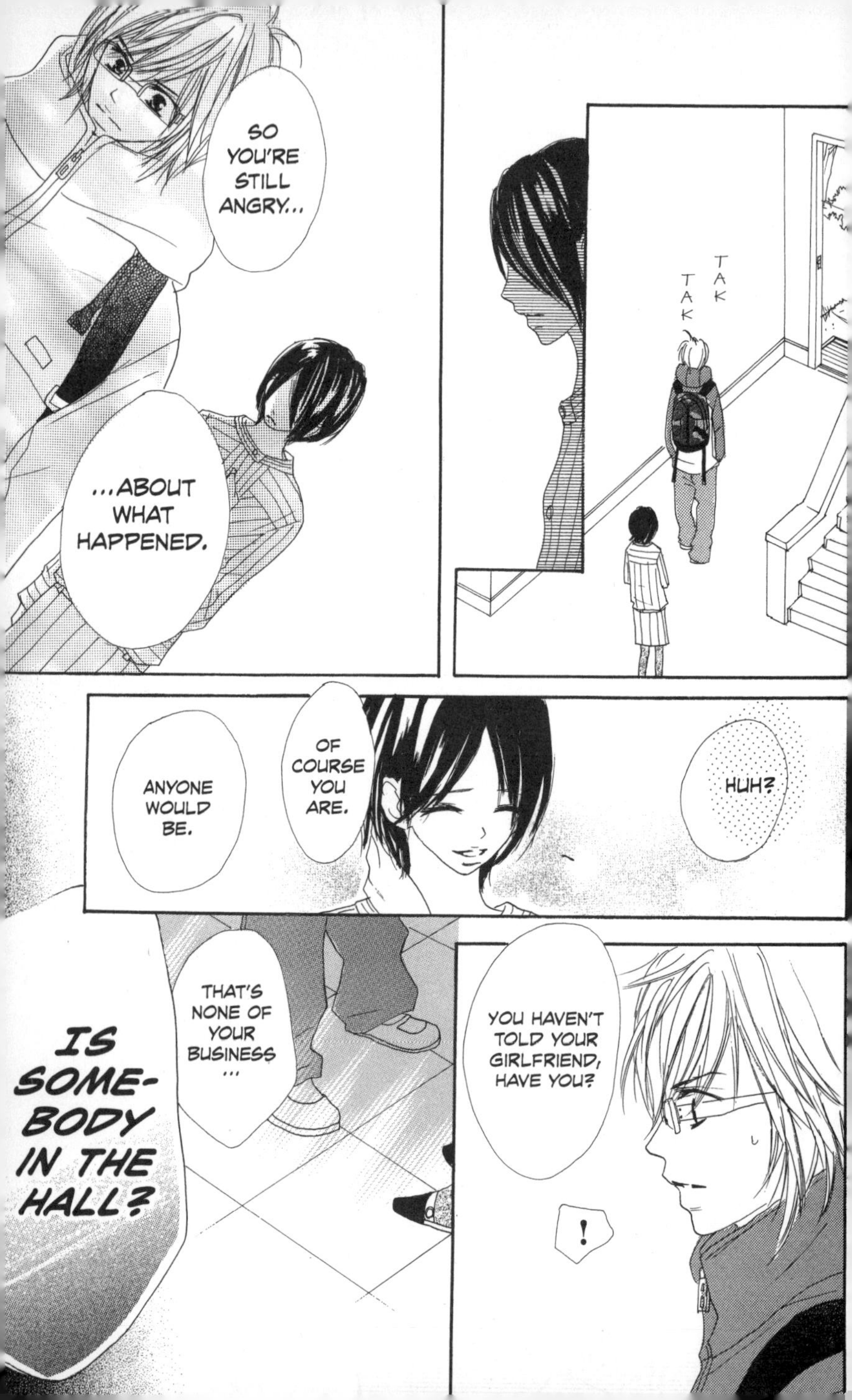
TAK TAK
SO YOU'RE STILL ANGRY...
...ABOUT WHAT HAPPENED.
HUH?
OF COURSE YOU ARE.
ANYONE WOULD BE.
YOU HAVEN'T TOLD YOUR GIRLFRIEND, HAVE YOU?
!
THAT'S NONE OF YOUR BUSINESS...
IS SOME-BODY IN THE HALL?

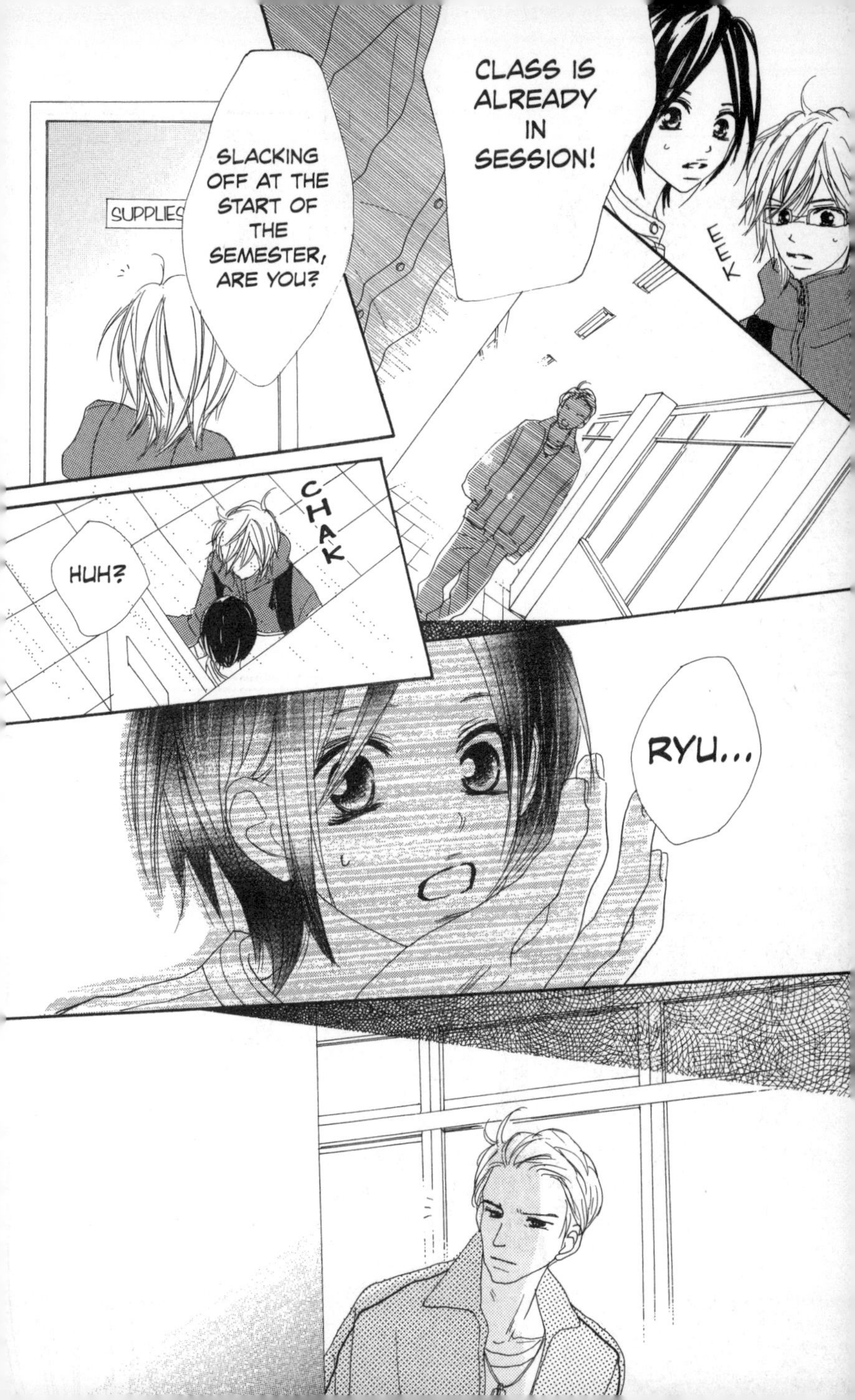

CLASS IS ALREADY IN SESSION!
EEK
SLACKING OFF AT THE START OF THE SEMESTER, ARE YOU?
SUPPLIES
CHAK
HUH?
RYU...

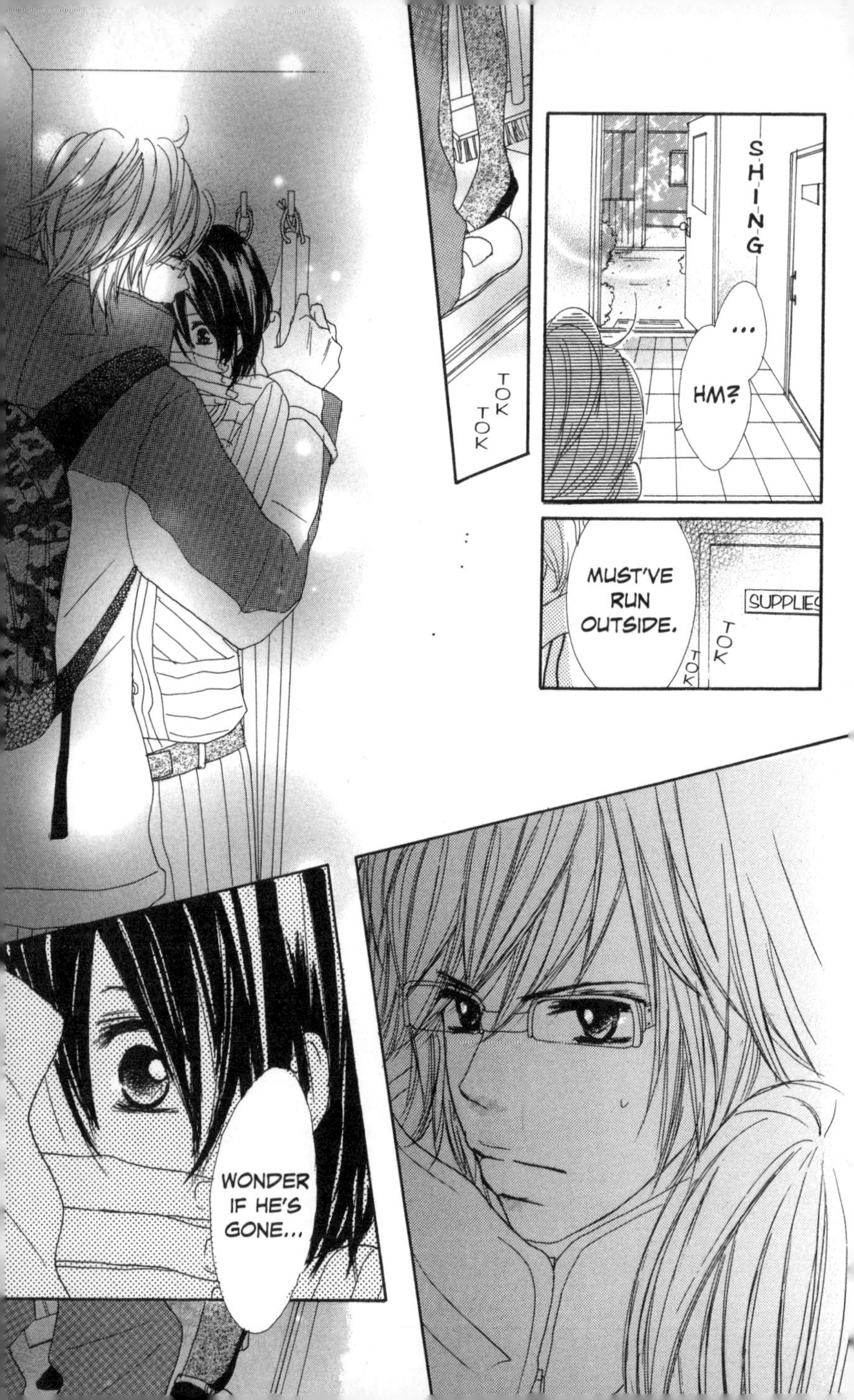
SHING
...
HM?
MUST'VE RUN OUTSIDE.
TOK TOK
TOK TOK
WONDER IF HE'S GONE...

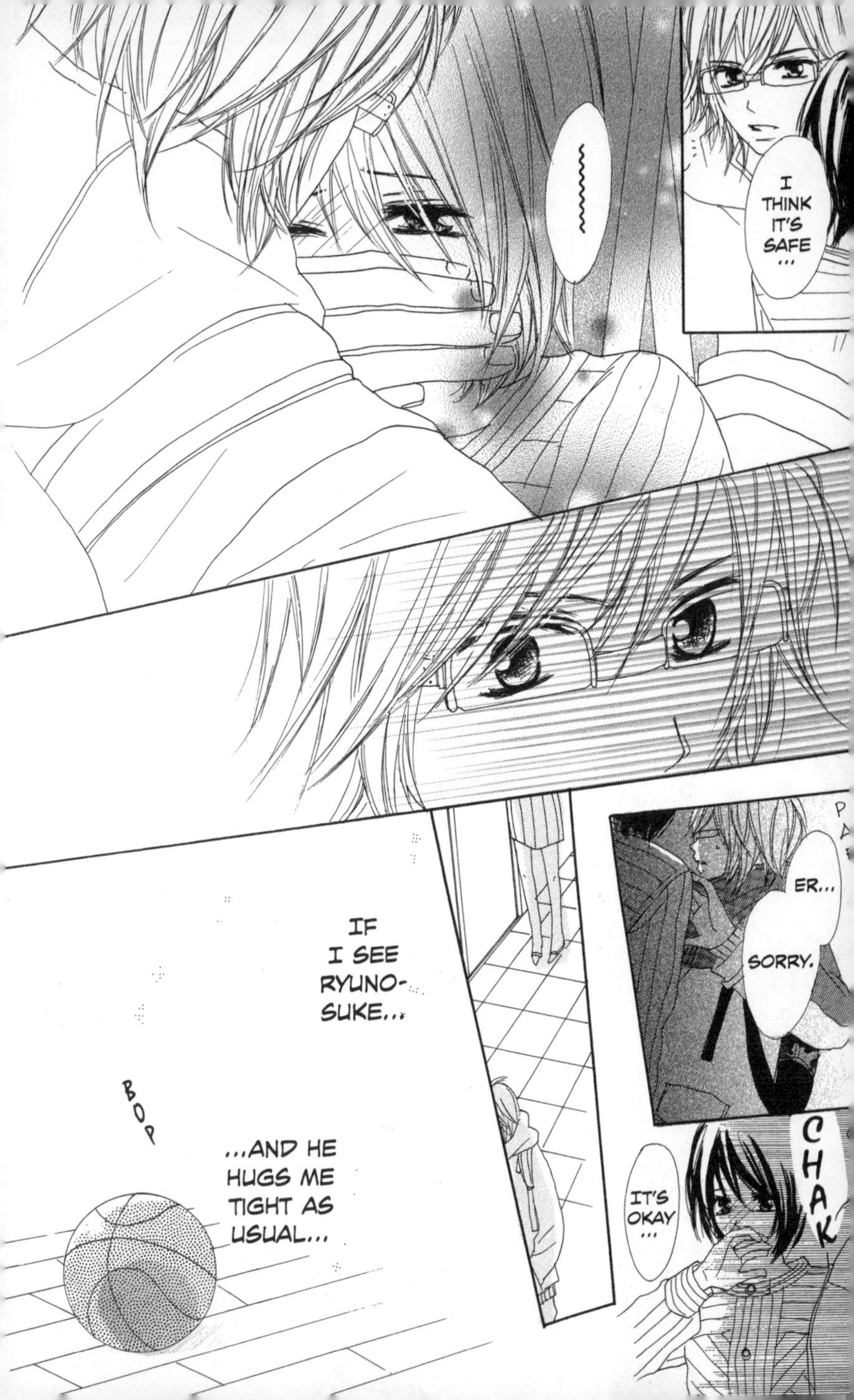

I THINK IT'S SAFE...
ER...
SORRY.
CHAK
IT'S OKAY...
IF I SEE RYUNO-SUKE...
BOP
...AND HE HUGS ME TIGHT AS USUAL...

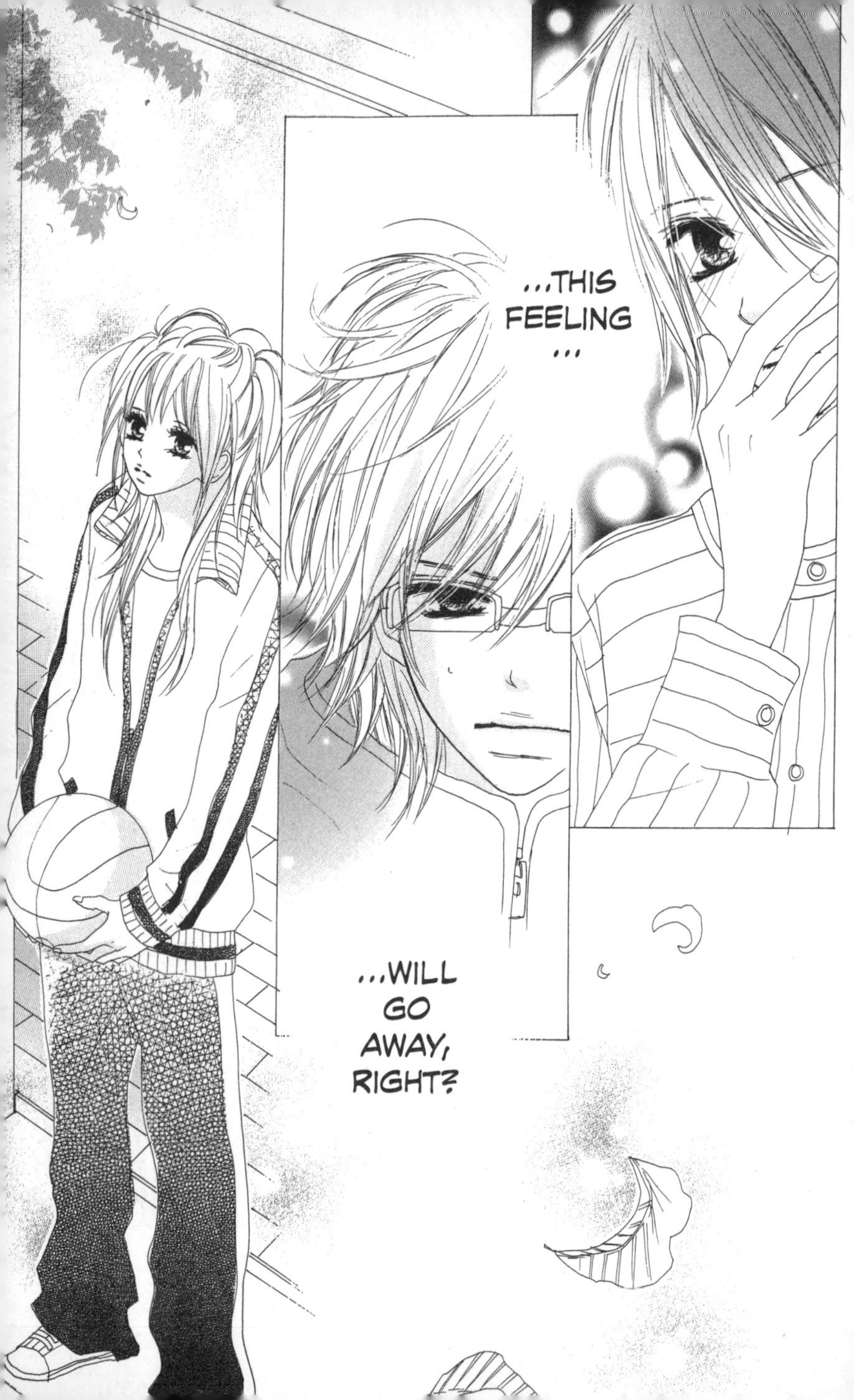
...THIS FEELING ...
...WILL GO AWAY, RIGHT?

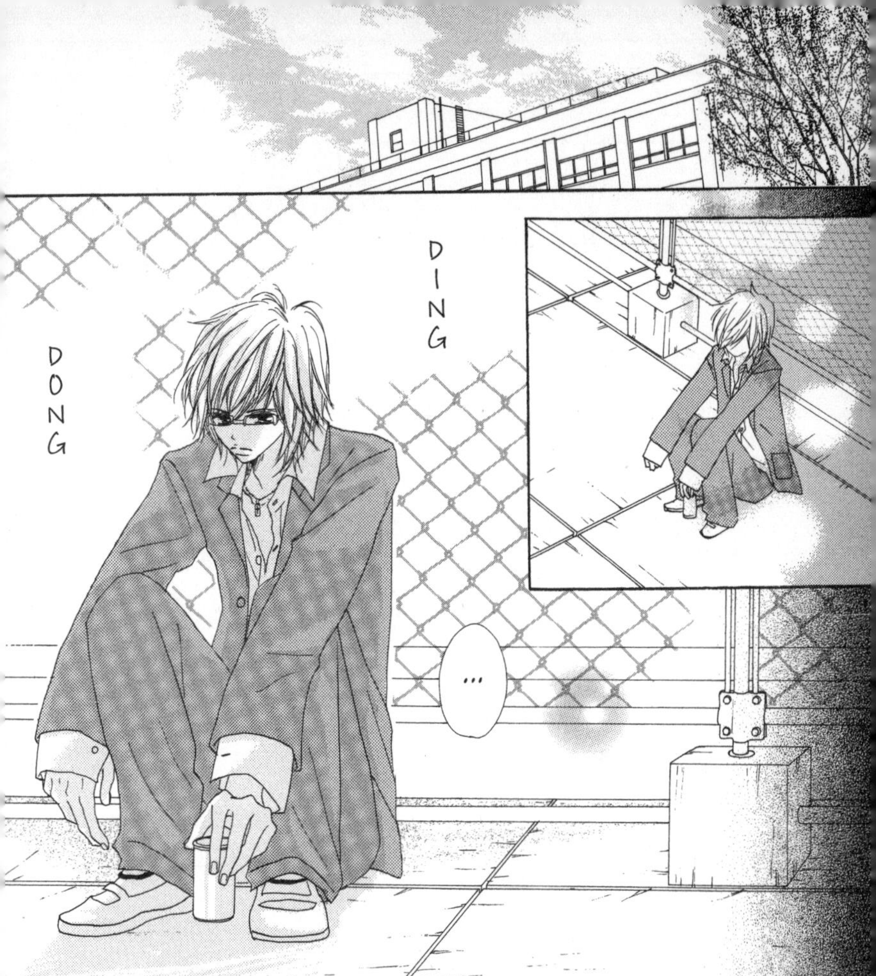
DING
DONG
...

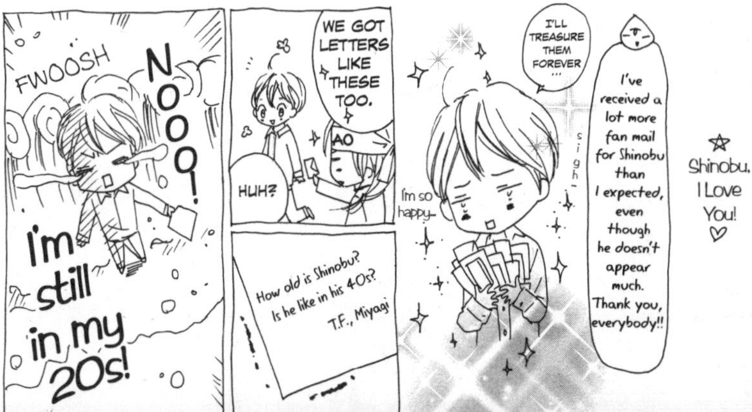
☆ Shinobu, I Love You! ♡
I've received a lot more fan mail for Shinobu than I expected, even though he doesn't appear much. Thank you, everybody!!
I'LL TREASURE THEM FOREVER...
sigh
I'm so happy
WE GOT LETTERS LIKE THESE TOO.
AO
HUH?
How old is Shinobu? Is he like in his 40s? T.F., Miyagi
FWOOSH
NOOO!
I'm still in my 20s!

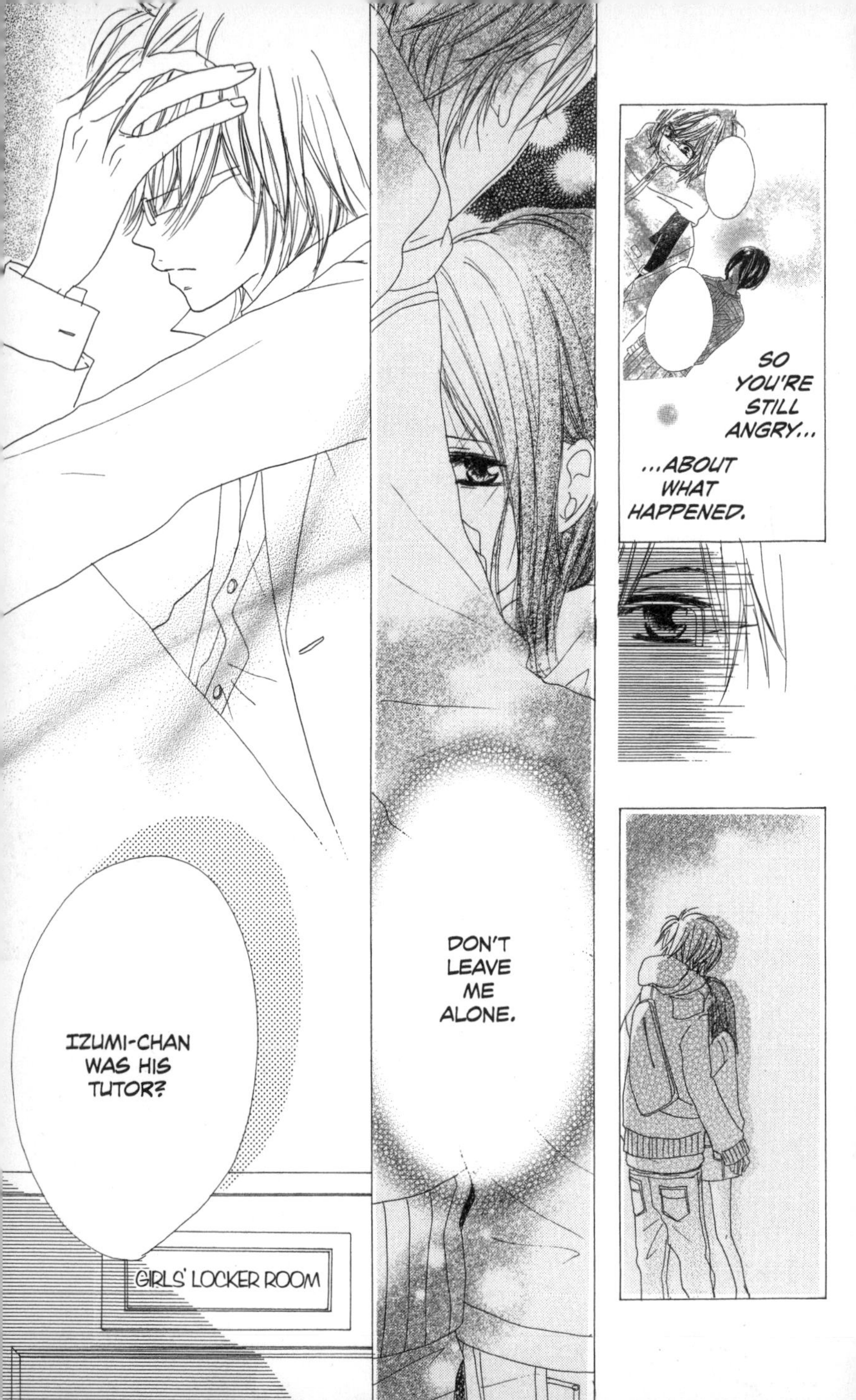
SO YOU'RE STILL ANGRY...
...ABOUT WHAT HAPPENED.
DON'T LEAVE ME ALONE.
IZUMI-CHAN WAS HIS TUTOR?
GIRLS' LOCKER ROOM

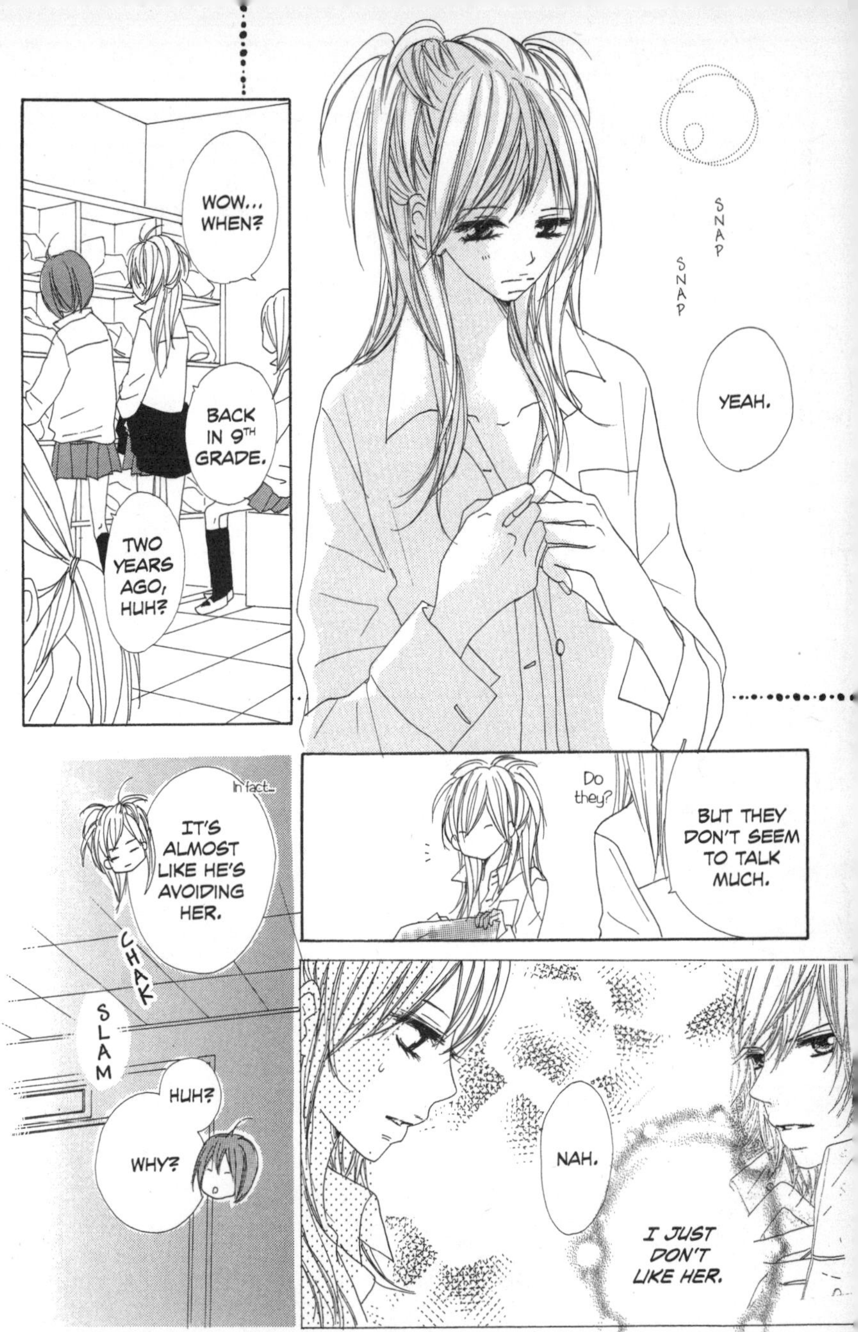
SNAP
SNAP
YEAH.
WOW... WHEN?
BACK IN 9TH GRADE.
TWO YEARS AGO, HUH?
BUT THEY DON'T SEEM TO TALK MUCH.
Do they?
NAH.
I JUST DON'T LIKE HER.
In fact...
IT'S ALMOST LIKE HE'S AVOIDING HER.
CHAK
SLAM
HUH?
WHY?

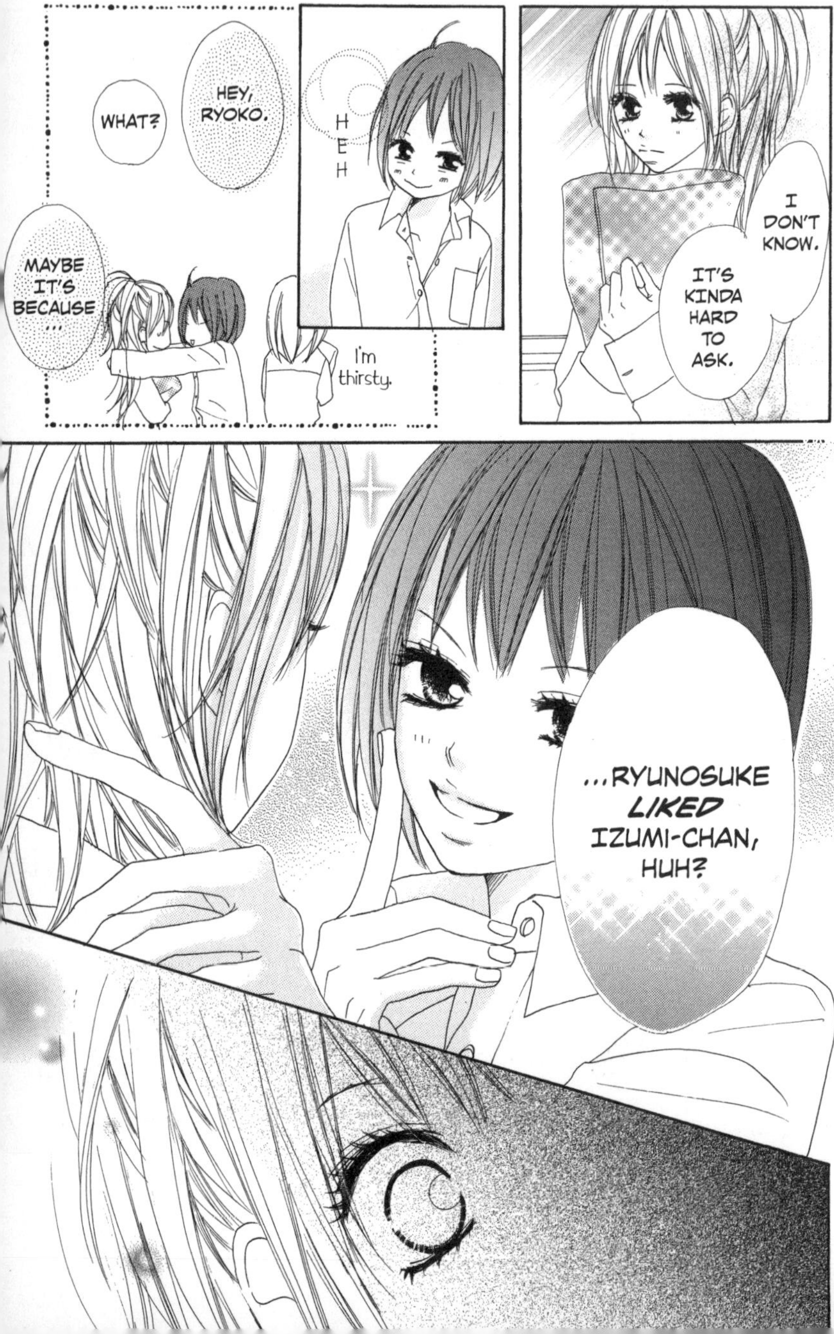
I DON'T KNOW.
IT'S KINDA HARD TO ASK.
HEH
HEY, RYOKO.
WHAT?
MAYBE IT'S BECAUSE...
I'm thirsty.
...RYUNOSUKE *LIKED* IZUMI-CHAN, HUH?

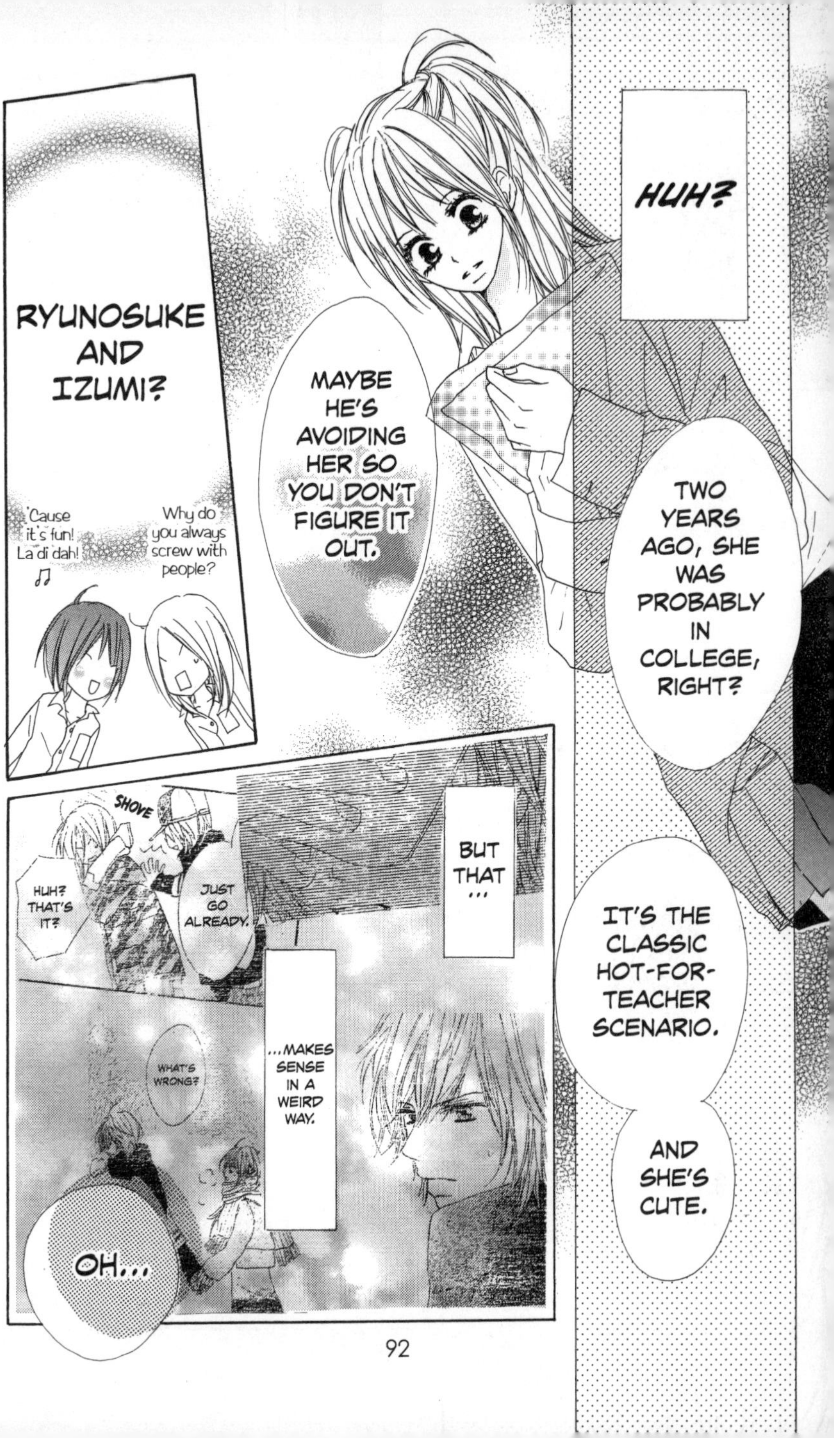
HUH?
TWO YEARS AGO, SHE WAS PROBABLY IN COLLEGE, RIGHT?
IT'S THE CLASSIC HOT-FOR-TEACHER SCENARIO.
AND SHE'S CUTE.
MAYBE HE'S AVOIDING HER SO YOU DON'T FIGURE IT OUT.
RYUNOSUKE AND IZUMI?
Why do you always screw with people?
'Cause it's fun! La di dah! ♫
BUT THAT...
SHOVE
JUST GO ALREADY.
HUH? THAT'S IT?
...MAKES SENSE IN A WEIRD WAY.
WHAT'S WRONG?
OH...

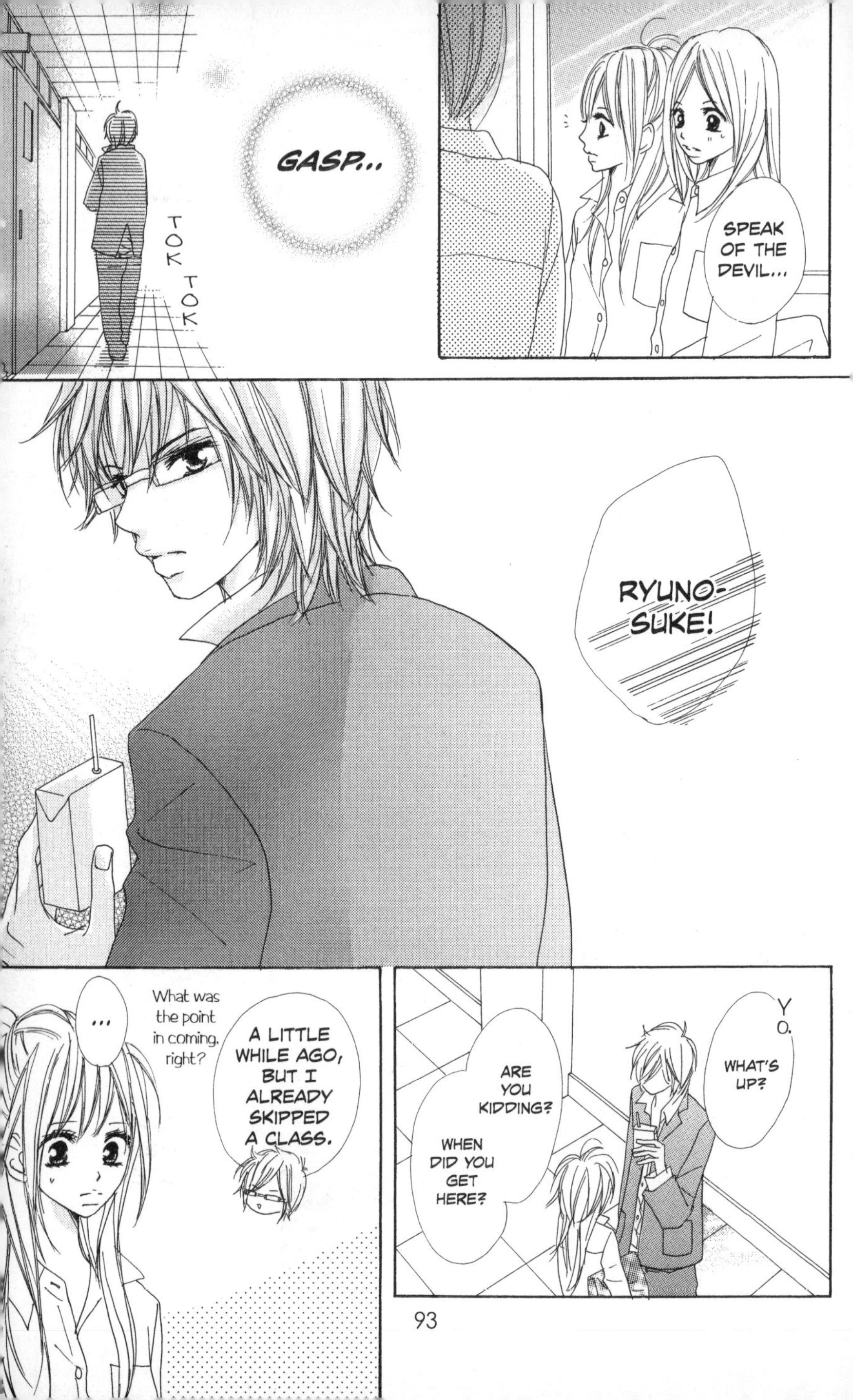
SPEAK OF THE DEVIL...
GASP...
TOK TOK
RYUNO-SUKE!
YO.
WHAT'S UP?
ARE YOU KIDDING?
WHEN DID YOU GET HERE?
A LITTLE WHILE AGO, BUT I ALREADY SKIPPED A CLASS.
What was the point in coming, right?
...

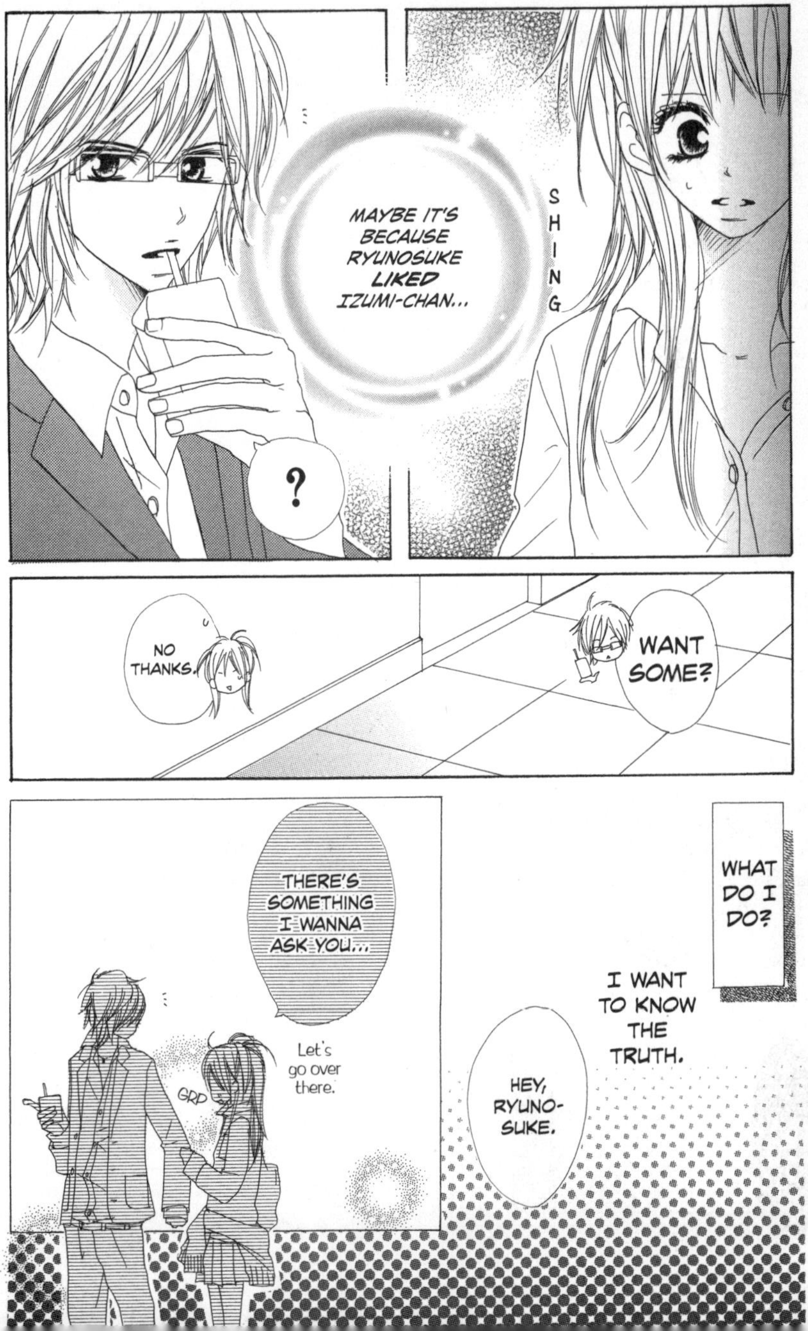
SHING
MAYBE IT'S BECAUSE RYUNOSUKE LIKED IZUMI-CHAN...
?
WANT SOME?
NO THANKS.
WHAT DO I DO?
I WANT TO KNOW THE TRUTH.
HEY, RYUNO-SUKE.
THERE'S SOMETHING I WANNA ASK YOU...
Let's go over there.
GRP

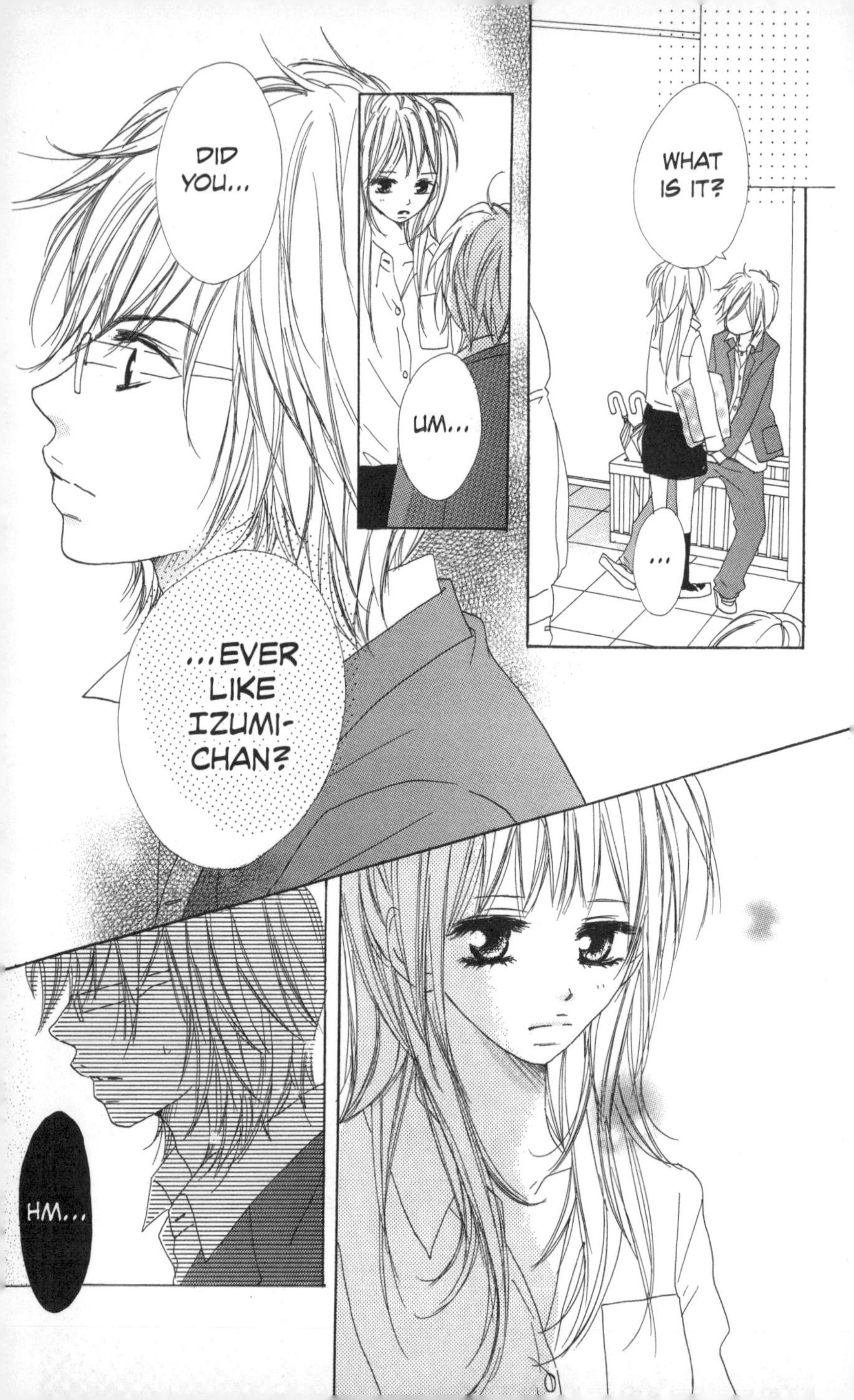
WHAT IS IT?
...
UM...
DID YOU...
...EVER LIKE IZUMI-CHAN?
HM...

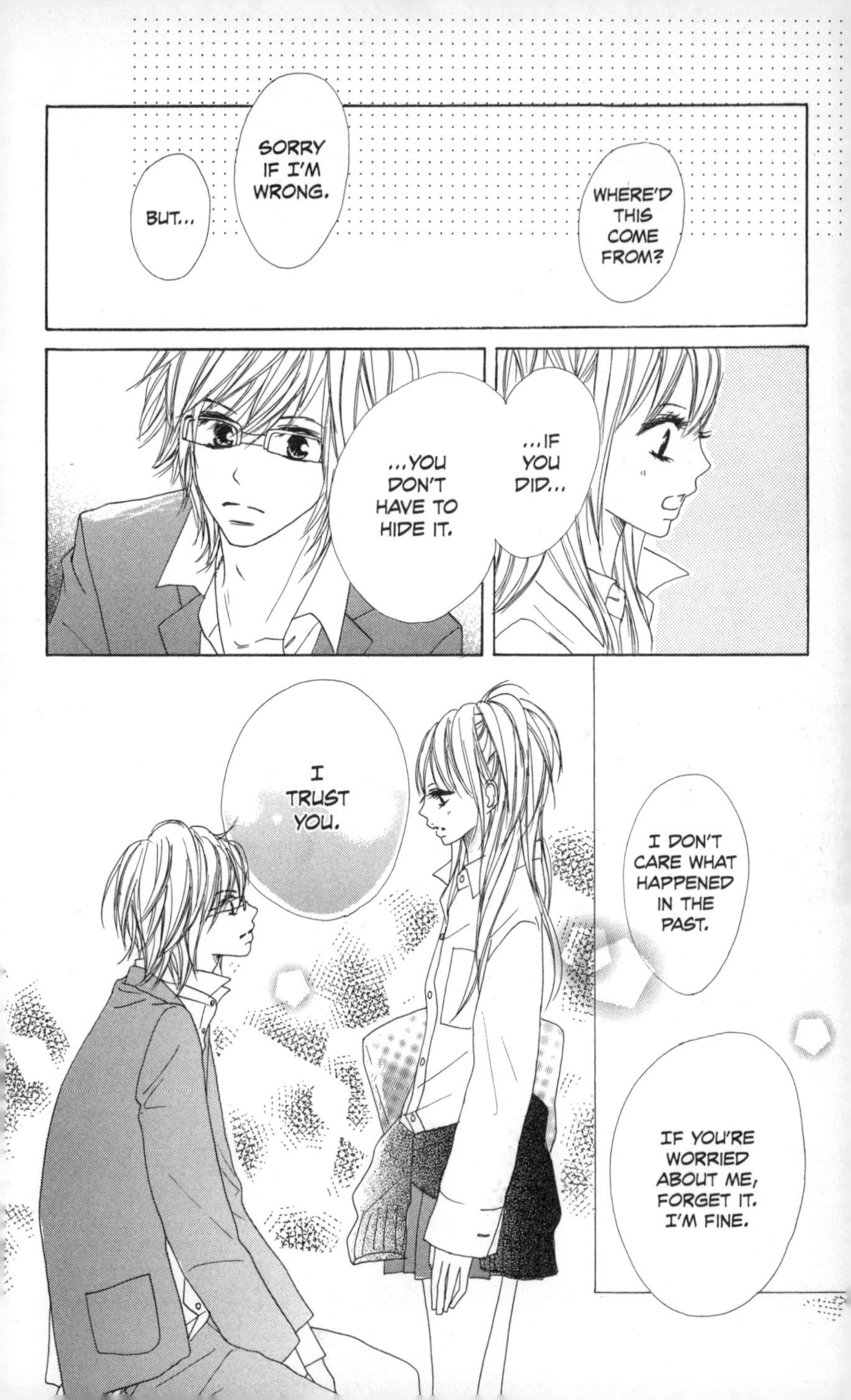
WHERE'D THIS COME FROM?
SORRY IF I'M WRONG.
BUT...
...IF YOU DID...
...YOU DON'T HAVE TO HIDE IT.
I DON'T CARE WHAT HAPPENED IN THE PAST.
IF YOU'RE WORRIED ABOUT ME, FORGET IT. I'M FINE.
I TRUST YOU.

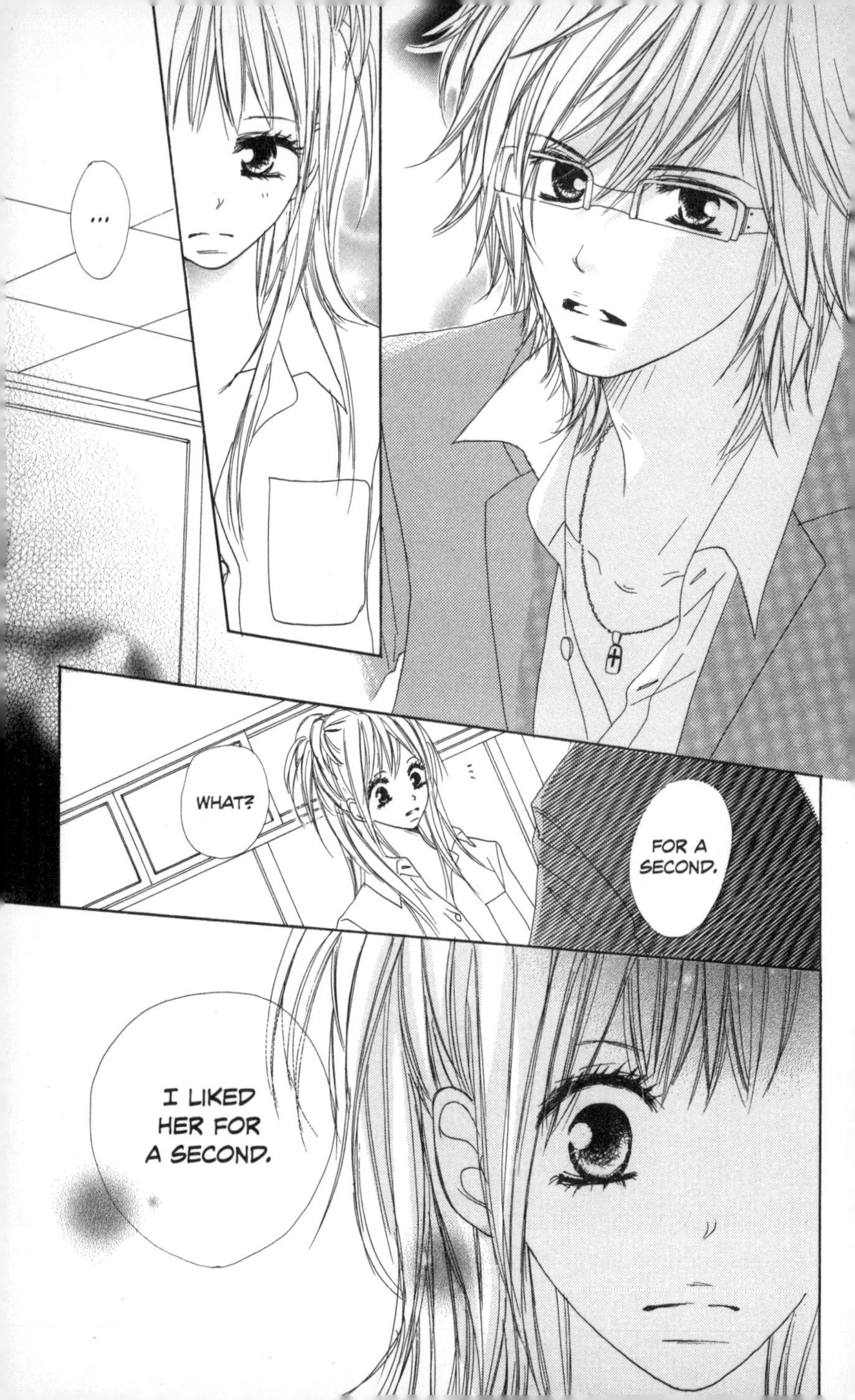
...
FOR A SECOND.
WHAT?
I LIKED HER FOR A SECOND.

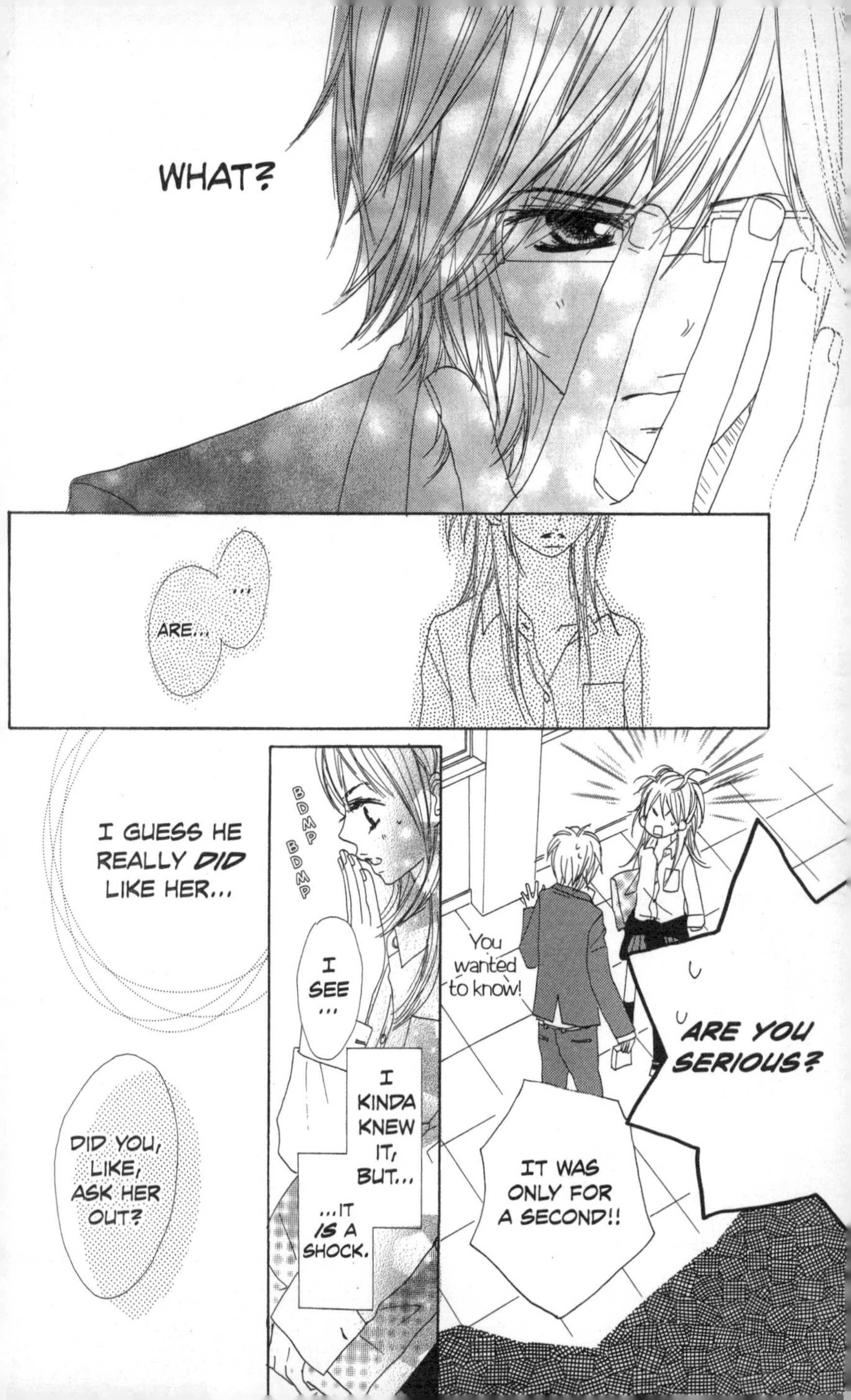
WHAT?
...
ARE...
ARE YOU SERIOUS?
You wanted to know!
IT WAS ONLY FOR A SECOND!!
BDMP BDMP
I SEE...
I KINDA KNEW IT, BUT...
...IT IS A SHOCK.
I GUESS HE REALLY DID LIKE HER...
DID YOU, LIKE, ASK HER OUT?

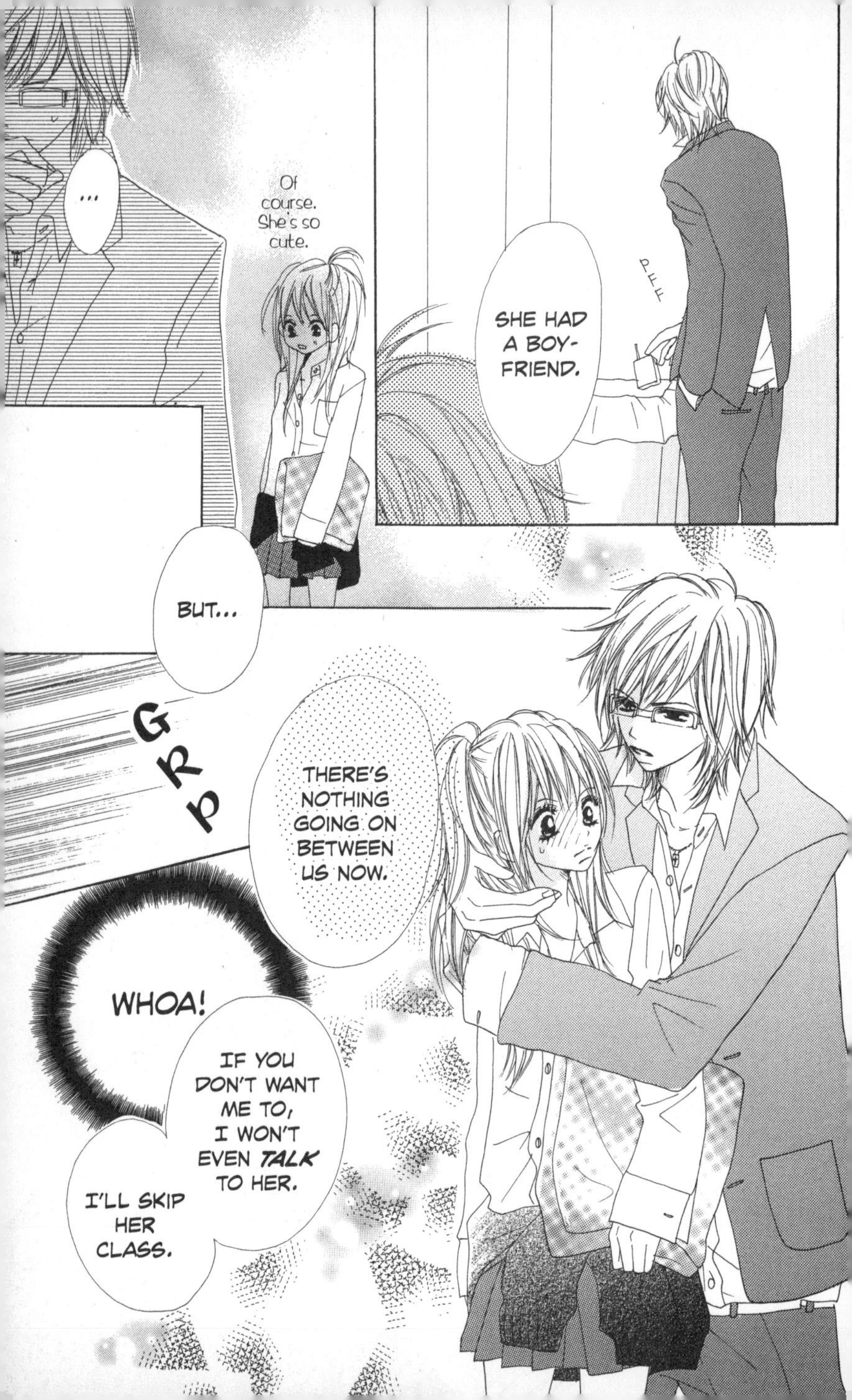
SHE HAD A BOY-FRIEND.
PFF
Of course. She's so cute.
...
BUT...
GRP
THERE'S NOTHING GOING ON BETWEEN US NOW.
WHOA!
IF YOU DON'T WANT ME TO, I WON'T EVEN TALK TO HER.
I'LL SKIP HER CLASS.

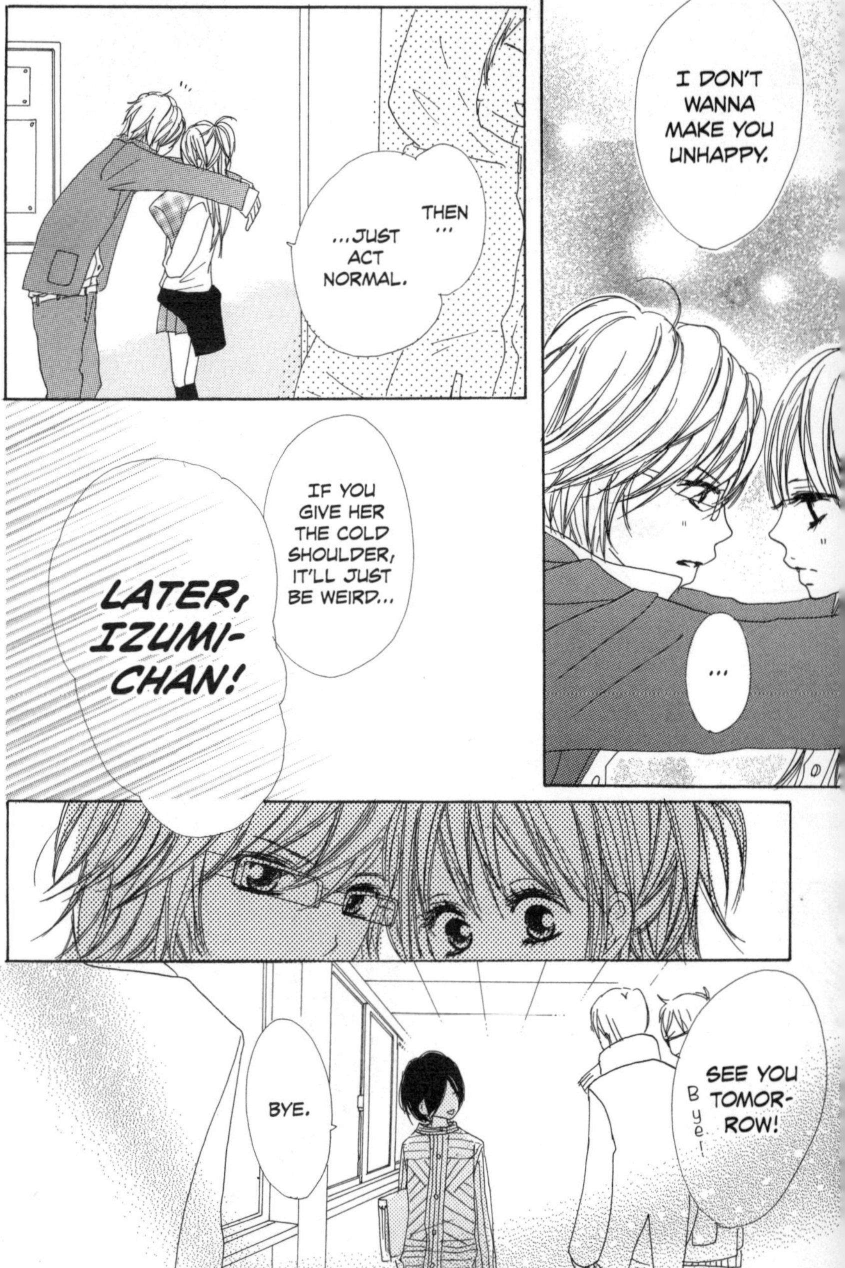
I DON'T WANNA MAKE YOU UNHAPPY.
...
THEN...
...JUST ACT NORMAL.
IF YOU GIVE HER THE COLD SHOULDER, IT'LL JUST BE WEIRD...
LATER, IZUMI-CHAN!
SEE YOU TOMOR-ROW!
Bye!
BYE.

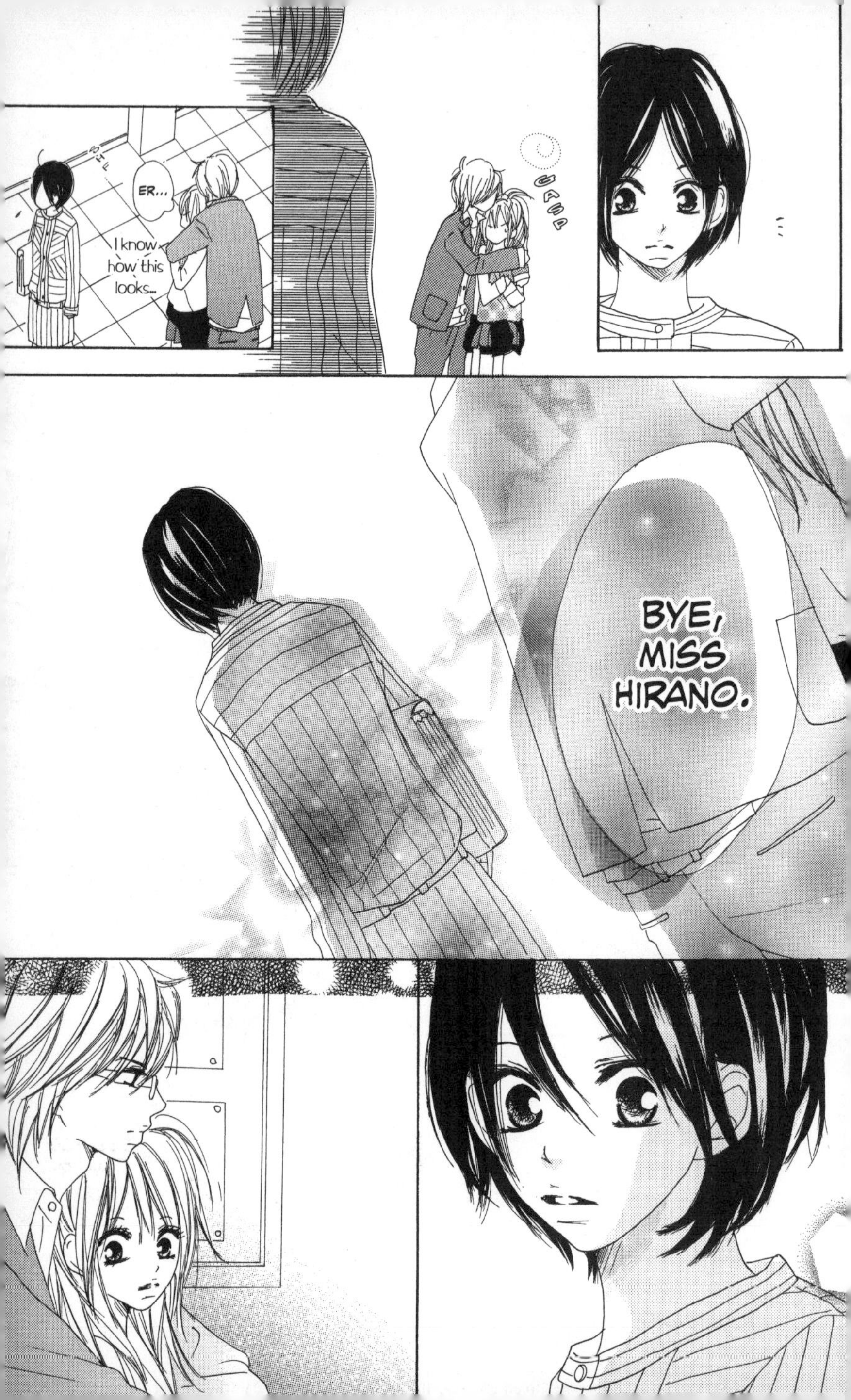

GASP
SHF
ER...
I know how this looks...
BYE, MISS HIRANO.

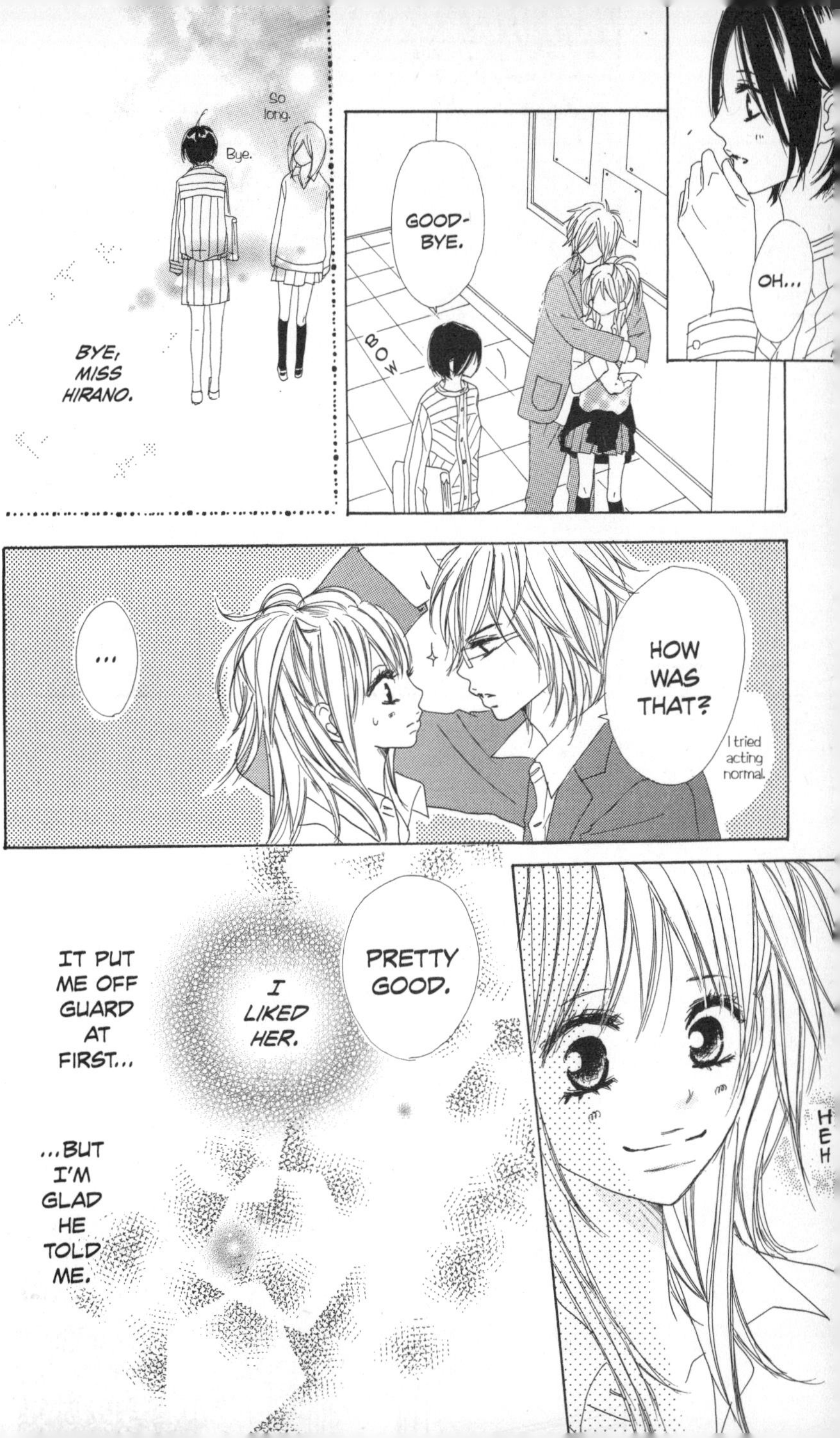
OH...
GOOD-BYE.
BOW
So long.
Bye.
BYE, MISS HIRANO.
HOW WAS THAT?
I tried acting normal.
...
HEH
PRETTY GOOD.
I LIKED HER.
IT PUT ME OFF GUARD AT FIRST...
...BUT I'M GLAD HE TOLD ME.

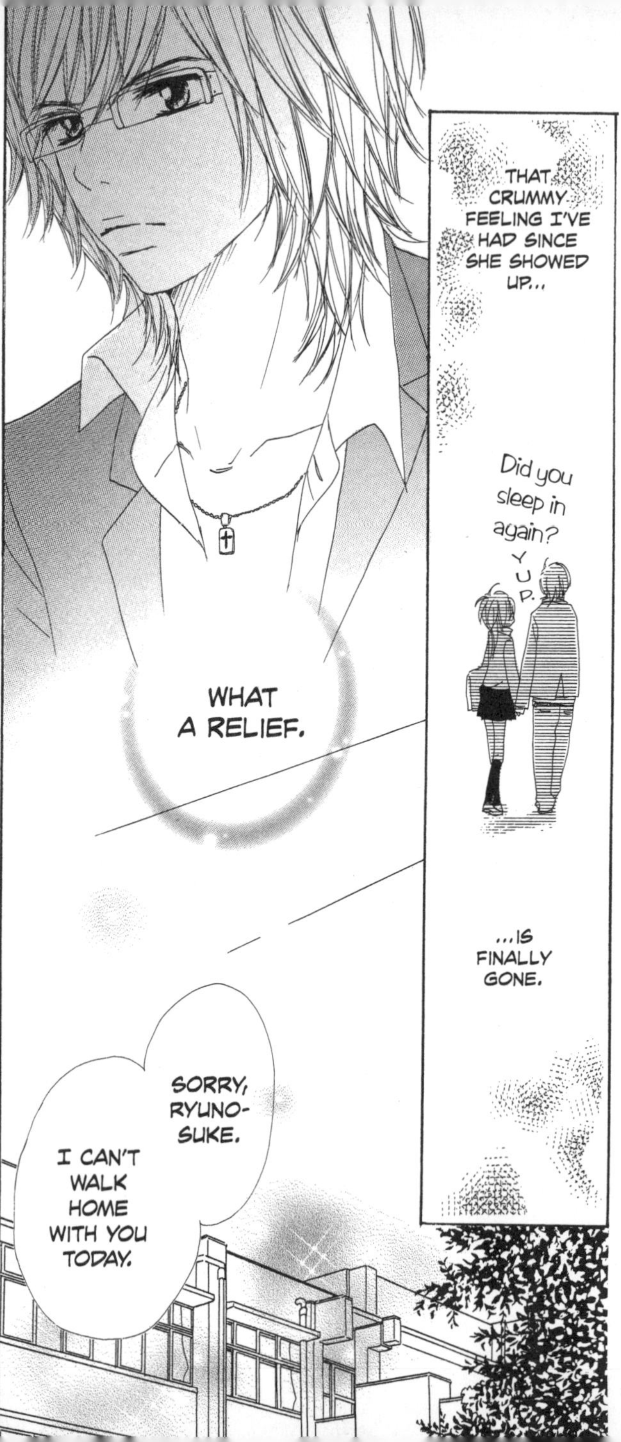
THAT CRUMMY FEELING I'VE HAD SINCE SHE SHOWED UP...
Did you sleep in again?
YUP.
...IS FINALLY GONE.
WHAT A RELIEF.
SORRY, RYUNOSUKE.
I CAN'T WALK HOME WITH YOU TODAY.

(3)

Ooh, I've been meaning to say this!! Guys!

Congratulations on finishing your exams!!

I bet a lot of you are thinking, "About time!!!" Sorry for not mentioning it!! I wanted to cheer you on in a more timely fashion, but I had a lot going on...

I got a lot of letters saying things like, "I have exams coming up," or "I'm reading B.O.D.Y. in between my studies." So I've been meaning to give you guys a shout-out...But it's already June!! Time to snap out of exam blues!! To those of you who got into the school of your dreams and to those who didn't, I hope you're all having fun...Are you guys joining clubs and falling in love?

I'm so jealous!! I'm so jealous!!

By the way, I was on the basketball team in junior high. I played basketball about 340 days a year.

CATCH!

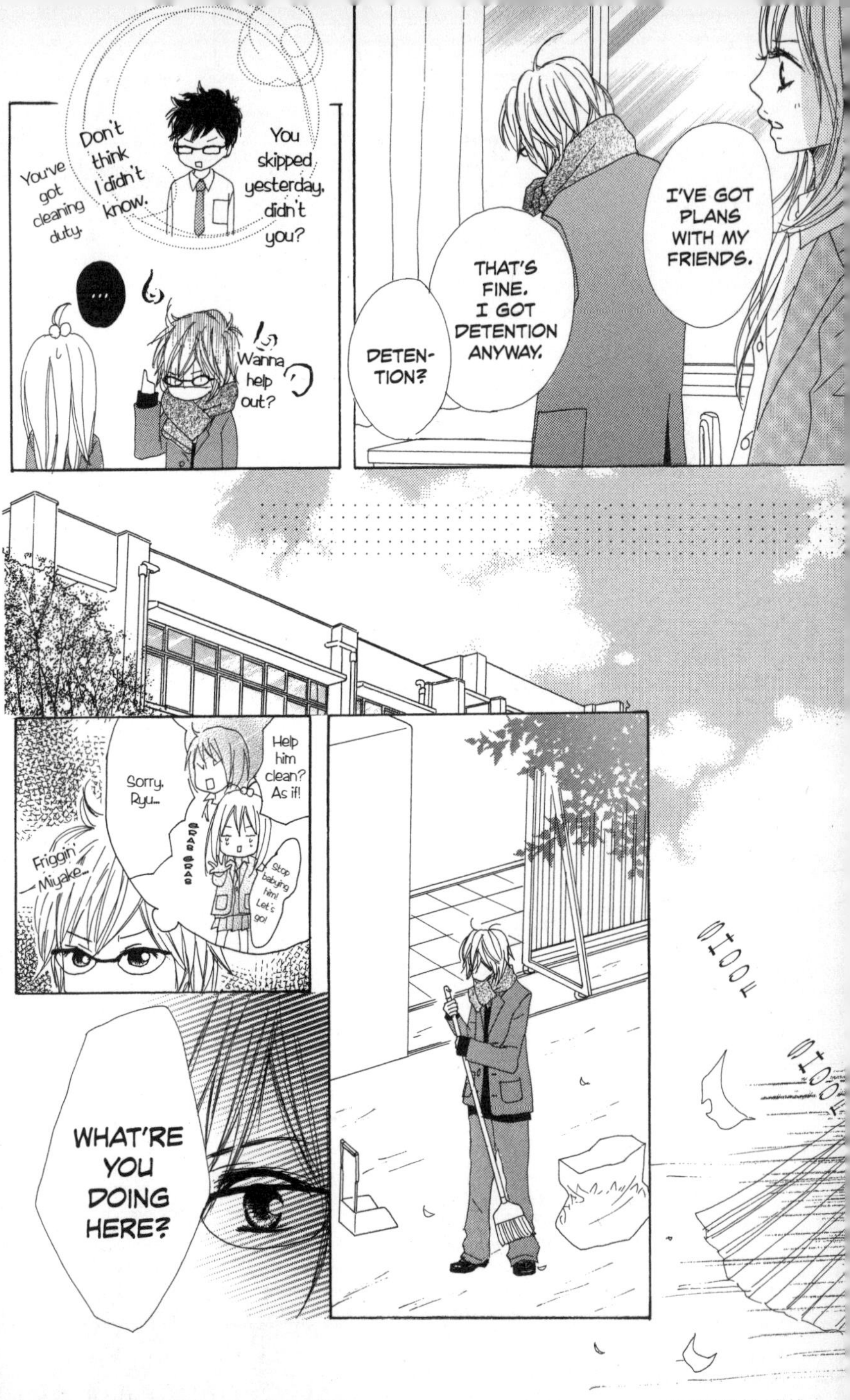
I'VE GOT PLANS WITH MY FRIENDS.
THAT'S FINE. I GOT DETENTION ANYWAY.
DETENTION?
You skipped yesterday, didn't you?
Don't think I didn't know.
You've got cleaning duty.
...
Wanna help out?
Help him clean? As if!
Sorry, Ryu...
Stop babying him! Let's go!
Friggin' Miyake...
WHAT'RE YOU DOING HERE?

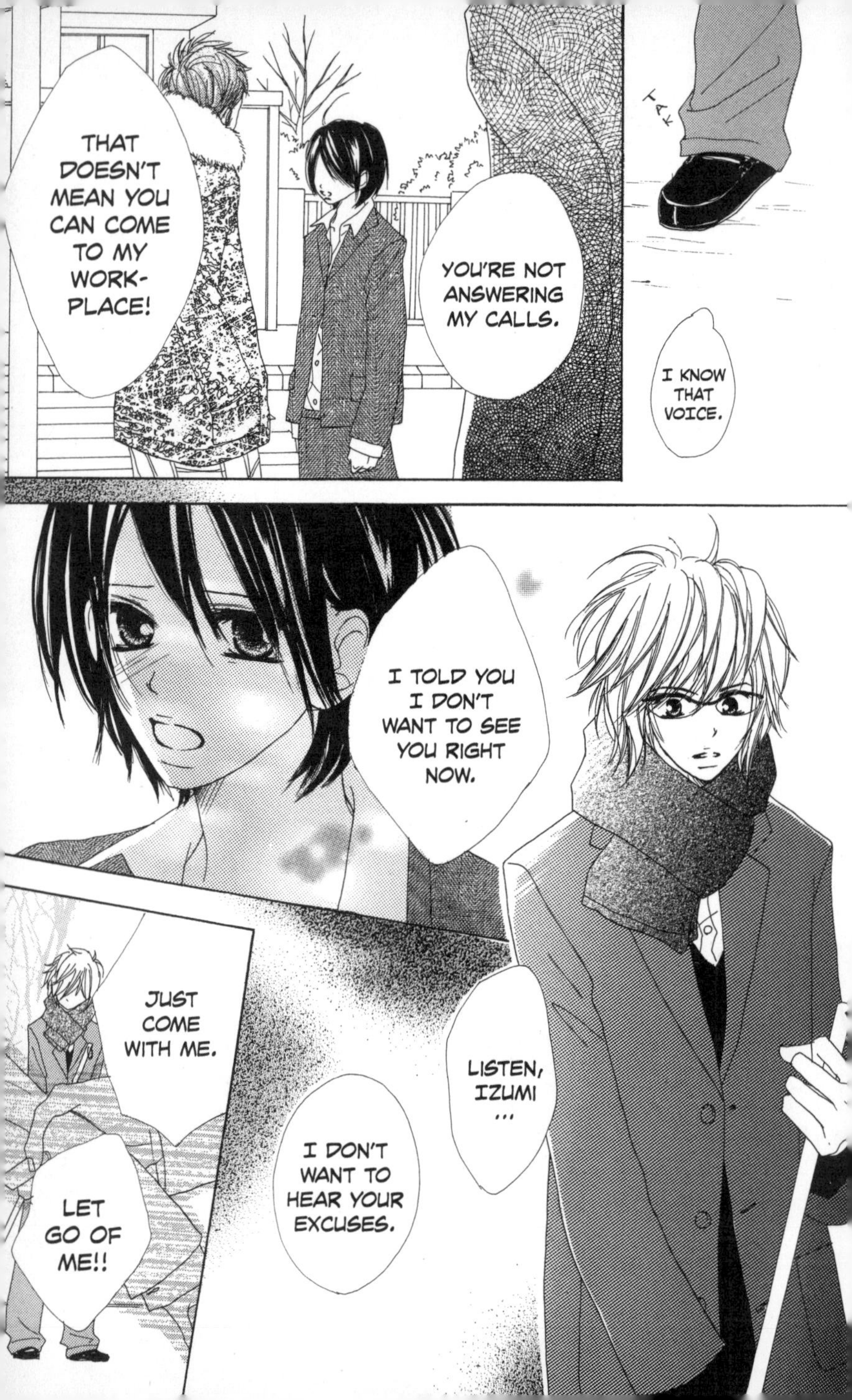
TAK
I KNOW THAT VOICE.
YOU'RE NOT ANSWERING MY CALLS.
THAT DOESN'T MEAN YOU CAN COME TO MY WORK-PLACE!
I TOLD YOU I DON'T WANT TO SEE YOU RIGHT NOW.
LISTEN, IZUMI ...
I DON'T WANT TO HEAR YOUR EXCUSES.
JUST COME WITH ME.
LET GO OF ME!!

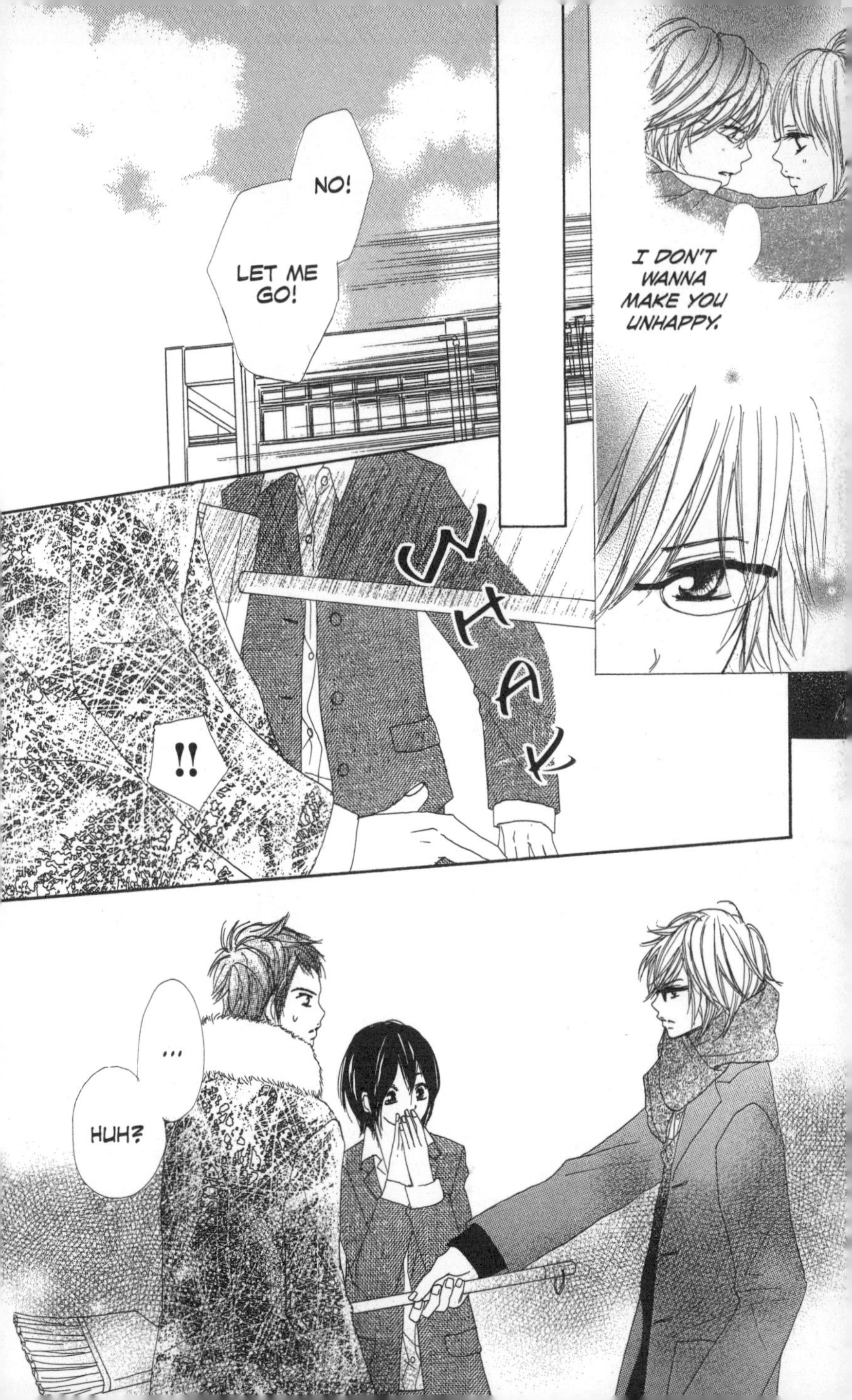
I DON'T WANNA MAKE YOU UNHAPPY.
NO!
LET ME GO!
WHAK
!!
...
HUH?

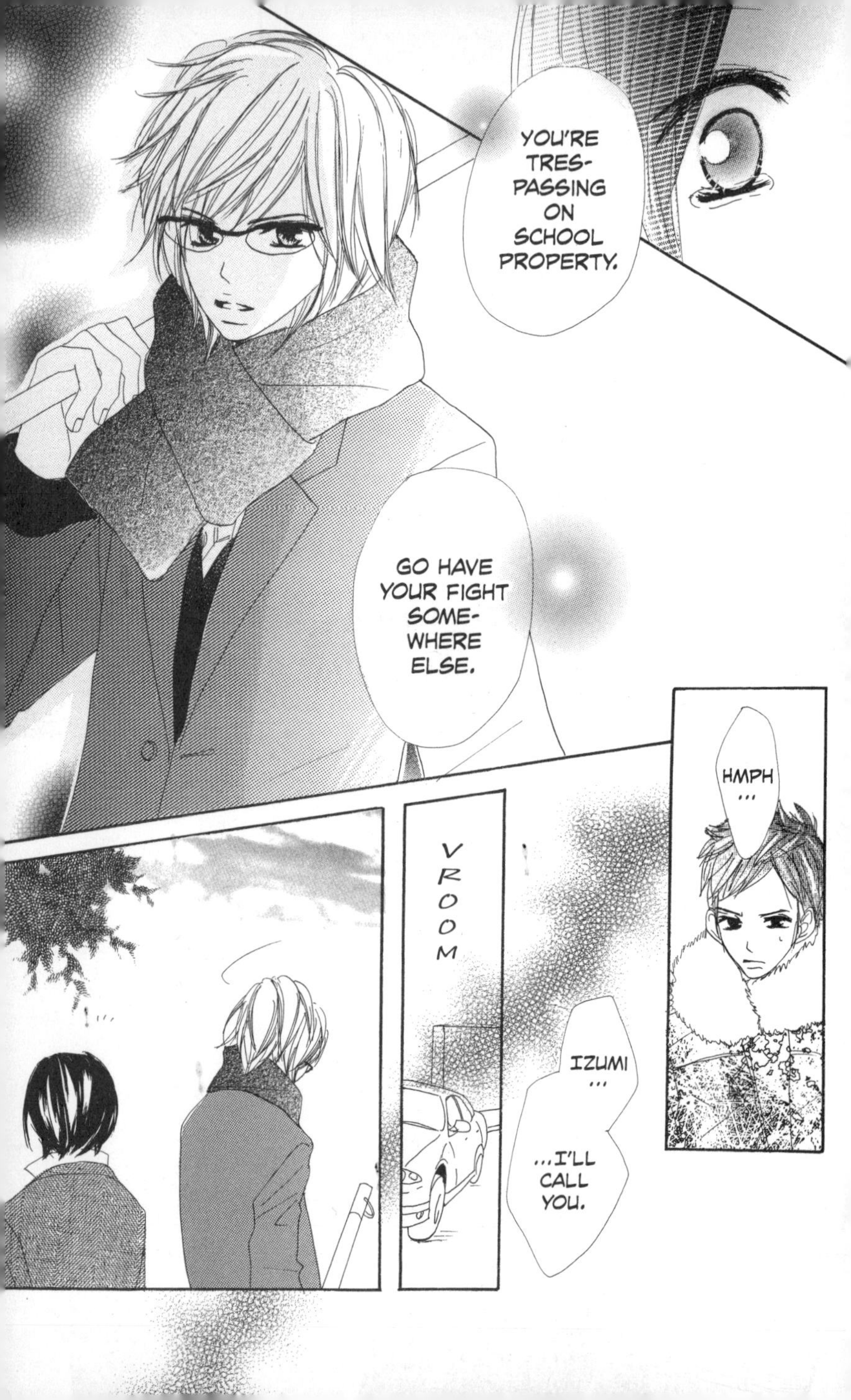
YOU'RE TRES-PASSING ON SCHOOL PROPERTY.
GO HAVE YOUR FIGHT SOME-WHERE ELSE.
HMPH ...
IZUMI ...
...I'LL CALL YOU.
VROOM

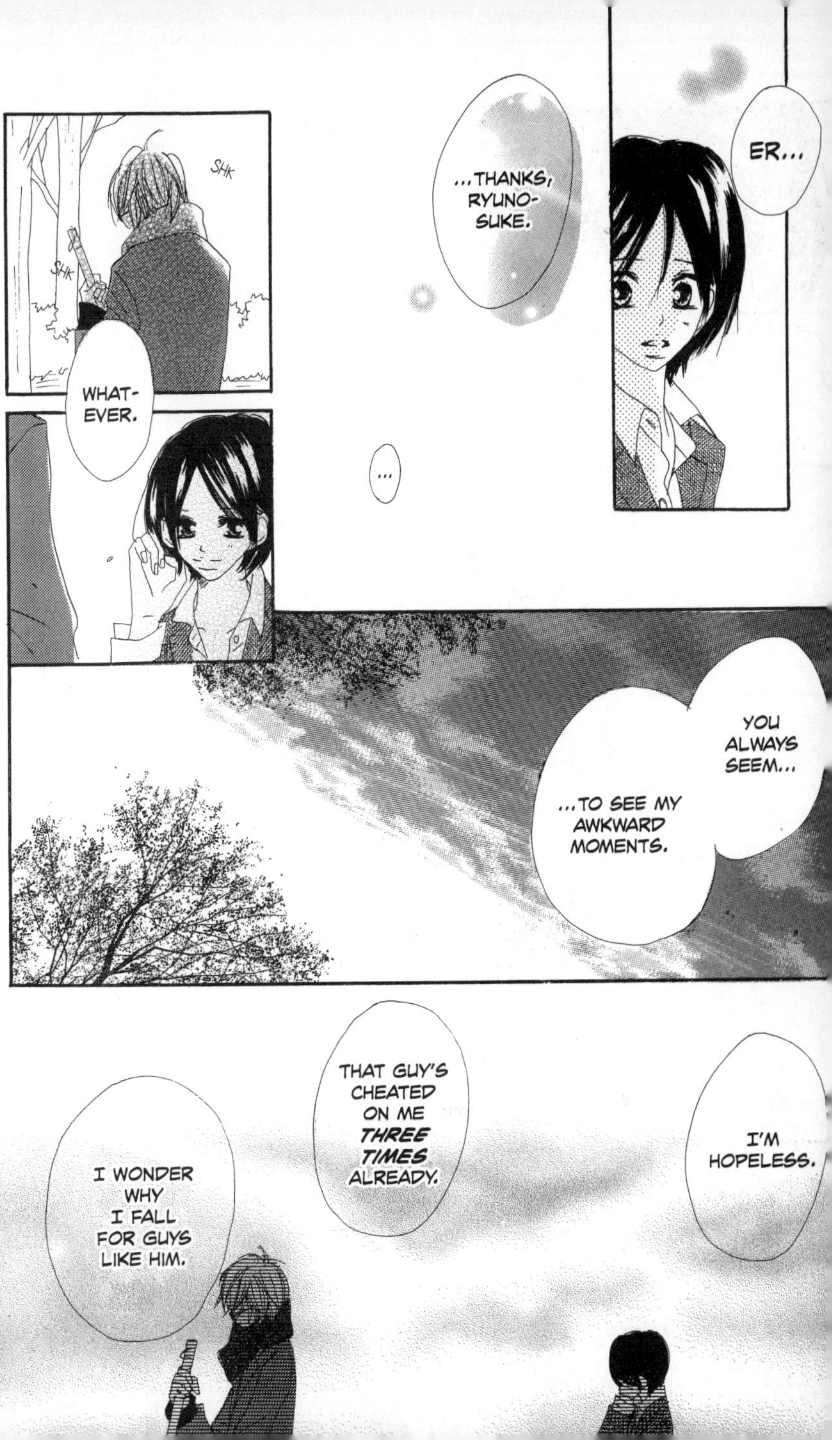
ER...
...THANKS, RYUNO-SUKE.
...
SHK
SHK
WHAT-EVER.
YOU ALWAYS SEEM...
...TO SEE MY AWKWARD MOMENTS.
I'M HOPELESS.
THAT GUY'S CHEATED ON ME *THREE TIMES* ALREADY.
I WONDER WHY I FALL FOR GUYS LIKE HIM.

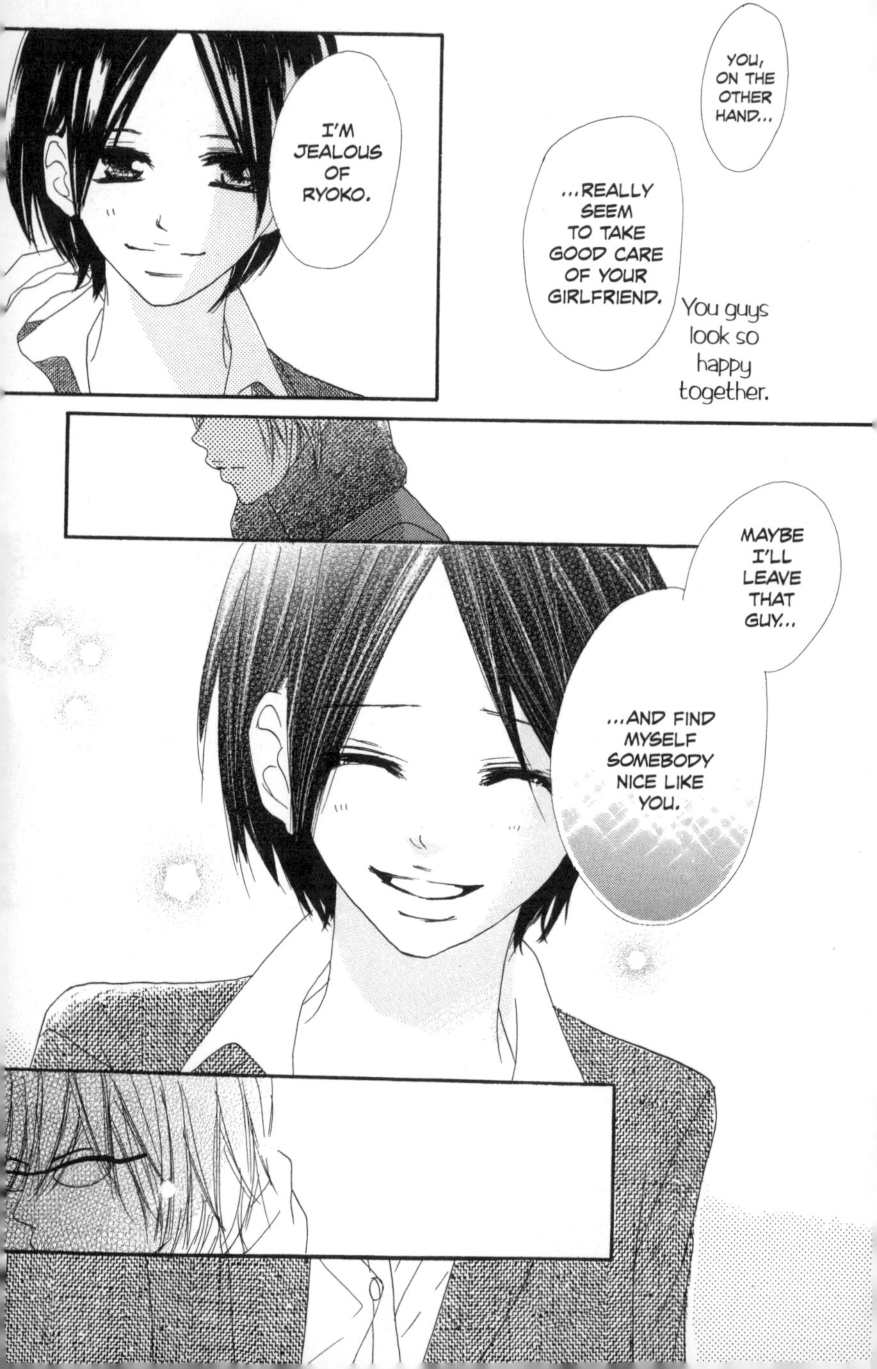
YOU, ON THE OTHER HAND...
...REALLY SEEM TO TAKE GOOD CARE OF YOUR GIRLFRIEND.
You guys look so happy together.
I'M JEALOUS OF RYOKO.
MAYBE I'LL LEAVE THAT GUY...
...AND FIND MYSELF SOMEBODY NICE LIKE YOU.

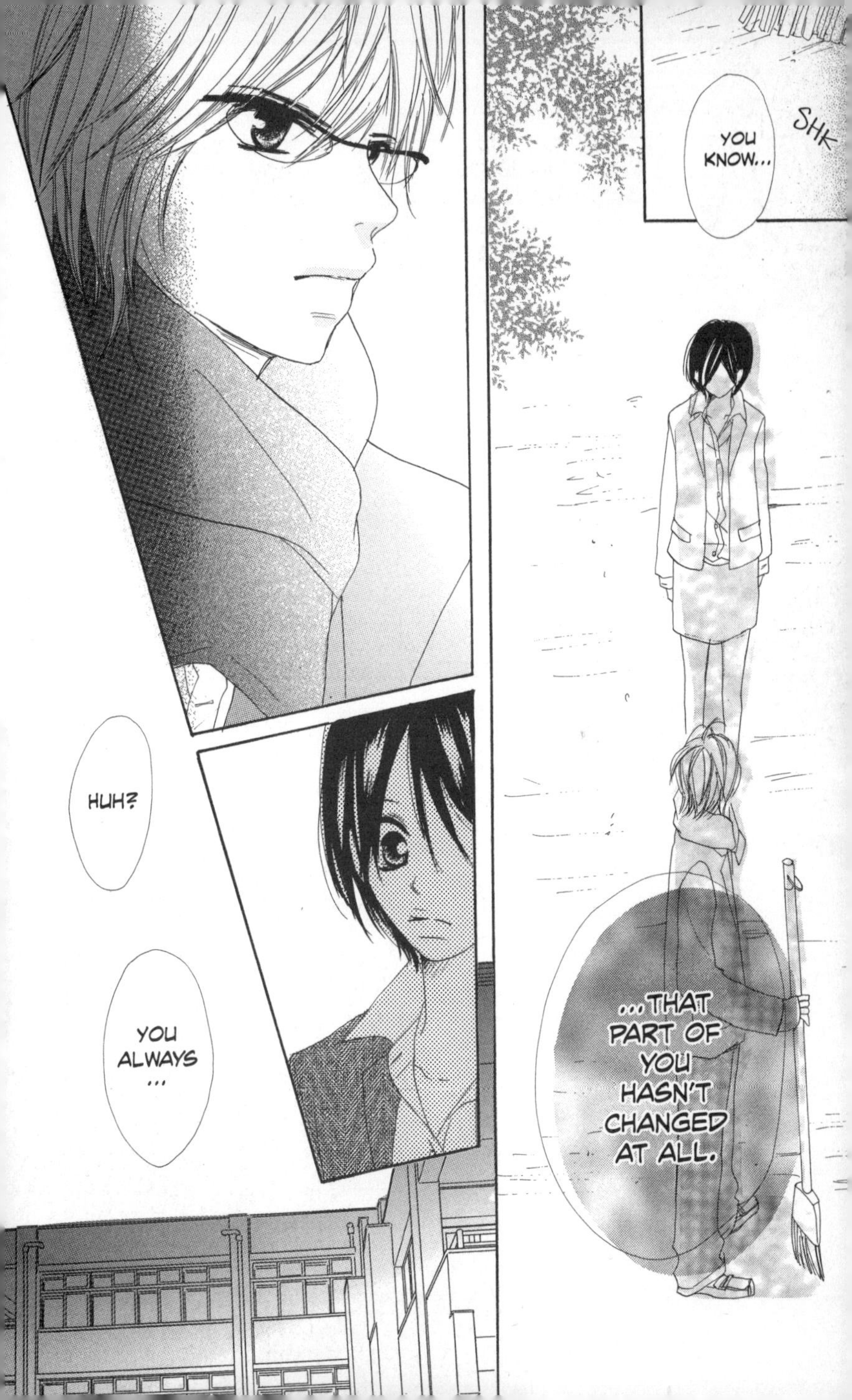
YOU KNOW...
SHK
...THAT PART OF YOU HASN'T CHANGED AT ALL.
HUH?
YOU ALWAYS ...

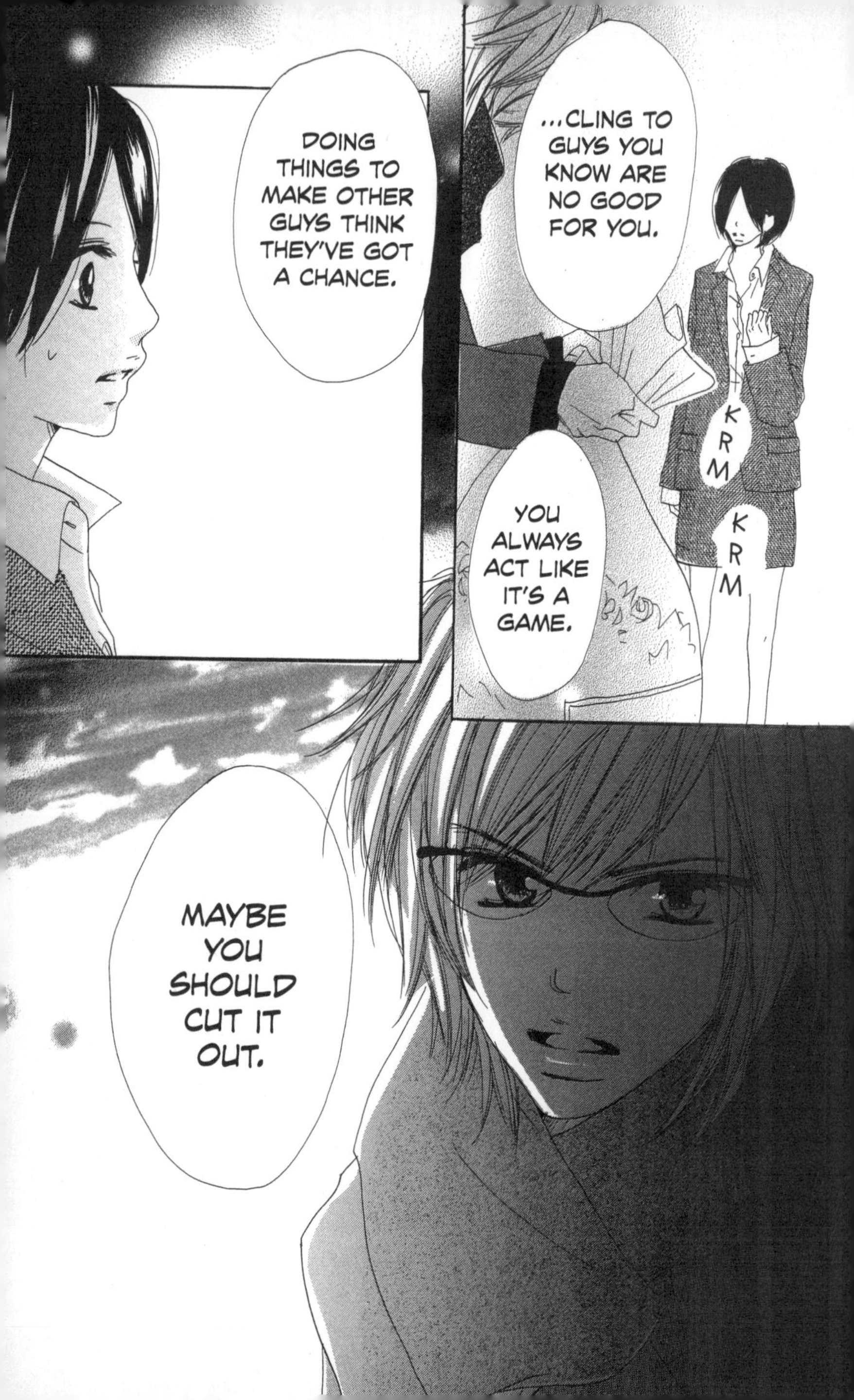
...CLING TO GUYS YOU KNOW ARE NO GOOD FOR YOU.
KRM
YOU ALWAYS ACT LIKE IT'S A GAME.
KRM
DOING THINGS TO MAKE OTHER GUYS THINK THEY'VE GOT A CHANCE.
MAYBE YOU SHOULD CUT IT OUT.

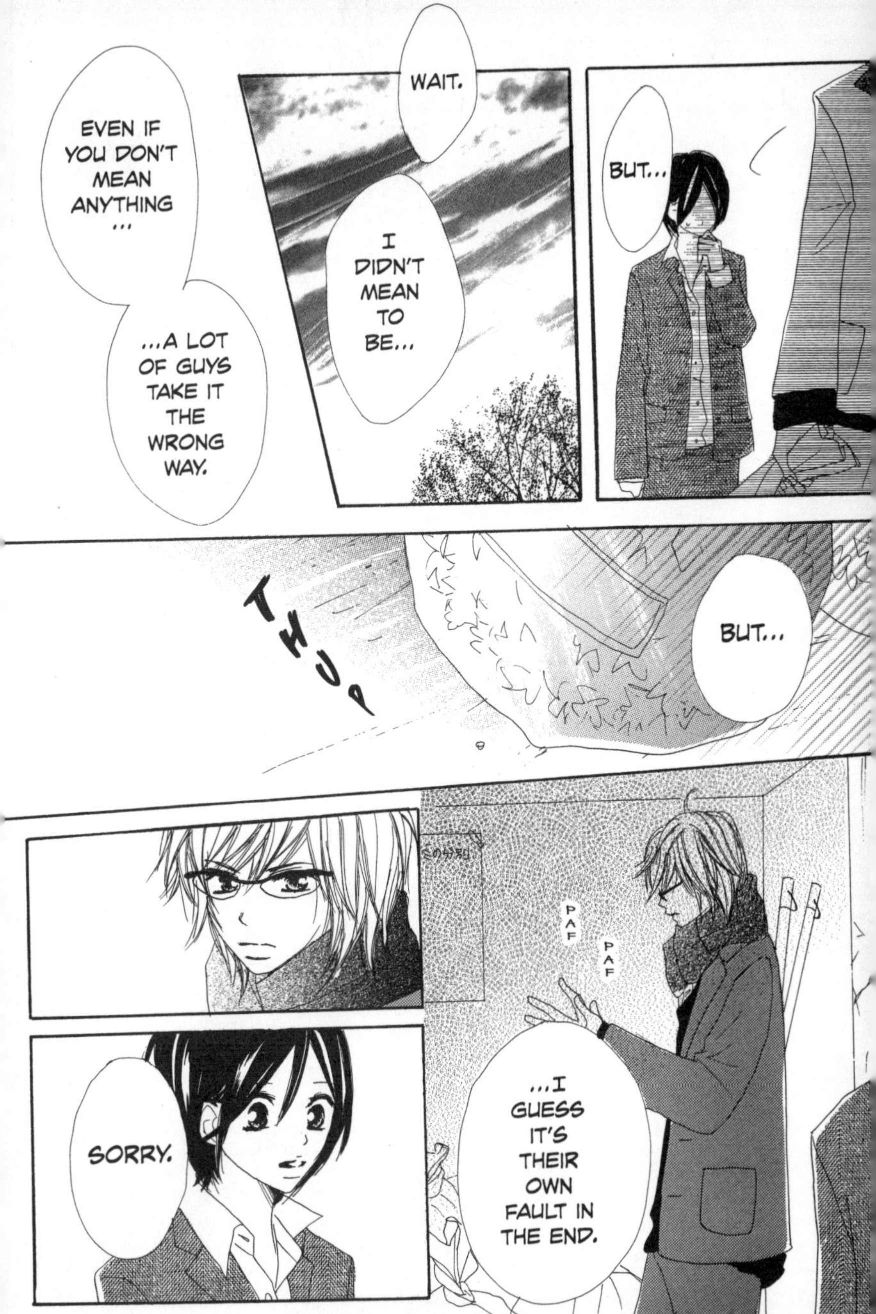
BUT...
WAIT.
I DIDN'T MEAN TO BE...
EVEN IF YOU DON'T MEAN ANYTHING...
...A LOT OF GUYS TAKE IT THE WRONG WAY.
BUT...
THUD
PAF
PAF
...I GUESS IT'S THEIR OWN FAULT IN THE END.
SORRY.

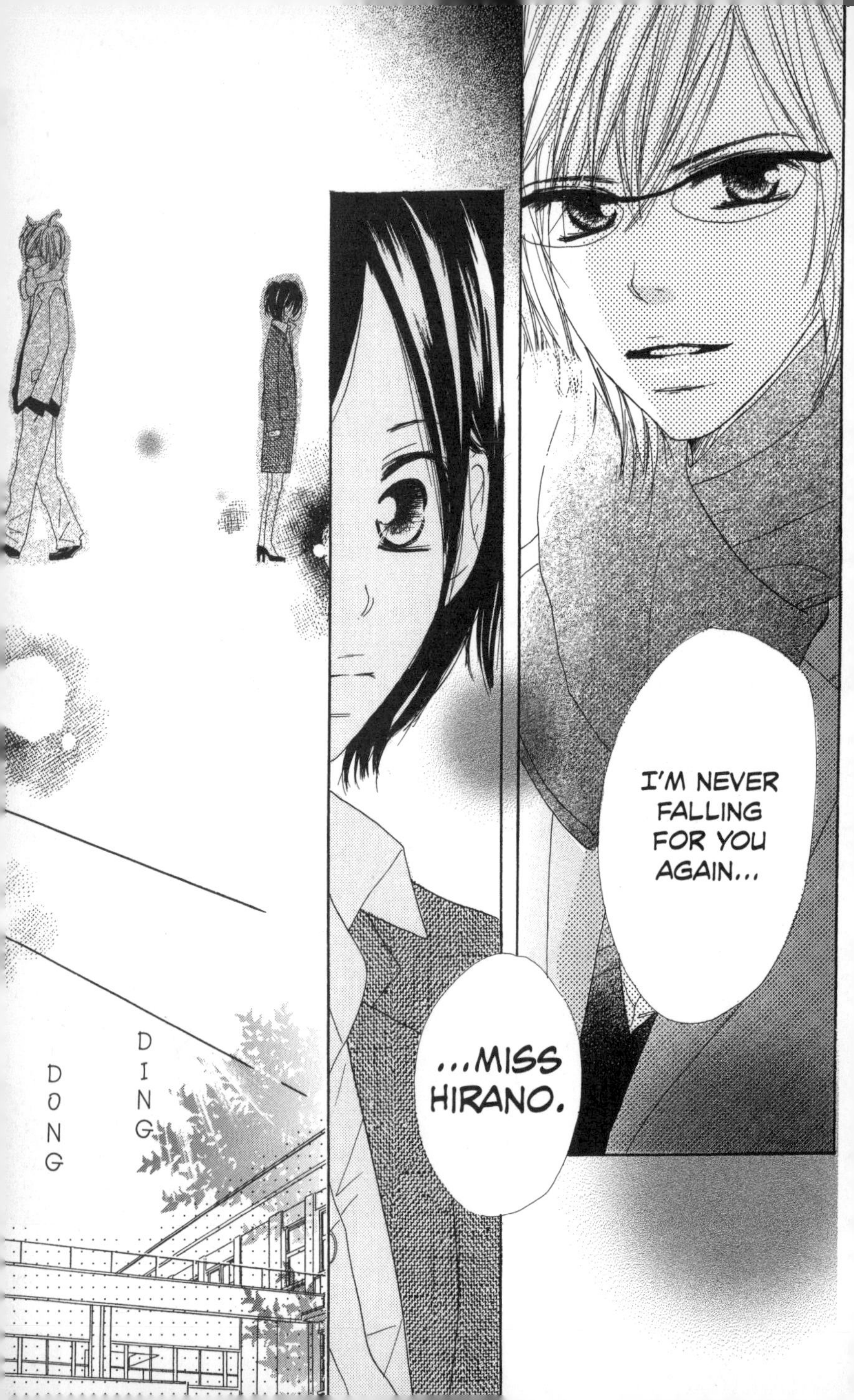
I'M NEVER FALLING FOR YOU AGAIN...
...MISS HIRANO.
DING
DONG

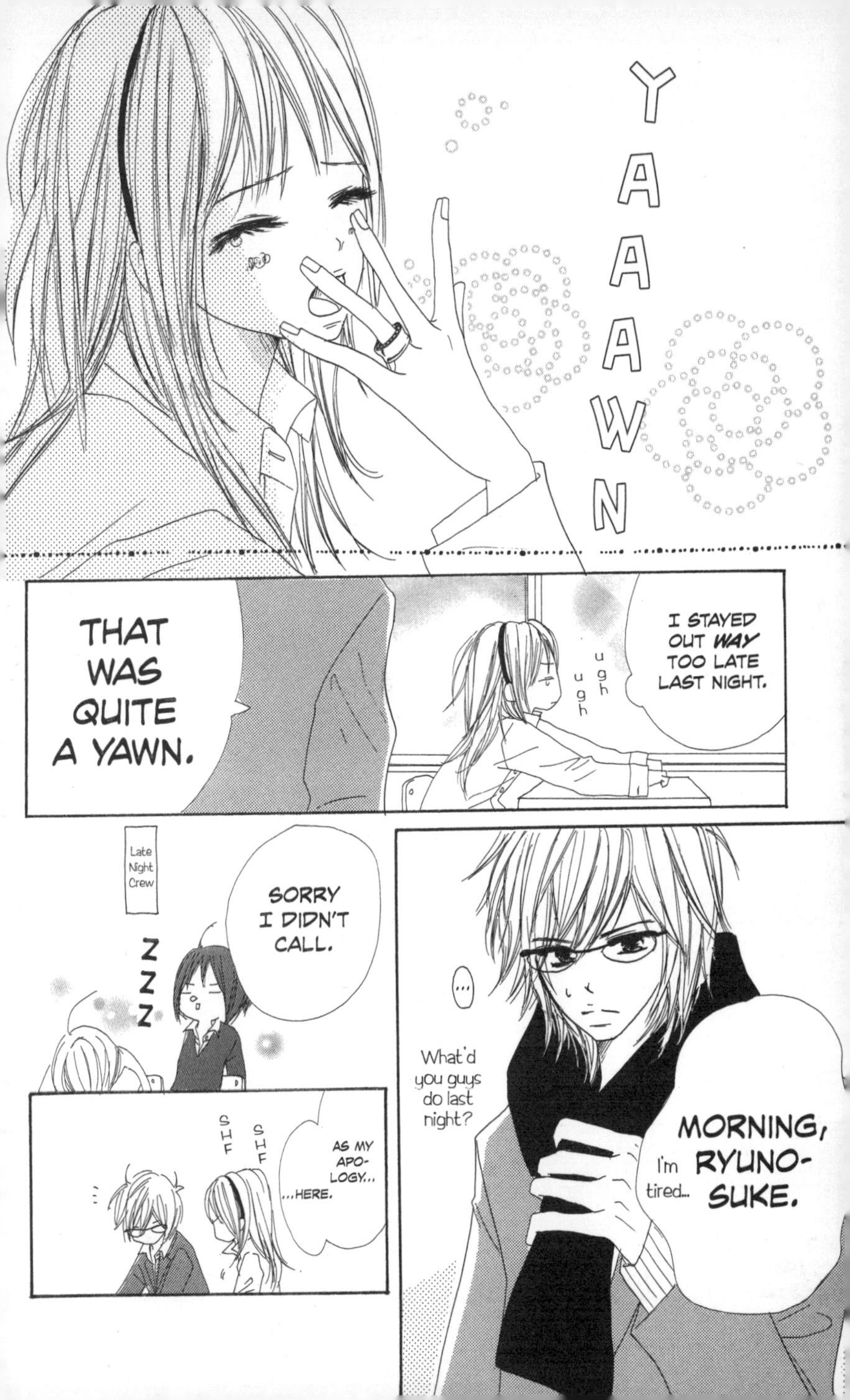
YAAAWN
I STAYED OUT WAY TOO LATE LAST NIGHT.
ugh ugh
THAT WAS QUITE A YAWN.
...
MORNING, RYUNO-SUKE.
I'm tired...
What'd you guys do last night?
Late Night Crew
SORRY I DIDN'T CALL.
ZZZ
AS MY APO-LOGY...
...HERE.
SHF SHF

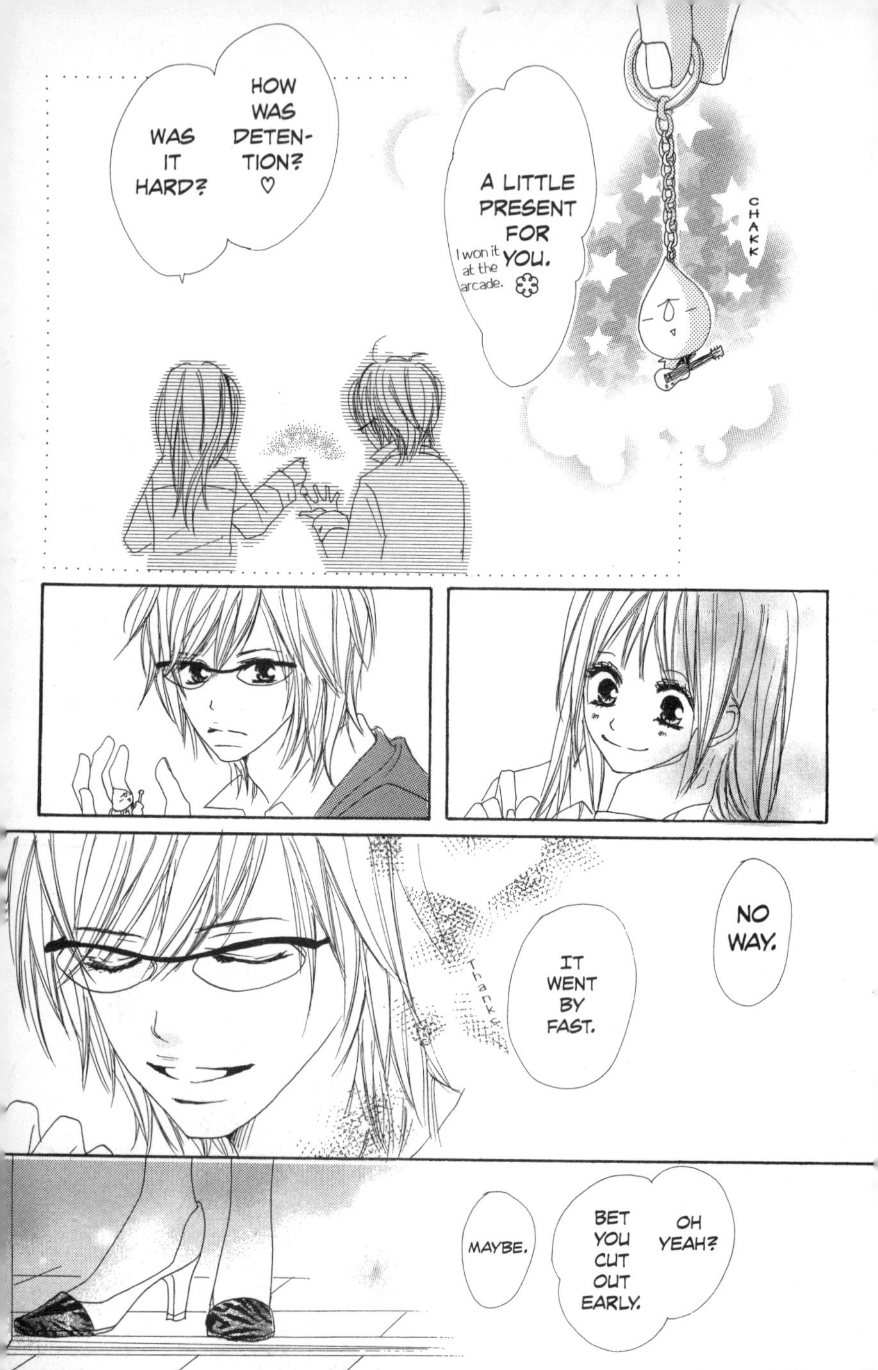
CHAKK
A LITTLE PRESENT FOR YOU.
I won it at the arcade.
HOW WAS DETENTION? ♡
WAS IT HARD?
NO WAY.
IT WENT BY FAST.
Thanks.
OH YEAH?
BET YOU CUT OUT EARLY.
MAYBE.

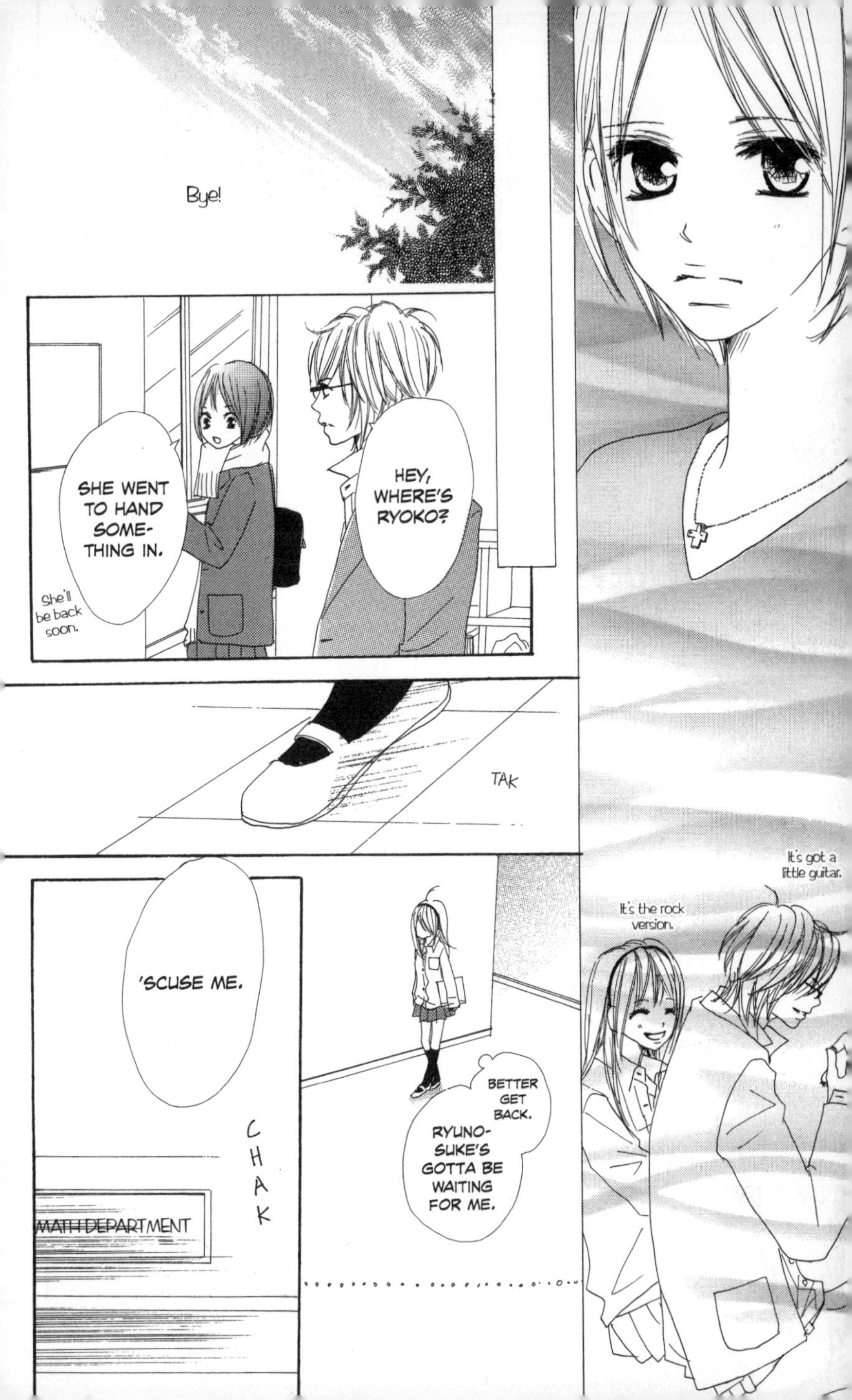

It's got a little guitar.
It's the rock version.
Bye!
HEY, WHERE'S RYOKO?
SHE WENT TO HAND SOME-THING IN.
She'll be back soon.
TAK
BETTER GET BACK.
RYUNO-SUKE'S GOTTA BE WAITING FOR ME.
'SCUSE ME.
CHAK
MATH DEPARTMENT

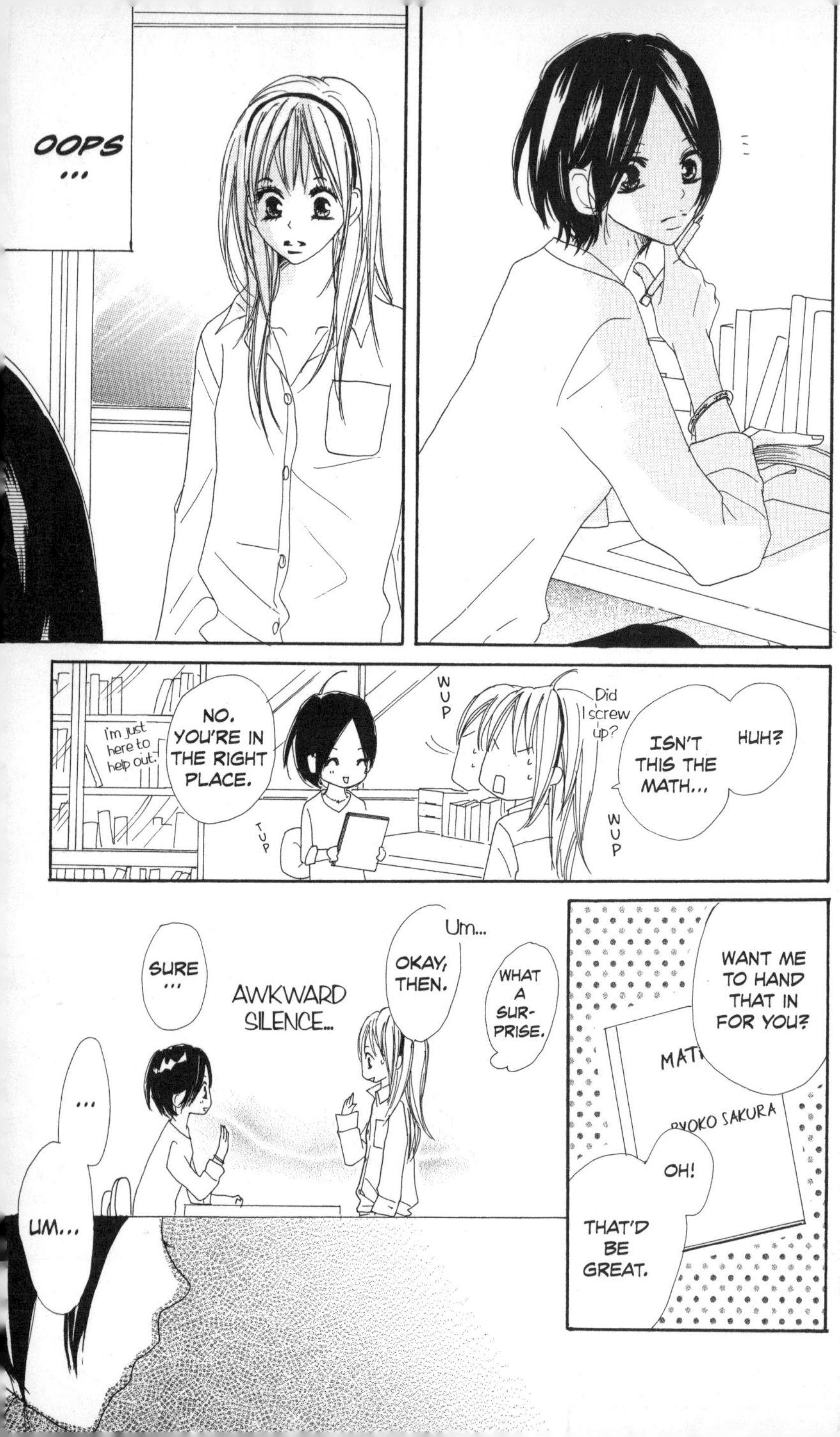
OOPS...
HUH?
ISN'T THIS THE MATH...
Did I screw up?
WUP
WUP
NO. YOU'RE IN THE RIGHT PLACE.
I'm just here to help out.
TUP
WANT ME TO HAND THAT IN FOR YOU?
MAT
RYOKO SAKURA
OH!
THAT'D BE GREAT.
Um...
OKAY, THEN.
WHAT A SURPRISE.
SURE...
AWKWARD SILENCE...
...
UM...

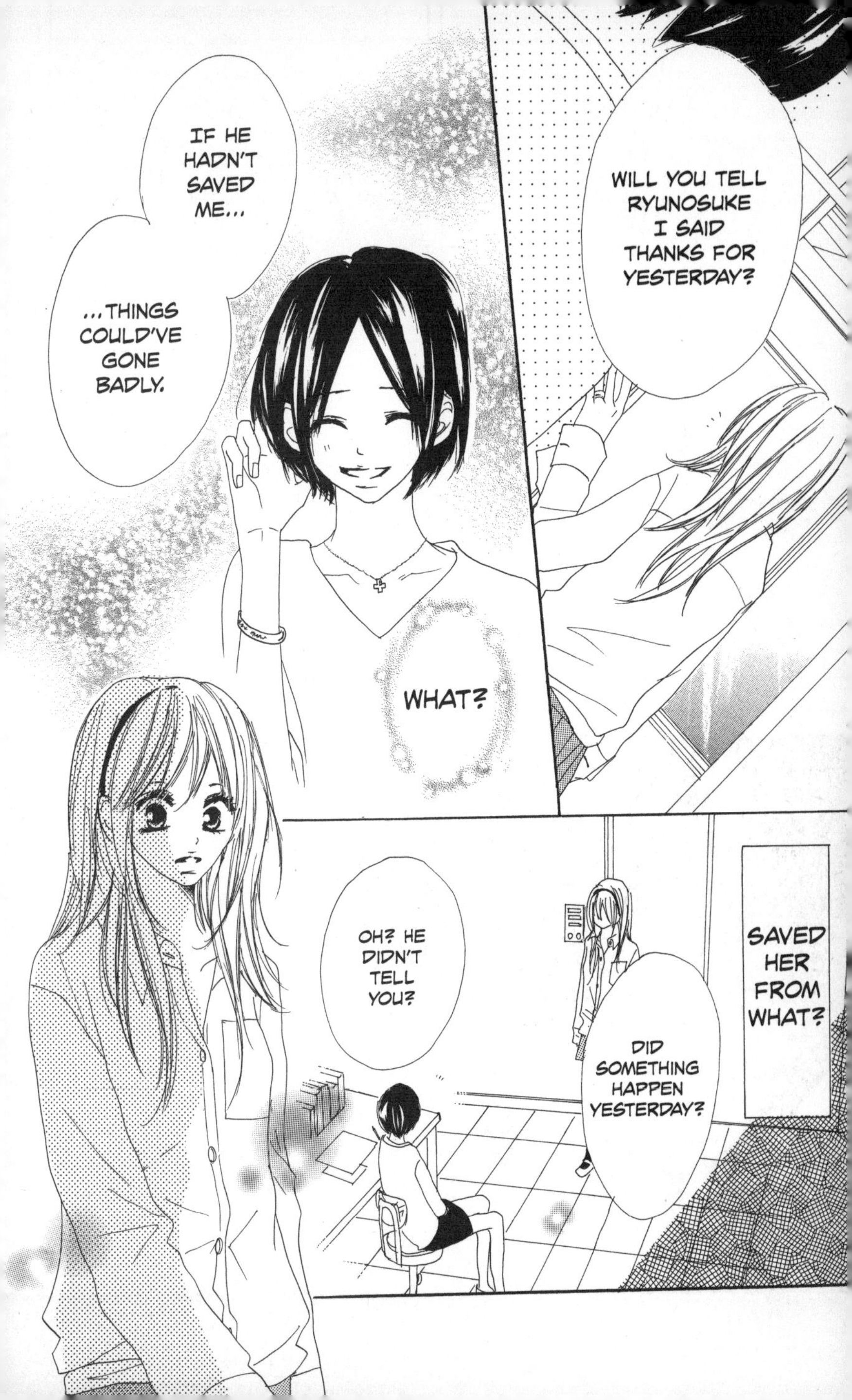
WILL YOU TELL RYUNOSUKE I SAID THANKS FOR YESTERDAY?
IF HE HADN'T SAVED ME...
...THINGS COULD'VE GONE BADLY.
WHAT?
SAVED HER FROM WHAT?
DID SOMETHING HAPPEN YESTERDAY?
OH? HE DIDN'T TELL YOU?

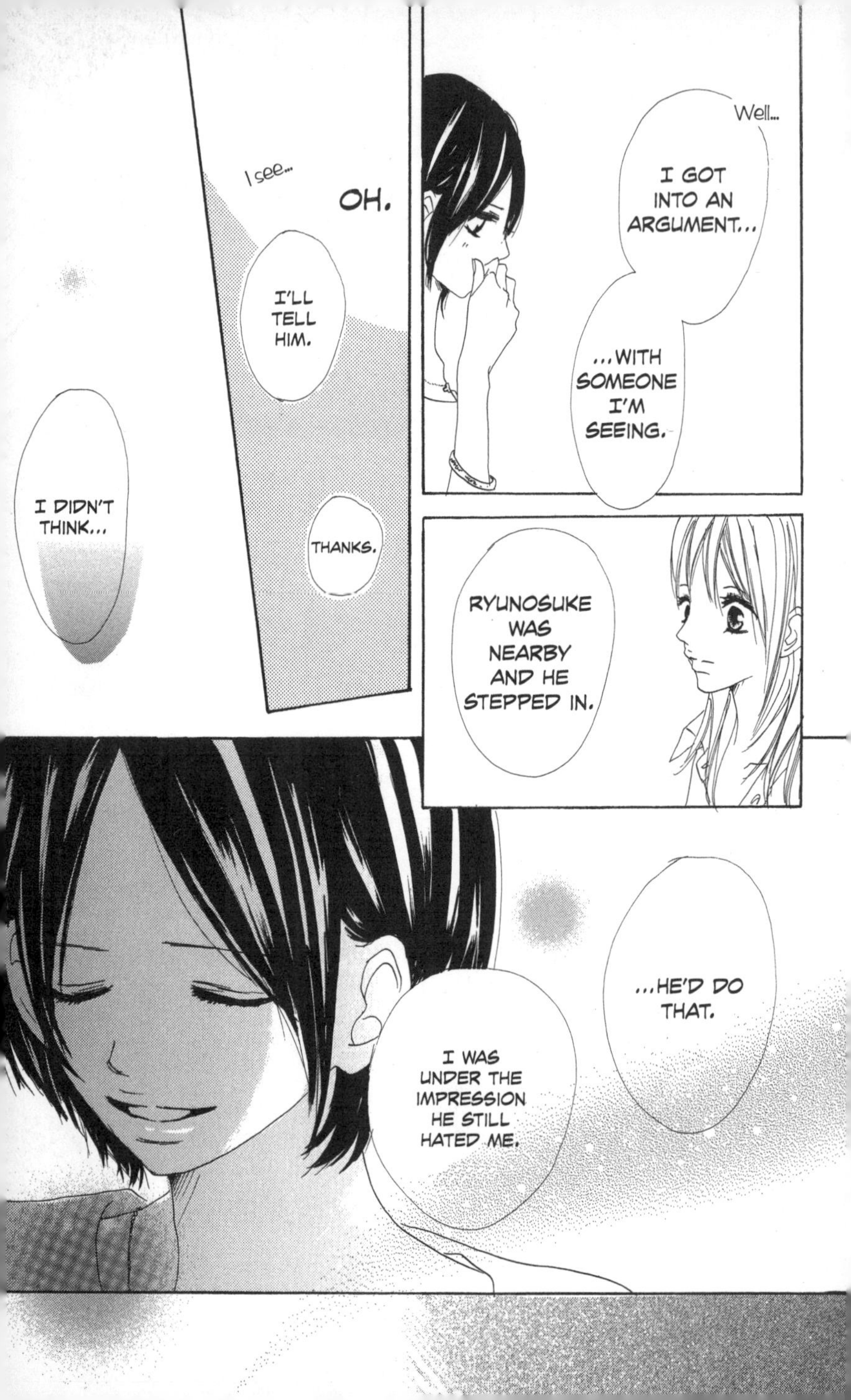
Well...
I GOT INTO AN ARGUMENT...
...WITH SOMEONE I'M SEEING.
RYUNOSUKE WAS NEARBY AND HE STEPPED IN.
OH.
I see...
I'LL TELL HIM.
THANKS.
I DIDN'T THINK...
...HE'D DO THAT.
I WAS UNDER THE IMPRESSION HE STILL HATED ME.

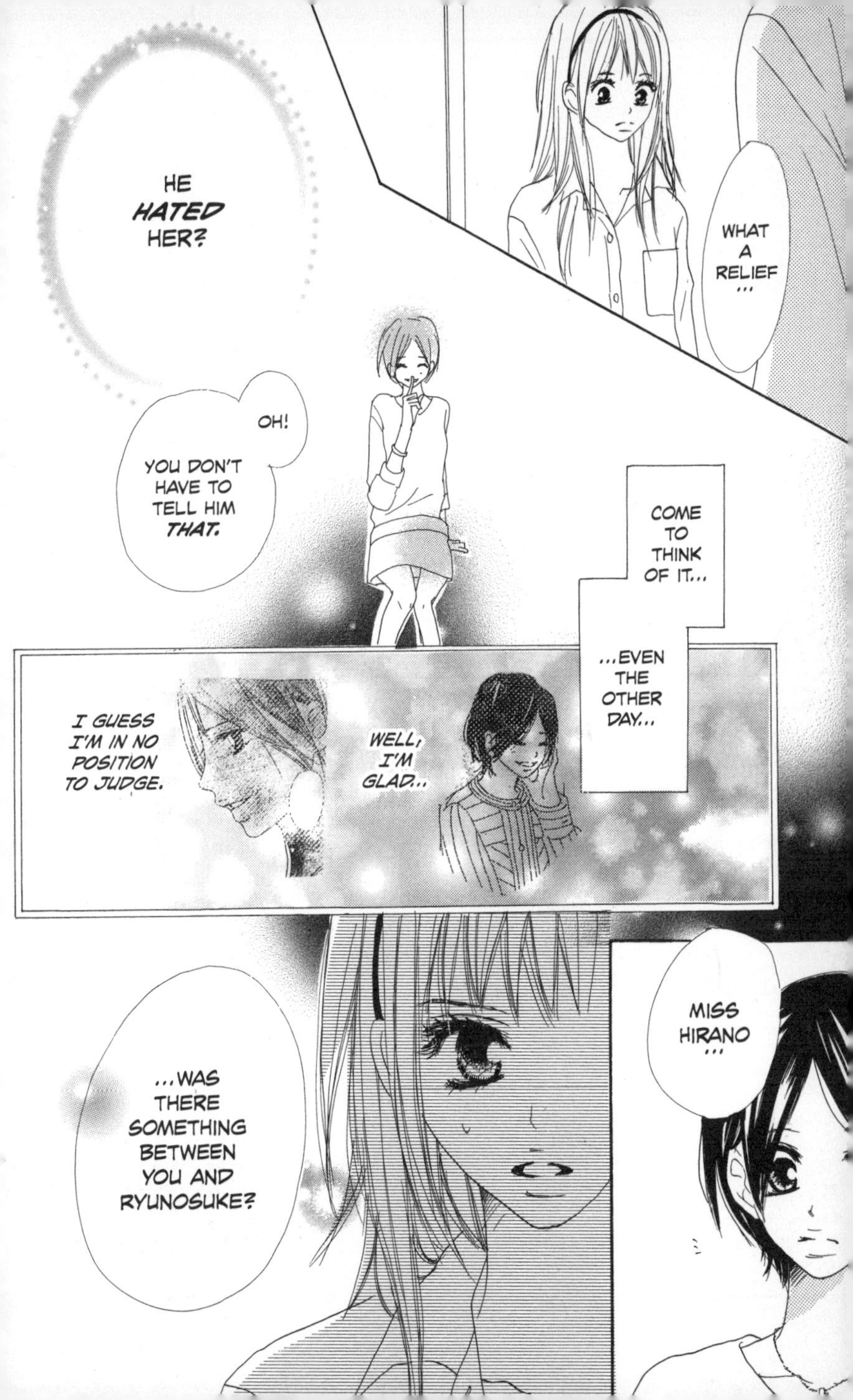

WHAT A RELIEF...
HE *HATED* HER?
OH!
YOU DON'T HAVE TO TELL HIM *THAT.*
COME TO THINK OF IT...
...EVEN THE OTHER DAY...
WELL, I'M GLAD...
I GUESS I'M IN NO POSITION TO JUDGE.
MISS HIRANO...
...WAS THERE SOMETHING BETWEEN YOU AND RYUNOSUKE?

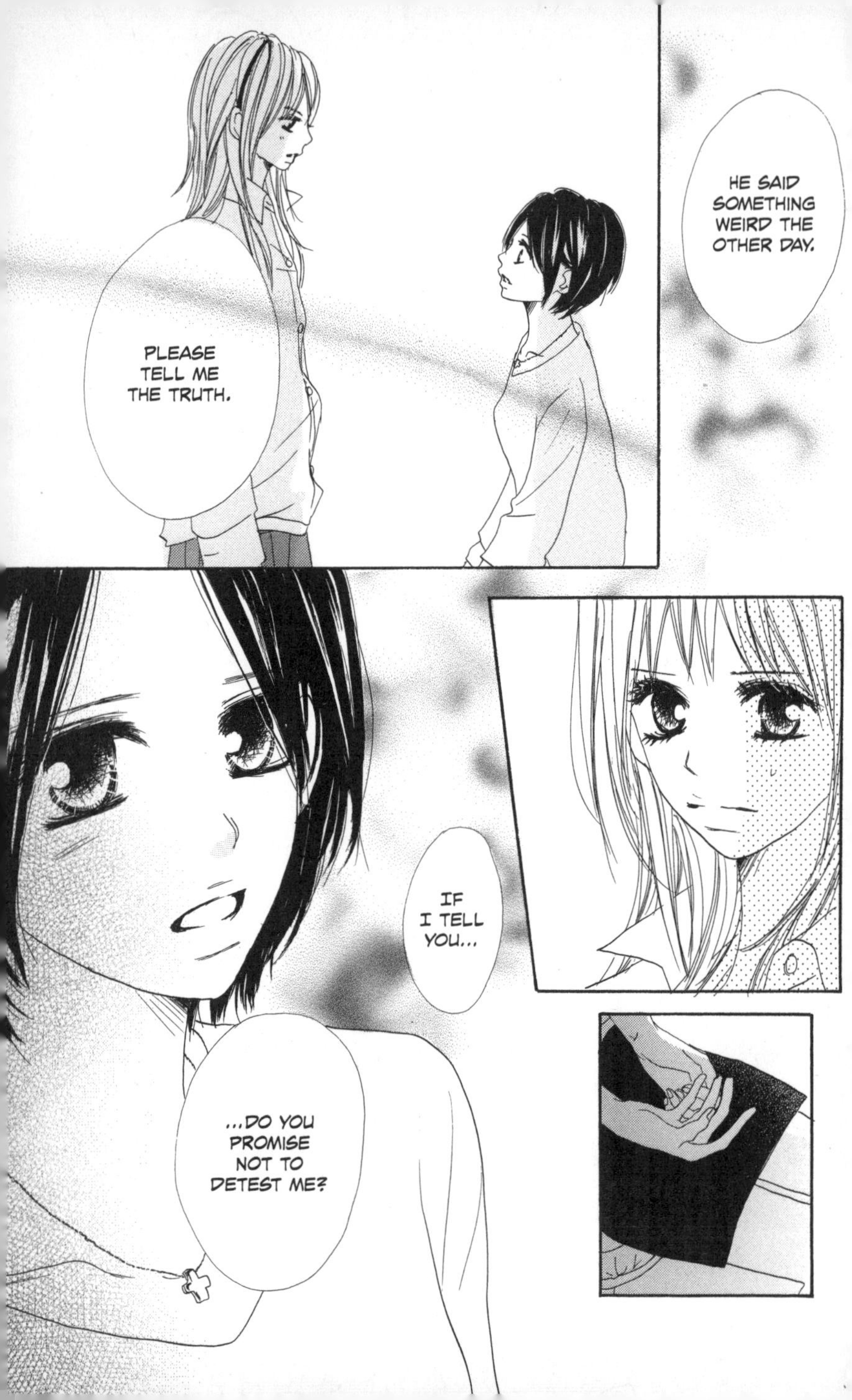
HE SAID SOMETHING WEIRD THE OTHER DAY.
PLEASE TELL ME THE TRUTH.
IF I TELL YOU...
...DO YOU PROMISE NOT TO DETEST ME?

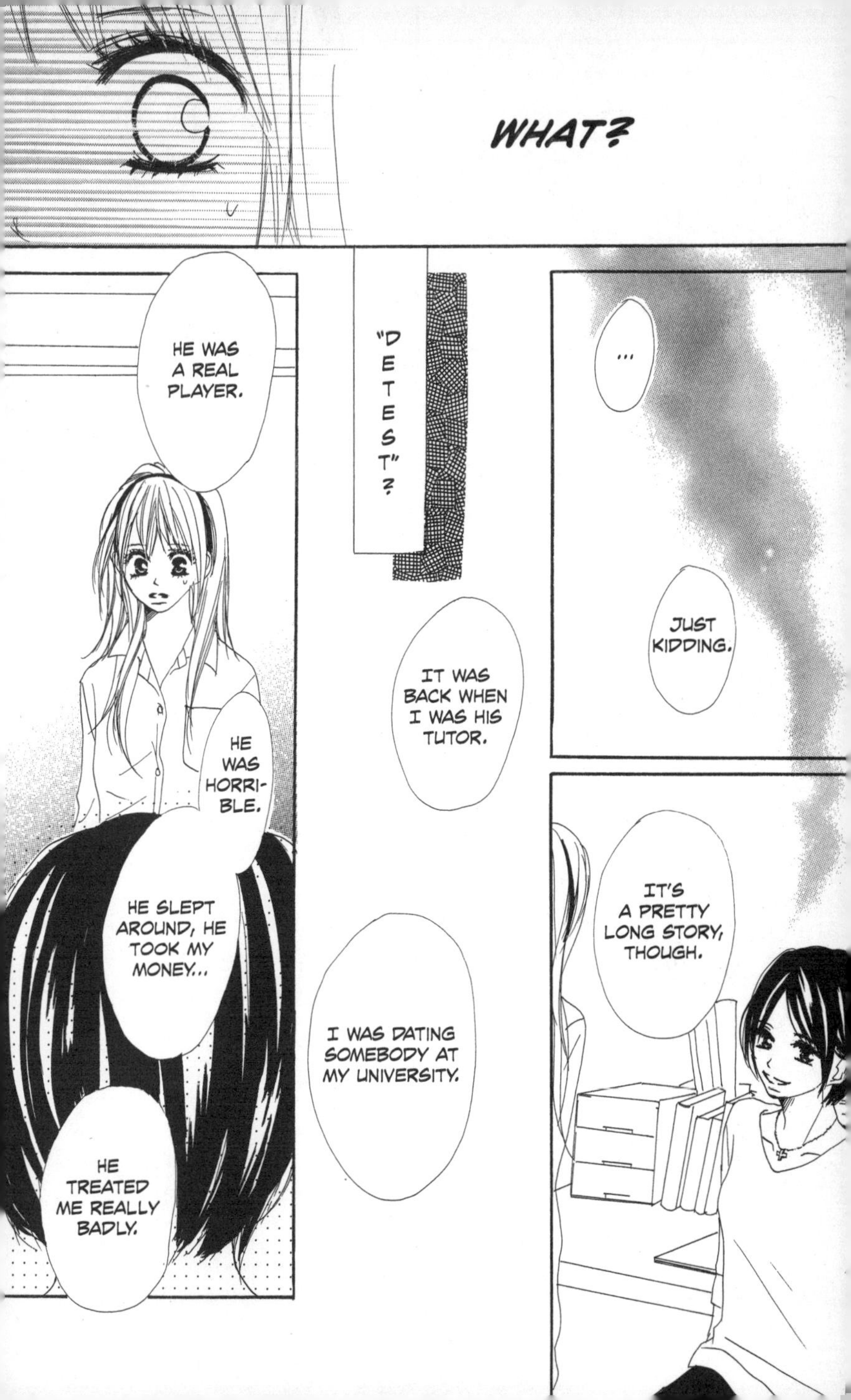
WHAT?
...
JUST KIDDING.
IT'S A PRETTY LONG STORY, THOUGH.
"DETEST"?
IT WAS BACK WHEN I WAS HIS TUTOR.
I WAS DATING SOMEBODY AT MY UNIVERSITY.
HE WAS A REAL PLAYER.
HE WAS HORRIBLE.
HE SLEPT AROUND, HE TOOK MY MONEY...
HE TREATED ME REALLY BADLY.

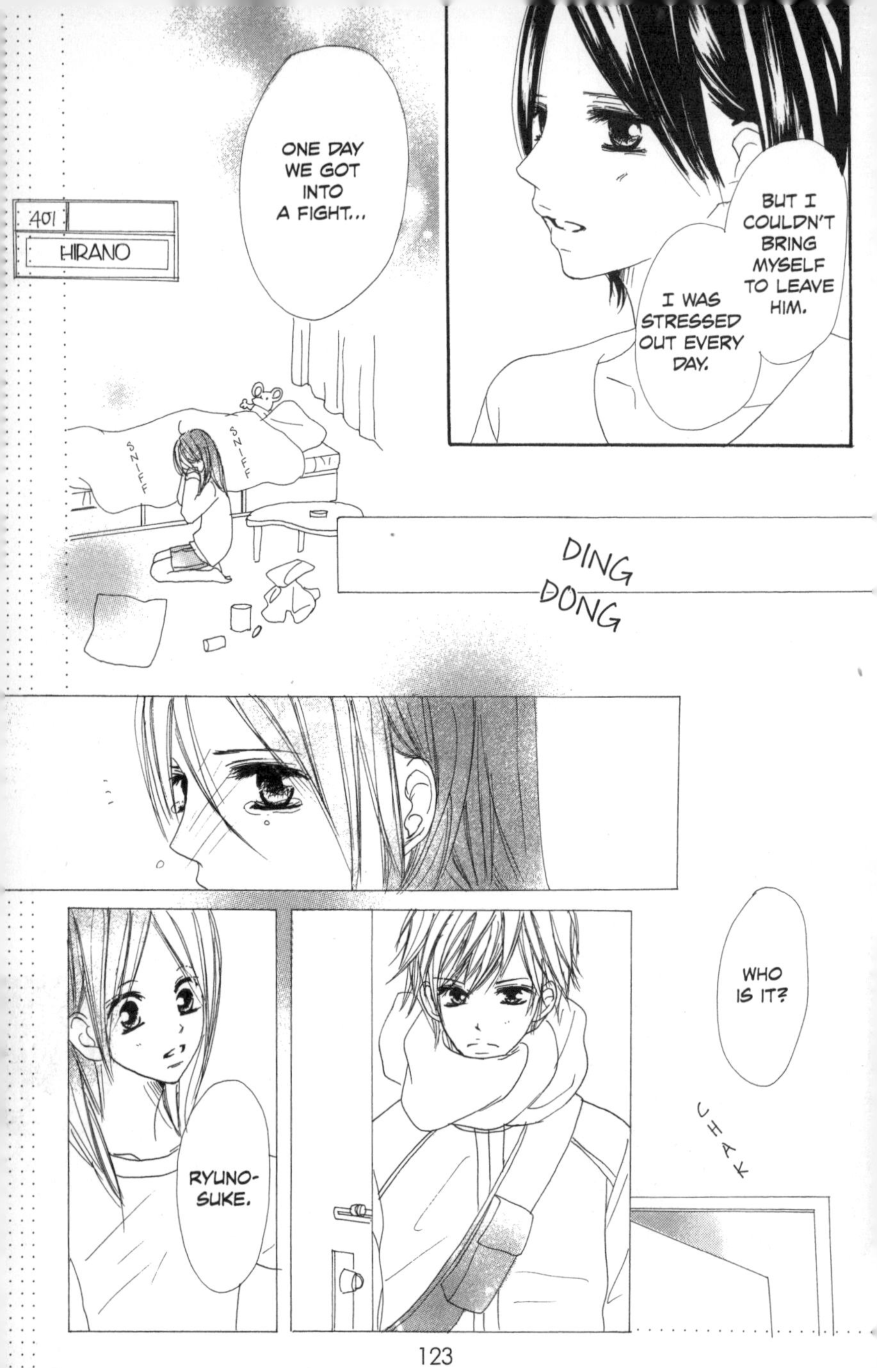
BUT I COULDN'T BRING MYSELF TO LEAVE HIM.
I WAS STRESSED OUT EVERY DAY.
ONE DAY WE GOT INTO A FIGHT...
401
HIRANO
SNIFF
SNIFF
DING DONG
WHO IS IT?
CHAK
RYUNO-SUKE.

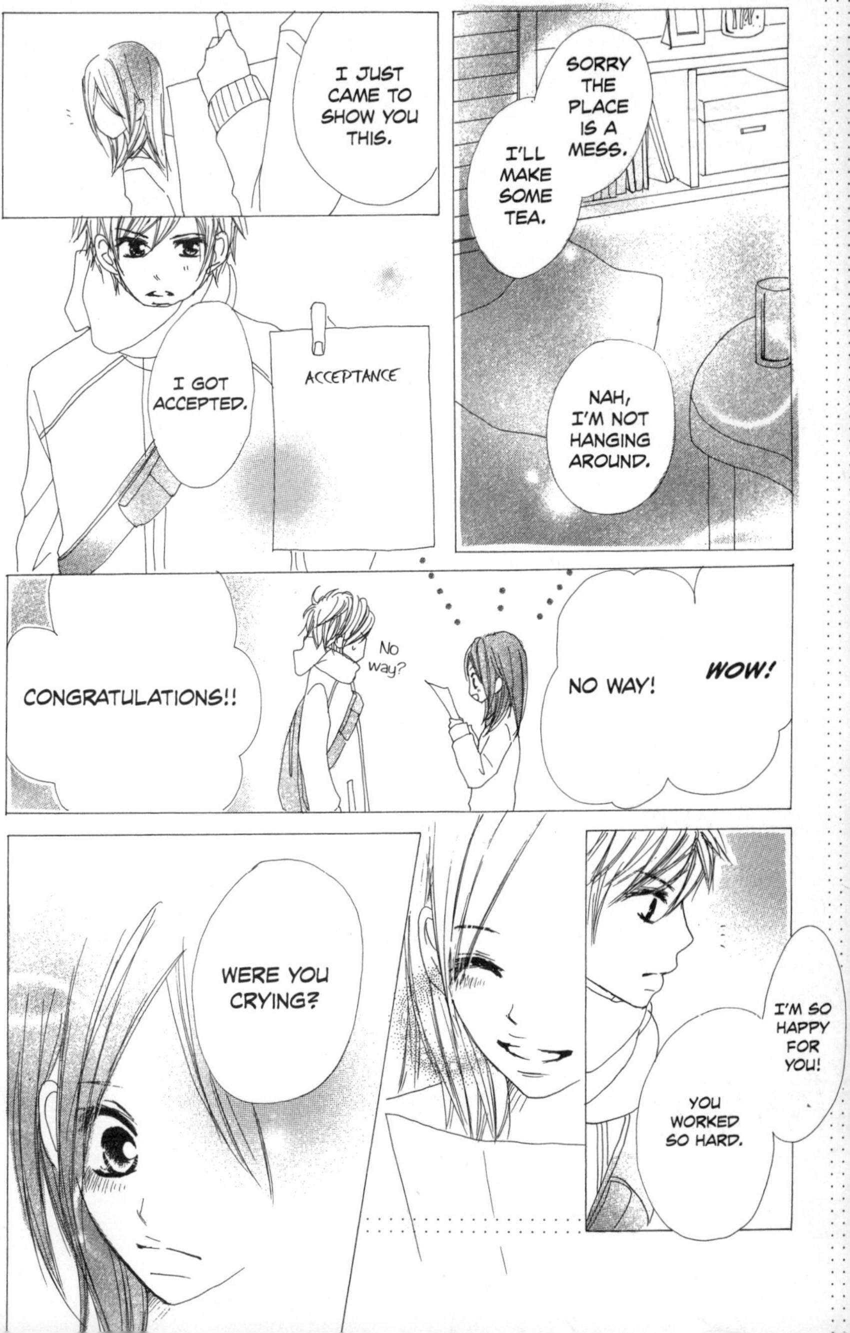
SORRY THE PLACE IS A MESS.
I'LL MAKE SOME TEA.
NAH, I'M NOT HANGING AROUND.
I JUST CAME TO SHOW YOU THIS.
I GOT ACCEPTED.
ACCEPTANCE
WOW!
NO WAY!
No way?
CONGRATULATIONS!!
I'M SO HAPPY FOR YOU!
YOU WORKED SO HARD.
WERE YOU CRYING?

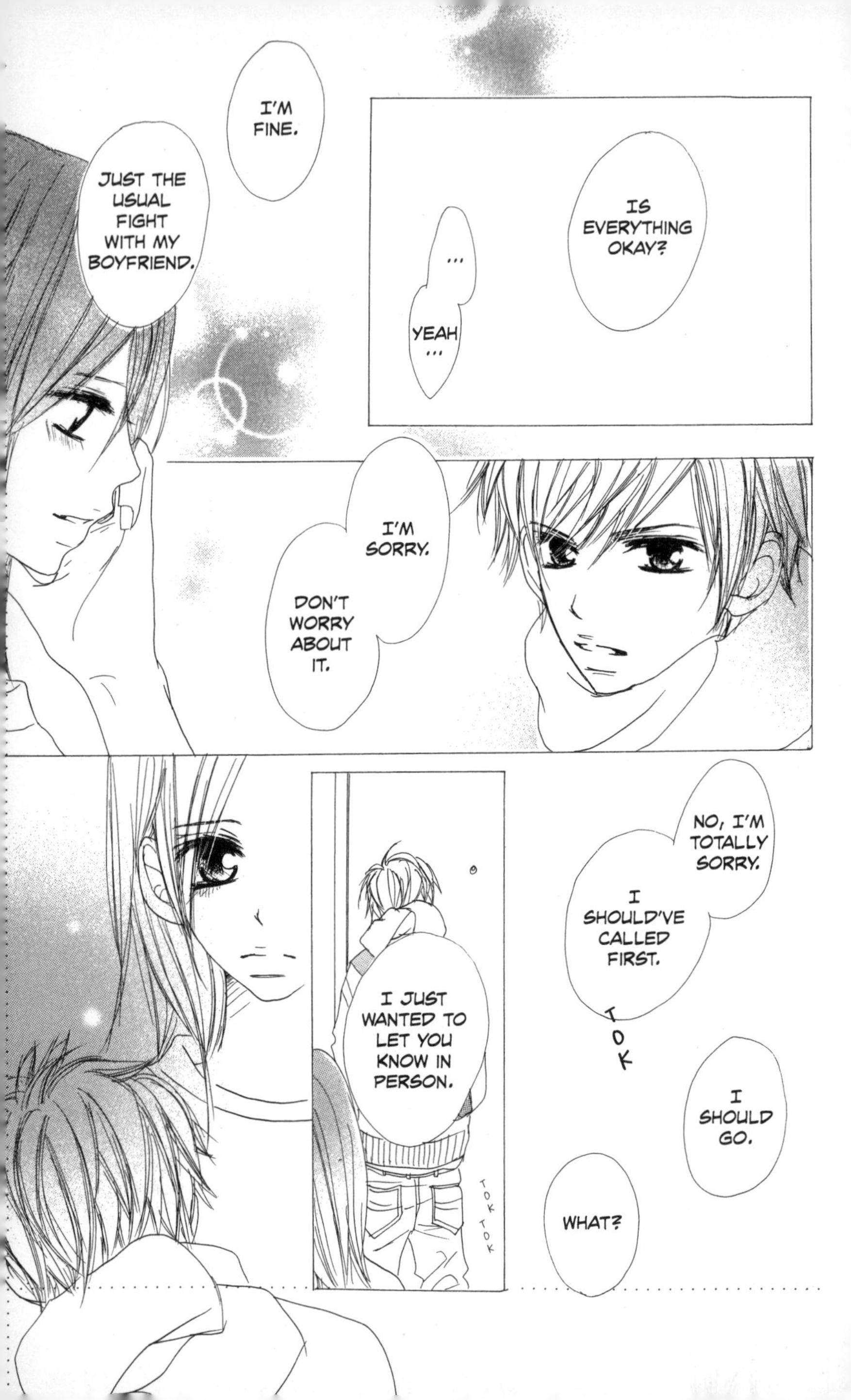
IS EVERYTHING OKAY?
...
YEAH...
I'M FINE.
JUST THE USUAL FIGHT WITH MY BOYFRIEND.
I'M SORRY.
DON'T WORRY ABOUT IT.
NO, I'M TOTALLY SORRY.
I SHOULD'VE CALLED FIRST.
TOK
I JUST WANTED TO LET YOU KNOW IN PERSON.
TOK TOK
I SHOULD GO.
WHAT?

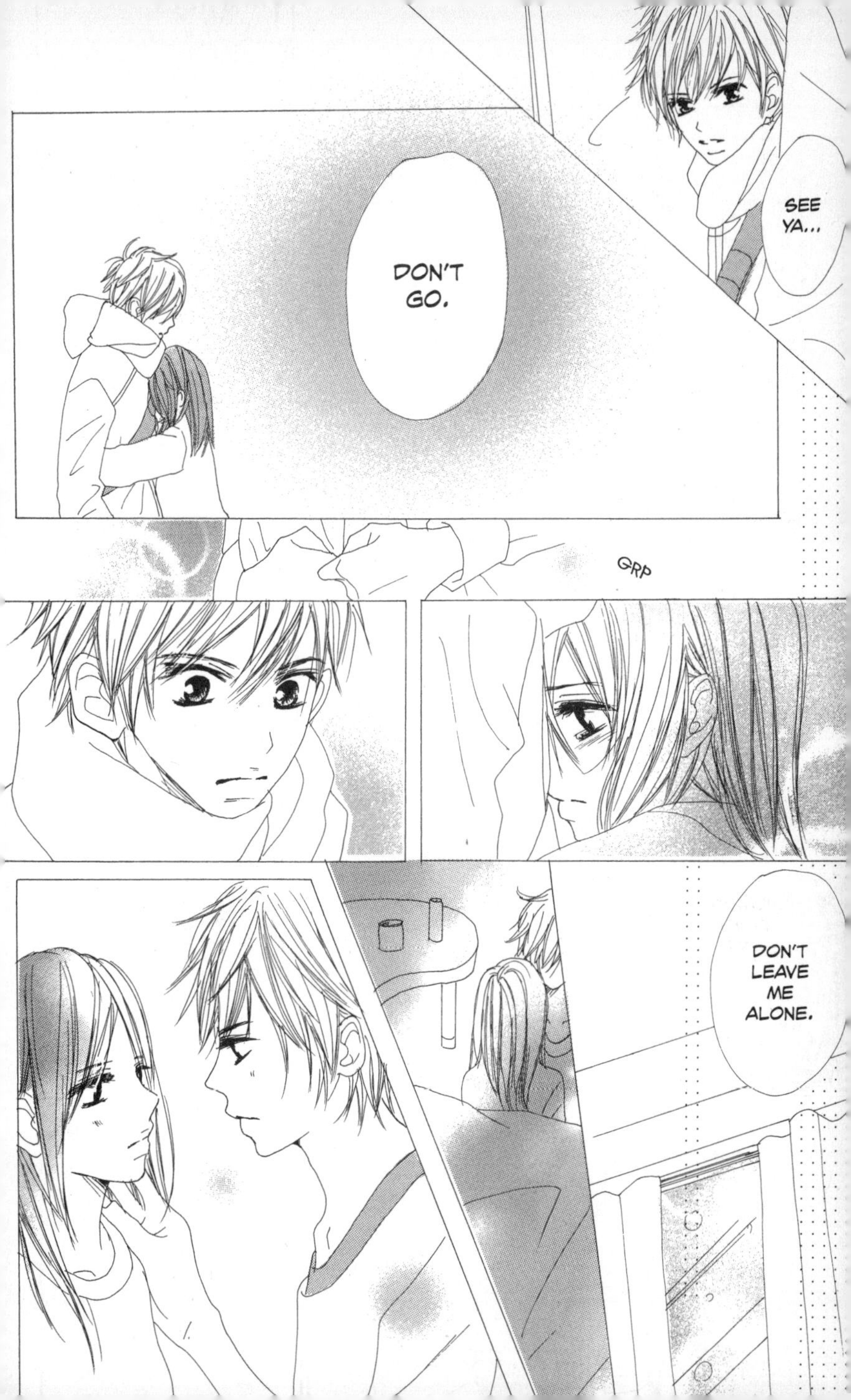
SEE YA...
DON'T GO.
GRP
DON'T LEAVE ME ALONE.

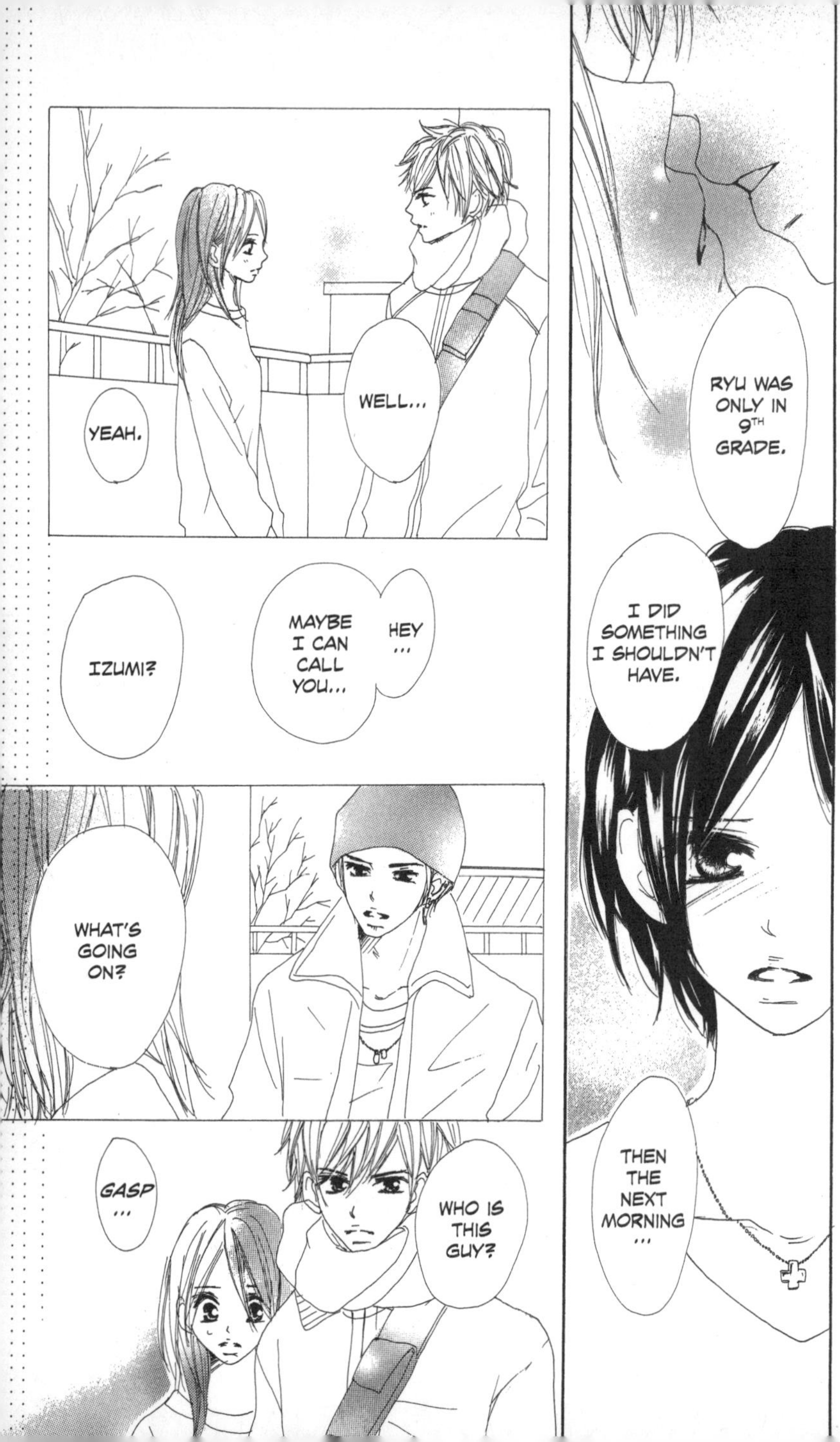
RYU WAS ONLY IN 9TH GRADE.
I DID SOMETHING I SHOULDN'T HAVE.
THEN THE NEXT MORNING...
WELL...
YEAH.
HEY...
MAYBE I CAN CALL YOU...
IZUMI?
WHAT'S GOING ON?
WHO IS THIS GUY?
GASP...

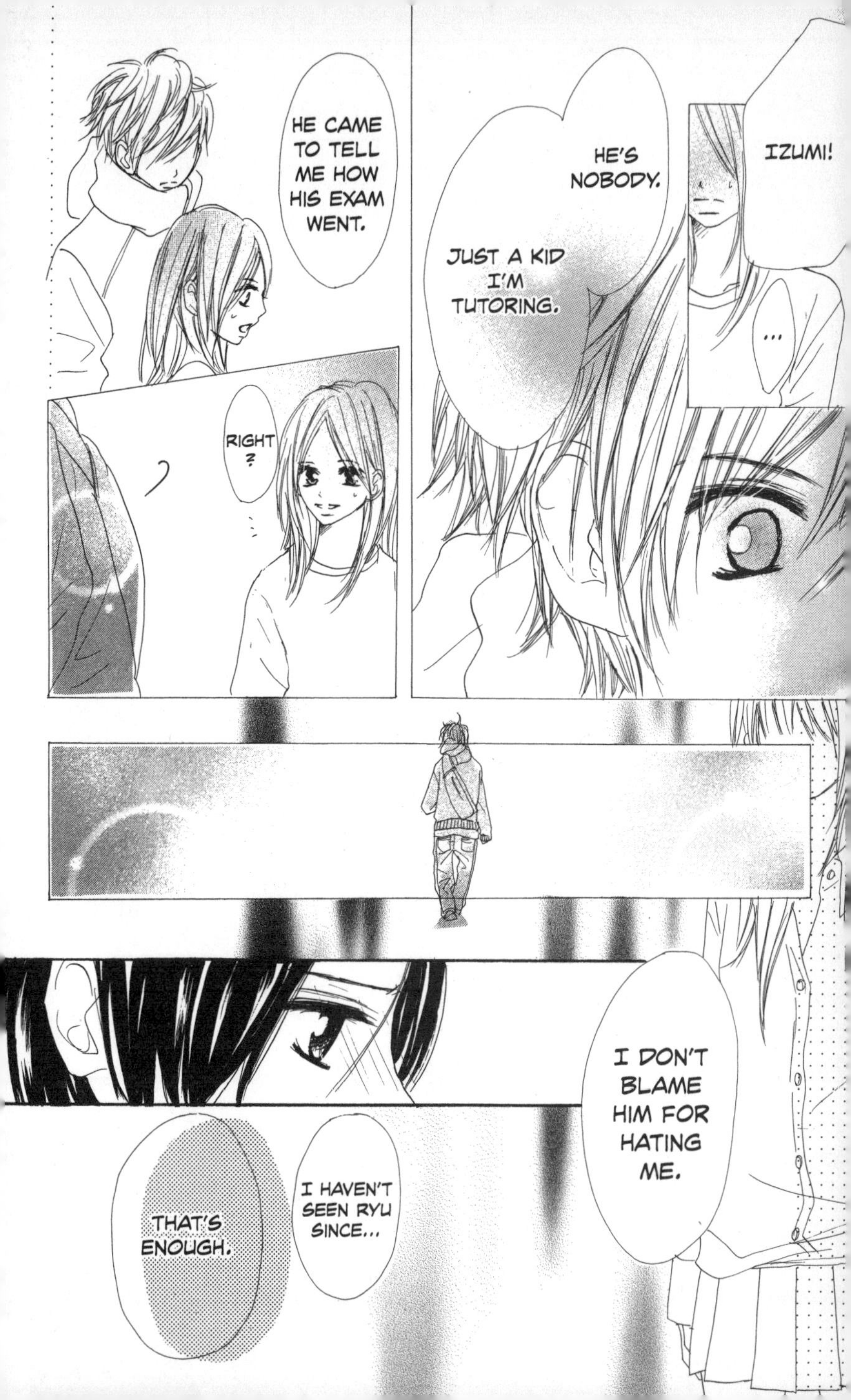
IZUMI!
...
HE'S NOBODY.
JUST A KID I'M TUTORING.
HE CAME TO TELL ME HOW HIS EXAM WENT.
RIGHT?
I DON'T BLAME HIM FOR HATING ME.
I HAVEN'T SEEN RYU SINCE...
THAT'S ENOUGH.

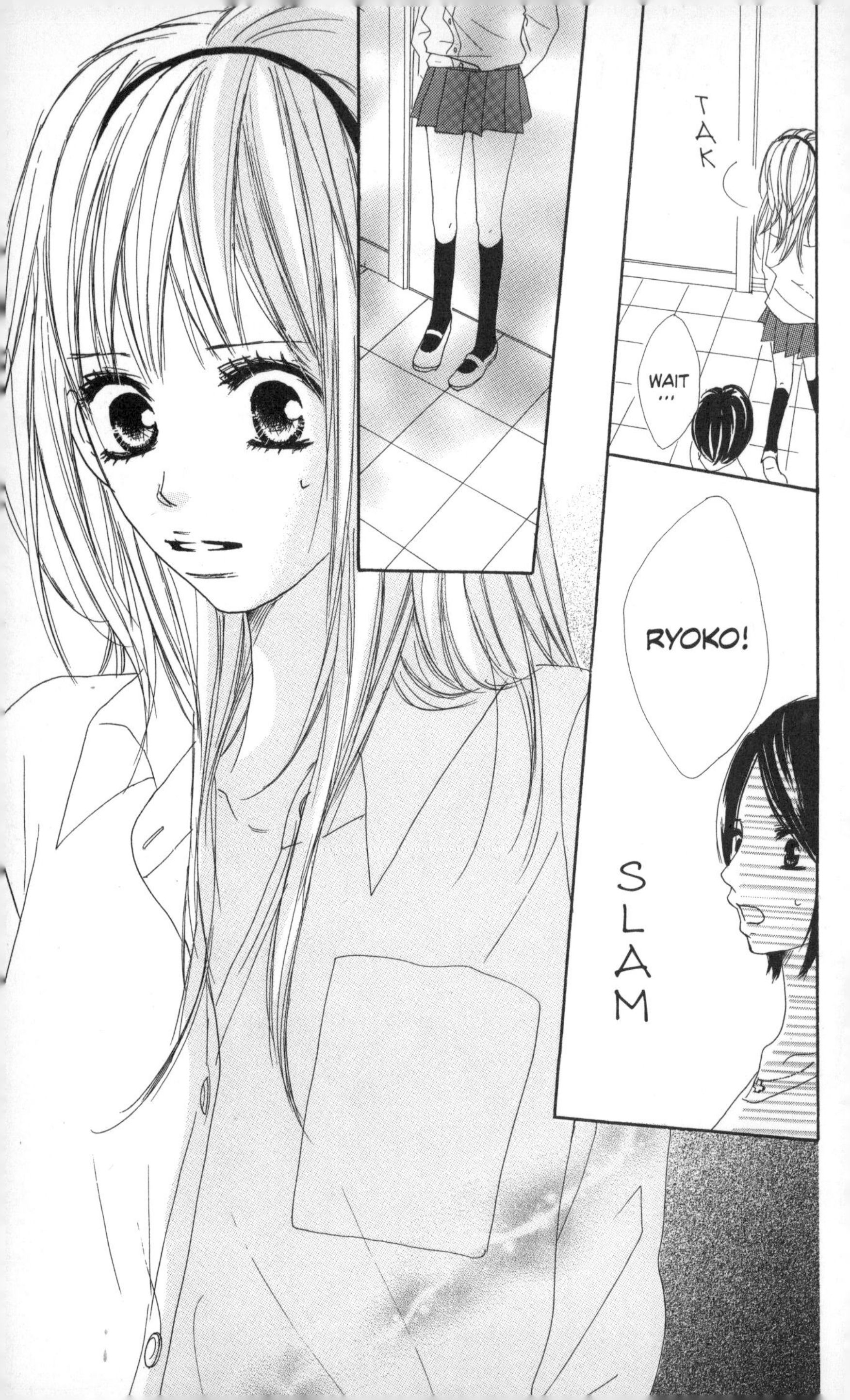
TAK
WAIT...
RYOKO!
SLAM

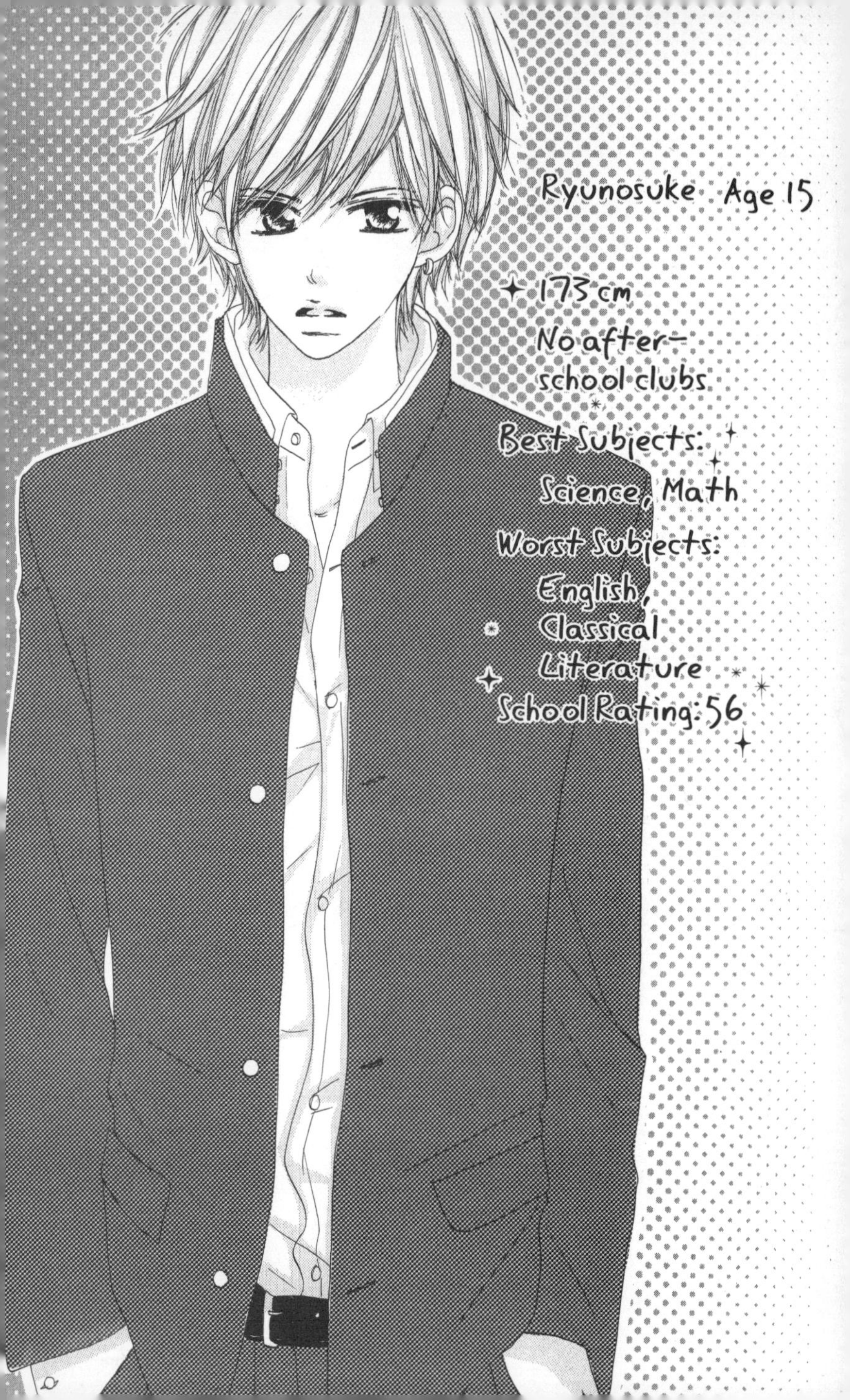
Ryunosuke Age 15
173 cm
No after-school clubs
Best Subjects:
Science, Math
Worst Subjects:
English, Classical Literature
School Rating: 56

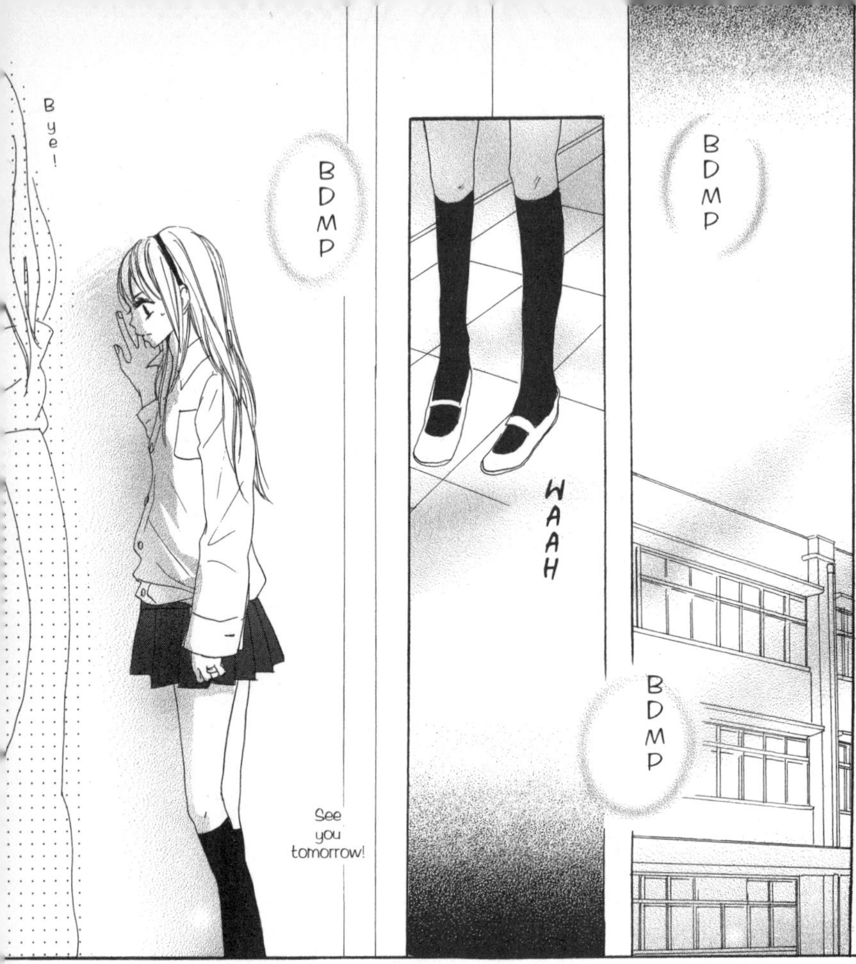
BDMP
BDMP
WAAAH
BDMP
Bye!
See you tomorrow!

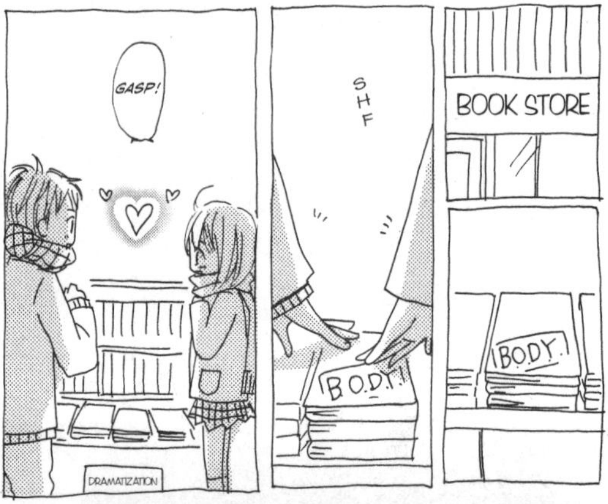
BOOK STORE
BODY
SHF
B.O.D.Y.
GASP!
DRAMATIZATION

☆ This is how my friend met her boyfriend.
—S.S., Mie Prefecture

IT'S LIKE A SOAP OPERA! HOW ROMANTIC!!! HOW DID THEY START DATING FROM THERE? ♡
KYAA! I'M SO HAPPY FOR THEM!! GOOD LUCK!
♡ ♡ ♡

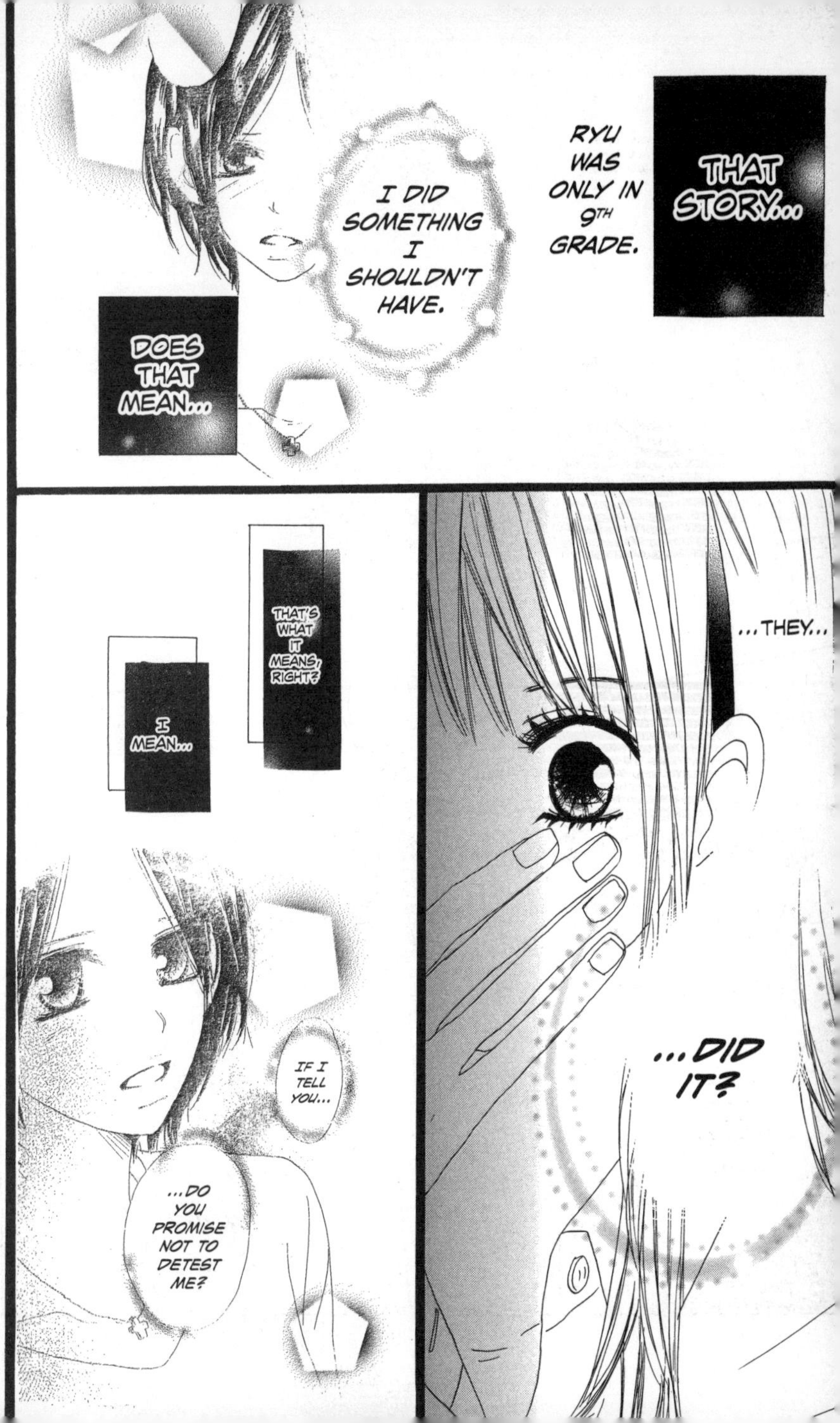
THAT STORY...
RYU WAS ONLY IN 9TH GRADE.
I DID SOMETHING I SHOULDN'T HAVE.
DOES THAT MEAN...
...THEY...
...DID IT?
THAT'S WHAT IT MEANS, RIGHT?
I MEAN...
IF I TELL YOU...
...DO YOU PROMISE NOT TO DETEST ME?

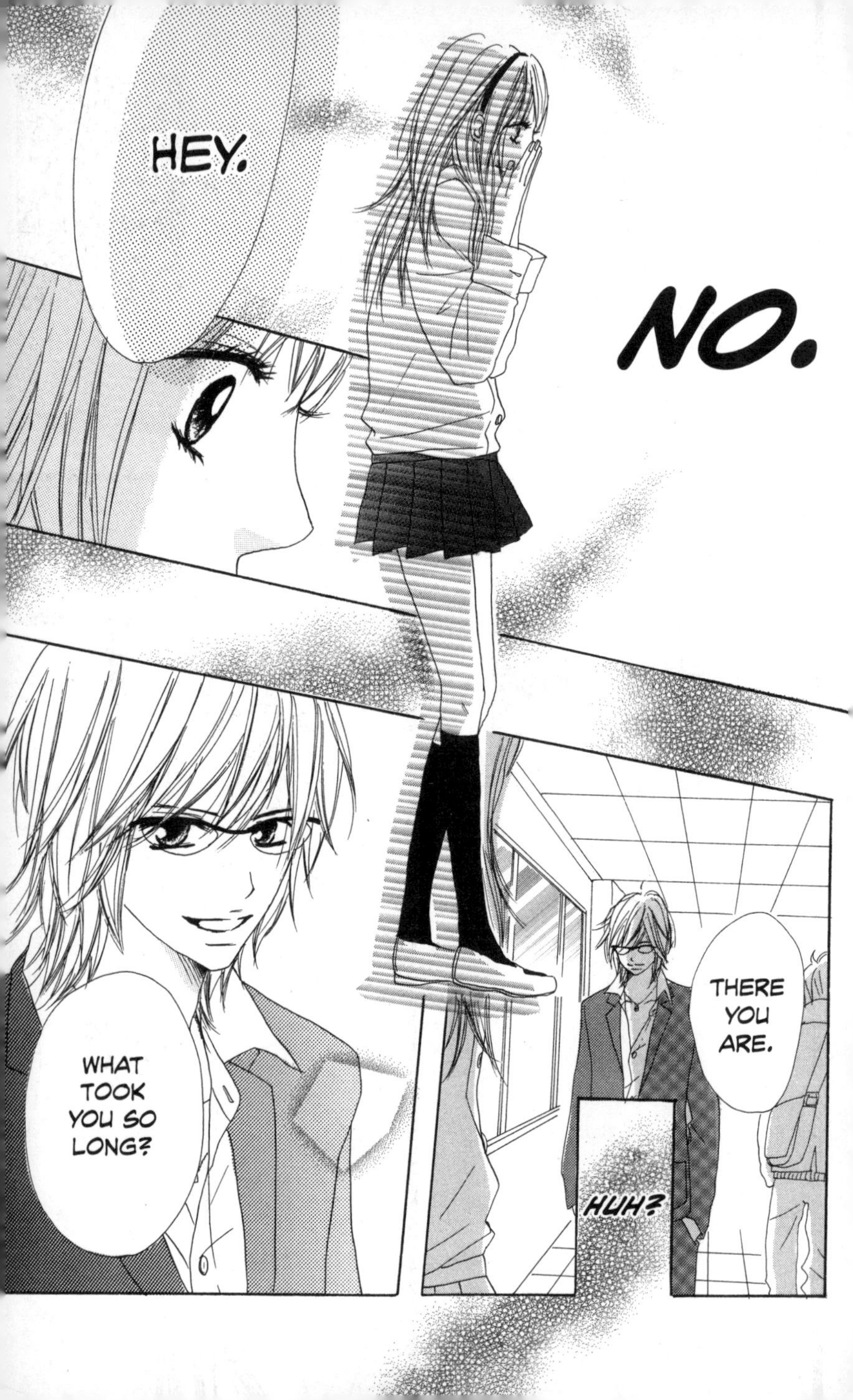
NO.
HEY.
THERE YOU ARE.
HUH?
WHAT TOOK YOU SO LONG?

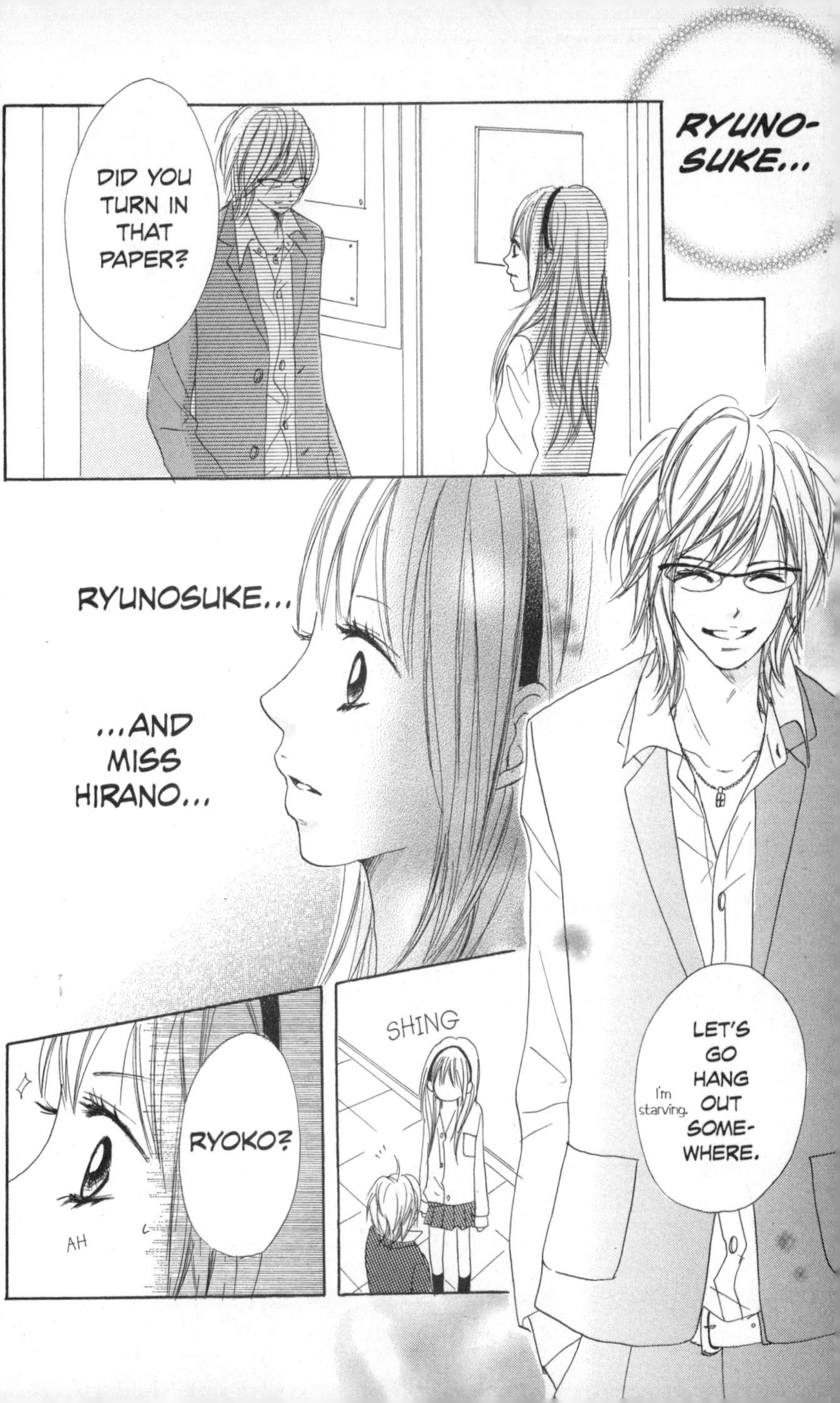
RYUNO-SUKE...
DID YOU TURN IN THAT PAPER?
RYUNOSUKE...
...AND MISS HIRANO...
LET'S GO HANG OUT SOMEWHERE.
I'm starving.
SHING
RYOKO?
AH

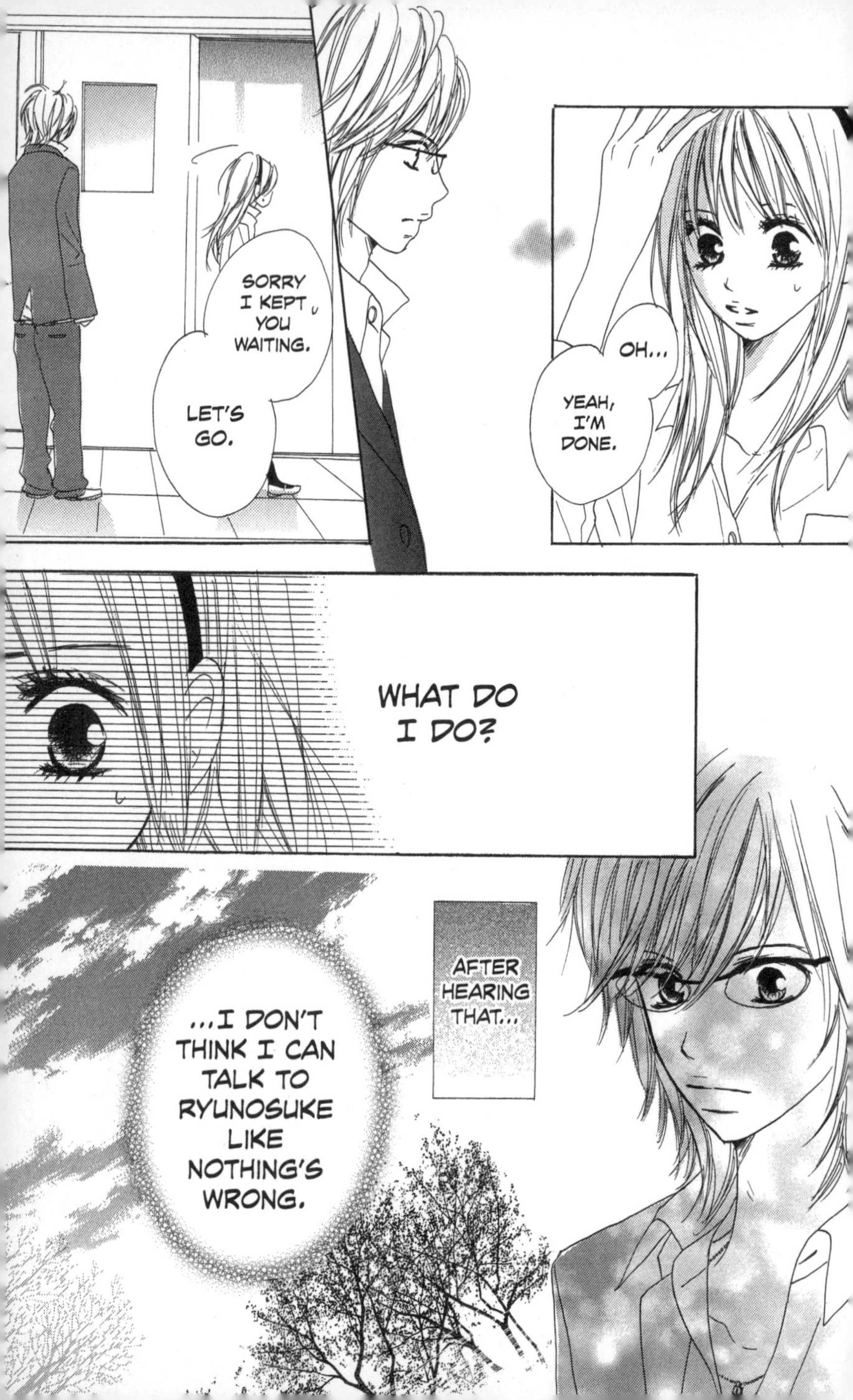
OH...
YEAH, I'M DONE.
SORRY I KEPT YOU WAITING.
LET'S GO.
WHAT DO I DO?
AFTER HEARING THAT...
...I DON'T THINK I CAN TALK TO RYUNOSUKE LIKE NOTHING'S WRONG.

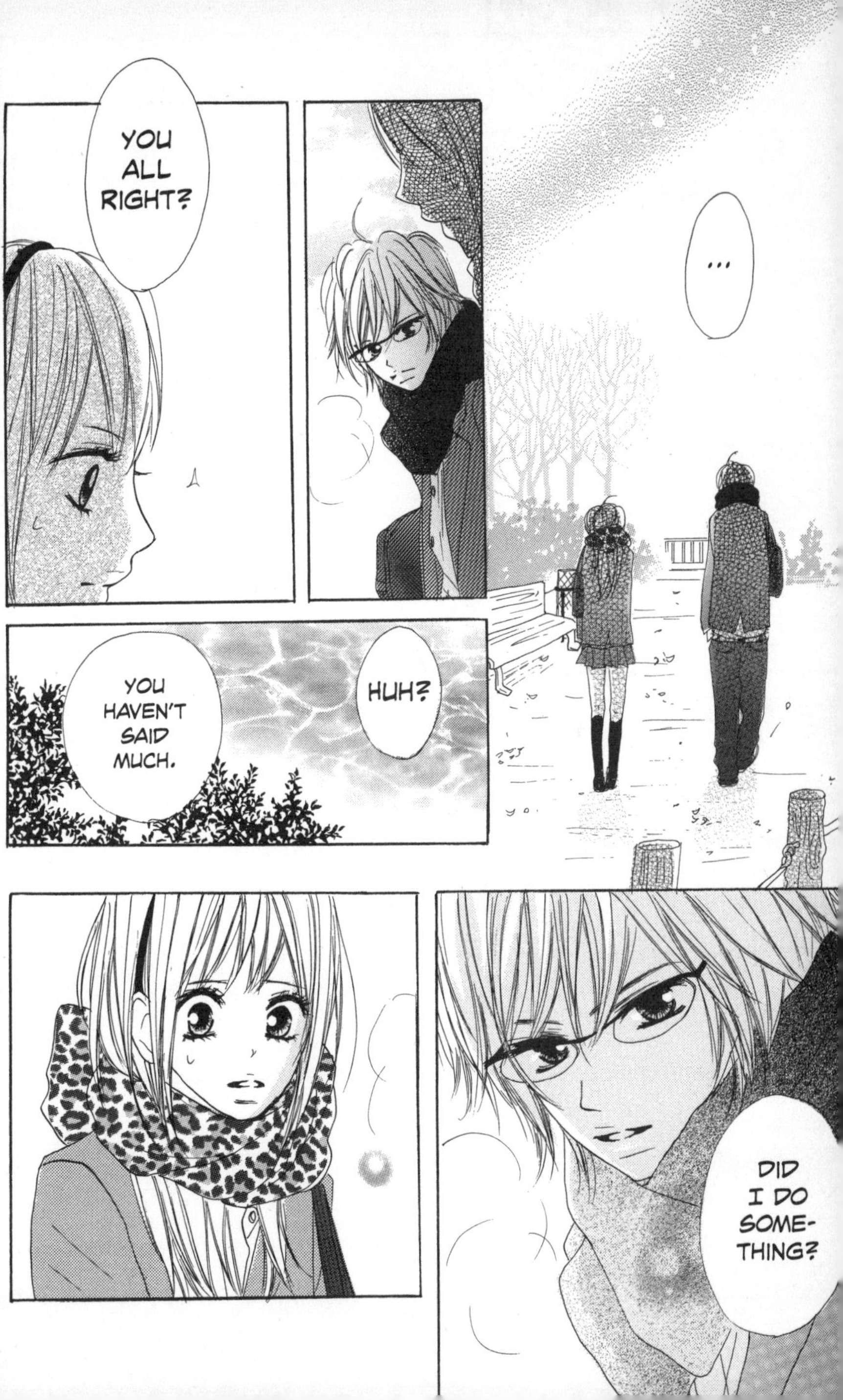
...
YOU ALL RIGHT?
HUH?
YOU HAVEN'T SAID MUCH.
DID I DO SOMETHING?

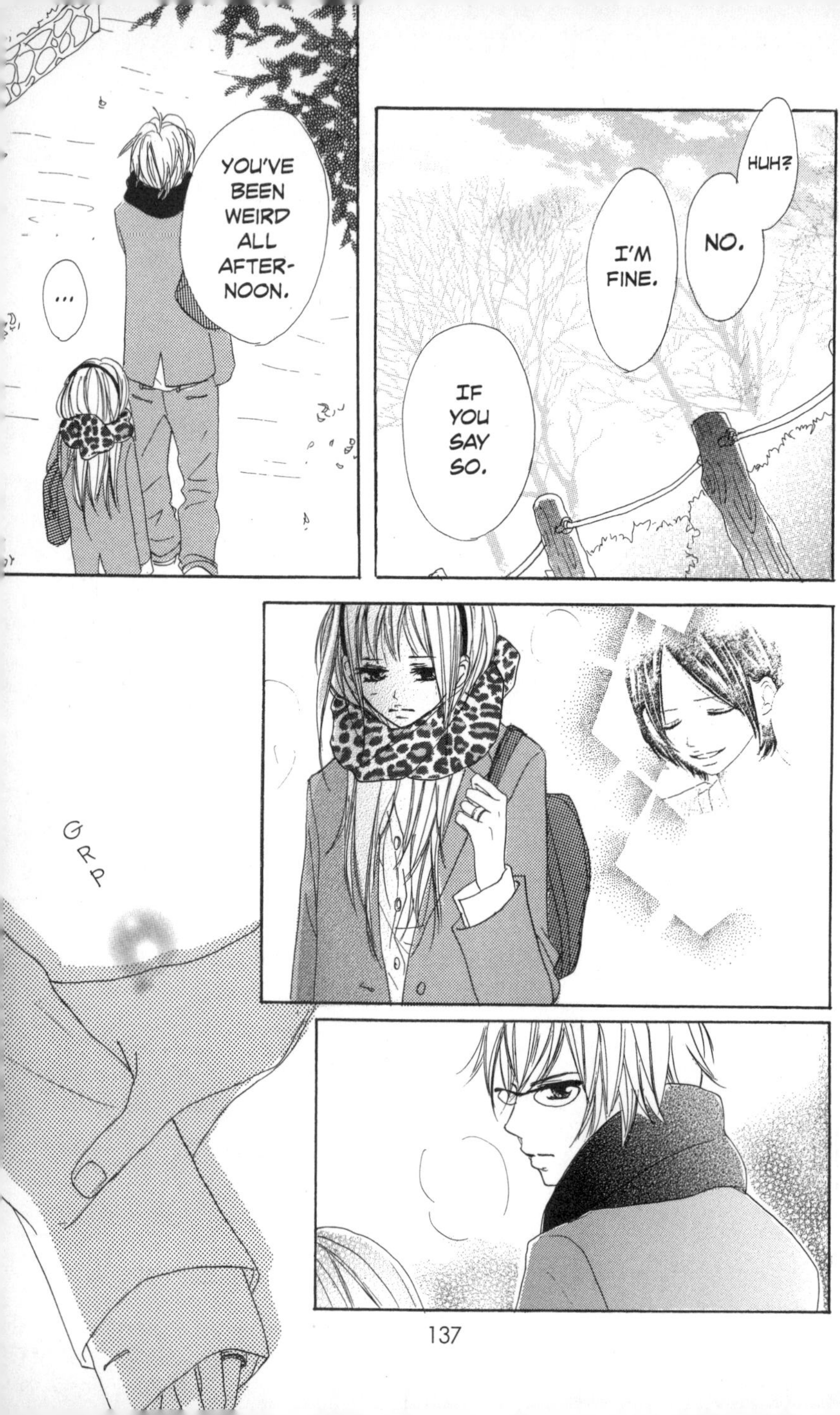
YOU'VE BEEN WEIRD ALL AFTER-NOON.
...
HUH?
NO.
I'M FINE.
IF YOU SAY SO.
GRP

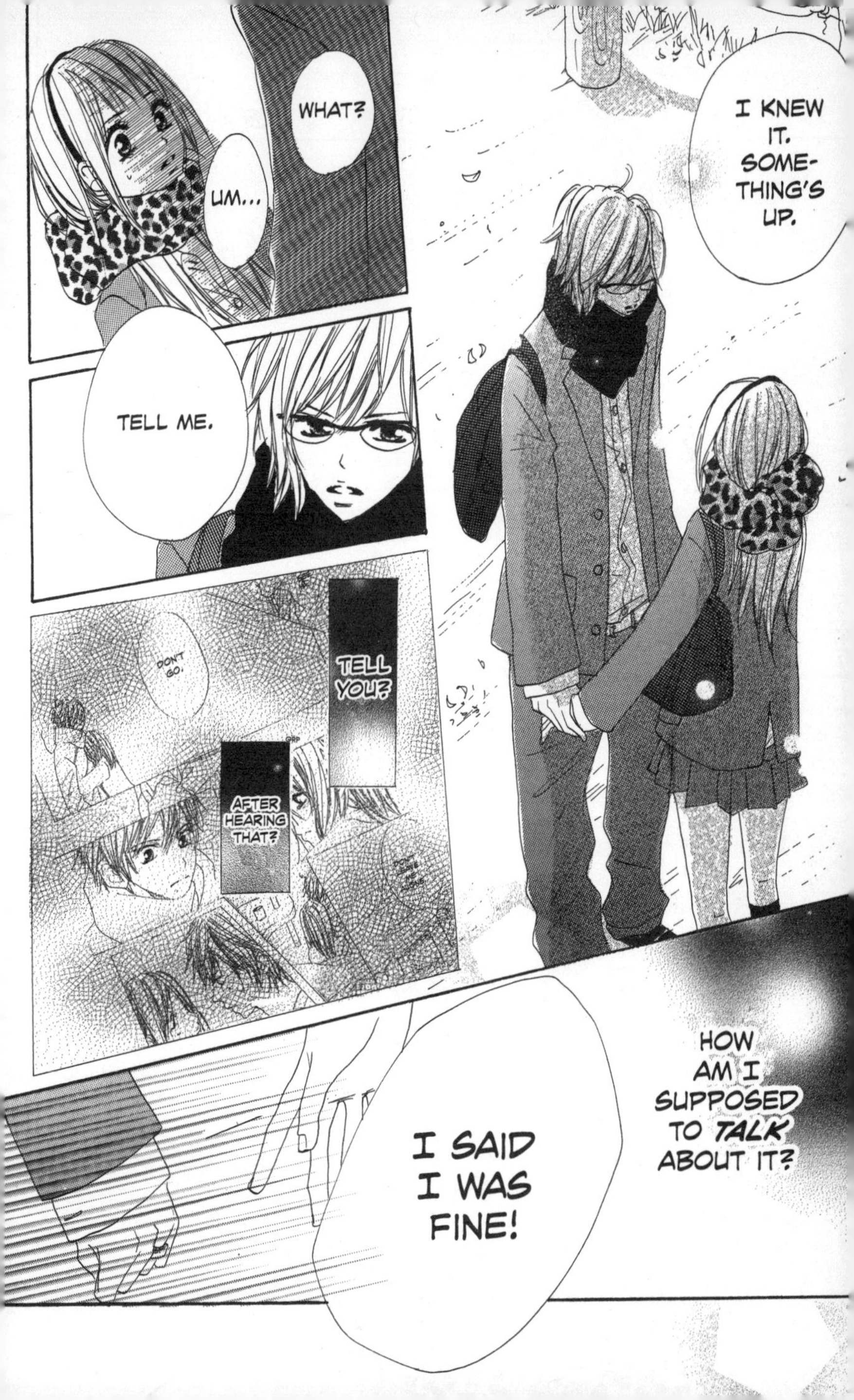
I KNEW IT. SOMETHING'S UP.
WHAT?
UM...
TELL ME.
TELL YOU?
AFTER HEARING THAT?
DON'T LEAVE ME ALONE
DON'T GO.
HOW AM I SUPPOSED TO *TALK* ABOUT IT?
I SAID I WAS FINE!

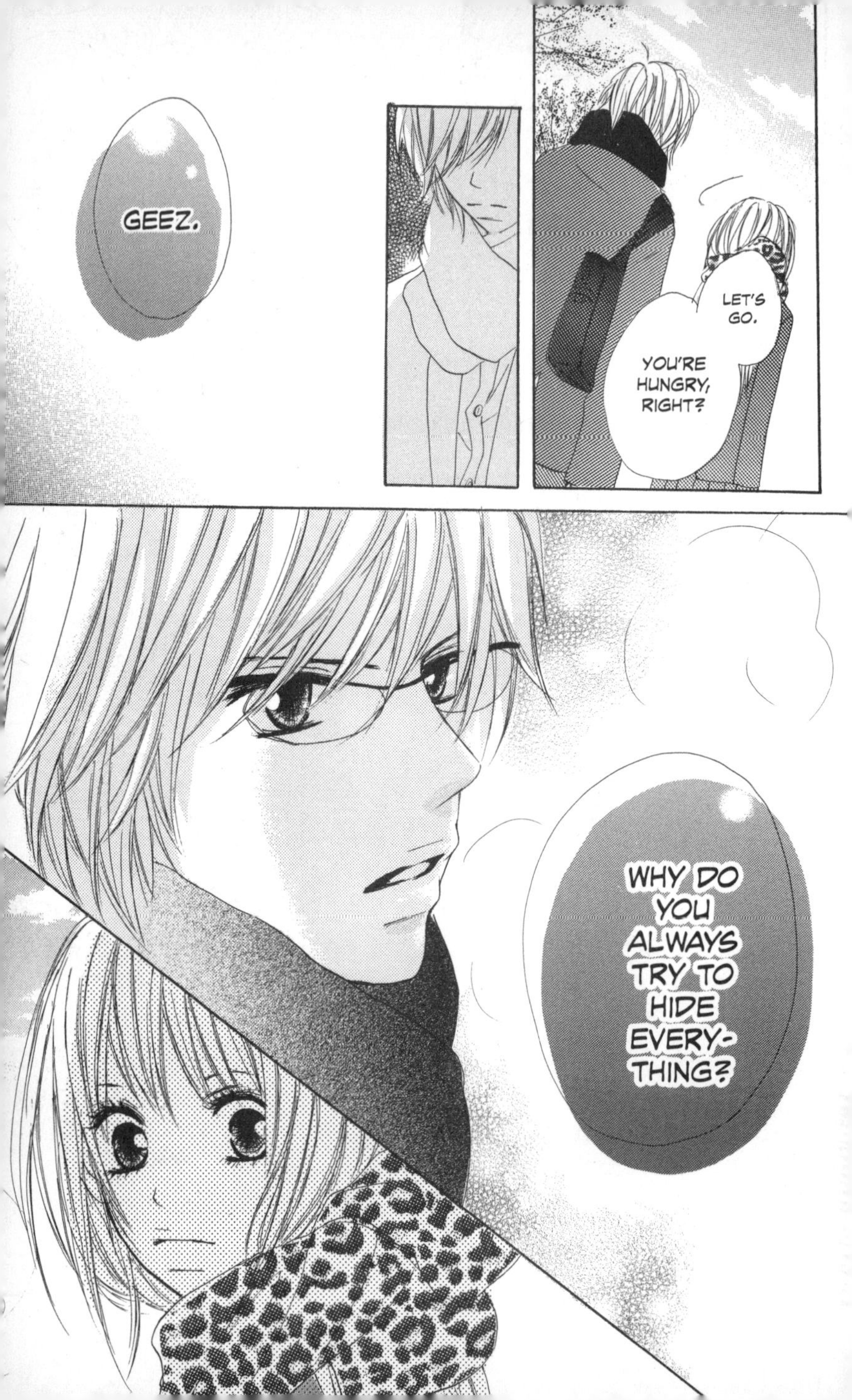
LET'S GO.
YOU'RE HUNGRY, RIGHT?
GEEZ.
WHY DO YOU ALWAYS TRY TO HIDE EVERY-THING?

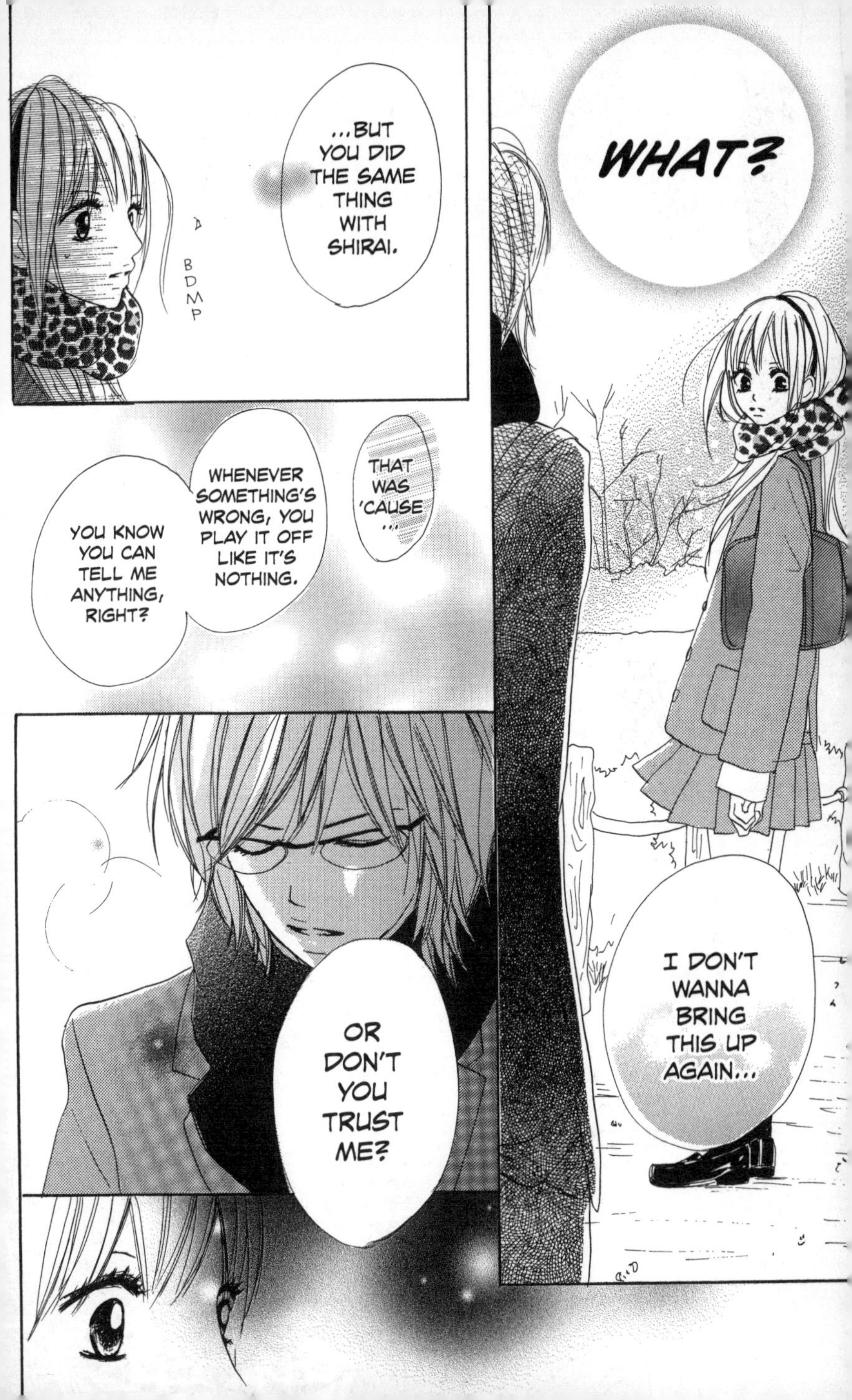
WHAT?
I DON'T WANNA BRING THIS UP AGAIN...
...BUT YOU DID THE SAME THING WITH SHIRAI.
BDMP
THAT WAS 'CAUSE...
WHENEVER SOMETHING'S WRONG, YOU PLAY IT OFF LIKE IT'S NOTHING.
YOU KNOW YOU CAN TELL ME ANYTHING, RIGHT?
OR DON'T YOU TRUST ME?

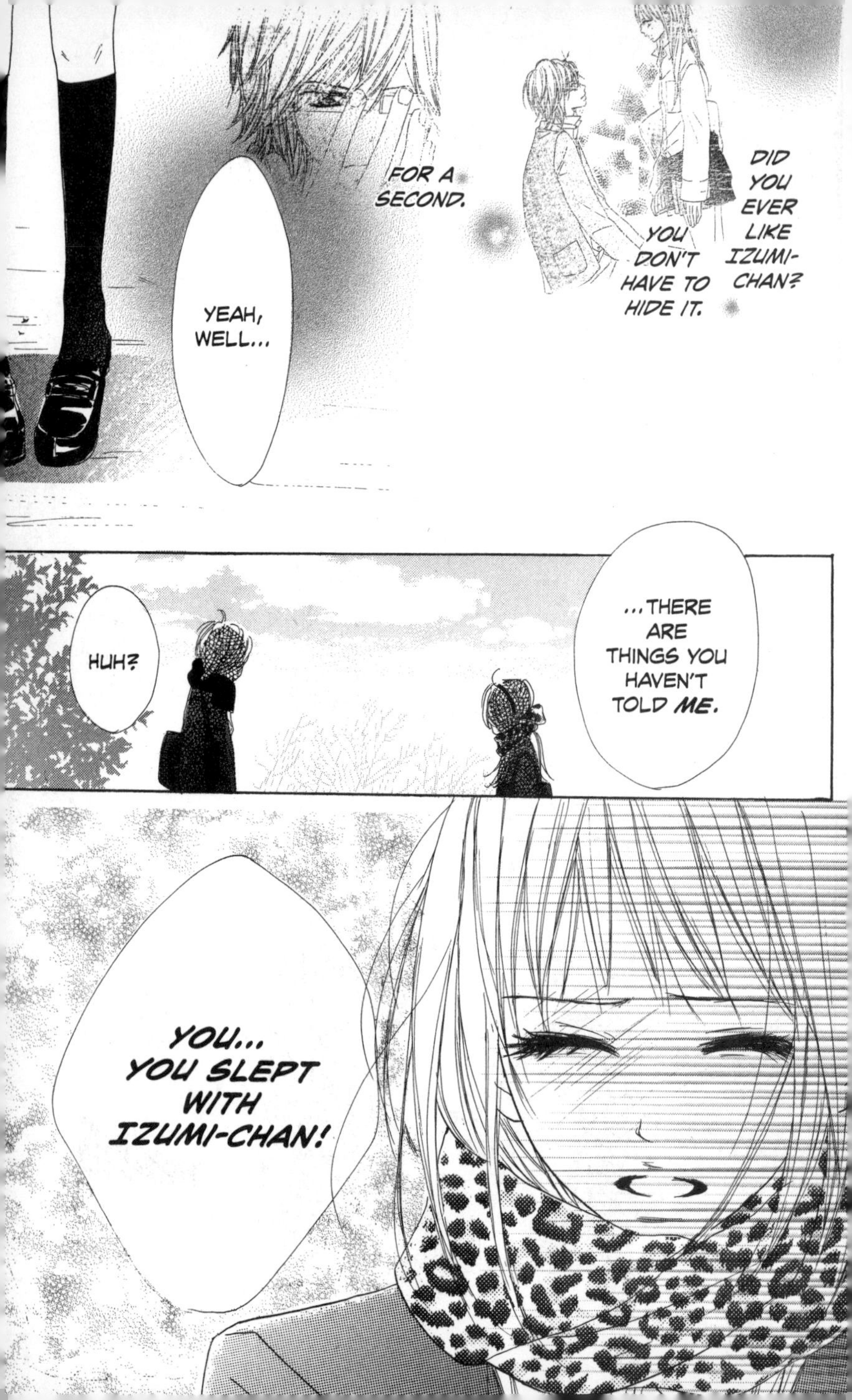
DID YOU EVER LIKE IZUMI-CHAN?
YOU DON'T HAVE TO HIDE IT.
FOR A SECOND.
YEAH, WELL...
...THERE ARE THINGS YOU HAVEN'T TOLD *ME*.
HUH?
YOU... YOU SLEPT WITH IZUMI-CHAN!

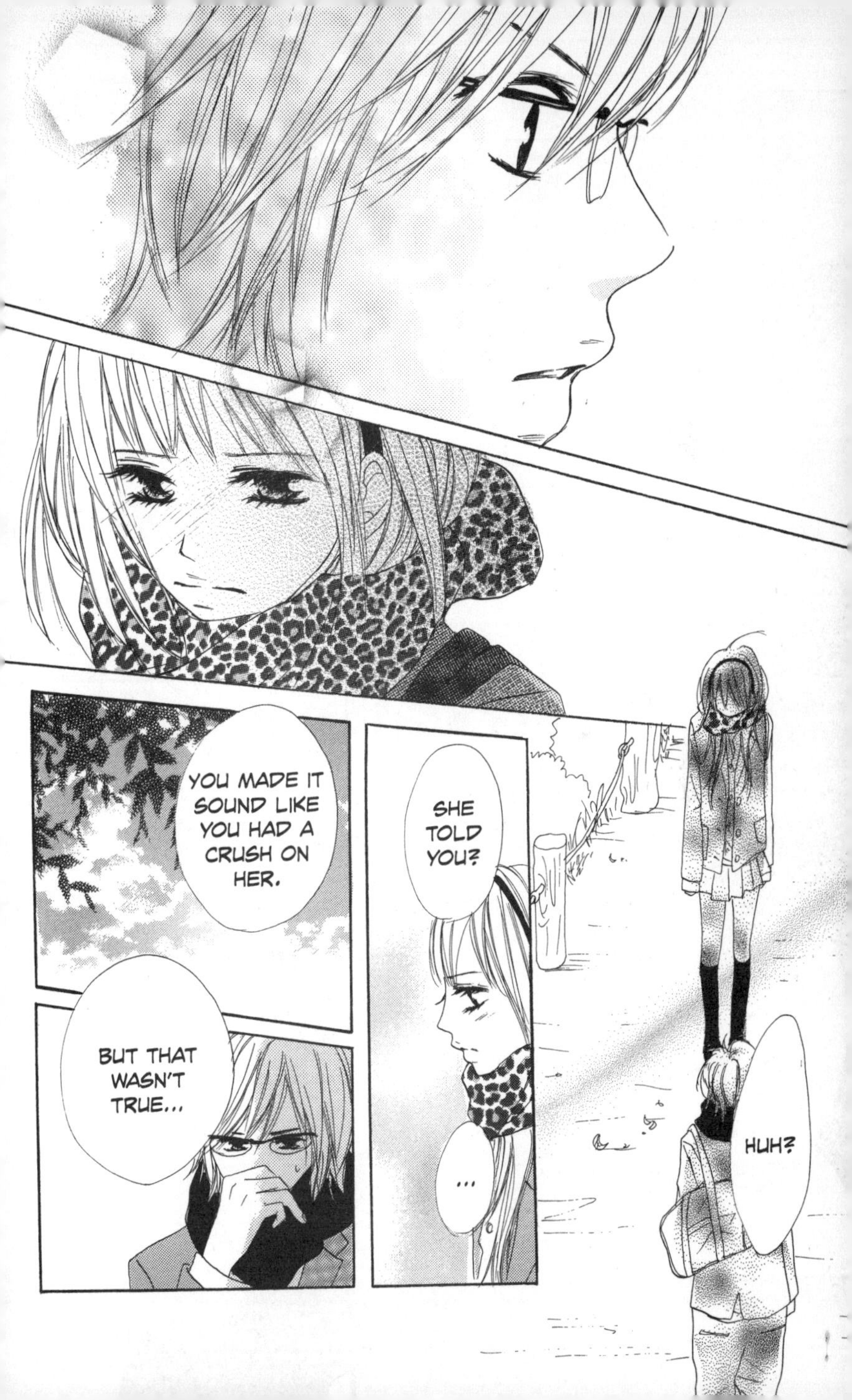
HUH?
SHE TOLD YOU?
...
YOU MADE IT SOUND LIKE YOU HAD A CRUSH ON HER.
BUT THAT WASN'T TRUE...

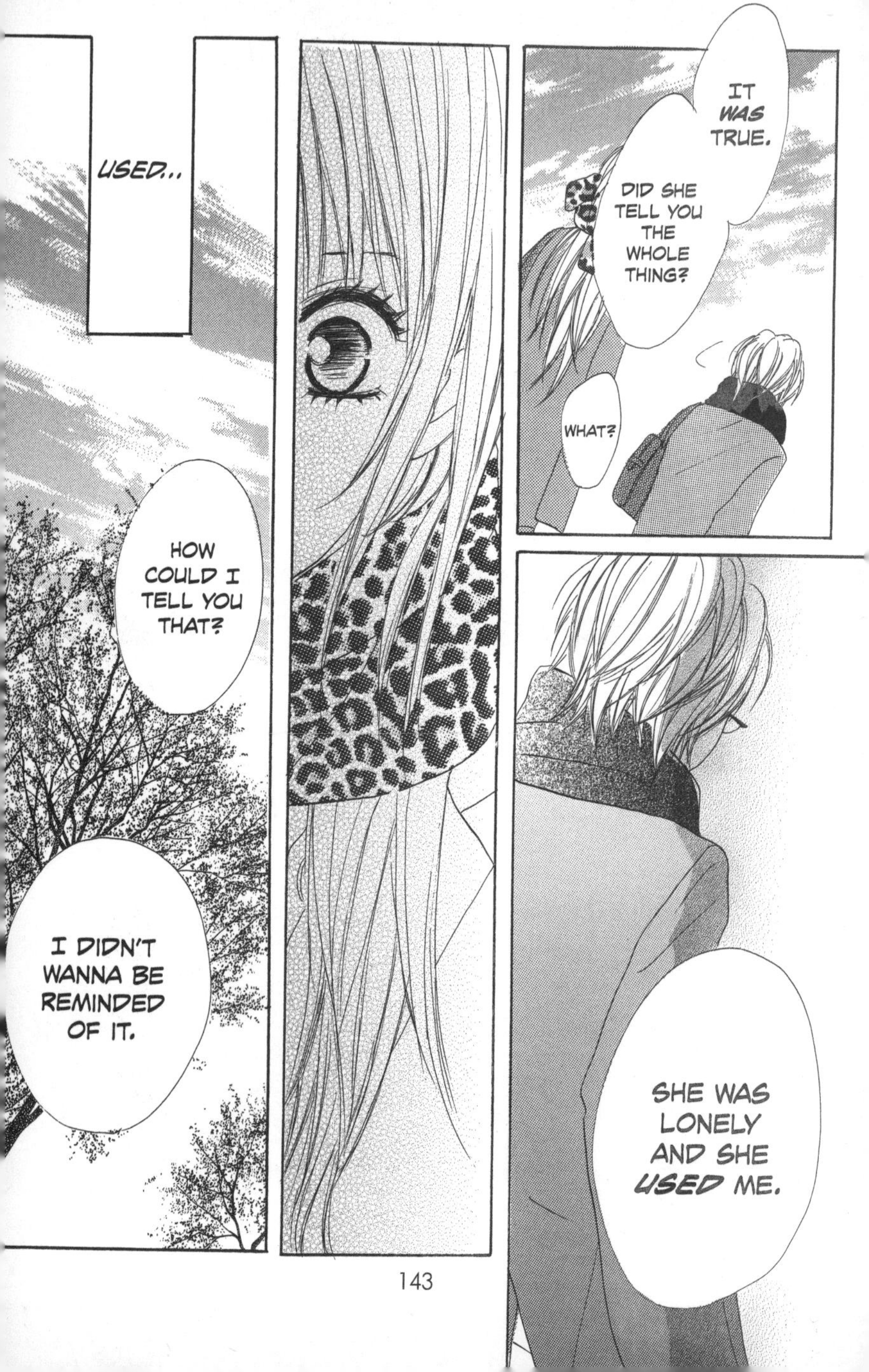
IT WAS TRUE.
DID SHE TELL YOU THE WHOLE THING?
WHAT?
SHE WAS LONELY AND SHE USED ME.
USED...
HOW COULD I TELL YOU THAT?
I DIDN'T WANNA BE REMINDED OF IT.

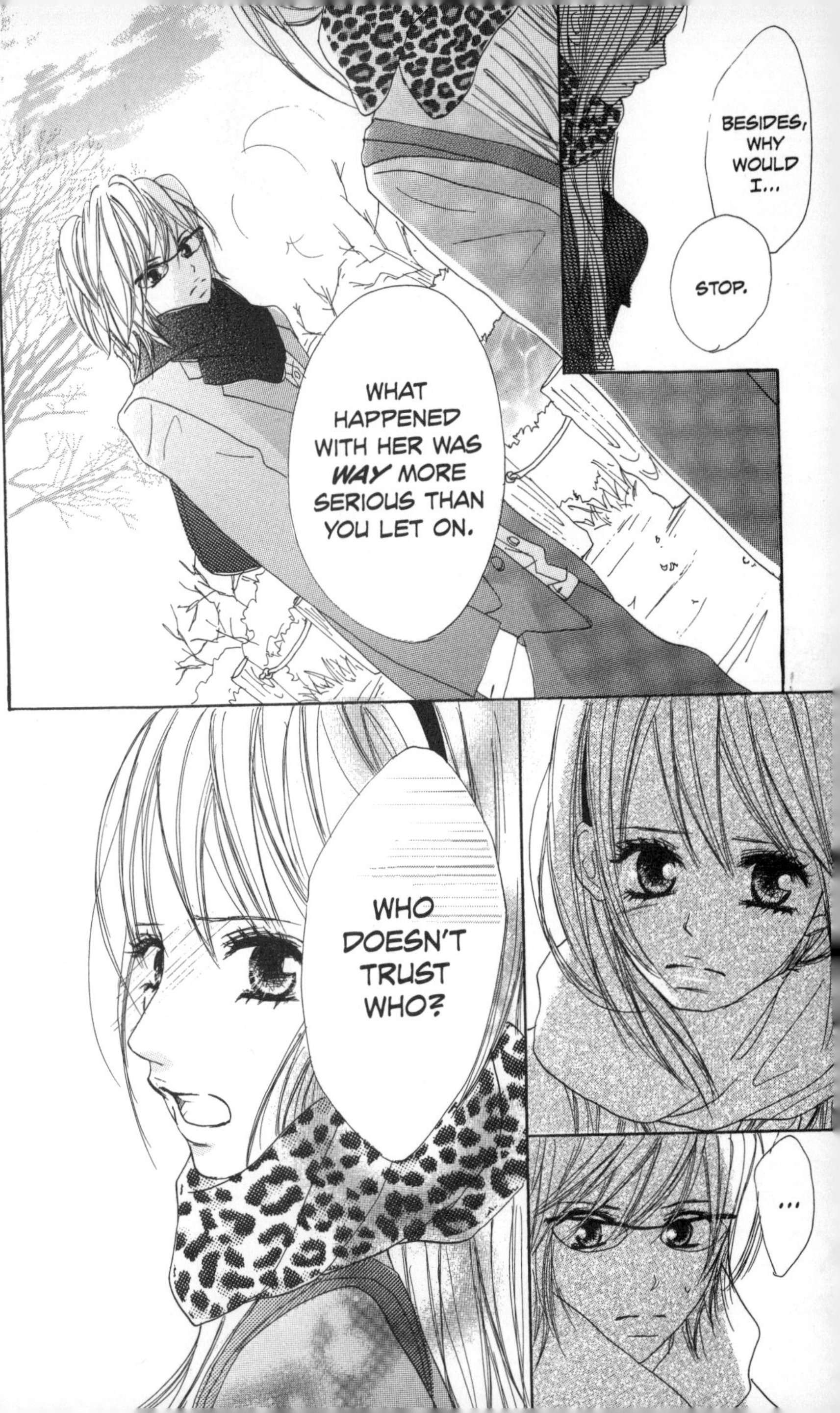
BESIDES, WHY WOULD I...
STOP.
WHAT HAPPENED WITH HER WAS *WAY* MORE SERIOUS THAN YOU LET ON.
...
WHO DOESN'T TRUST WHO?

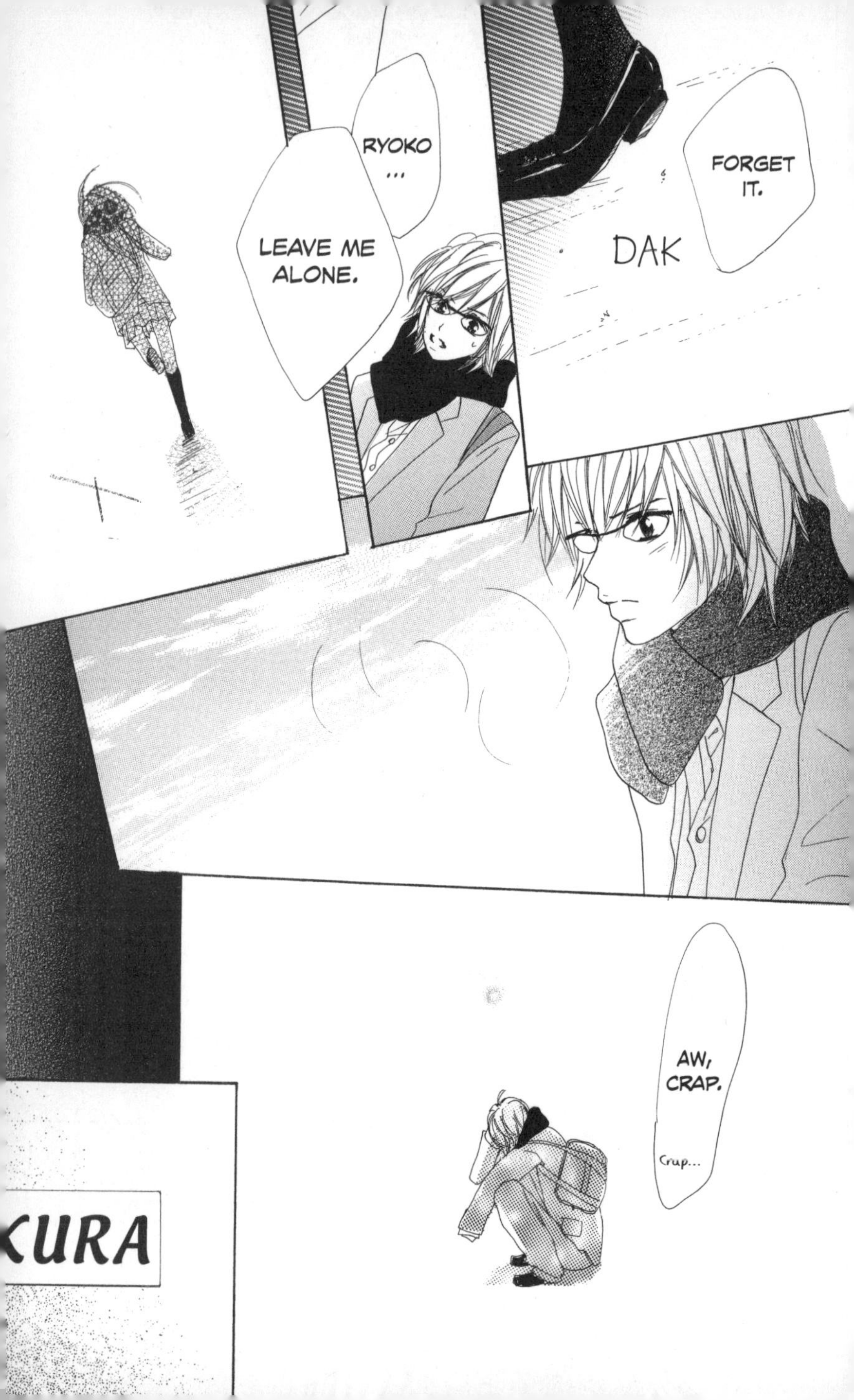
FORGET IT.
DAK
RYOKO ...
LEAVE ME ALONE.
AW, CRAP.
Crap...

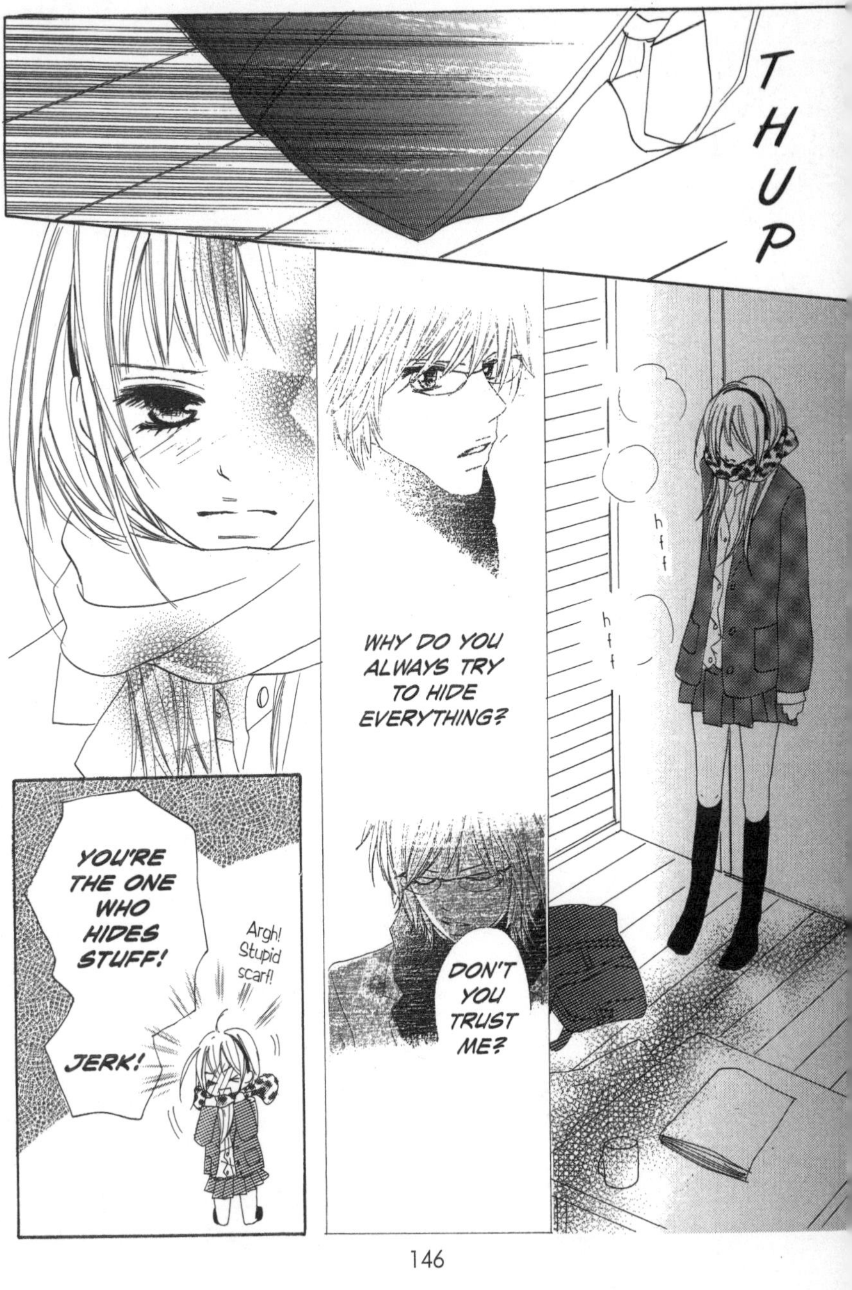
THUP
hff
hff
WHY DO YOU ALWAYS TRY TO HIDE EVERYTHING?
DON'T YOU TRUST ME?
YOU'RE THE ONE WHO HIDES STUFF!
Argh! Stupid scarf!
JERK!

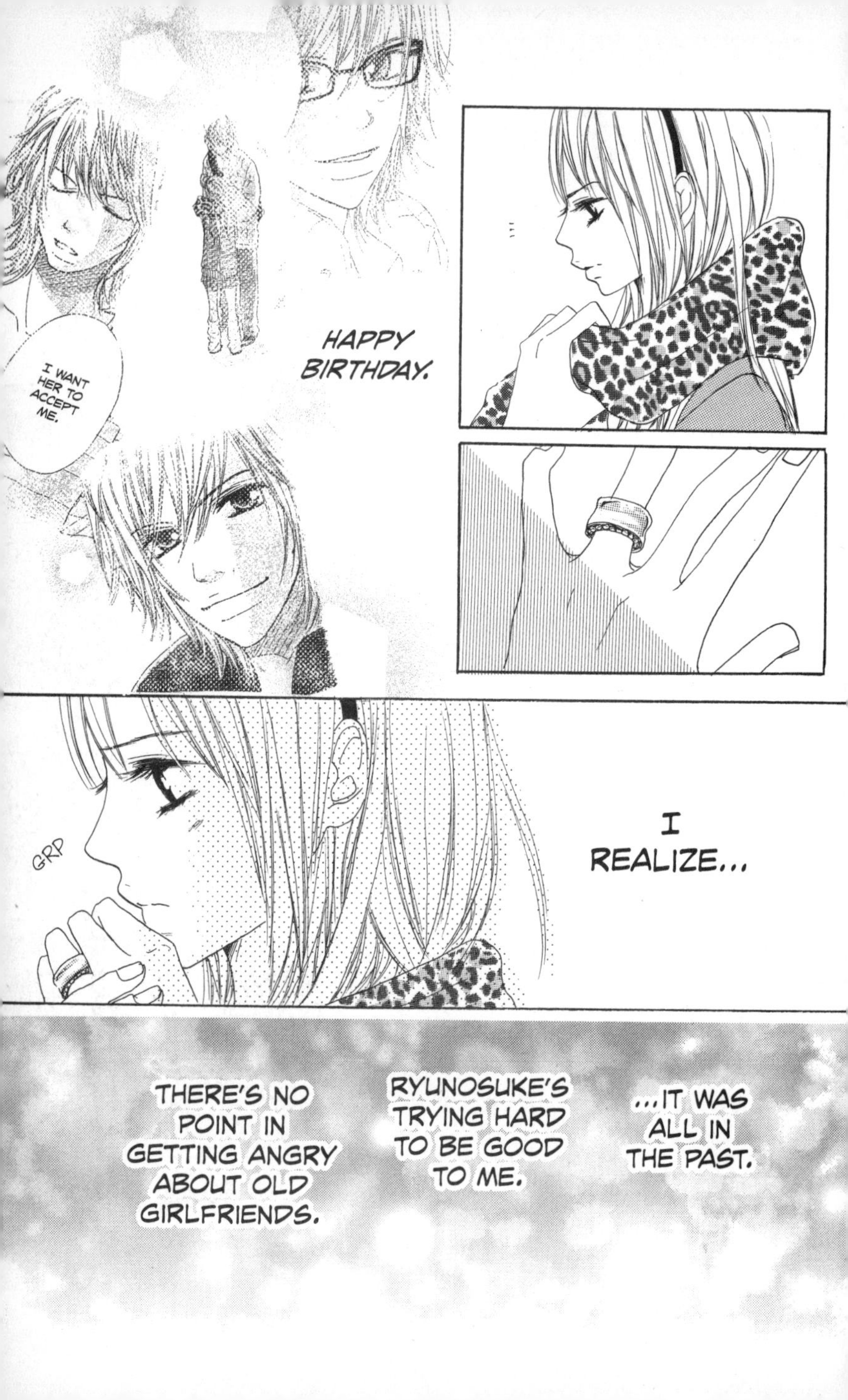
HAPPY BIRTHDAY.
I WANT HER TO ACCEPT ME.
I REALIZE...
GRP
...IT WAS ALL IN THE PAST.
RYUNOSUKE'S TRYING HARD TO BE GOOD TO ME.
THERE'S NO POINT IN GETTING ANGRY ABOUT OLD GIRLFRIENDS.

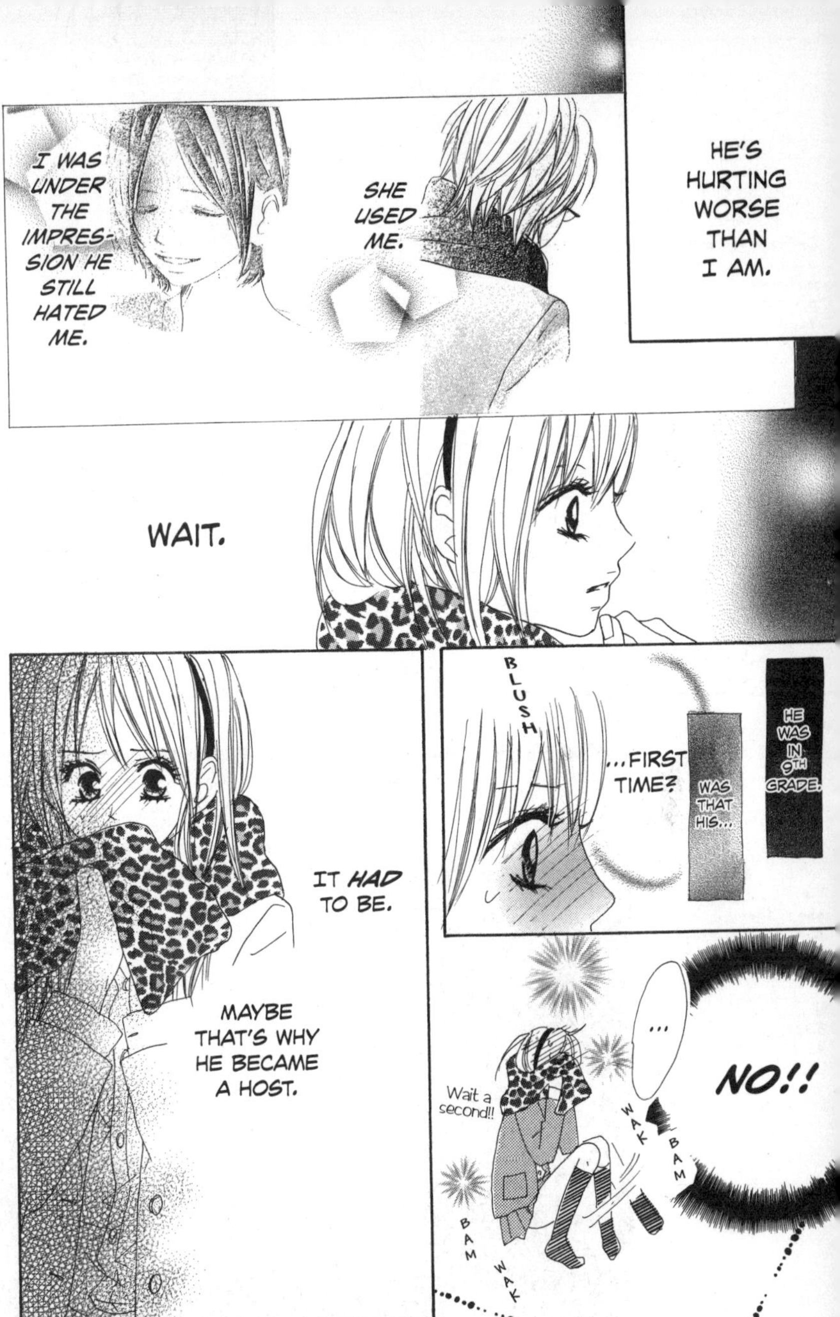
HE'S HURTING WORSE THAN I AM.
SHE USED ME.
I WAS UNDER THE IMPRESSION HE STILL HATED ME.
WAIT.
HE WAS IN 9TH GRADE.
WAS THAT HIS...
...FIRST TIME?
BLUSH
NO!!
...
WAK BAM
Wait a second!!
BAM WAK
IT *HAD* TO BE.
MAYBE THAT'S WHY HE BECAME A HOST.

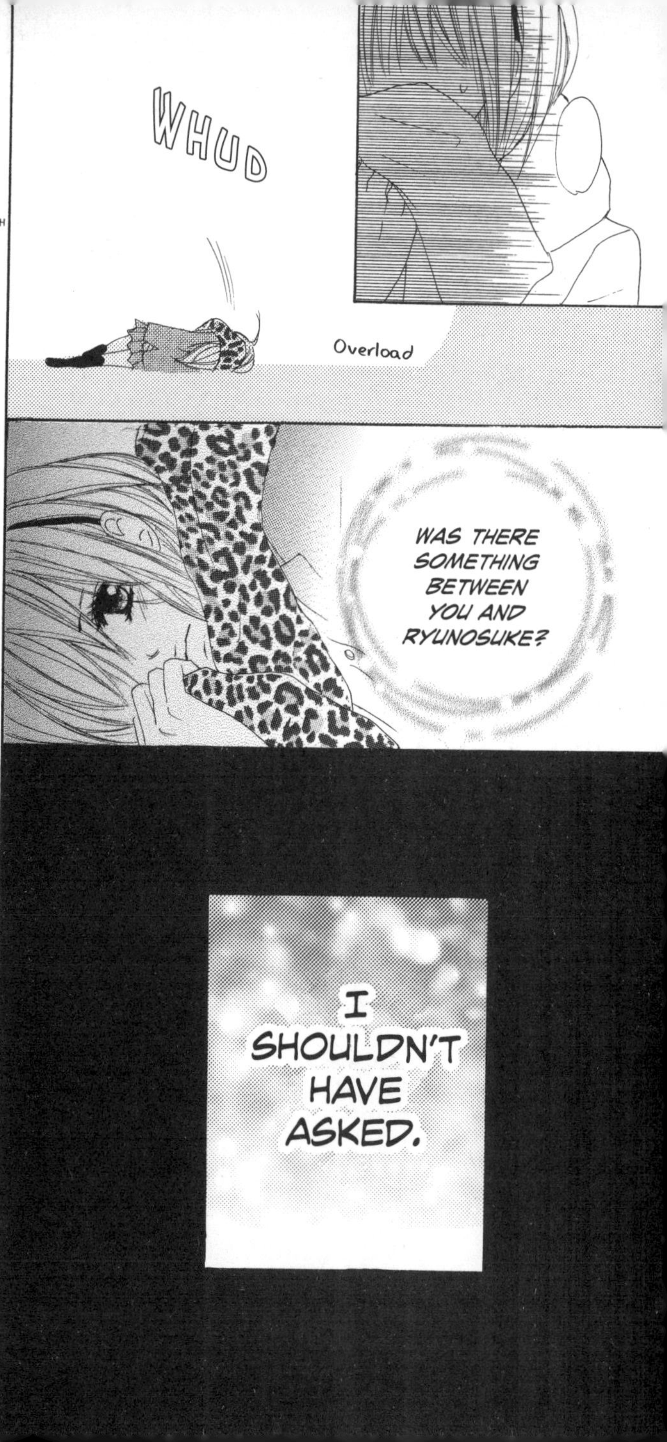
WHUD
Overload
WAS THERE SOMETHING BETWEEN YOU AND RYUNOSUKE?
I SHOULDN'T HAVE ASKED.

4

On the boys' team there was this guy I liked. On co-ed practice days I'd blow-dry my hair early in the morning! But no matter how much I styled it, once I started sweating it'd frizz out...heh...

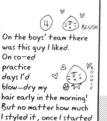

My friends gave me the nickname "Perm," which I couldn't deny. Eventually the guy went out with a friend of mine on the team!! That was my youth!! Damn the fates!!

Why did I share this tale of heartbreak? I get a lot of letters asking what school clubs I was in, so that's my answer.

There's a bonus story about Ryunosuke's parents at the end of the volume. Please check it out.

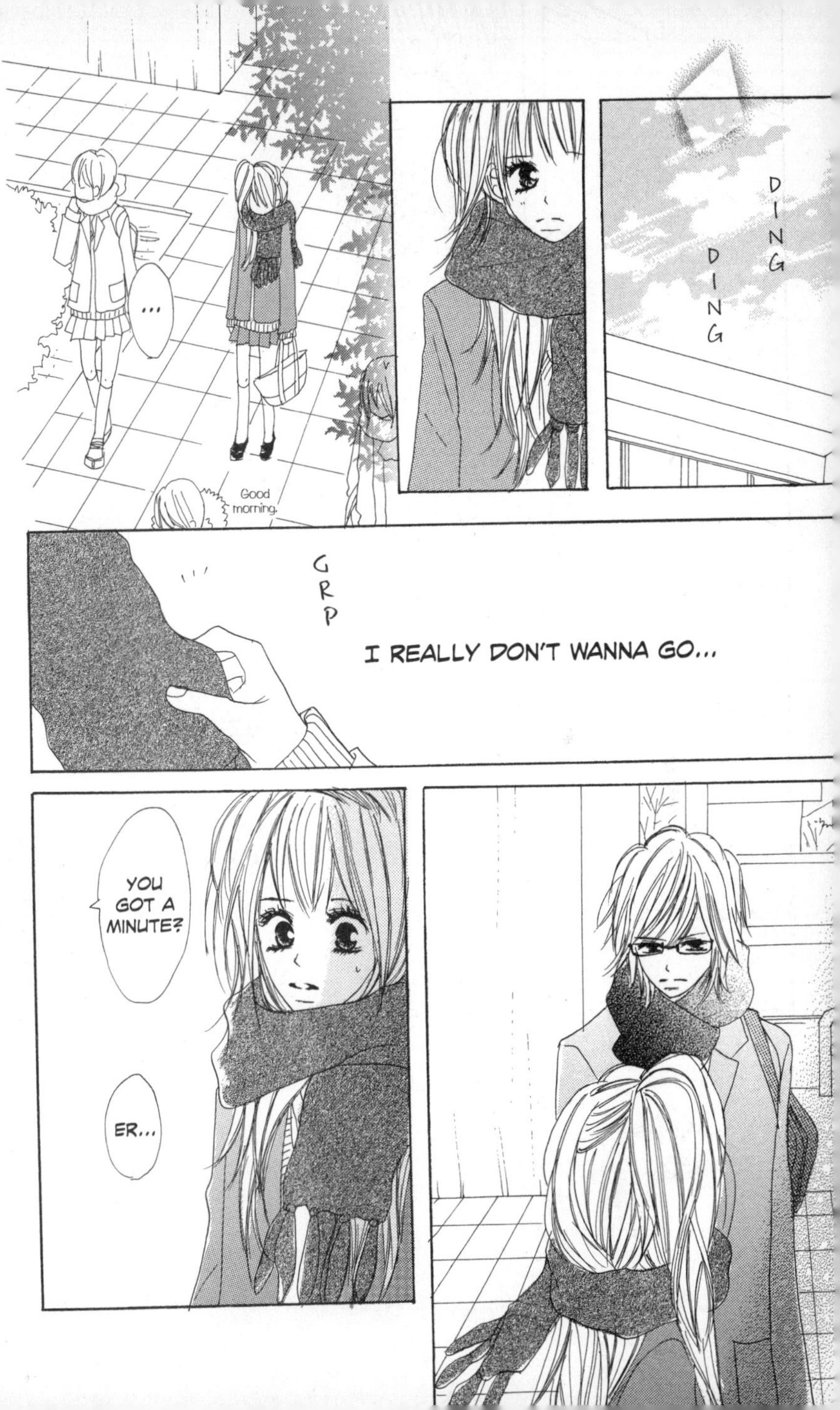
DING
DING
...
Good morning.
GRP
I REALLY DON'T WANNA GO...
YOU GOT A MINUTE?
ER...

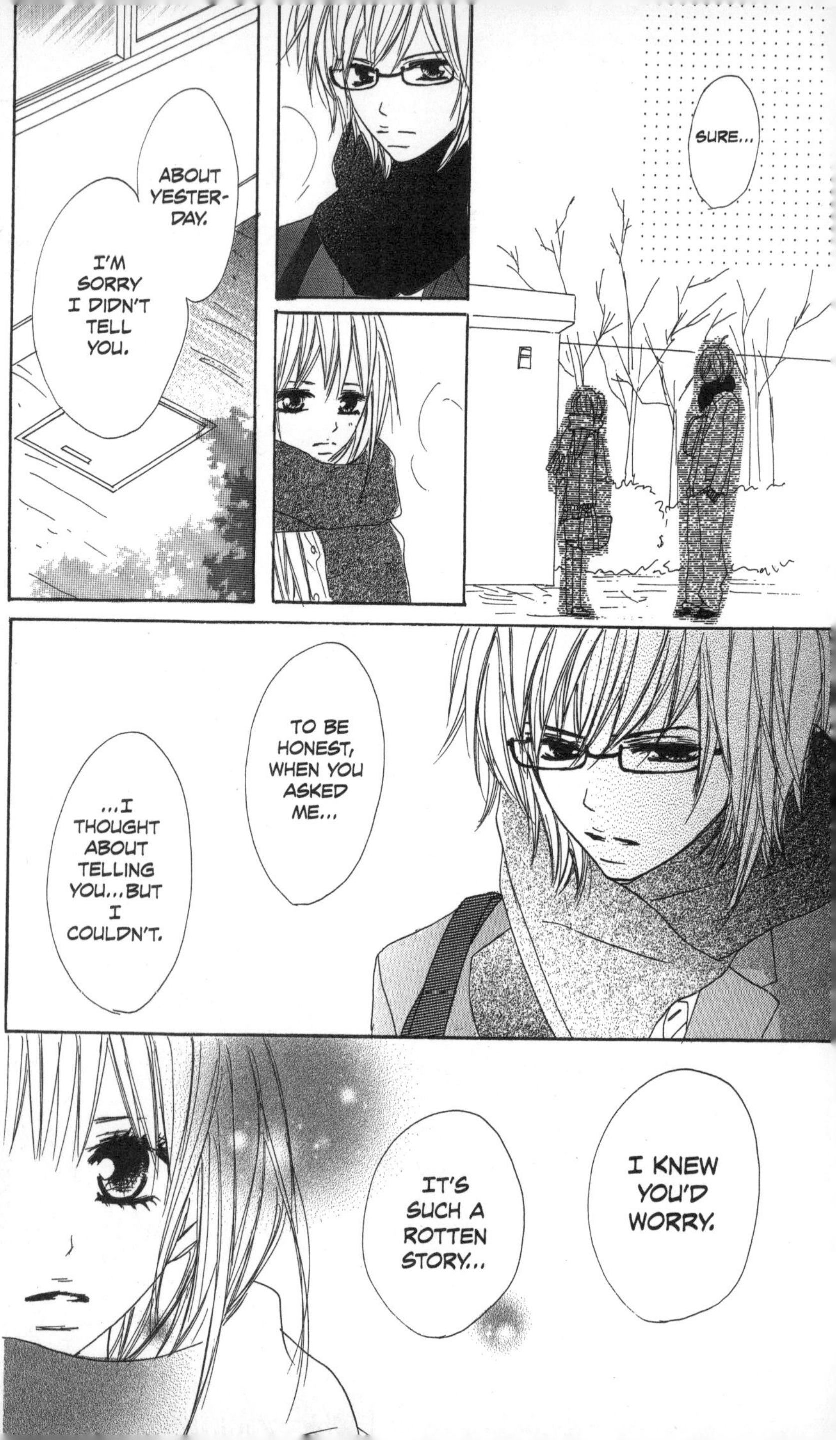
SURE...
ABOUT YESTER-DAY.
I'M SORRY I DIDN'T TELL YOU.
TO BE HONEST, WHEN YOU ASKED ME...
...I THOUGHT ABOUT TELLING YOU...BUT I COULDN'T.
I KNEW YOU'D WORRY.
IT'S SUCH A ROTTEN STORY...

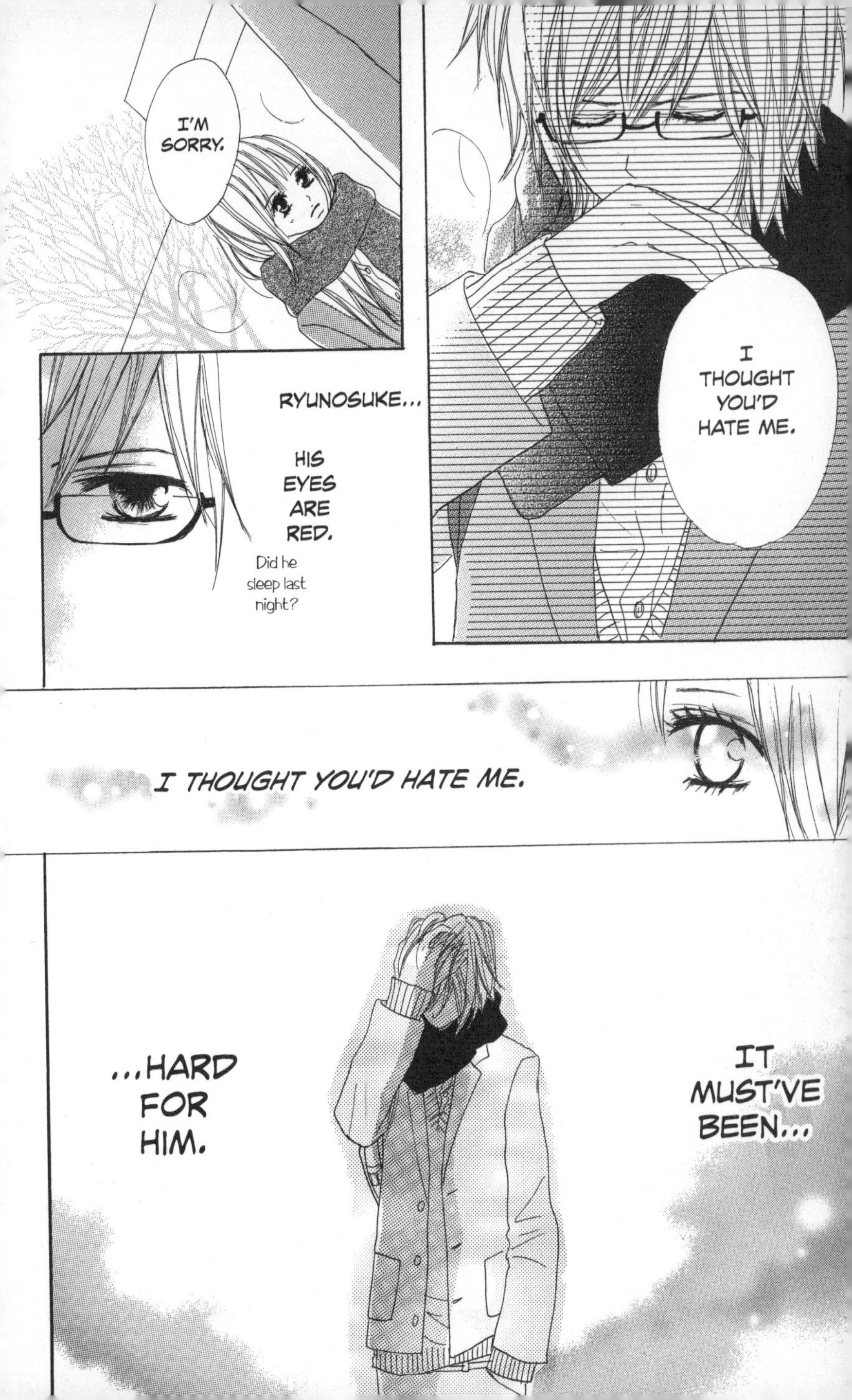
I THOUGHT YOU'D HATE ME.
I'M SORRY.
RYUNOSUKE...
HIS EYES ARE RED.
Did he sleep last night?
I THOUGHT YOU'D HATE ME.
IT MUST'VE BEEN...
...HARD FOR HIM.

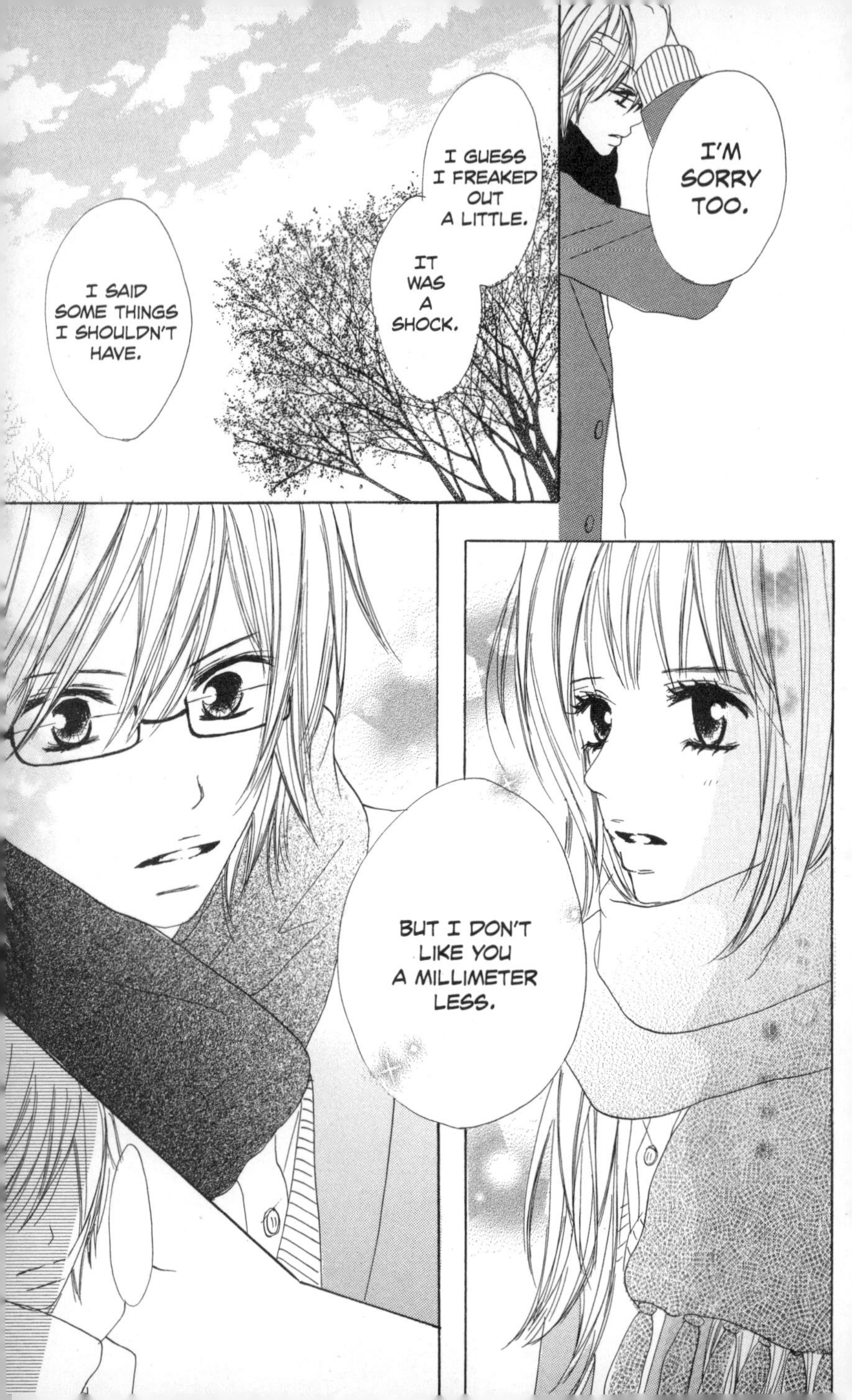
I'M SORRY TOO.
I GUESS I FREAKED OUT A LITTLE.
IT WAS A SHOCK.
I SAID SOME THINGS I SHOULDN'T HAVE.
BUT I DON'T LIKE YOU A MILLIMETER LESS.

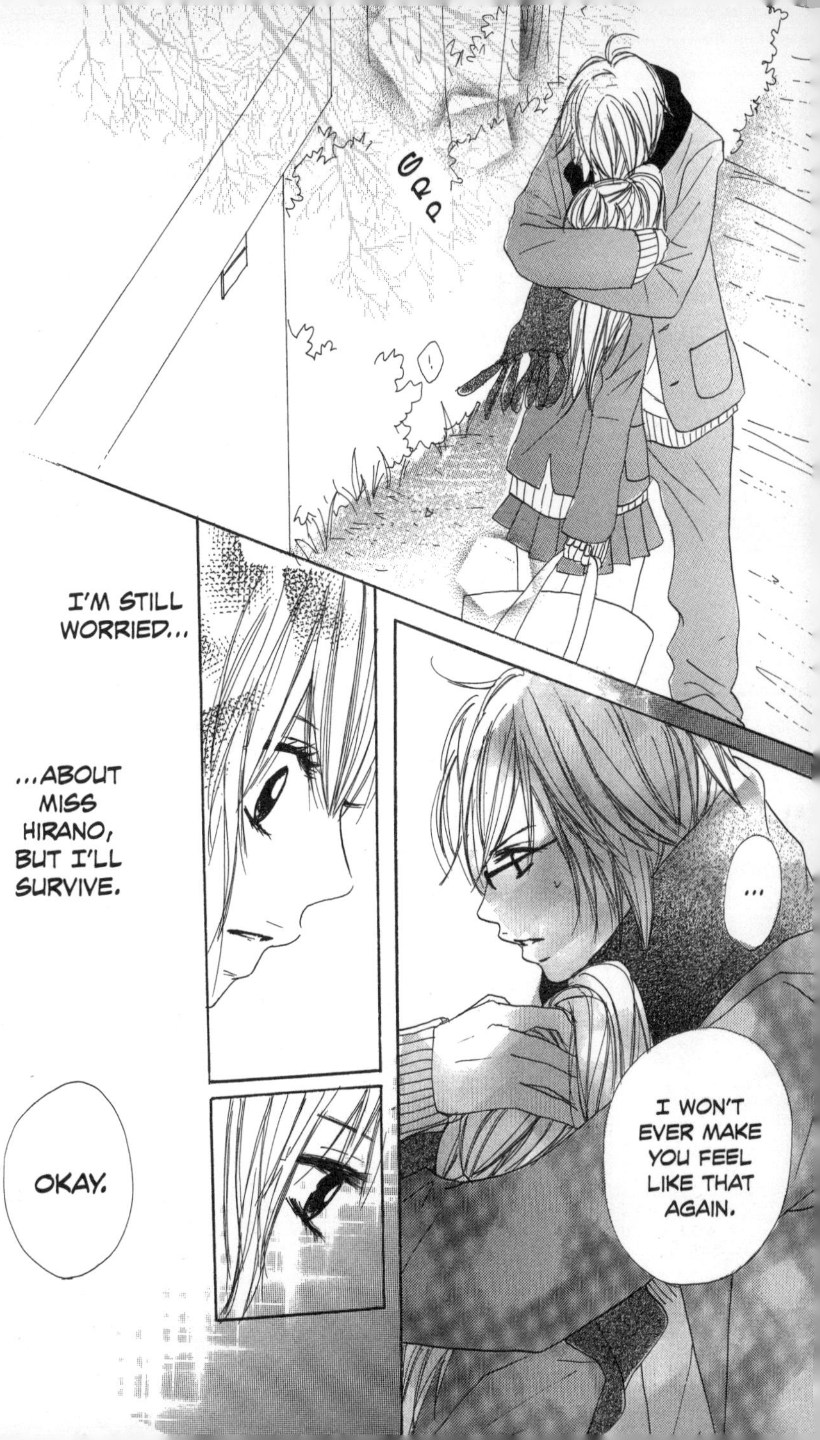
GRR
!
...
I WON'T EVER MAKE YOU FEEL LIKE THAT AGAIN.
I'M STILL WORRIED...
...ABOUT MISS HIRANO, BUT I'LL SURVIVE.
OKAY.

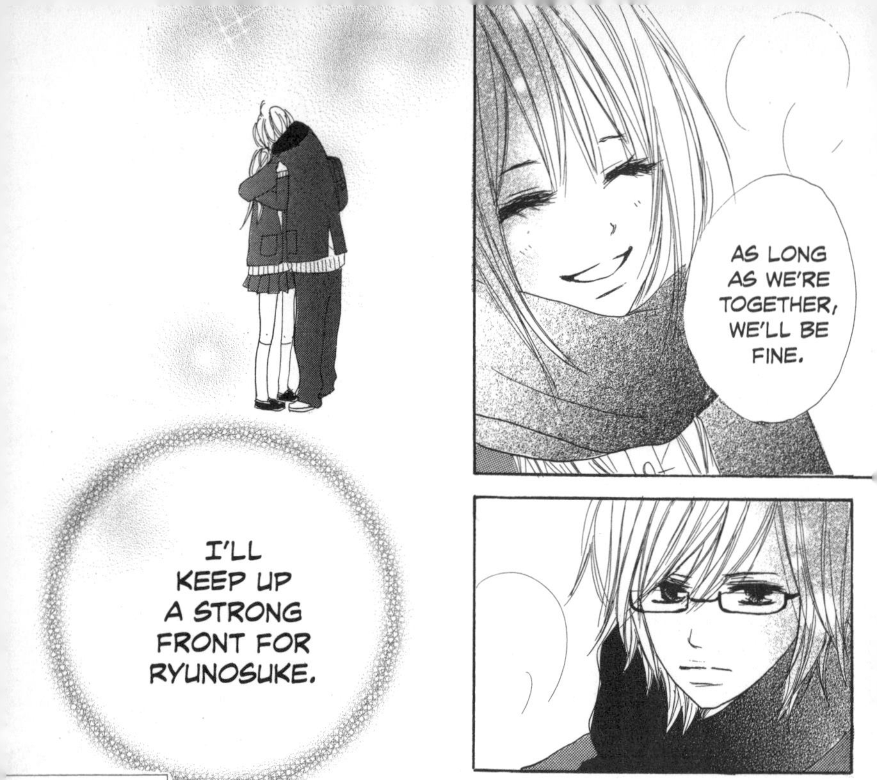
AS LONG AS WE'RE TOGETHER, WE'LL BE FINE.
I'LL KEEP UP A STRONG FRONT FOR RYUNOSUKE.

2 — 2

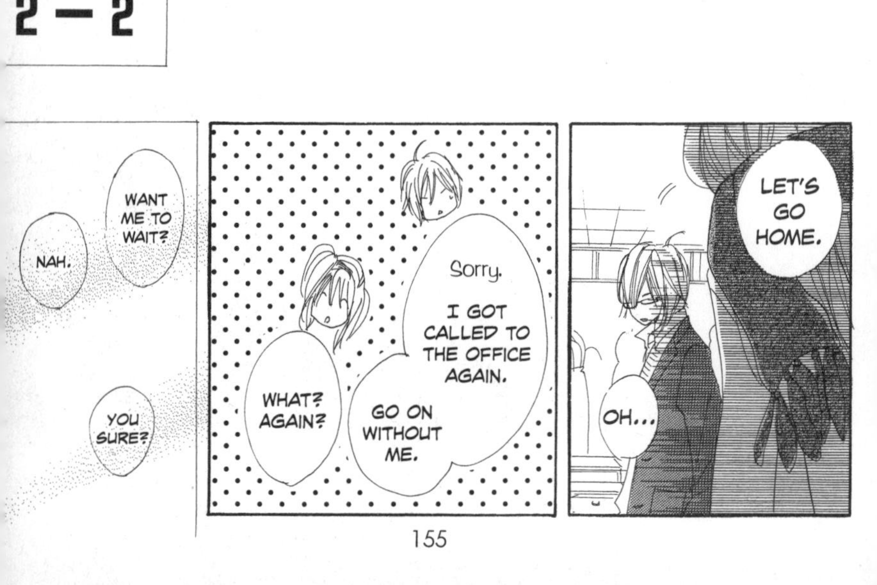
LET'S GO HOME.
OH...
Sorry.
I GOT CALLED TO THE OFFICE AGAIN.
GO ON WITHOUT ME.
WHAT? AGAIN?
WANT ME TO WAIT?
NAH.
YOU SURE?

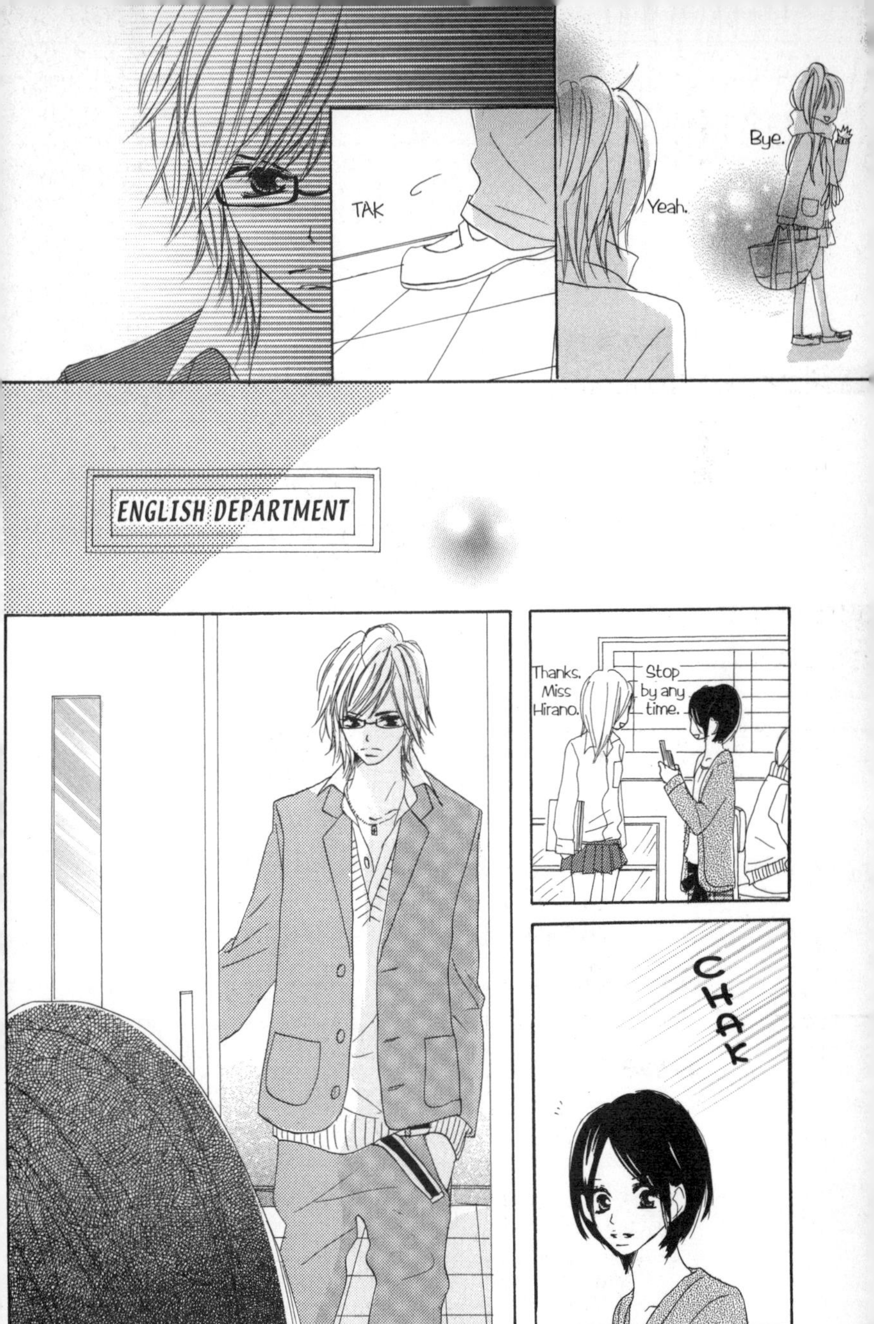
Bye.
Yeah.
TAK
ENGLISH DEPARTMENT
Stop by any time.
Thanks, Miss Hirano.
CHAK

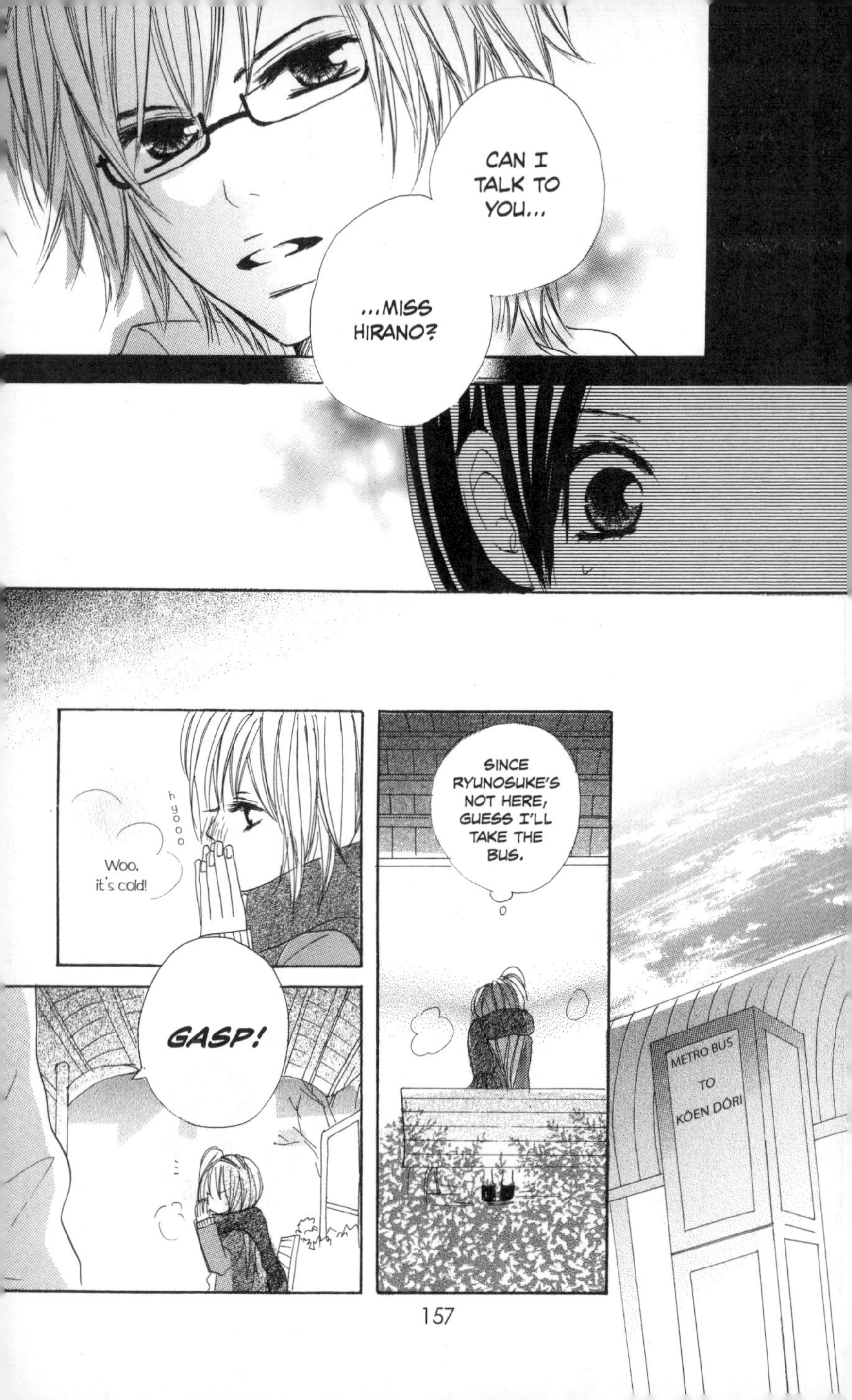
CAN I TALK TO YOU...
...MISS HIRANO?
METRO BUS TO KÔEN DÔRI
SINCE RYUNOSUKE'S NOT HERE, GUESS I'LL TAKE THE BUS.
hyooo
Woo, it's cold!
GASP!

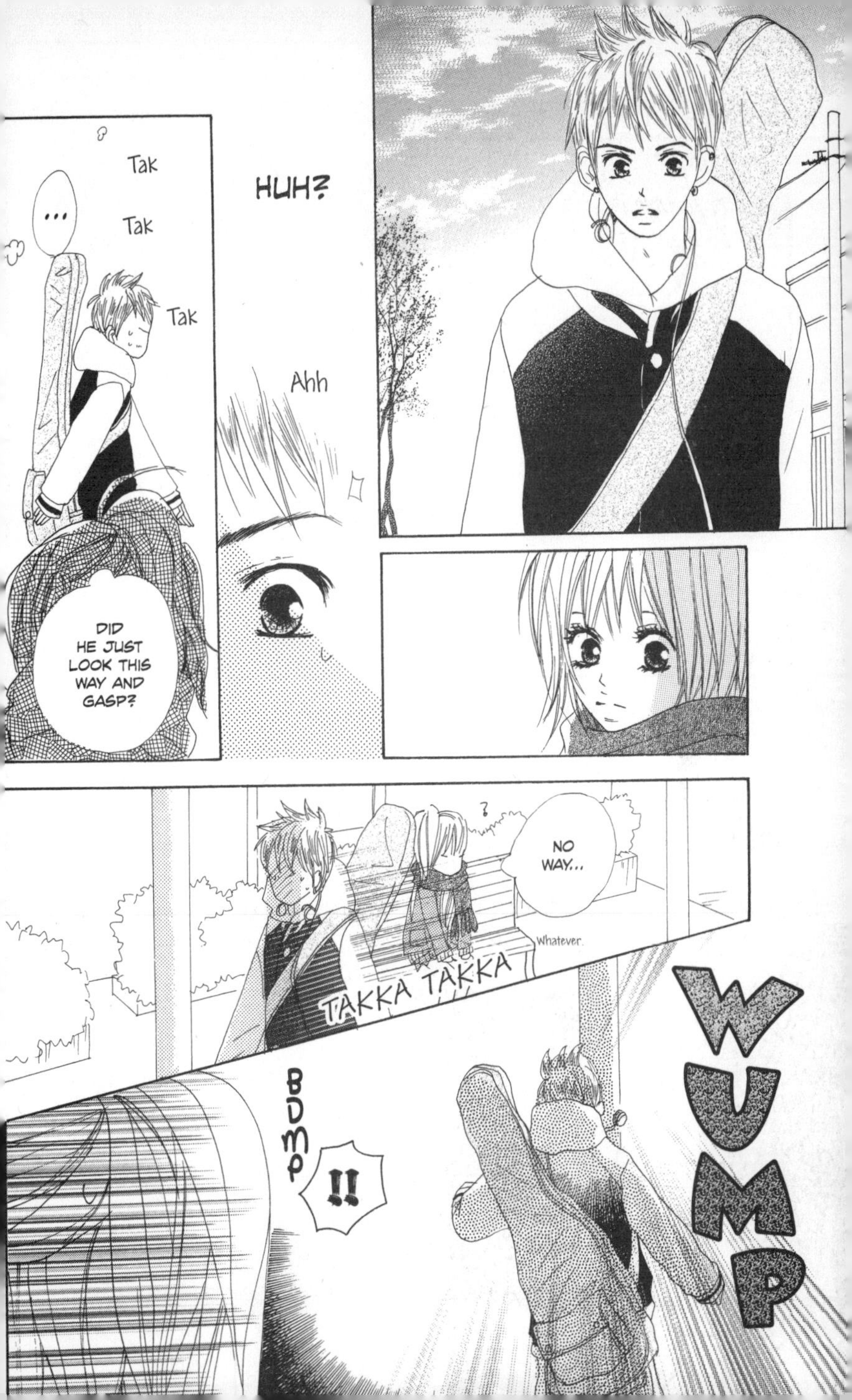
HUH?
Ahh
Tak
Tak
Tak
...
DID HE JUST LOOK THIS WAY AND GASP?
?
NO WAY...
Whatever.
TAKKA TAKKA
WUMP
BUMP
!!

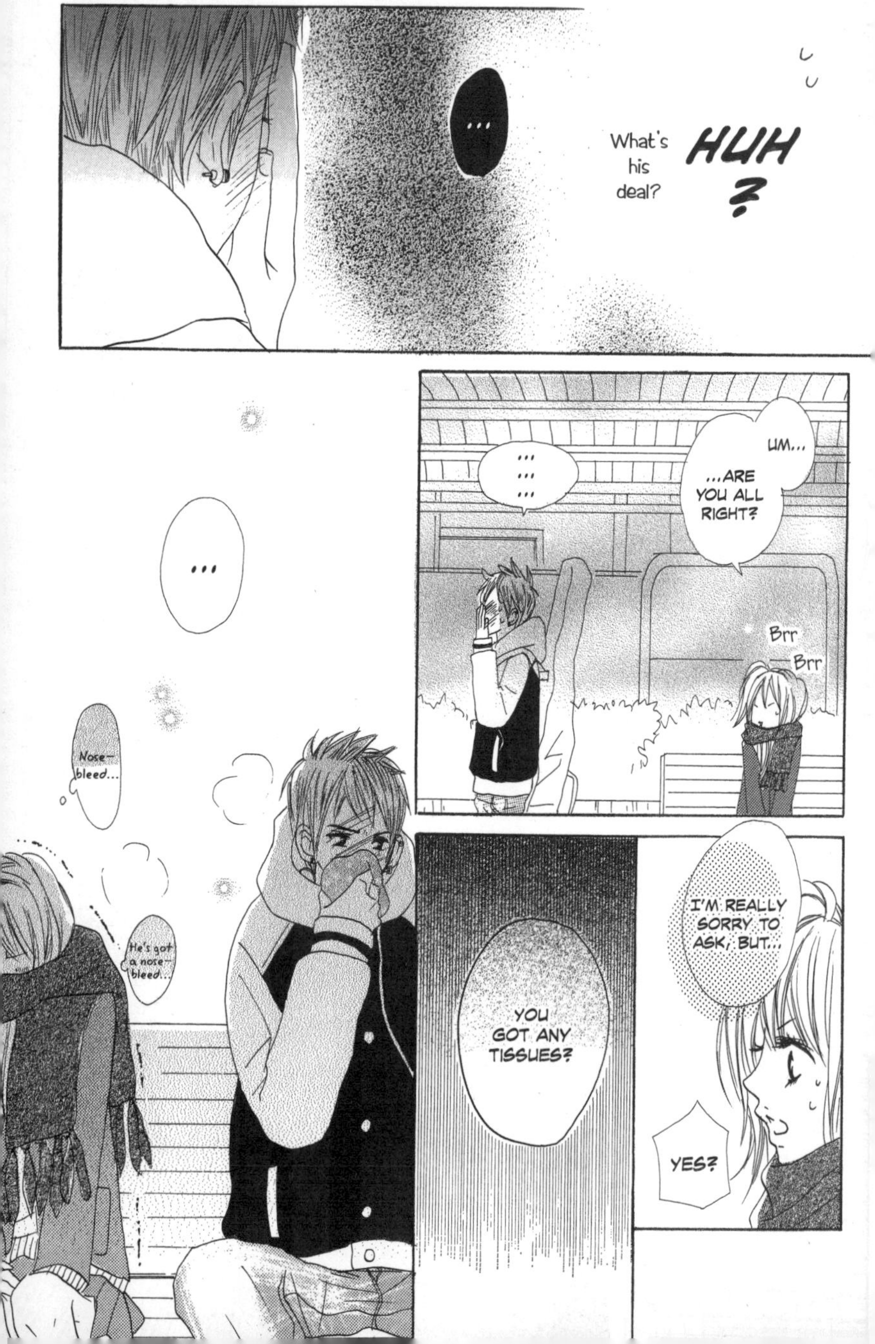
HUH?
What's his deal?
...
UM... ...ARE YOU ALL RIGHT?
Brr Brr
... ...
I'M REALLY SORRY TO ASK, BUT...
YES?
YOU GOT ANY TISSUES?
...
Nose-bleed...
He's got a nose-bleed...

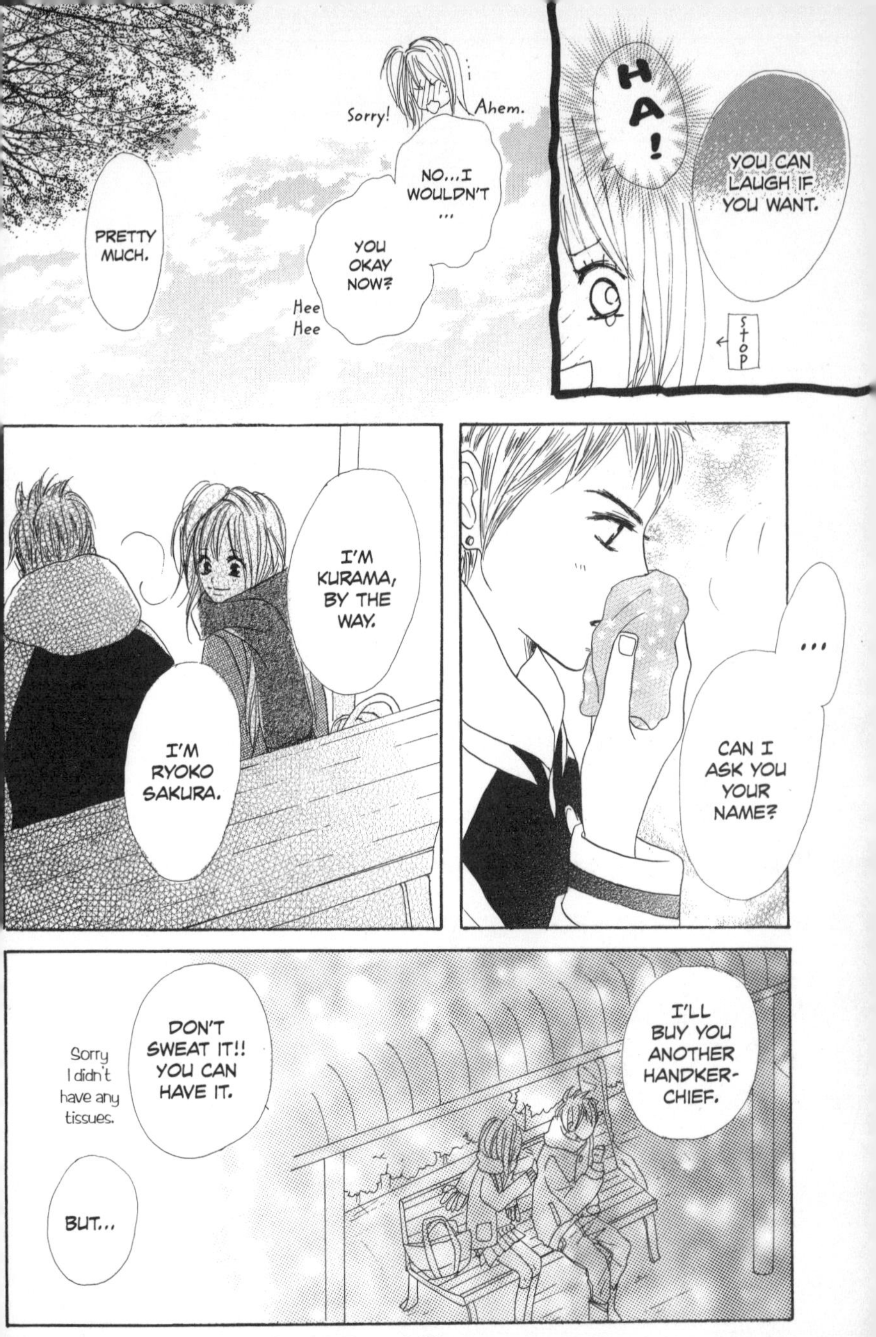

HA!
YOU CAN LAUGH IF YOU WANT.
stop
Ahem.
Sorry!
NO...I WOULDN'T ...
YOU OKAY NOW?
Hee Hee
PRETTY MUCH.
...
CAN I ASK YOU YOUR NAME?
I'M KURAMA, BY THE WAY.
I'M RYOKO SAKURA.
I'LL BUY YOU ANOTHER HANDKER-CHIEF.
DON'T SWEAT IT!! YOU CAN HAVE IT.
Sorry I didn't have any tissues.
BUT...

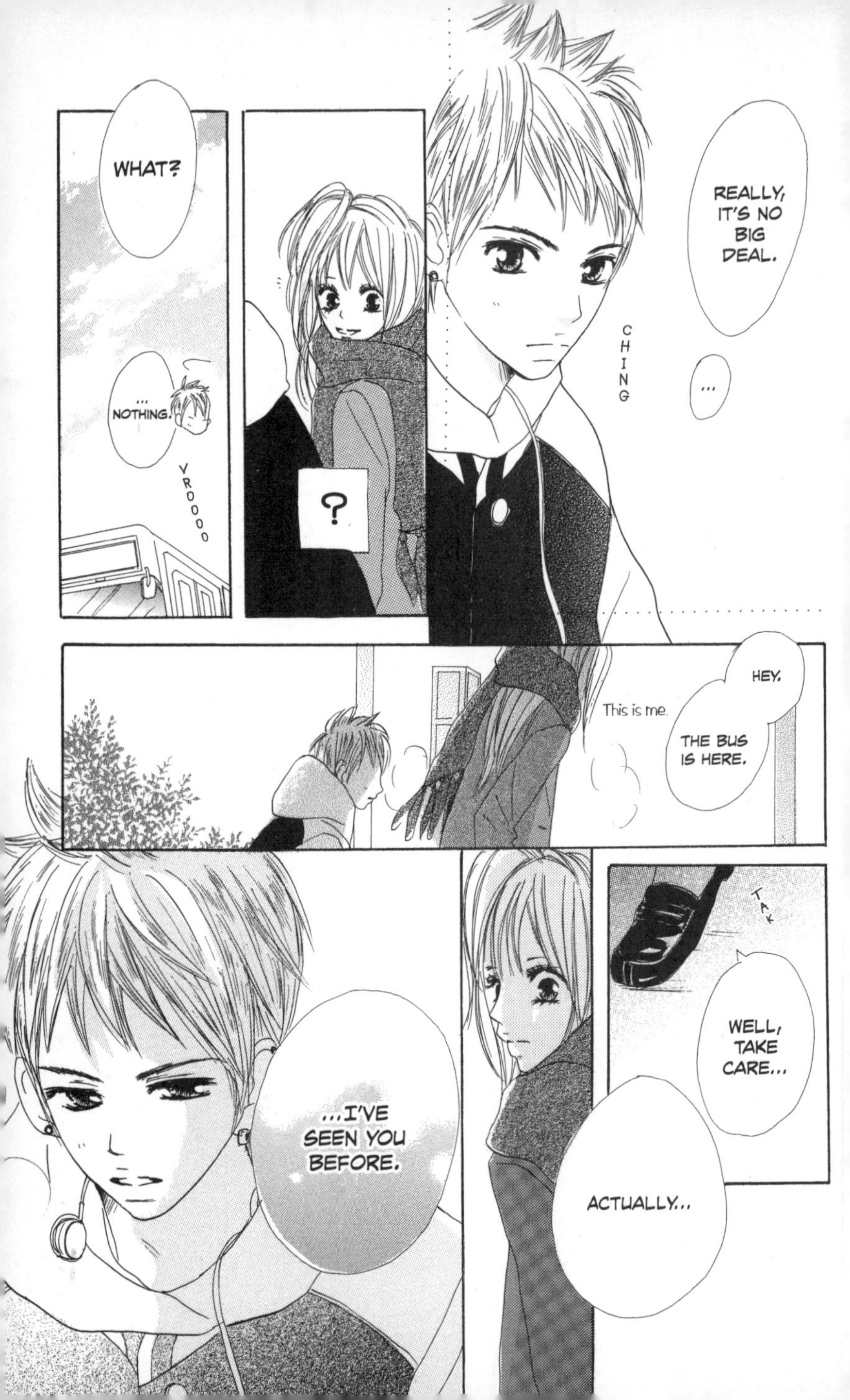
REALLY, IT'S NO BIG DEAL.
CHING
...
?
WHAT?
... NOTHING.
VROOOOO
HEY.
THE BUS IS HERE.
This is me.
TAK
WELL, TAKE CARE...
ACTUALLY...
...I'VE SEEN YOU BEFORE.

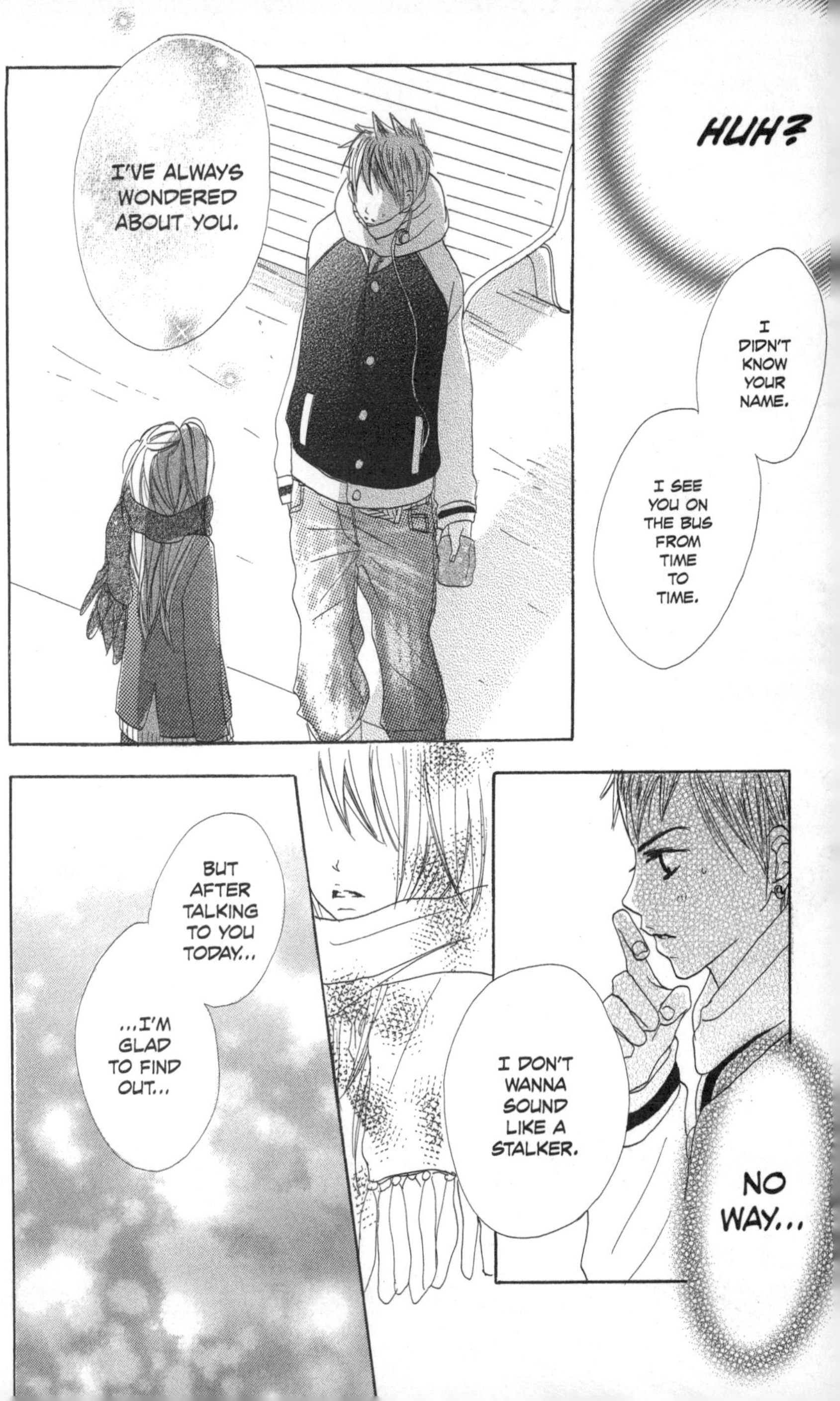
HUH?
I DIDN'T KNOW YOUR NAME.
I SEE YOU ON THE BUS FROM TIME TO TIME.
I'VE ALWAYS WONDERED ABOUT YOU.
I DON'T WANNA SOUND LIKE A STALKER.
NO WAY...
BUT AFTER TALKING TO YOU TODAY...
...I'M GLAD TO FIND OUT...

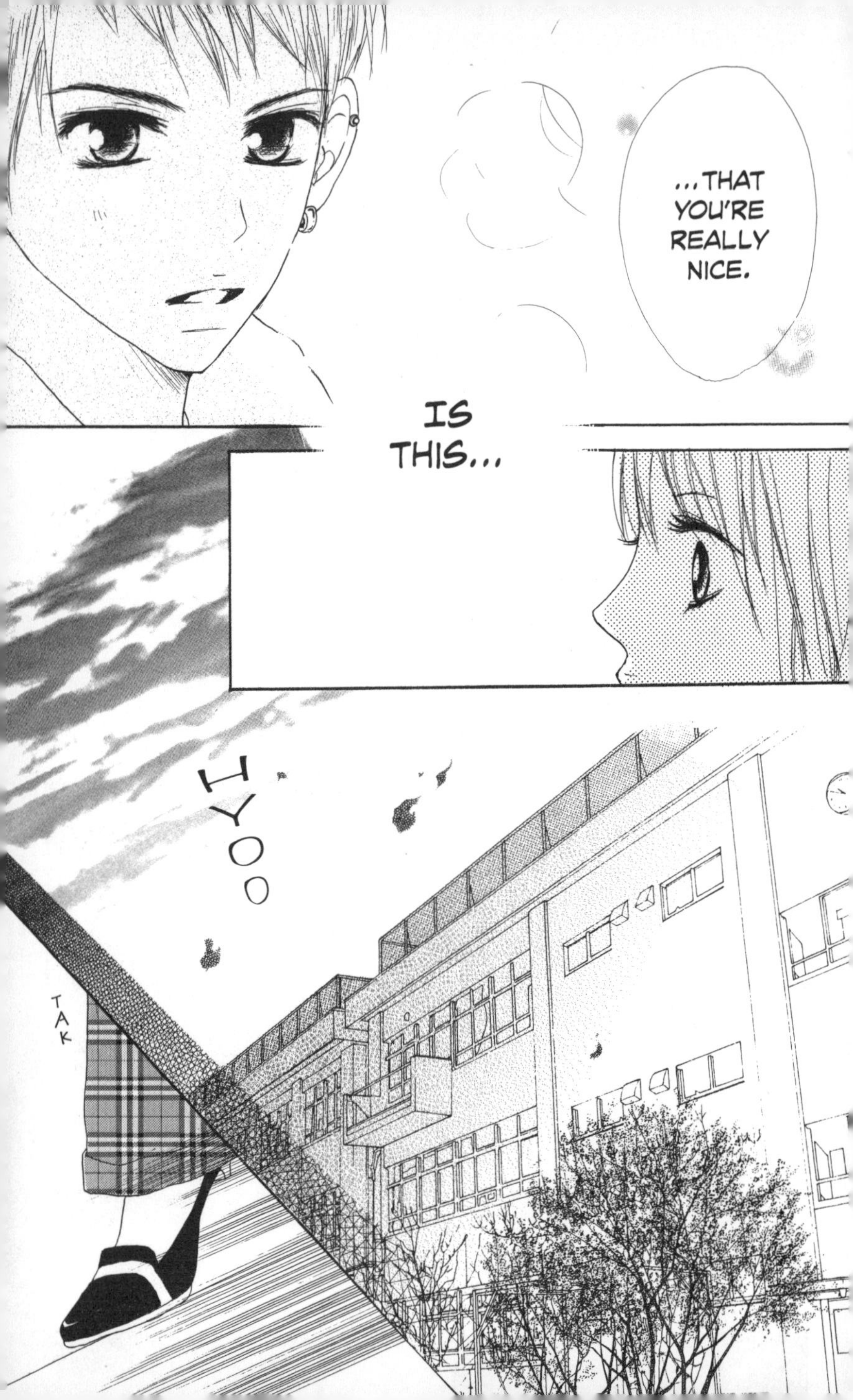

...THAT YOU'RE REALLY NICE.
IS THIS...
HYOO
TAK

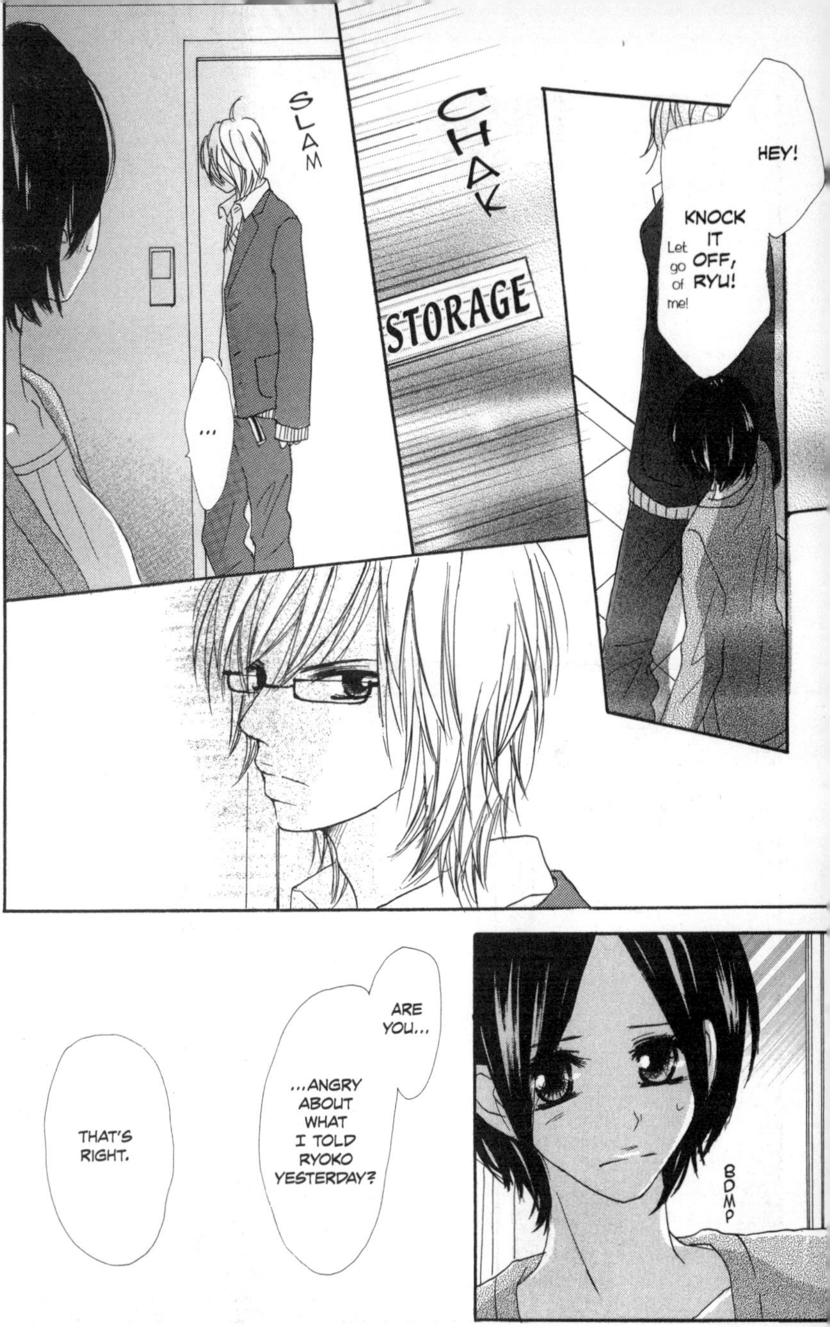
HEY!
KNOCK IT OFF, RYU!
Let go of me!
CHAK
STORAGE
SLAM
...
BDMP
ARE YOU...
...ANGRY ABOUT WHAT I TOLD RYOKO YESTERDAY?
THAT'S RIGHT.

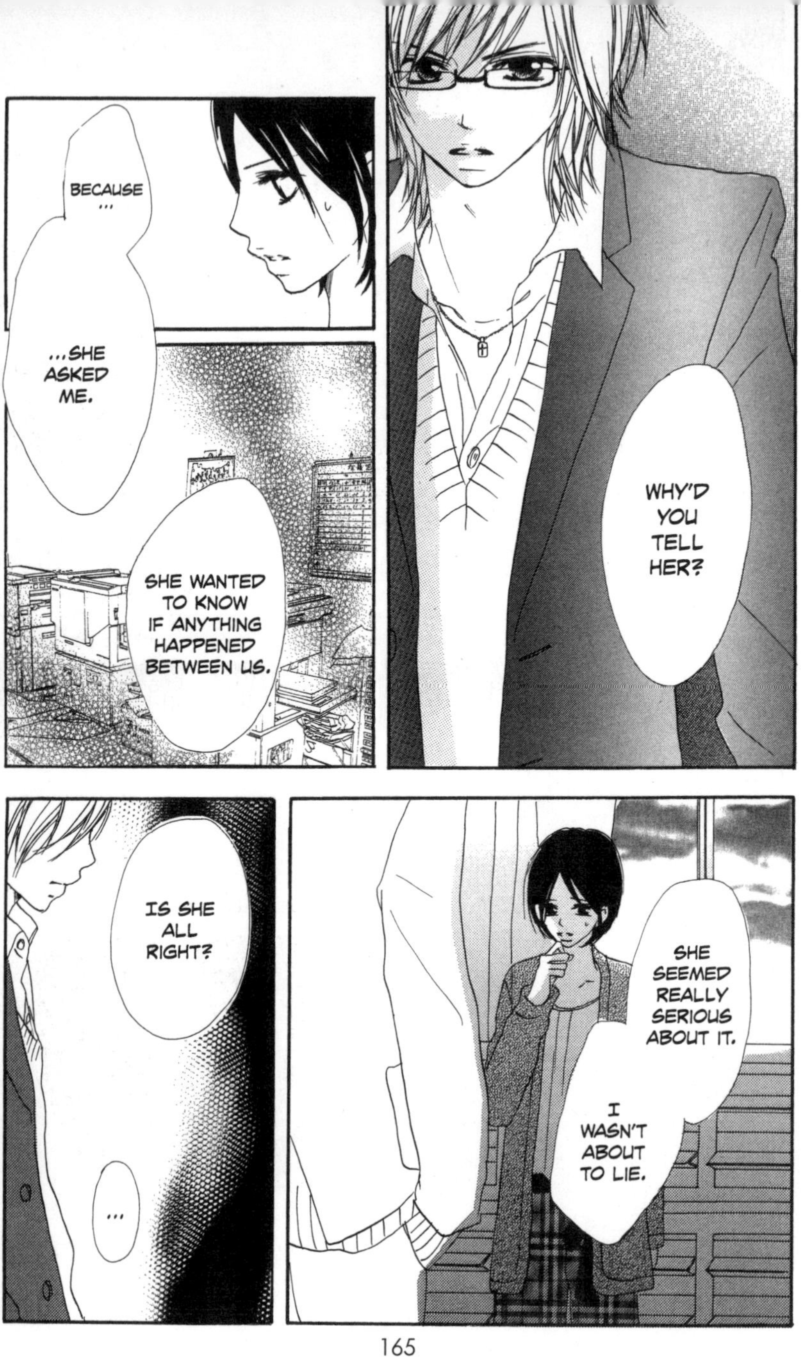
WHY'D YOU TELL HER?
BECAUSE ...
...SHE ASKED ME.
SHE WANTED TO KNOW IF ANYTHING HAPPENED BETWEEN US.
SHE SEEMED REALLY SERIOUS ABOUT IT.
I WASN'T ABOUT TO LIE.
IS SHE ALL RIGHT?
...

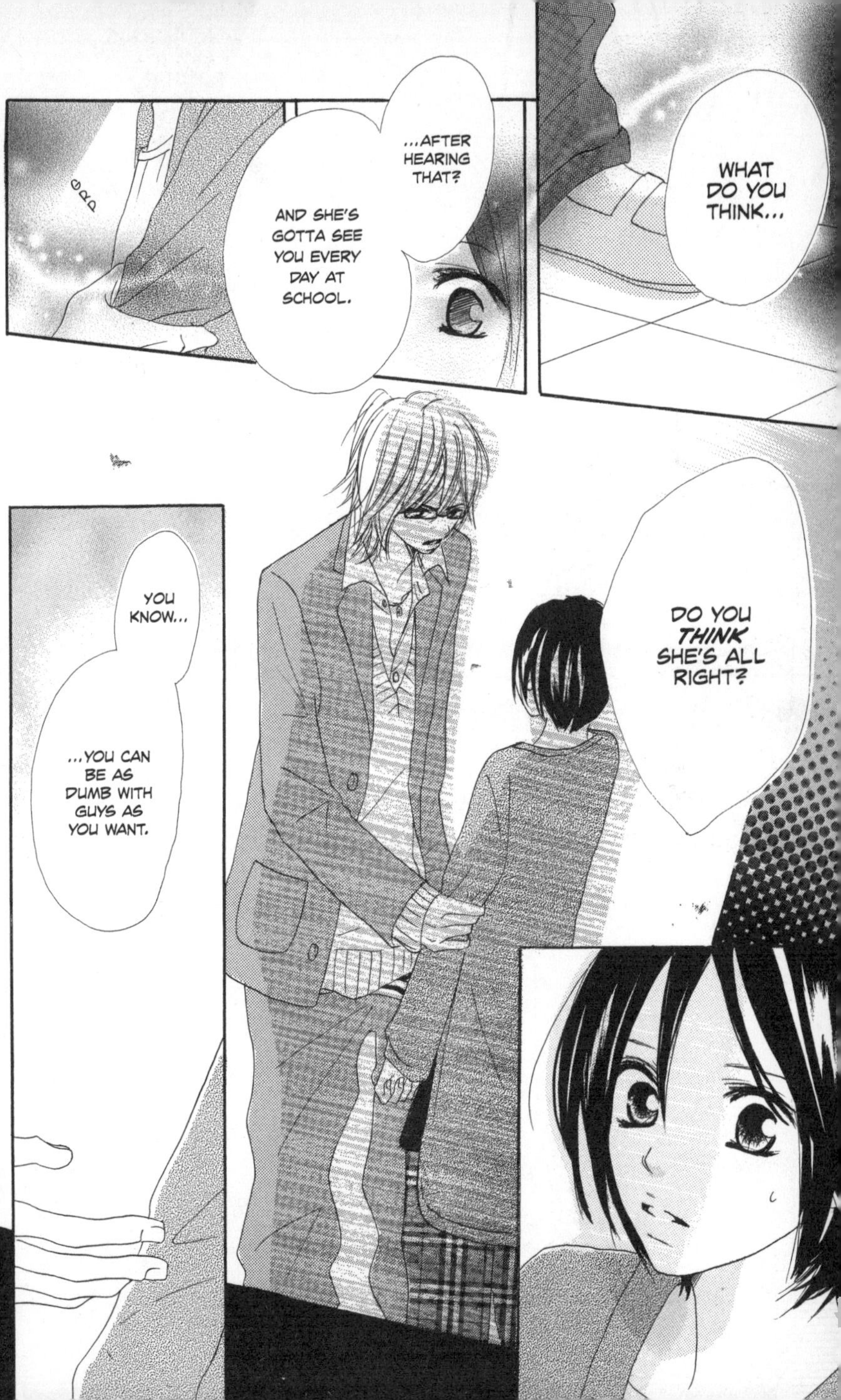
WHAT DO YOU THINK...
...AFTER HEARING THAT?
AND SHE'S GOTTA SEE YOU EVERY DAY AT SCHOOL.
DO YOU *THINK* SHE'S ALL RIGHT?
YOU KNOW...
...YOU CAN BE AS DUMB WITH GUYS AS YOU WANT.

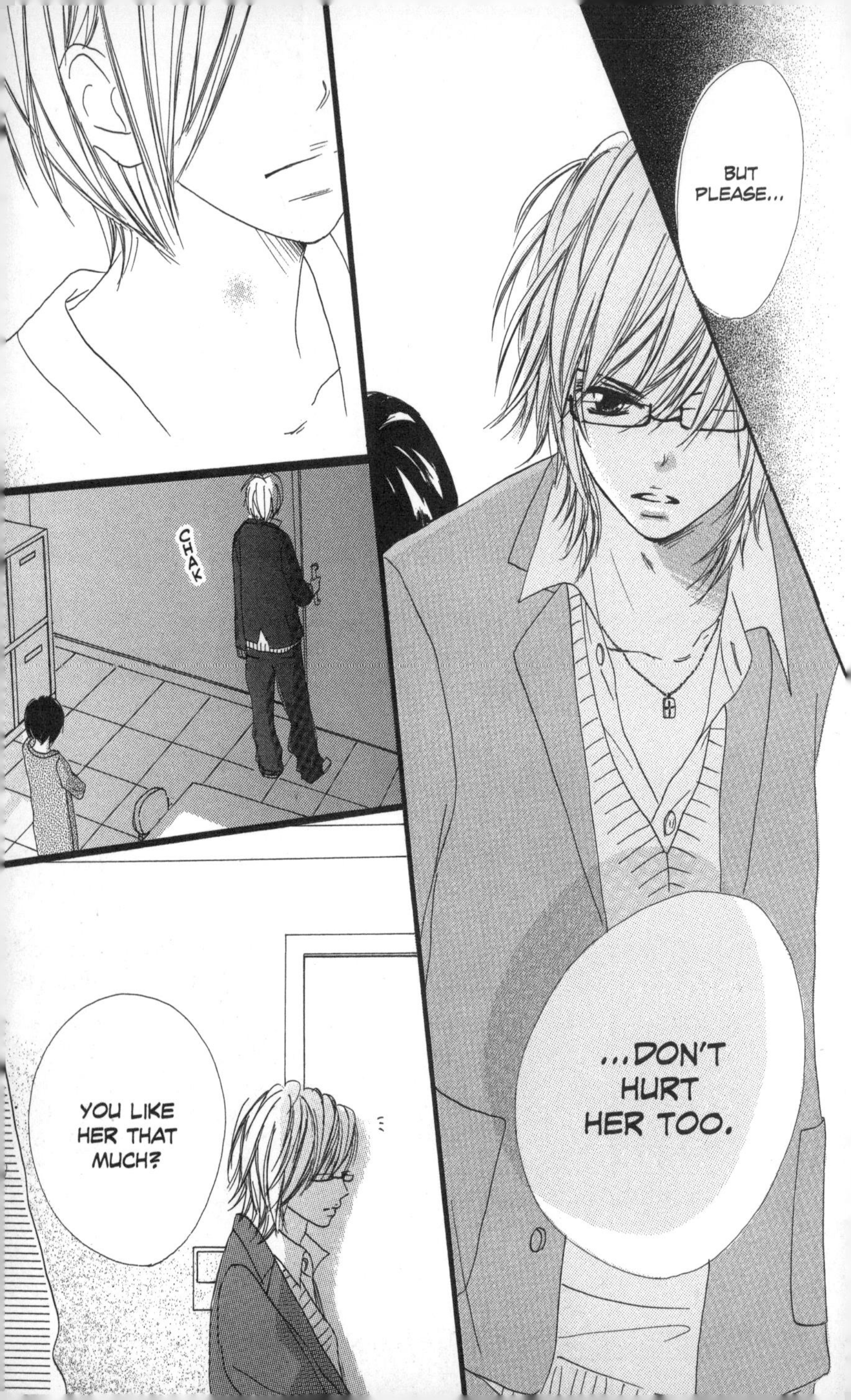
BUT PLEASE...
...DON'T HURT HER TOO.
CHAK
YOU LIKE HER THAT MUCH?

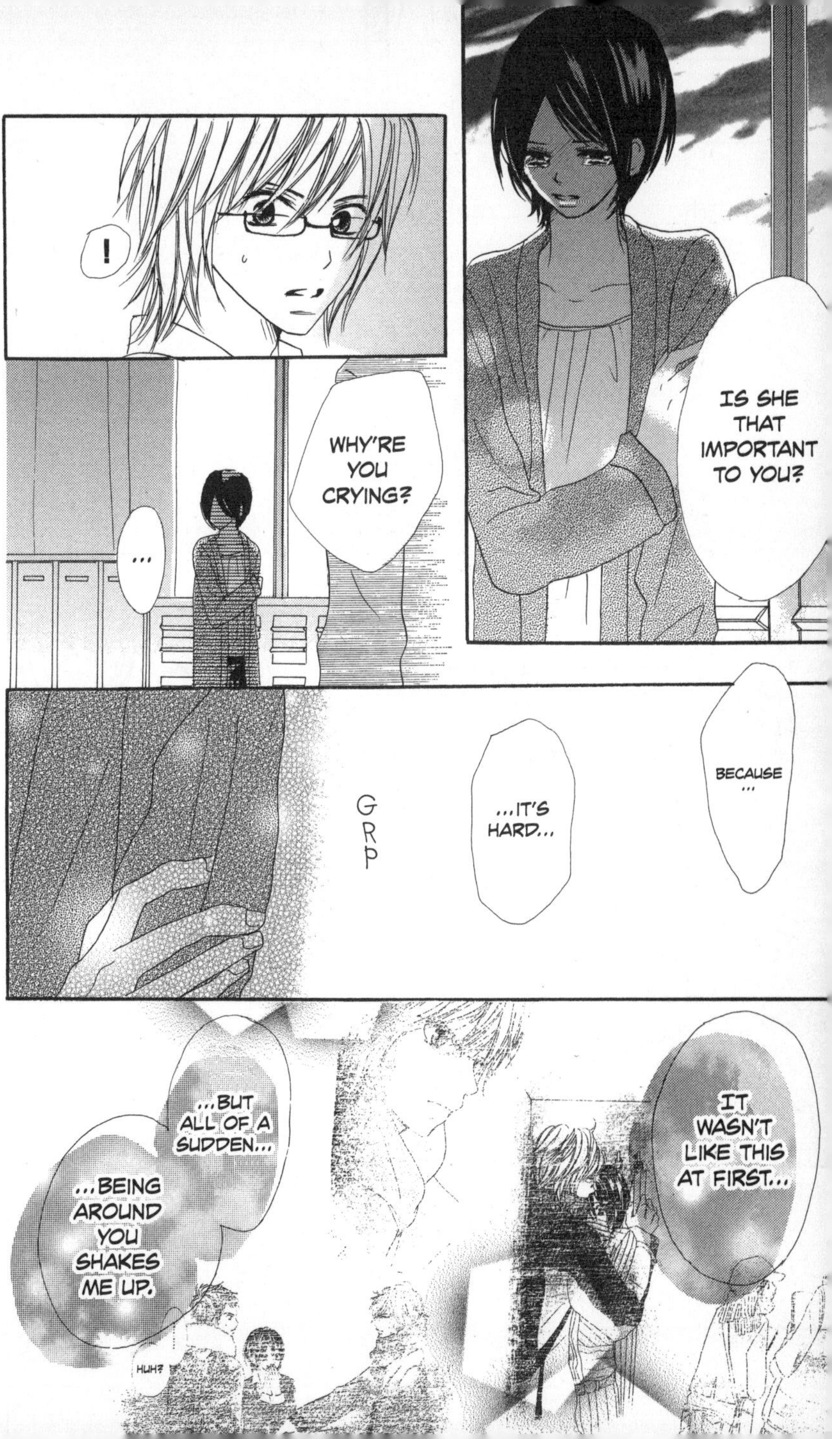
IS SHE THAT IMPORTANT TO YOU?
!
WHY'RE YOU CRYING?
...
BECAUSE ...
...IT'S HARD...
GRP
IT WASN'T LIKE THIS AT FIRST...
...BUT ALL OF A SUDDEN...
...BEING AROUND YOU SHAKES ME UP.
HUH?

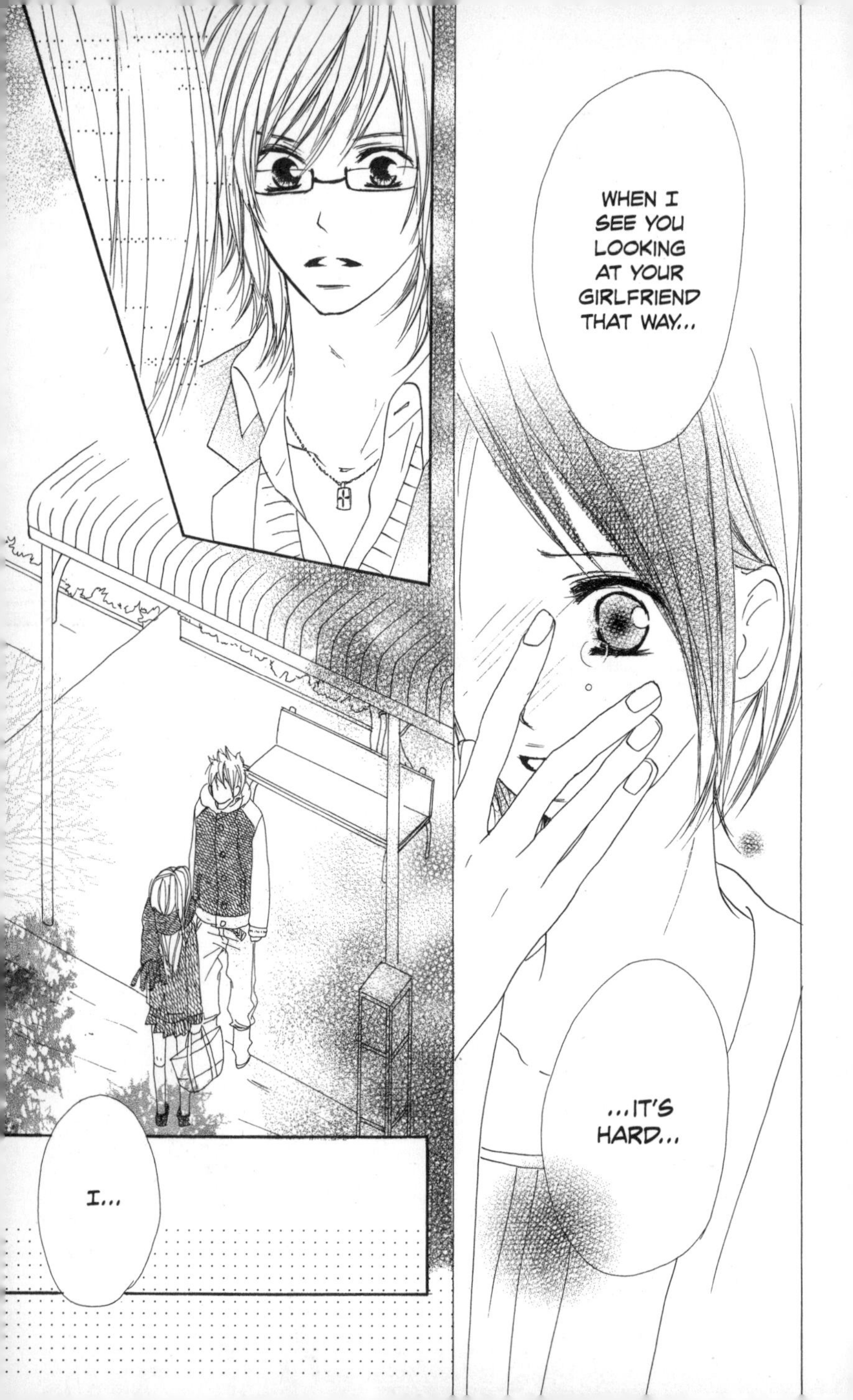
WHEN I SEE YOU LOOKING AT YOUR GIRLFRIEND THAT WAY...
...IT'S HARD...
I...

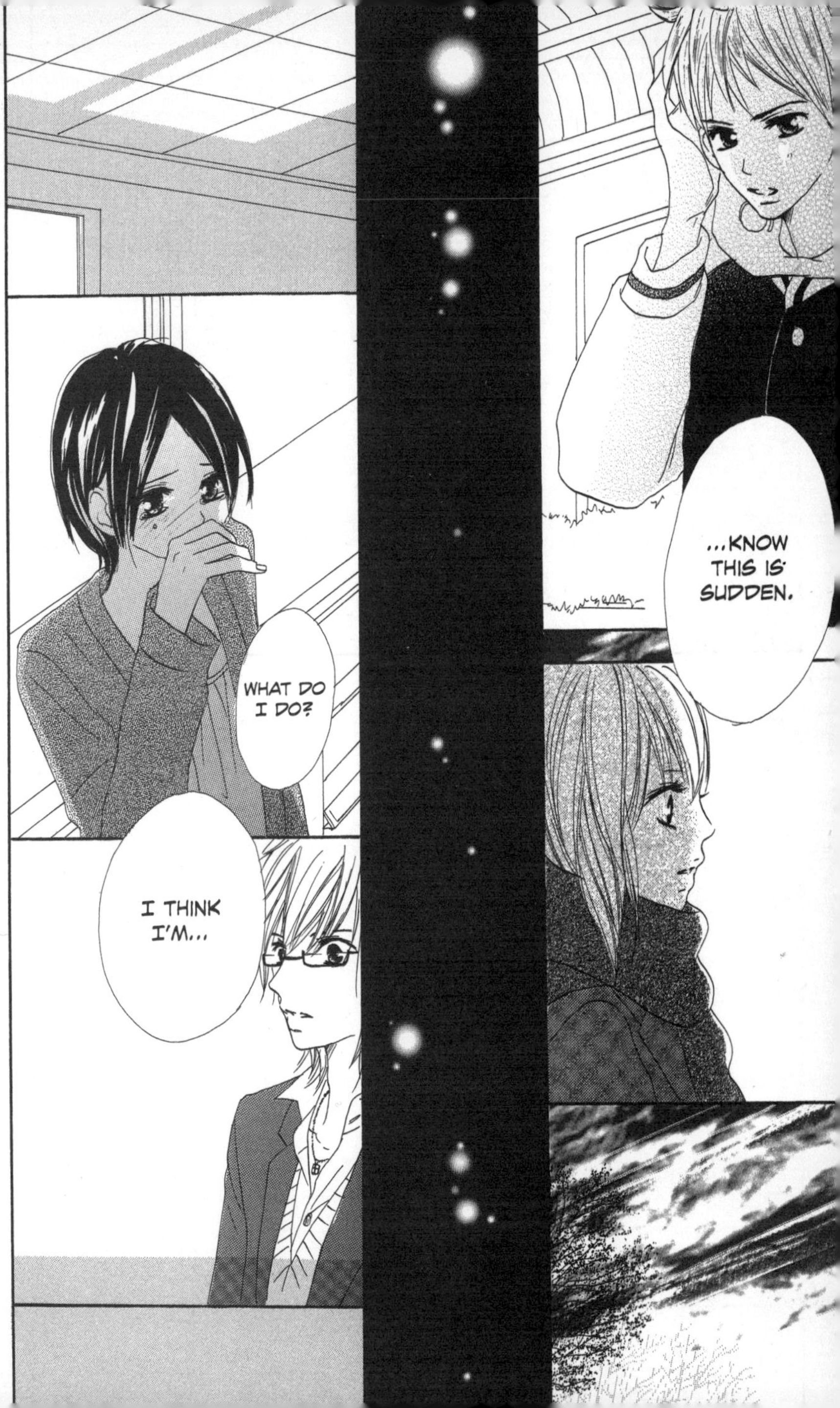
...KNOW THIS IS SUDDEN.
WHAT DO I DO?
I THINK I'M...

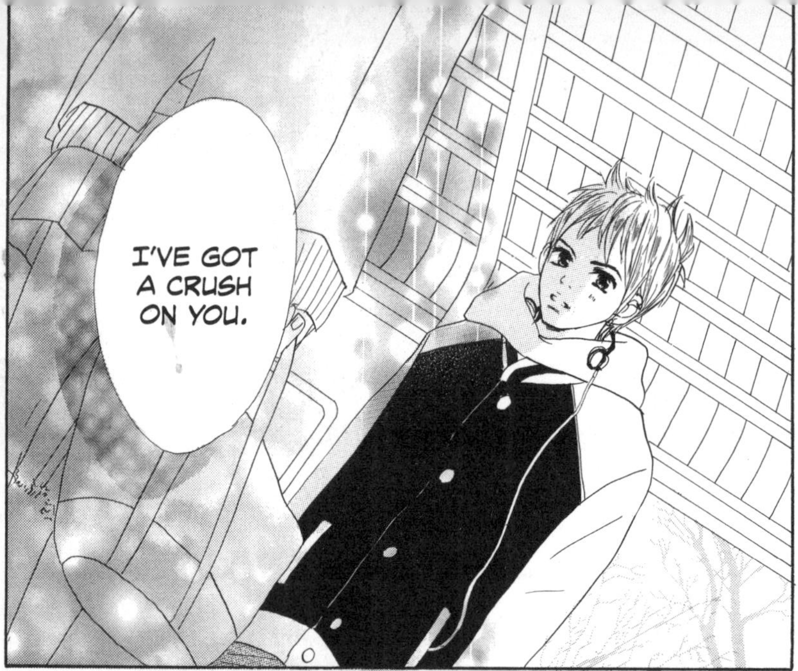
I'VE GOT A CRUSH ON YOU.
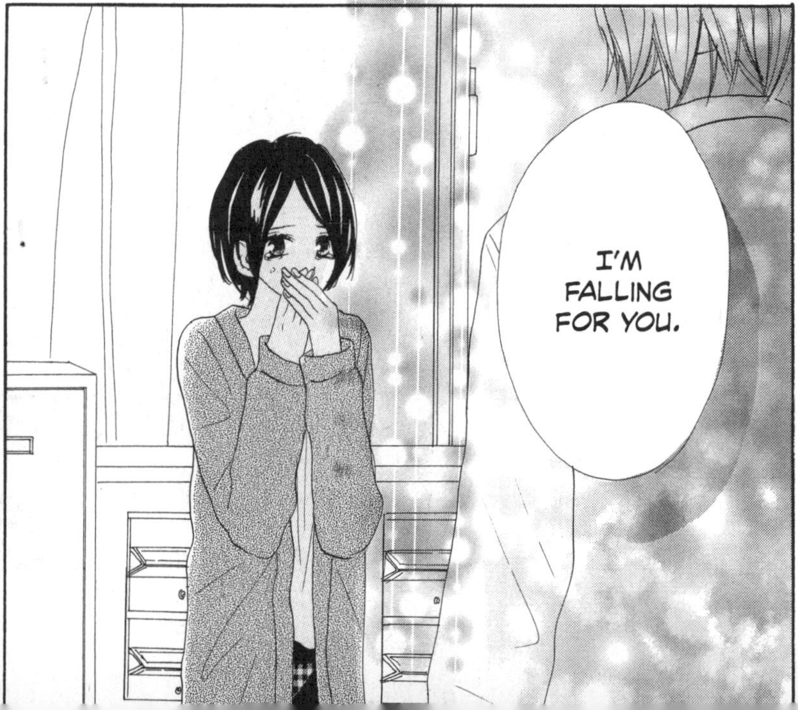
I'M FALLING FOR YOU.

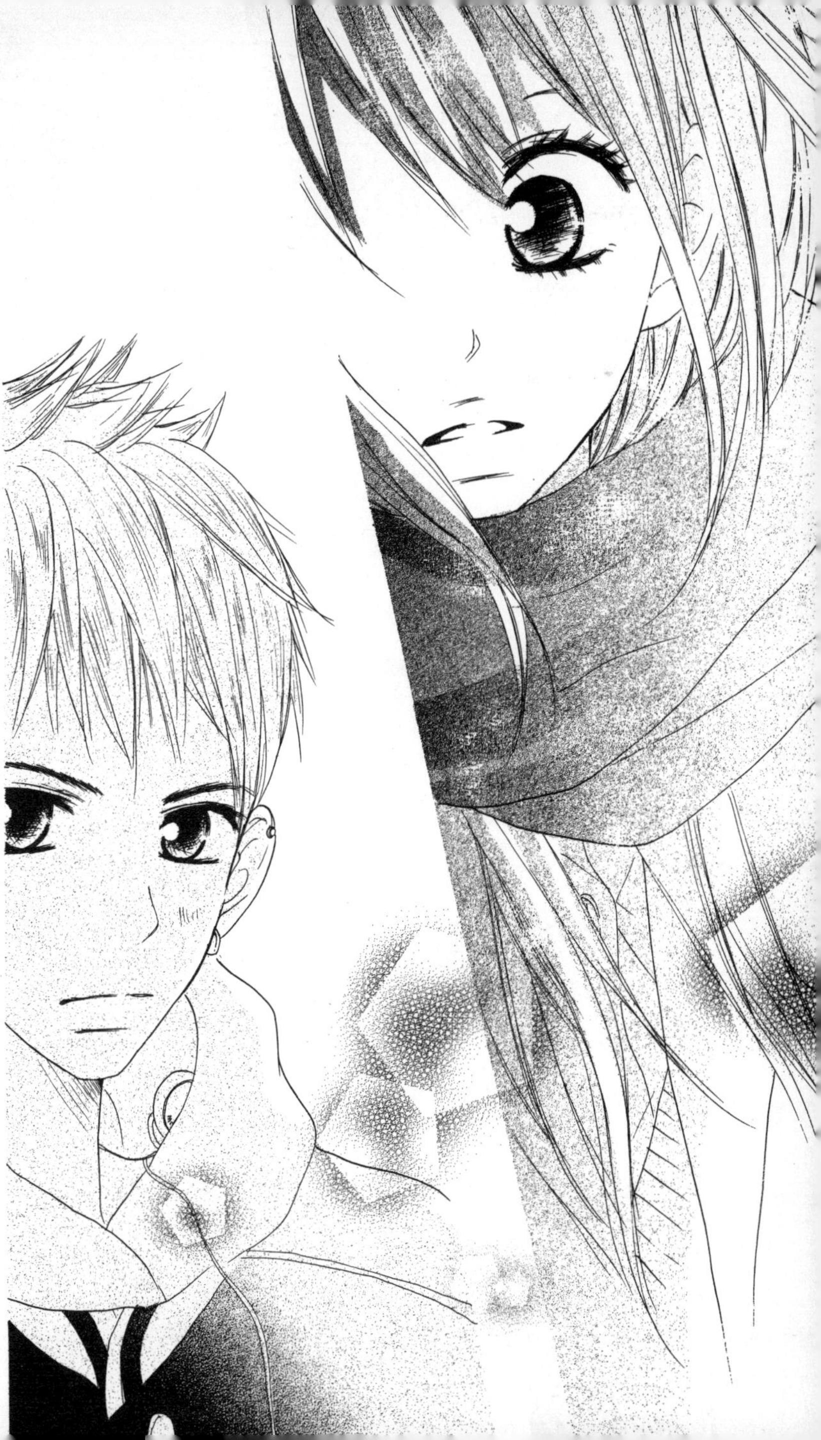

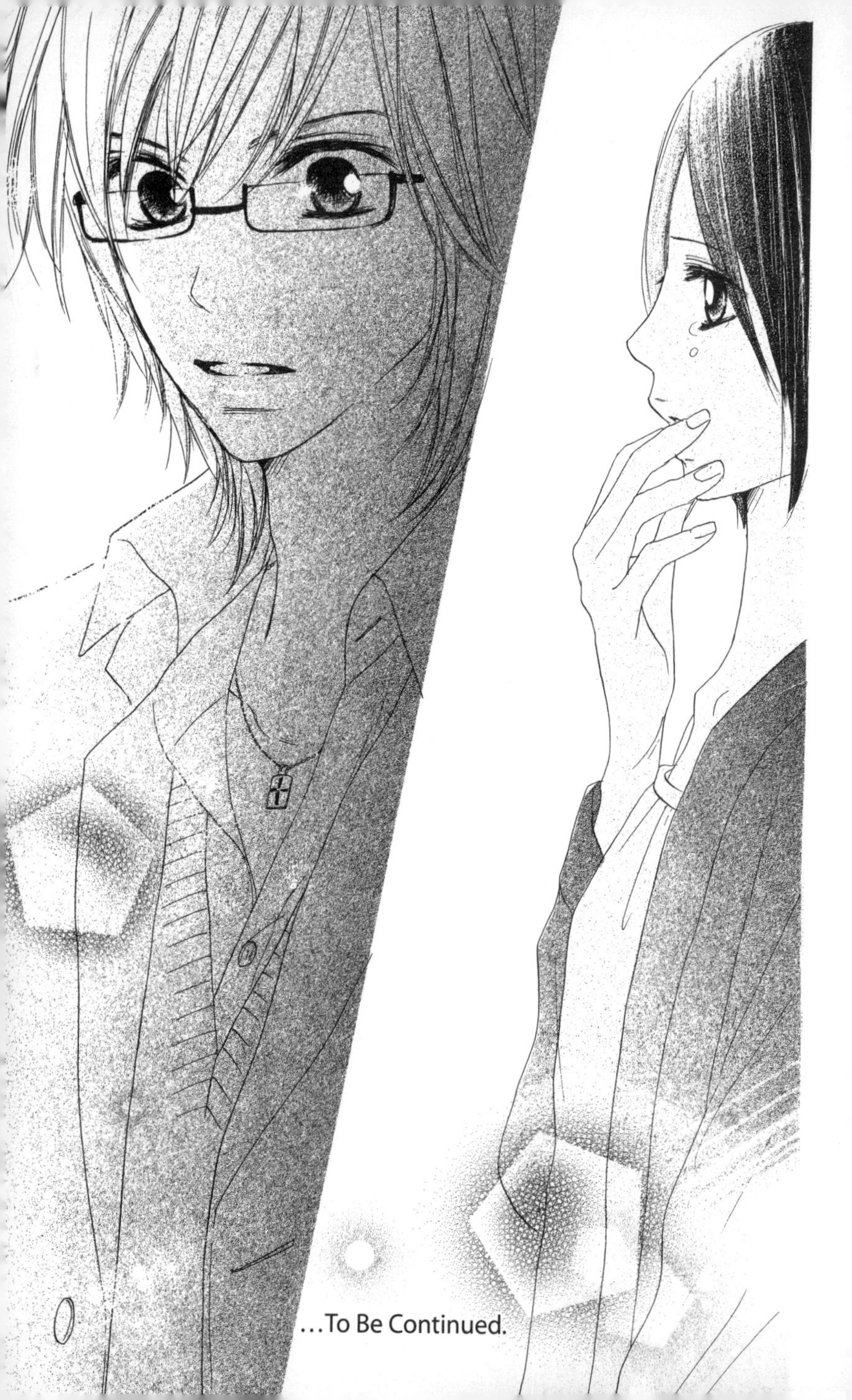
...To Be Continued.

Hello, everybody!!

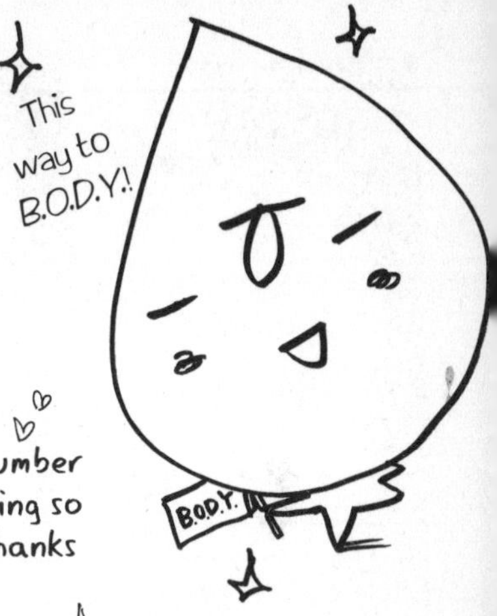
This way to B.O.D.Y.!
B.O.D.Y.

Volume 7's finally here! Lucky number seven!! I'm glad you're still reading so we can keep meeting like this. Thanks so much!

The bonus features for this volume are...

- How Ryunosuke's Parents Met Short Story
- Ao Does a Radio Show
- Drama CD Info
- Mailbag

That's right... I went on the radio...

I worked hard on all of this, so I'd be really grateful if you took your time reading it. Ha ha ha!

GO!!

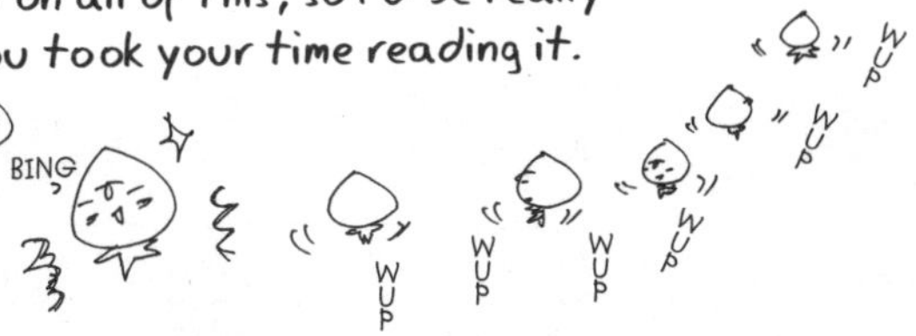
BING
WUP
WUP
WUP
WUP
WUP
WUP

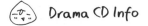

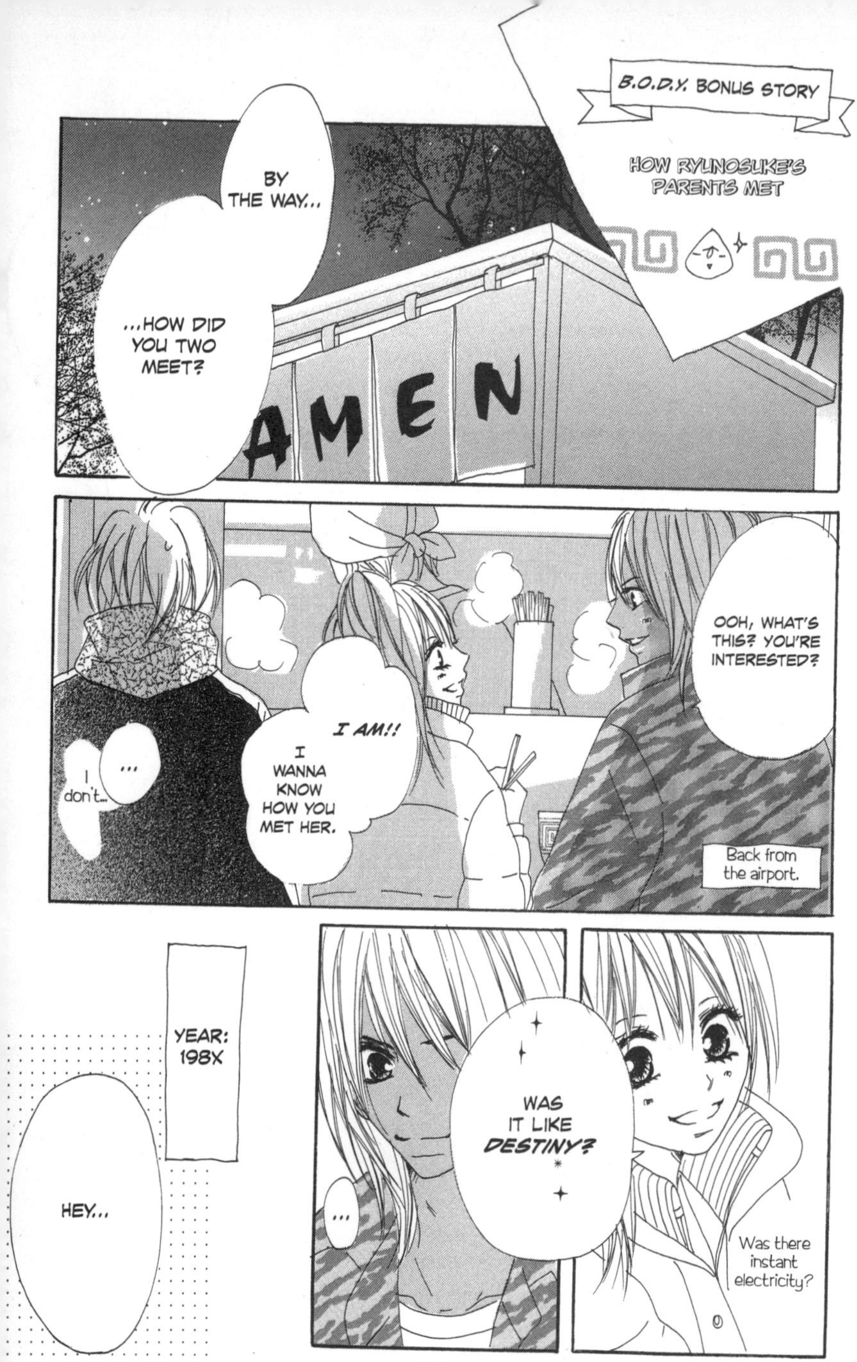
B.O.D.Y. BONUS STORY
HOW RYUNOSUKE'S PARENTS MET
BY THE WAY...
...HOW DID YOU TWO MEET?
AMEN
OOH, WHAT'S THIS? YOU'RE INTERESTED?
Back from the airport.
I AM!! I WANNA KNOW HOW YOU MET HER.
...
I don't...
WAS IT LIKE DESTINY?
Was there instant electricity?
...
YEAR: 198X
HEY...

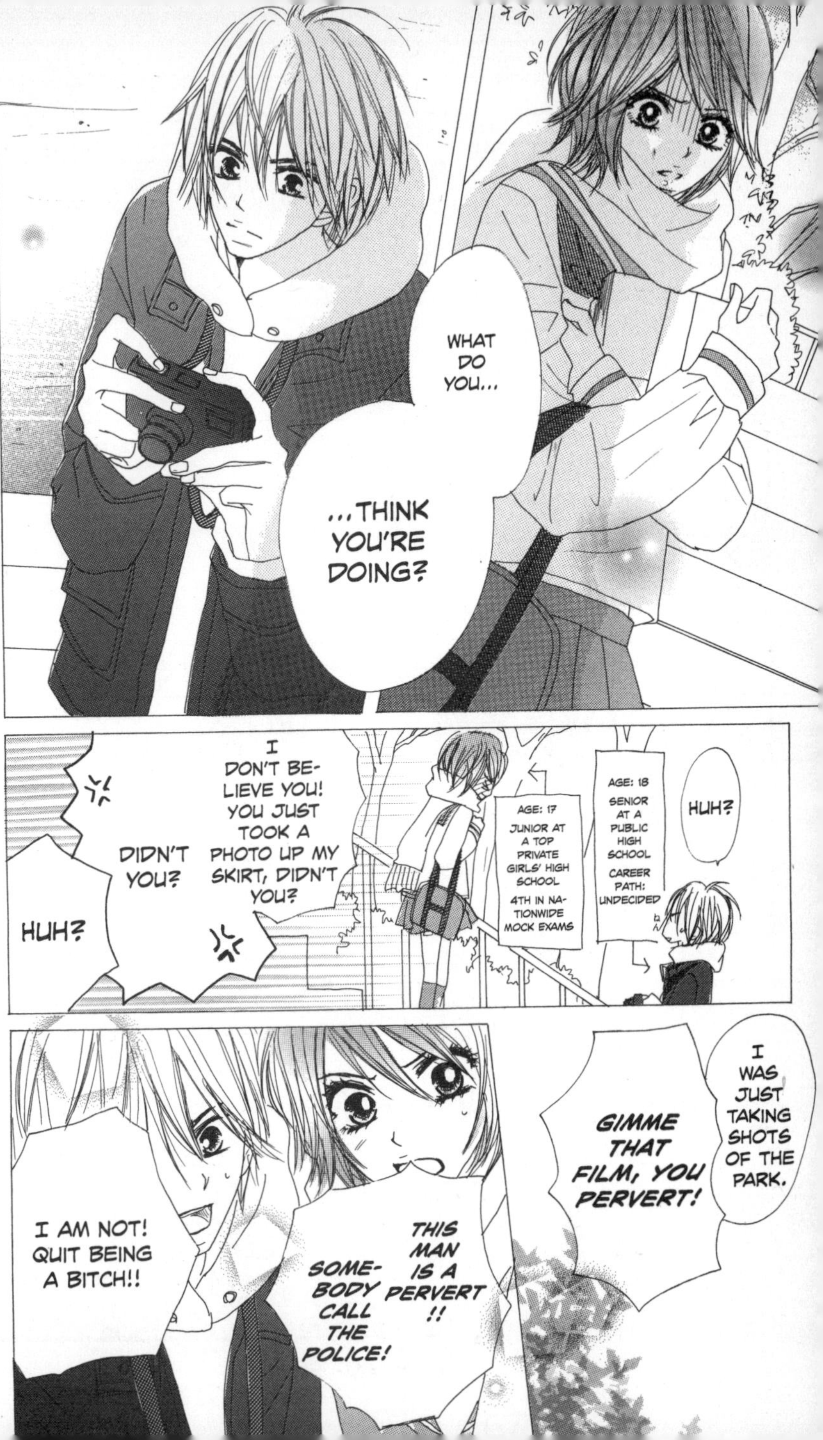
WHAT DO YOU...
...THINK YOU'RE DOING?
HUH?
AGE: 18 SENIOR AT A PUBLIC HIGH SCHOOL CAREER PATH: UNDECIDED
AGE: 17 JUNIOR AT A TOP PRIVATE GIRLS' HIGH SCHOOL 4TH IN NATIONWIDE MOCK EXAMS
I DON'T BELIEVE YOU! YOU JUST TOOK A PHOTO UP MY SKIRT, DIDN'T YOU?
DIDN'T YOU?
HUH?
I WAS JUST TAKING SHOTS OF THE PARK.
GIMME THAT FILM, YOU PERVERT!
THIS MAN IS A PERVERT!!
SOMEBODY CALL THE POLICE!
I AM NOT! QUIT BEING A BITCH!!

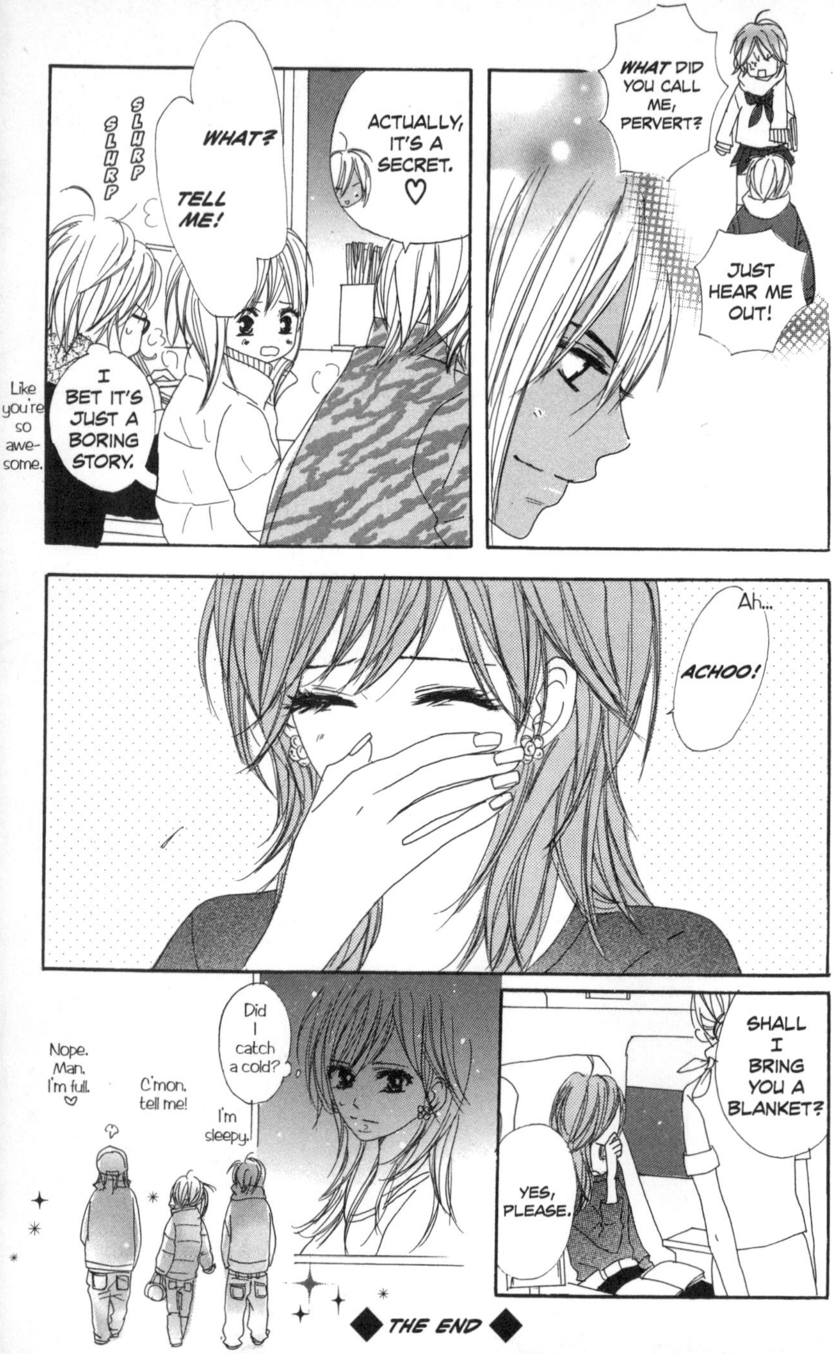
WHAT DID YOU CALL ME, PERVERT?
JUST HEAR ME OUT!
ACTUALLY, IT'S A SECRET. ♥
WHAT? TELL ME!
SLURP SLURP
I BET IT'S JUST A BORING STORY.
Like you're so awesome.
Ah...
ACHOO!
SHALL I BRING YOU A BLANKET?
YES, PLEASE.
Did I catch a cold?
I'm sleepy.
C'mon, tell me!
Nope. Man, I'm full. ♥
THE END

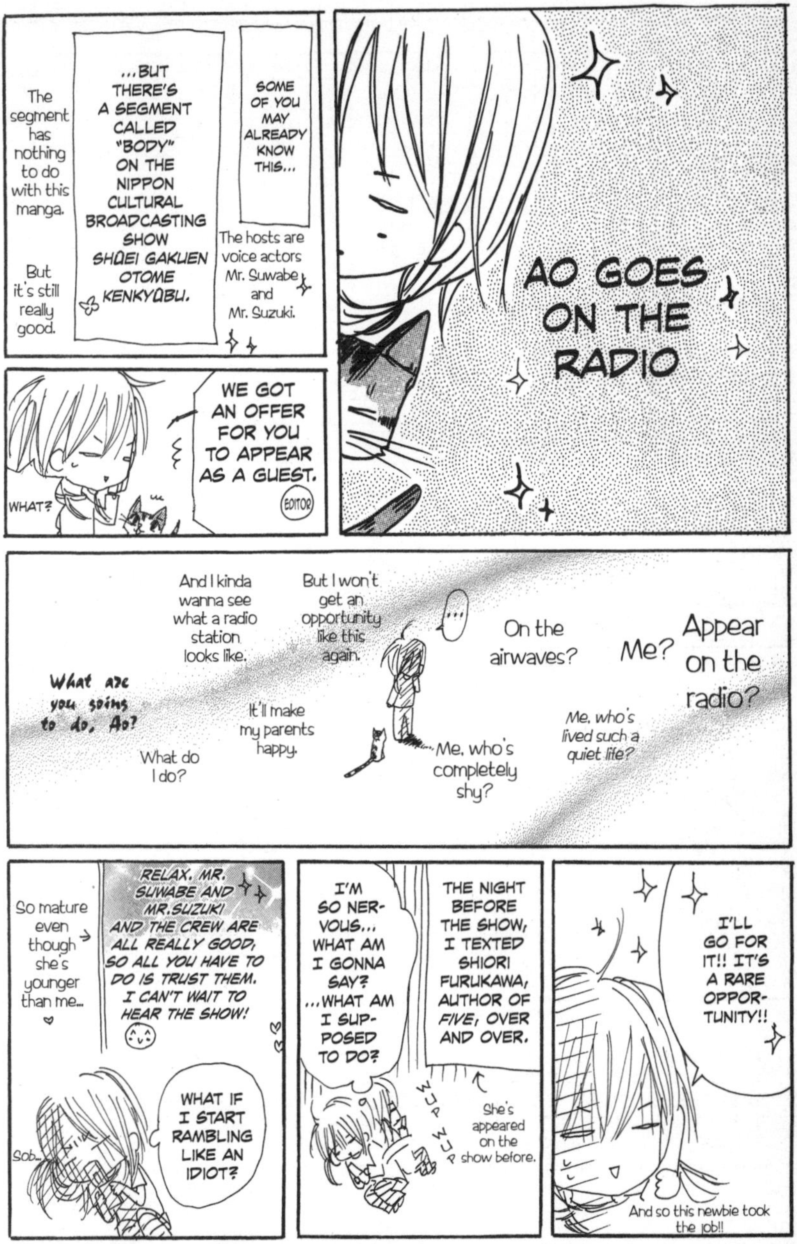
AO GOES ON THE RADIO
SOME OF YOU MAY ALREADY KNOW THIS...
The hosts are voice actors Mr. Suwabe and Mr. Suzuki.
...BUT THERE'S A SEGMENT CALLED "BODY" ON THE NIPPON CULTURAL BROADCASTING SHOW SHŪEI GAKUEN OTOME KENKYŪBU.
The segment has nothing to do with this manga.
But it's still really good.
WE GOT AN OFFER FOR YOU TO APPEAR AS A GUEST.
EDITOR
WHAT?
Appear on the radio?
Me?
On the airwaves?
Me, who's lived such a quiet life?
Me, who's completely shy?
...
But I won't get an opportunity like this again.
And I kinda wanna see what a radio station looks like.
It'll make my parents happy.
What do I do?
What are you going to do, Ao?
I'LL GO FOR IT!! IT'S A RARE OPPORTUNITY!!
And so this newbie took the job!!
THE NIGHT BEFORE THE SHOW, I TEXTED SHIORI FURUKAWA, AUTHOR OF FIVE, OVER AND OVER.
She's appeared on the show before.
I'M SO NERVOUS... WHAT AM I GONNA SAY? ...WHAT AM I SUPPOSED TO DO?
WUP WUP WUP
RELAX. MR. SUWABE AND MR.SUZUKI AND THE CREW ARE ALL REALLY GOOD, SO ALL YOU HAVE TO DO IS TRUST THEM. I CAN'T WAIT TO HEAR THE SHOW!
So mature even though she's younger than me...
WHAT IF I START RAMBLING LIKE AN IDIOT?
Sob...

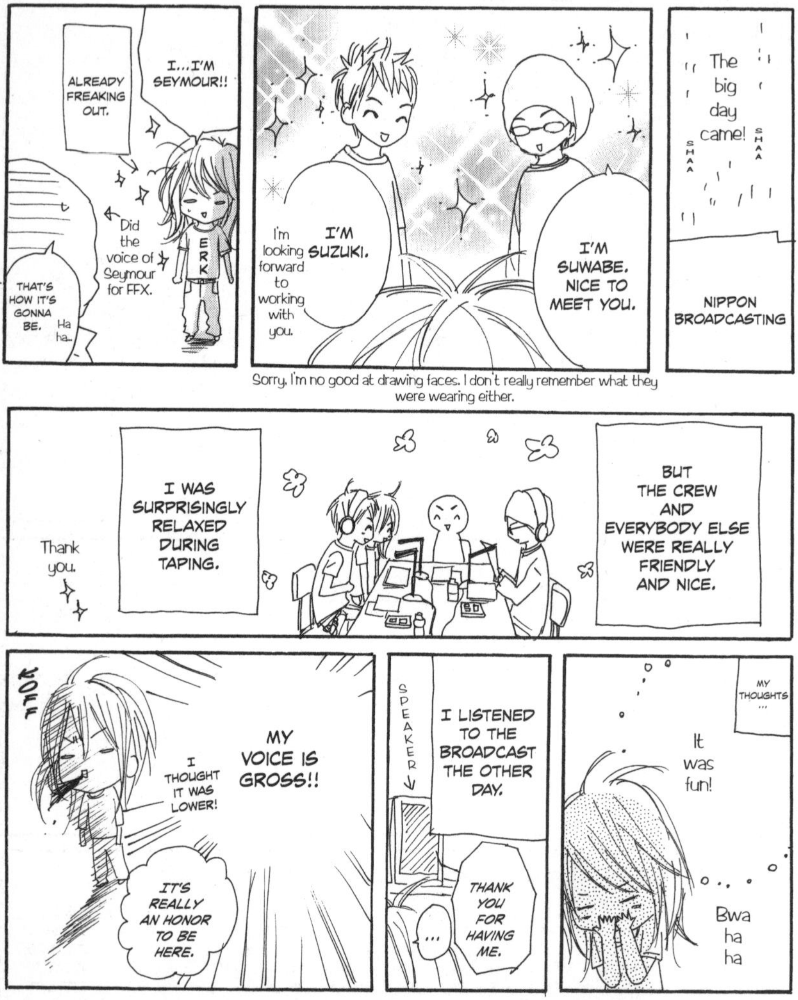
The big day came!
SHAA
SHAA
NIPPON BROADCASTING
I'M SUWABE. NICE TO MEET YOU.
I'M SUZUKI.
I'm looking forward to working with you.
I...I'M SEYMOUR!!
ALREADY FREAKING OUT.
Did the voice of Seymour for FFX.
ERK
THAT'S HOW IT'S GONNA BE.
Ha ha...
I'm really sorry...
Sorry, I'm no good at drawing faces. I don't really remember what they were wearing either.
BUT THE CREW AND EVERYBODY ELSE WERE REALLY FRIENDLY AND NICE.
I WAS SURPRISINGLY RELAXED DURING TAPING.
Thank you.
MY THOUGHTS...
It was fun!
Bwa ha ha
SPEAKER
I LISTENED TO THE BROADCAST THE OTHER DAY.
THANK YOU FOR HAVING ME.
...
MY VOICE IS GROSS!!
I THOUGHT IT WAS LOWER!
IT'S REALLY AN HONOR TO BE HERE.

WE DID A CASTING CALL OVER THE RADIO FOR SOMEONE TO PLAY RYOKO'S CLASSMATE IN THE DRAMA CD, BUT I THINK THE DEADLINE WILL HAVE PASSED BY THE TIME THIS MANGA COMES OUT. I'M REALLY HAPPY ABOUT THE CHANCE TO MEET A BUNCH OF FANS. THERE'LL BE MORE NEWS LIKE THIS COMING UP, SO KEEP AN EYE OUT!!

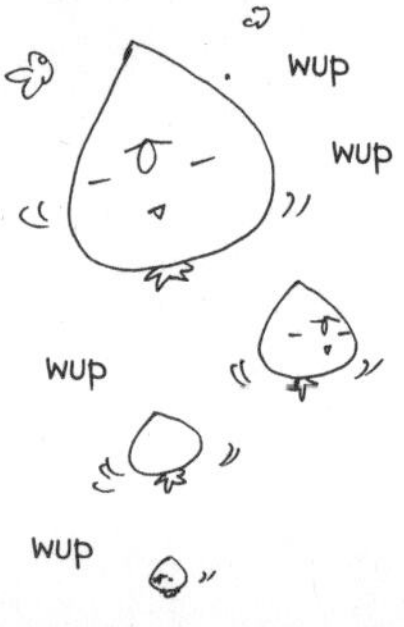
wup
wup
wup
wup

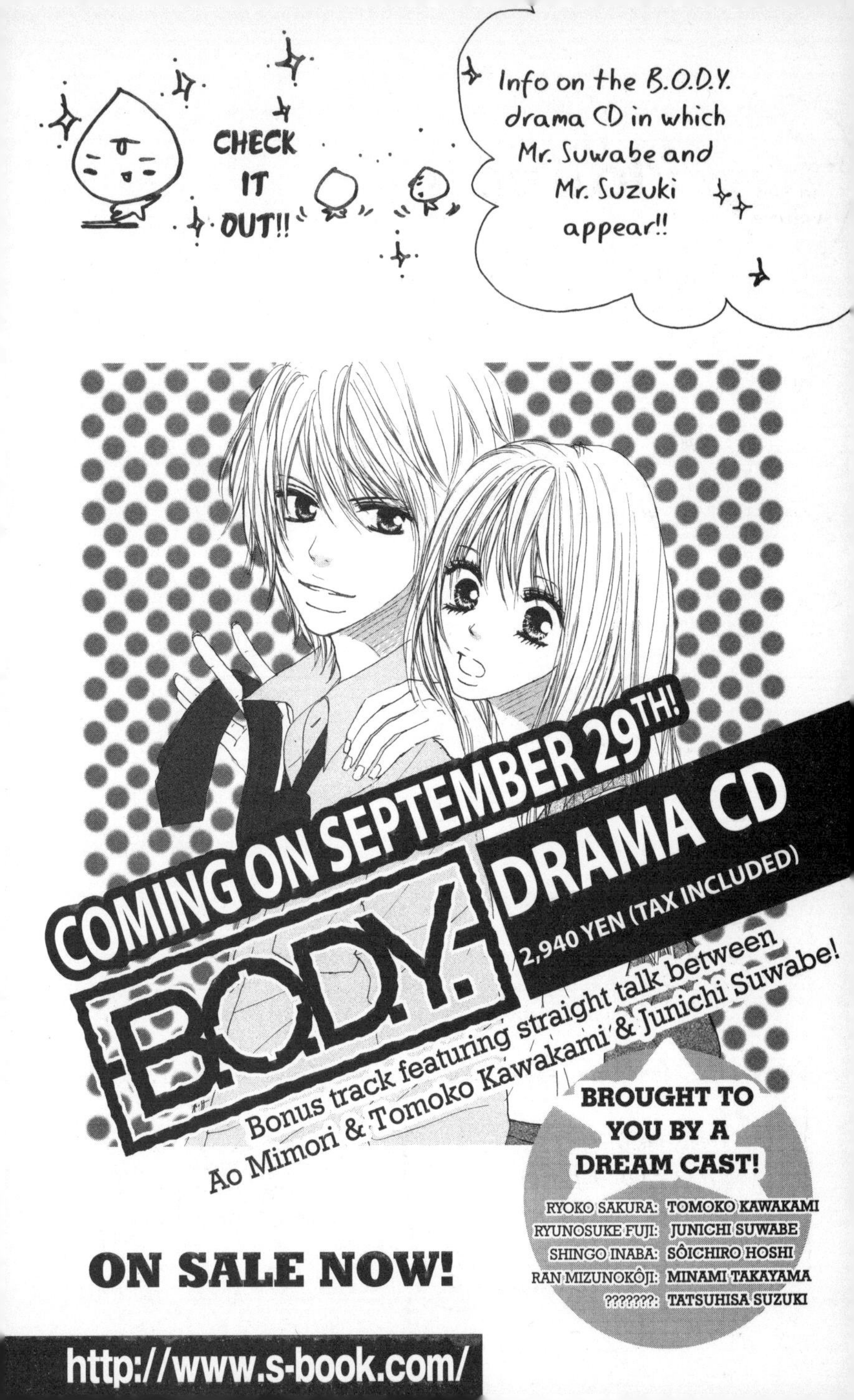
CHECK IT OUT!!
Info on the B.O.D.Y. drama CD in which Mr. Suwabe and Mr. Suzuki appear!!
COMING ON SEPTEMBER 29TH!
B.O.D.Y.
DRAMA CD
2,940 YEN (TAX INCLUDED)
Bonus track featuring straight talk between Ao Mimori & Tomoko Kawakami & Junichi Suwabe!
BROUGHT TO YOU BY A DREAM CAST!
RYOKO SAKURA: TOMOKO KAWAKAMI
RYUNOSUKE FUJI: JUNICHI SUWABE
SHINGO INABA: SÔICHIRO HOSHI
RAN MIZUNOKÔJI: MINAMI TAKAYAMA
???????: TATSUHISA SUZUKI
ON SALE NOW!
http://www.s-book.com/

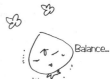
Balance...

Also seen earlier in this volume.

Mailbag —

"I hesitated to send this letter, but it seemed like you actually read our letters, so I decided to go for it."

K.M., IBARAKI

I DO READ THEM!! I TOTALLY READ THEM! I ALSO GET A LOT OF LETTERS SAYING, "I WROTE THIS ON PAPER THAT STANDS OUT SO YOU'D READ IT," BUT YOU DON'T HAVE TO WORRY!! I OPEN EVEN THE MOST ORDINARY ENVELOPES!

"I wrote my book report on B.O.D.Y. (I didn't tell them it was a comic) and won an award!!"

WOW! CONGRATULATIONS!! IS THAT OKAY, THOUGH? OH, WHATEVER! I'M REALLY INTERESTED TO KNOW HOW YOU SUMMARIZED THIS CRAZY STORY AS LITERATURE. THANK YOU!!

These days I get letters telling me, "Don't worry about replying and just keep up the good work. I'll write again." I'm really sorry!! I hate to admit it, but I don't think I can write back to everyone for a while. Sigh...I suck at writing. But I'll get back to you one of these days.

VIZ MEDIA, LLC
P.O. BOX 77010
SAN FRANCISCO, CA 94107

I'M ALWAYS HAPPY TO RECEIVE LETTERS. IT'S THE OASIS OF MY SOUL.

I'll be waiting.

The end.

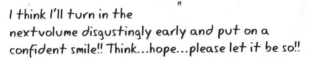

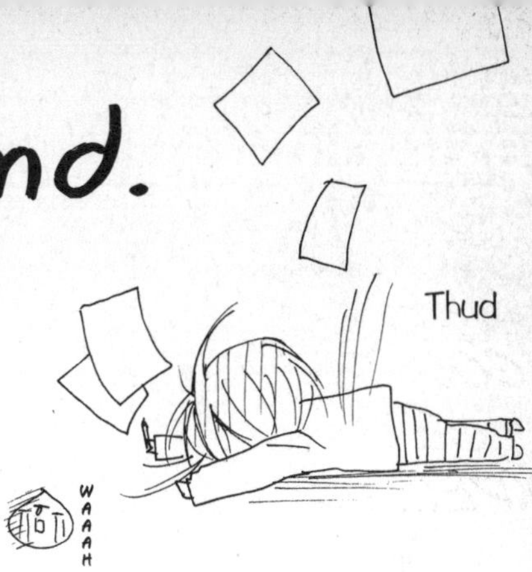

Thank you for sticking around to the end!!

I just barely met my deadline again...

Thud

WAAAH

I think I'll turn in the next volume disgustingly early and put on a confident smile!! Think...hope...please let it be so!!

I didn't touch on this too much in my notes, but this volume introduces some new characters. Izumi...heh heh heh...Kurama...ha ha ha... I don't know how things are going to unfold, but I'll do my best.

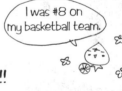

I was #8 on my basketball team.

I'll be waiting for you guys in Volume 8!!

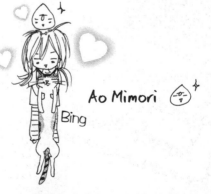

Bing

2006.5.19

Ao Mimori

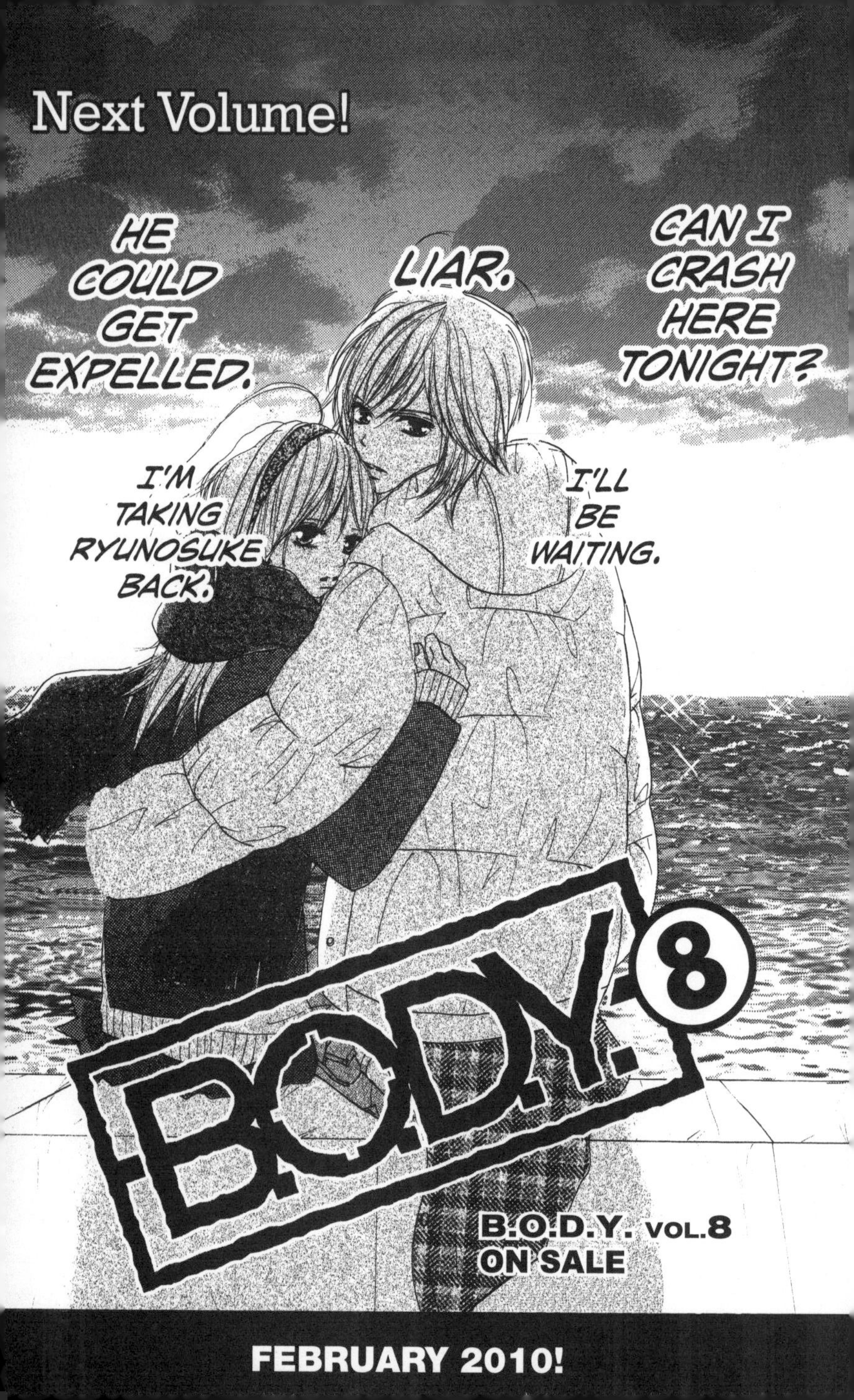
Next Volume!
CAN I CRASH HERE TONIGHT?
LIAR.
HE COULD GET EXPELLED.
I'LL BE WAITING.
I'M TAKING RYUNOSUKE BACK.
B.O.D.Y. 8
B.O.D.Y. VOL.8 ON SALE
FEBRUARY 2010!

B.O.D.Y. Language

Page 57, Author's Note: Karuho Shiina's *Kimi ni Todoke*
Shojo manga about the relationship between a girl considered weird
and spooky by her classmates and a cool, popular guy she looks up to
as a model of normal behavior.

Page 62, panel 6: When I was in 9th grade
Japanese high schools include grades 10 through 12, so 9th grade is the
last year of junior high. Izumi was hired to tutor Ryunosuke for his high
school entrance exams.

Page 130: School Rating
This is Ryunosuke's *hensachi*, or standardized school ranking.
Hensachi for schools and students are calculated using a formula
based on test scores. The average score is 50, so a hensachi of 56 is
slightly above average.

Page 178, panel 2: *Shûei Gakuen Otome Kenkyûbu*
The show's title means "Shuei Academy Girl Research Department."
Shuei is a play on the name of manga publisher Sheuisha.

Page 178, panel 6: Shiori Furukawa
Shojo manga artist. Her series *Five* is about a girl who transfers to a
new school and lands in a class made up entirely of boys, five of whom
take an interest in her.

Page 179, panel 3: Seymour
Seymour Guado, a character in *Final Fantasy X*.

Page 180: 2,940 yen
About $29.

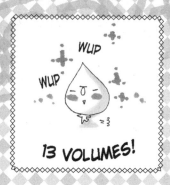

WUP

WUP

13 VOLUMES!

Author's Commentary

It's almost summer. I love this time of year—the feeling that summer's right around the corner...♡ All this meaningless excitement.

Ao Mimori began creating manga during her junior year of college, and her work debuted when she was only 23. *B.O.D.Y.*, her third series, was first published in *Bessatsu Margaret* in 2003 and is also available in Japanese as an audio CD. Her other work includes *Sonnano Koi Jyanai* (That's Not Love), *Anta Nanka Iranai* (I Don't Need You), *Dakishimetaiyo Motto* (I Want to Hold You More), *I LOVE YOU* and *Kamisama no Iu Toori* (As the God of Death Dictates).

B.O.D.Y. VOL 7
Shojo Beat Manga Edition

STORY & ART BY
AO MIMORI

Translation/Joe Yamazaki
Touch-up Art & Lettering/HudsonYards
Design/Sean Lee
Editor/Shaenon K. Garrity

VP, Production/Alvin Lu
VP, Publishing Licensing/Rika Inouye
VP, Sales & Product Marketing/Gonzalo Ferreyra
VP, Creative/Linda Espinosa
Publisher/Hyoe Narita

Printed in Canada

Published by VIZ Media, LLC
P.O. Box 77010
San Francisco, CA 94107

10 9 8 7 6 5 4 3 2 1
First printing, November 2009

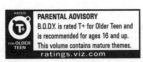

www.viz.com   www.shojobeat.com

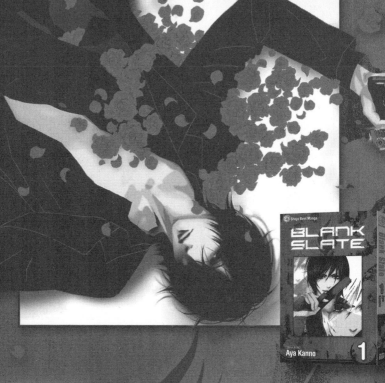

A Past Shrouded in Mystery

BLANK SLATE
by Aya Kanno

Zen's memory has been wiped, and he can't remember if he's a killer or a hero. How far will he go—and how hard will he have to fight—to uncover the secrets of his identity?

Find out in *Blank Slate*—manga on sale now!

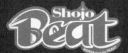

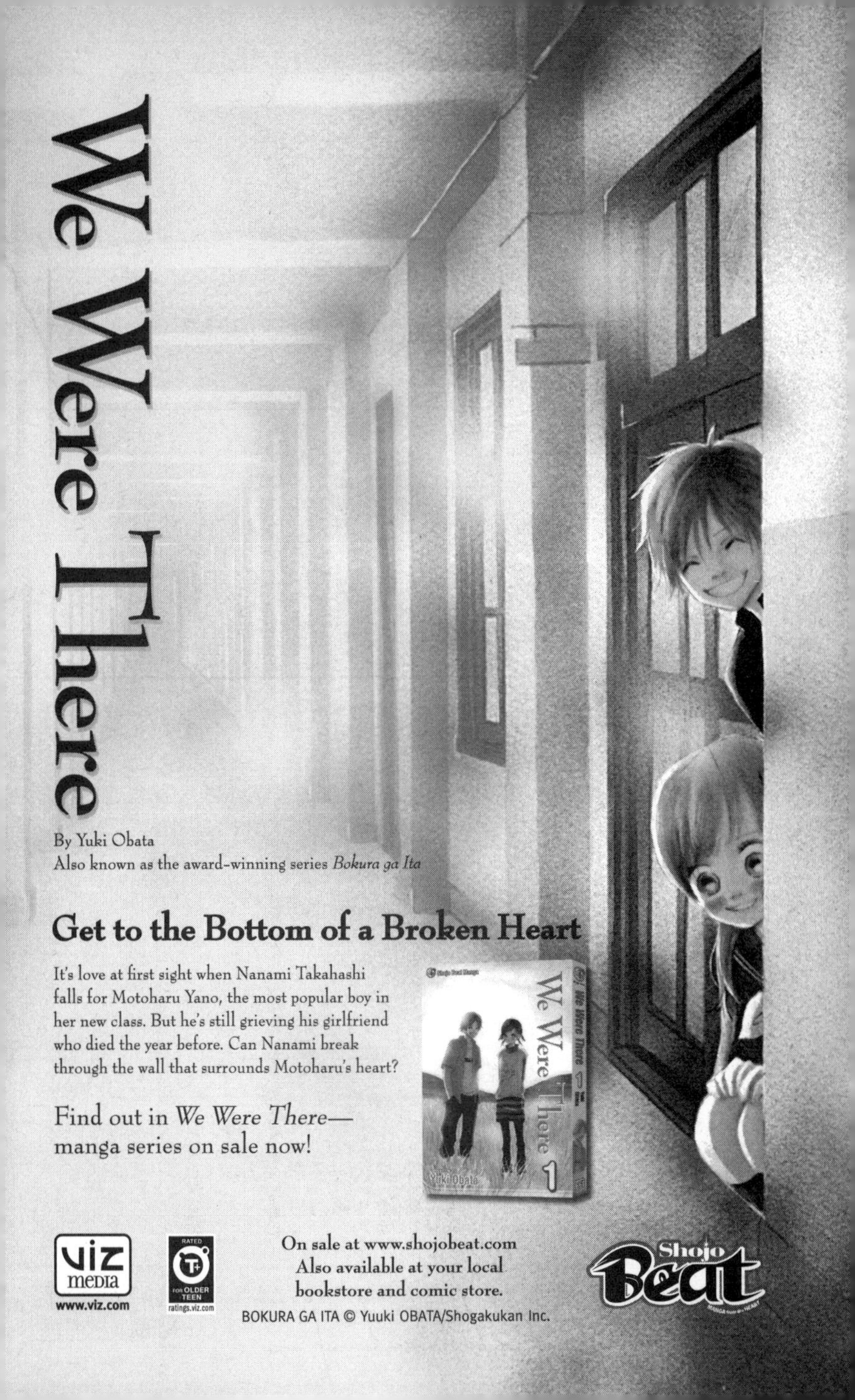

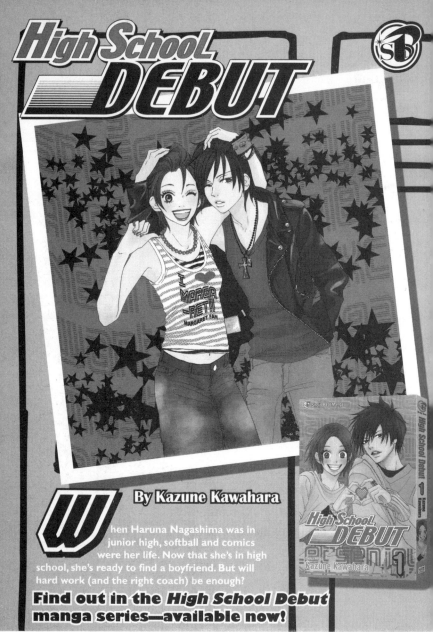
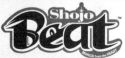

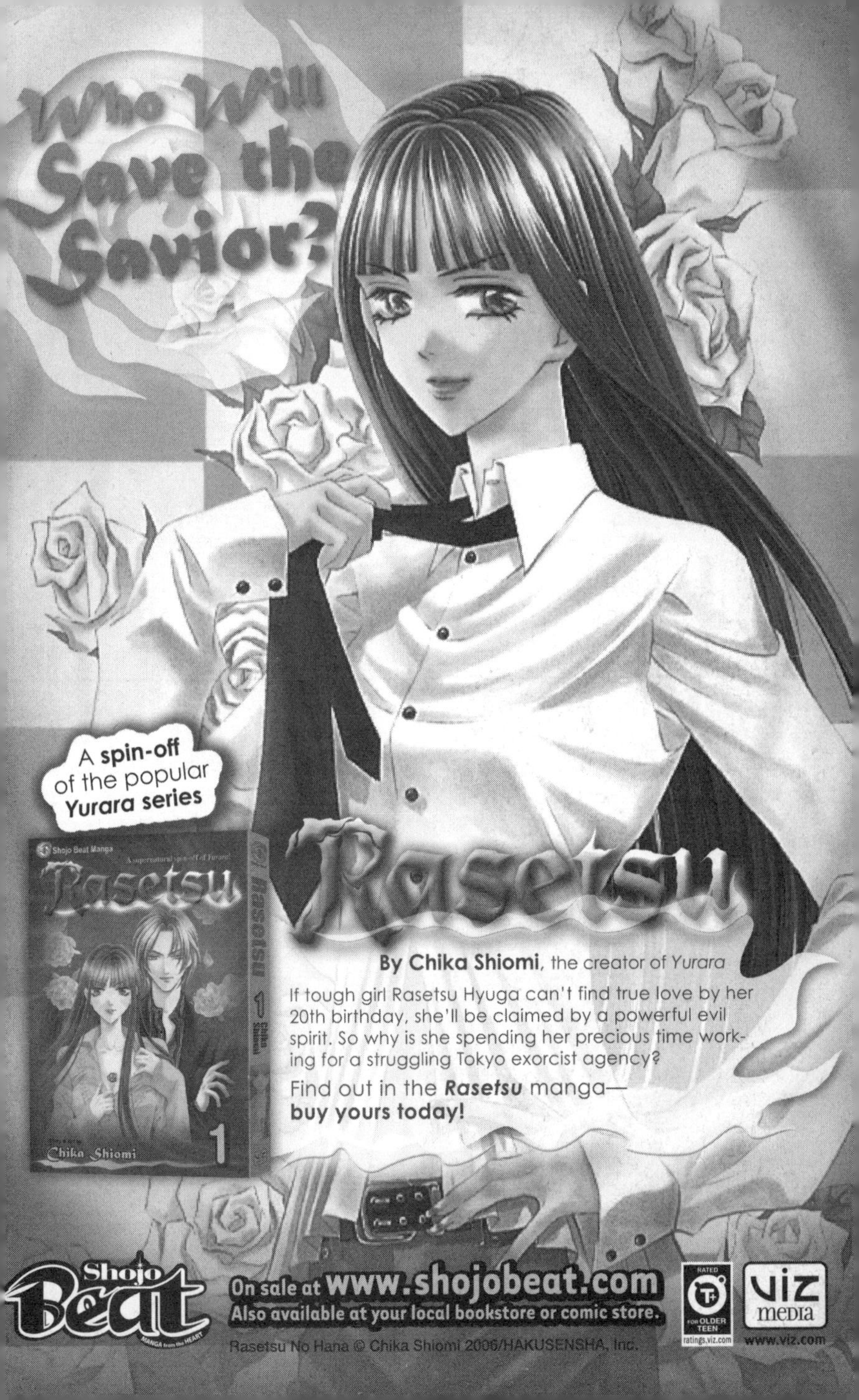
Who Will Save the Savior?
A spin-off of the popular Yurara series
Shojo Beat Manga
Rasetsu
1
Chika Shiomi
Rasetsu
By Chika Shiomi, the creator of Yurara
If tough girl Rasetsu Hyuga can't find true love by her 20th birthday, she'll be claimed by a powerful evil spirit. So why is she spending her precious time working for a struggling Tokyo exorcist agency?
Find out in the Rasetsu manga—buy yours today!
Shojo Beat
MANGA from the HEART
On sale at www.shojobeat.com
Also available at your local bookstore or comic store.
Rasetsu No Hana © Chika Shiomi 2006/HAKUSENSHA, Inc.
RATED T+ FOR OLDER TEEN
ratings.viz.com
VIZ media
www.viz.com

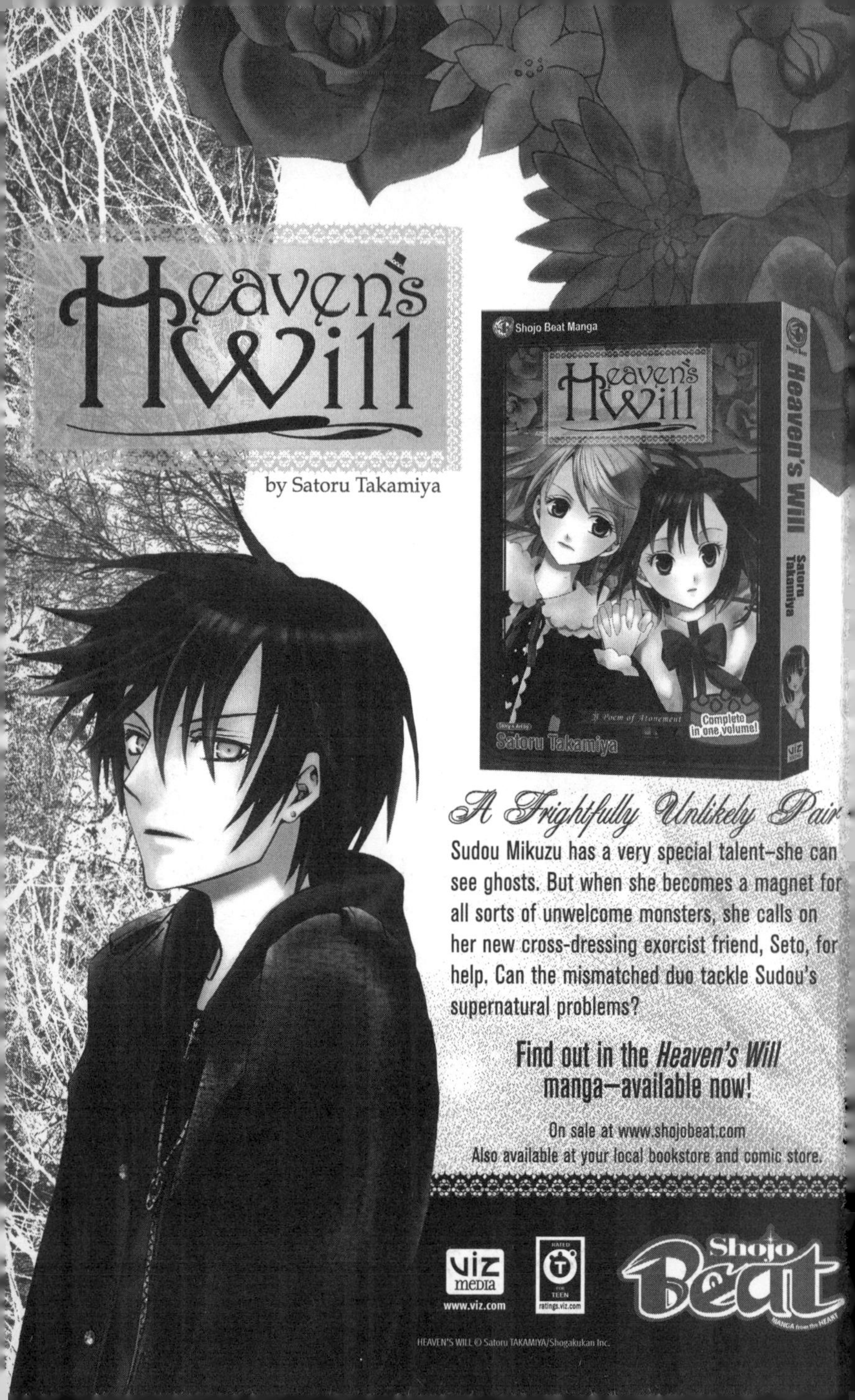
Heaven's Will
by Satoru Takamiya
Shojo Beat Manga
Heaven's Will
Satoru Takamiya
A Poem of Atonement
Complete in one volume!
A Frightfully Unlikely Pair
Sudou Mikuzu has a very special talent–she can see ghosts. But when she becomes a magnet for all sorts of unwelcome monsters, she calls on her new cross-dressing exorcist friend, Seto, for help. Can the mismatched duo tackle Sudou's supernatural problems?
Find out in the Heaven's Will manga—available now!
On sale at www.shojobeat.com
Also available at your local bookstore and comic store.
viz media
www.viz.com
RATED T FOR TEEN
ratings.viz.com
Shojo Beat
MANGA from the HEART
HEAVEN'S WILL © Satoru TAKAMIYA/Shogakukan Inc.

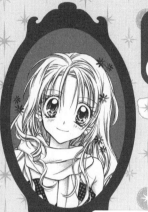
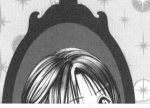
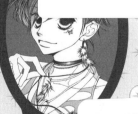
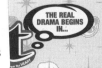

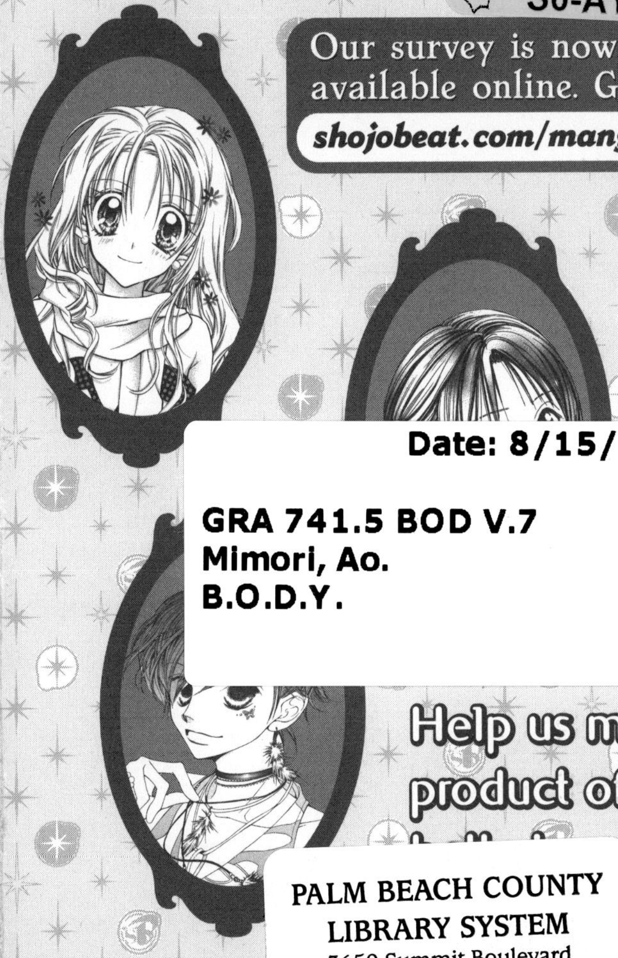